CITY OF ENTERPRISE

CITY OF ENTERPRISE

PERSPECTIVES ON AUCKLAND BUSINESS HISTORY

edited by
IAN HUNTER and DIANA MORROW

AUCKLAND UNIVERSITY PRESS

To Emeritus Professor Russell Stone

First published 2006

Auckland University Press
University of Auckland
Private Bag 92019
Auckland
New Zealand
www.auckland.ac.nz/aup

© the authors, 2006

ISBN 1 86940 351 7

National Library of New Zealand Cataloguing-in-Publication Data
City of enterprise : perspectives on Auckland business history /
edited by Ian Hunter and Diana Morrow.
Includes bibliographical references and index.
ISBN 1-86940-351-7
1. Business enterprises—New Zealand—Auckland—History.
2. Industries—New Zealand—Auckland—History. 3. Auckland
(N.Z.)—Commerce—History. 4. New Zealand—Economic
conditions. I. Hunter, Ian, 1967- II. Morrow, Diana.
330.99324—dc 22

Publication is assisted by The University of Auckland Business School
to commemorate 100 years of business and economics education.

Cover design by Christine Hansen

Printed in China through Colorcraft Ltd, Hong Kong

CONTENTS

ACKNOWLEDGEMENTS

This book forms part of the University of Auckland Business History Project. Commenced in 2003 by the Dean of the University of Auckland Business School, Professor Barry Spicer, the project has the ultimate aim of reinvigorating and fostering the research, teaching and dissemination of business history in New Zealand. This publication is one of the initial outcomes of the project. Others include the creation of static and interactive displays throughout the new University of Auckland Business School building (due to open 2008), the establishment of an annual business history conference (held for the first time in September 2004), the creation of an oral history archive, development of a historic discovery trail in conjunction with Auckland City, and the publication of individual corporate histories.

We would like to acknowledge and give our thanks to the numerous people who have provided assistance and support to this project: Professor Michael Powell, Emeritus Professor Russell Stone, Paul Gilberd, Professor James Belich, Felicity Lamm, Manuka Henare, Warwick Nicoll, Rachel Morley, Ken Jackson, Professor Simon Ville, Steve Jones, Bill Thurston, David Levene (foundation sponsor), John Banks (former Auckland City Mayor), George Farrant (Auckland City Heritage), Peter Berrett, Peter Deutschle, Stephen Innes, David Verran, Charlie Fahy and Alex Felker.

We would also like to acknowledge the Hunter family and the Morrow family, without whose patience and support, this book would not have come about.

Ian Hunter and Diana Morrow
Editors

A Welcome Renaissance:
Business History in New Zealand

IAN HUNTER AND DIANA MORROW

Pre-eminent here was commerce: the word embraces everything
from warehousing, retailing, and manufacturing to investment.[1]

Proclamation town

The 'proclamation town' established in September 1840 by Lieutenant-Governor Hobson quickly gained notoriety as a settlement where commerce reigned supreme. Early Auckland was a place where fortunes could be won. It rapidly became, and remains to this day, a key *entrepôt* and the nation's commercial and financial capital. Understanding how and why business has flourished in Auckland offers a vital insight into New Zealand's economic development, past and present.

In the latter part of the nineteenth century, as the town crept up the gullies branching out from the coastal bays, Auckland seemed to gather a momentum all its own. Commerce, in various forms and with all its virtues and vices, continued to play a dominant role. At times extractive industries – such as Coromandel gold, or timber and gum from the Northland forests – enjoyed brief bursts of prominence, but commerce remained the dominant influence in the city, defining and shaping its character. Then, as now, much business had a global dimension, with ships bearing sugar from Mauritius, salt from Liverpool, suits from London and silks from Japan. New Zealand was part of a web of international interchange and Auckland a central node of trade and transportation.

Infrastructure and urbanisation, as much as they are challenges for the present, were issues faced in the late nineteenth century. They remained to the forefront in the twentieth century, as at different times a growing population's transport and communication needs outpaced development. House building, school building, roading, drainage: none of these are particularly glamorous industries, yet all of them, because of their prolonged intensity, have played an important role in Auckland's business history. Each improvement, investment or innovation in turn yielded a secondary complementary demand. The social, educational and mercantile needs of the city's ever-expanding population had to be met. Mercantile and retail markets needed to keep up with that demand and to be supported by adequate warehousing and importing infrastructure. The latter relied on efficient capital and banking markets, supported by insurance and information. To achieve all of these diverse ends, in a way that was both timely and did not impede urban development, presented numerous, ongoing challenges.

This book offers a range of perspectives and insights into how Auckland business has responded to these challenges. The first in a series of works on New Zealand business history, it owes its existence to the University of Auckland Business History Project. This multifaceted project, which commenced in 2003, aims to reinvigorate and foster the research, teaching and dissemination of business history in New Zealand.

Business history

The resurgence of interest in the potential of business history, and an appreciation of its fundamental importance in this country's history, mirrors a recent renaissance and reassessment of the subject internationally. When, in the 1920s, 'business history' located itself in the Harvard Business School, it found a natural home in the Harvard case method, an approach that has since spread widely. By careful analysis of company response to difficulty, alternative strategies, entrepreneurial behaviours and the study of successful firms, the student of history can gain insight into present and future direction. The manager may be aided in decision-making. But to study business history for this reason alone would impoverish the discipline. More recent research trends in business history, which have rapidly gathered momentum since the early 1990s, approach the subject from a more encompassing perspective.

Business history is no longer synonymous with the firm. The organisation, the partnership, the cooperative, the industrial association, the entrepreneur – these are all important components in the business historian's lexicon. So too is industry and the national and global economy. Covering such broad territory does not mean that business history loses its focus or precision – rather there is a recognition that the best business history, like the best history, is written with sympathy for its broader context. It is insufficient for individual firms to be written up as if their history were indicative of broader industrial or economic patterns without reference to those patterns. Equally, it is misleading to focus exclusively on the economic superstructure with no reference to what is happening on the ground.

Alfred Chandler's classic work *Strategy and Structure*,[2] a careful and revealing account of the emergence and effectiveness of the multi-divisional form in American corporate history, has provided a reference point for many business historians in the past. It is salutary to note, however, that a new generation of business historians has alerted the historical world to other forms of organisation with equal economic potency, notably, the network, the entrepreneur and, in Britain especially, the family firm.

These other types of economic actors have historically played an important part in Australasia. The large-scale multi-divisional form was not typically a colonial response to the challenges and opportunities of colonisation. Instead, colonies forged ahead as cities and towns of enterprise, pushed forward by small firms, family firms, proprietors, adventurers and industry clusters. Although there was large-scale organisation in shipping, mining, finance, stock and station agency and timber, the Australasian response to economic development was predominantly one involving types of organisational forms other than Chandler's multi-divisional structure.

New Zealand: potential research

In New Zealand the need to know more about our commercial past, to understand what has made it distinctive and what characteristics it shared with other colonies, is particularly pressing. While the country has benefited from important works on politics, on Maori, on society, on women, on race, and on war, the history of business is largely absent. There are fleeting glances, but the kind of in-depth research upon which other branches of national history rest has not been done. Commercial activity is a vital part of the national identity, and it is the role of business history to add this dimension to the understanding of our past.

The existing historiography as it relates to New Zealand economic and business history generally falls into four observable categories: company and industrial histories, regional histories, biographies, and economic history. In each of the four categories, while there are some outstanding pieces and authors, scholarly works which endeavour to offer critical analysis or a broader historical context are noticeably lacking. Company histories, for example, tend to be commissioned as projects to mark some milestone or centenary, and are often given to a past member of the company or a practising journalist to write. At their worst, such works run out a laudatory, and quickly tiring, list of past chairmen and leaders, missing both the undercurrent of change in the firm and the general economic context. Many are just too brief. The result is that the opportunity for incisive analysis or learning is lost. Indeed, much has been allowed to lie fallow that holds productive potential.

With regard to Auckland business history, for example, there have been no comprehensive thematically or chronologically inclusive studies with a city or regional focus. R. C. J. Stone in *Makers of Fortune* looked at Auckland's business community during a few crucial decades in the latter nineteenth century; his most recent work focuses on early Maori history in the region and concludes shortly after the advent of European settlement. A comprehensive business history of Auckland that surveys its commercial sector and unique 'enterprise culture' from about 1840 to the present day would be a challenging but worthwhile undertaking. Less ambitiously, the opportunity awaits to augment Stone's work with studies that focus on shorter time periods in Auckland's business past (for example, on a single or several decades, or even key years or epochs). Such works could either take the form of a traditional chronological narrative or focus on a particular theme or groups of themes.

While some recent academic research has examined New Zealand–Australian economic relations and overseas trade relations generally, comparative work on New Zealand/Auckland business history has been relatively neglected to date. Such work could have a broad international focus: comparing and contrasting the colonial business histories/development patterns of former British colonies such as Australia, Canada, New Zealand and South Africa, for example. Alternatively, it could have an internal regional or parochial focus, comparing Auckland's business history and development with that of Christchurch or Dunedin. More narrowly focused industry- or occupation-based comparative investigations and methodologies might also prove rewarding.

Similarly, although there have been some significant biographies of major New Zealand business figures, there are numerous individuals and/or families of note about whom nothing has been written, and whose lives and influence, both economic and social, remain unexplored. There are innumerable companies and business concerns, both in Auckland and elsewhere in New Zealand, that have also never had their histories researched or their legacy assessed. Works of this kind should ideally be undertaken not just when commissioned for the occasion of a centenary or other such milestone. Rather, professional historians should be encouraged to undertake such topics, and to approach them in such a way as to highlight their broader import and impact for both the region and the country as a whole. This aim should extend to studies (again relatively few to date) of particular professions, related business interests and financial institutions.

The complex historic links between local politics and local business, and between local business and national politics, is another area that warrants further academic research. Similarly, micro-studies of particular business districts or even particular streets over different time periods, the history of various ethnic and/or religious groups' contributions to business culture and economic climate, of how and why the banking sector as a whole has helped to shape and/or interacted with business interests over time – all are potentially fruitful and as yet largely unexplored aspects of this country's business history.

To produce works of this kind of high academic quality, it will be necessary for all those interested in fostering business history to work together to define aims and methodologies, promote requisite interdisciplinary approaches, enhance skills and knowledge, familiarise students, academics and professional authors with the kinds of archival and secondary sources that can be utilised, encourage initiatives to ensure adequate archival retention, arrangement and description among the business sector, and generally work to raise awareness of the nature and importance of business history as an important and richly potential field of study.

City of Enterprise

City of Enterprise: Perspectives on Auckland Business History is a first step toward achieving these goals. It is a collection of essays by scholars from New Zealand and overseas which aims to introduce readers to the diversity and interest of business history. The book is structured in a basically chronological fashion, commencing with an introductory chapter which gives an overview of the broader national and international context. Following this, the authors explore particular aspects of Auckland's business development, with the aim of better understanding the city's distinctive commercial heritage.

John Singleton's opening chapter offers a survey of the Auckland commercial economy and considers the symbiosis between Auckland's growth and development and that of the wider New Zealand economy. The question he considers is: would Auckland's economic impact have been even more dramatic had New Zealand's economy taken a different course?

In Chapter 2, Hazel Petrie examines the question of Maori commercial enterprise from the time of first European contact. In particular, she explores the extraordinary early engagement of Maori with business and trade in the Auckland Province, and considers the reasons for its equally rapid demise in the latter part of the century.

Maritime historian Gavin McLean surveys Auckland's maritime development and examines how the centrality of the port and maritime commerce contributed to the city's prosperity. In particular, he looks at continuity and change in shipping practices. Michael Keenan's chapter – using a classic approach to business history – undertakes an exhaustive analysis of company archives to reveal the financial practices and strategies of the Auckland Gas Company, a public utility which was to have far-reaching effects on the social and economic life of the city.

Timber – vital in the development of the colonial economy – is the subject of Ken Jackson's chapter on the Kauri Timber Company. As Jackson reveals, government policy toward industrial associations had a significant impact on the way the industry itself could operate. Gordon Winder, a historical geographer, offers an example of another type of business history, which involves the application of sophisticated computer mapping technology to archival records. Plotting company listings from Auckland postal directories, Winder is able to examine why industrial clusters originated and why they were discarded. In doing so, he opens new windows for future research into the 1889–1908 period.

In Chapter 7, economic historian Simon Ville looks at the provision of the stock and station business in the Auckland region, using this as a platform from which to explore the strategies of key corporate players and the business linkages that emerged. Ville shows how, in a colonial economy that was not characterised by large-scale industrial investment, alternative organisational forms – notably the business network – assisted economic development.

Chapter 8 provides an insight into a successful business enterprise that has previously escaped examination by historians of business. Diana Morrow focuses on how the Auckland newspaper industry and the Auckland business community grew up and prospered together in a close and mutually beneficial relationship.

In Chapter 9, Ian Hunter considers the retail and management innovations of one of Auckland's most significant retail firms: the Farmers Trading Company. He assesses the impact of the entrepreneur leading the firm, Robert Laidlaw, whose innovation is shown to be a means both for market entry and competitive leadership.

In his study of Ross and Glendining, in Chapter 10, Steve Jones introduces the reader to the reality of commercial failure. The company's failure is due to its incapacity to adapt to New Zealand's changing industrial conditions. Its belated focus on the Auckland market comes too late; in the end, the story of Ross & Glendining is a vivid account of generals fighting the last war.

In the concluding chapter, accounting historian Rachel Morley focuses on one of the key trends shaping the city at present: the movement of accounting firms from traditional professional partnerships to global corporate professional networks. Morley provides two case studies as a way to illustrate the competition between partnerships in the Auckland region and considers the impact on organisational culture of these dramatic ownership changes.

The afterword, a keynote address given by Emeritus Professor Russell Stone at the University of Auckland Business History Conference 2004, investigates the ongoing legacy of Auckland's early years of entrepreneurial speculation. Discussing the images that the city has conjured up for the rest of New Zealand, Professor Stone examines why the 'exceptionalism' of Auckland has never dissipated.

As editors, we have attempted in this volume to blend interest with relevance, keeping before us the simple but salient dictum of American business historian Alfred Chandler: What made for change? Why did it come when it did, and in the way it did? In exploring the answers to these questions, the contributors shed light on fundamental historical issues of origin and identity.

CHAPTER ONE

Auckland Business:
The National and International Context

JOHN SINGLETON

Over the past 150 years, the Auckland economy has outpaced that of New Zealand as a whole. Nowadays Auckland plays a larger role in the New Zealand economy than London does in the British economy or Paris does in the French economy. As a metropolis, Auckland has also become increasingly differentiated from the rest of New Zealand, a country that in the early 1960s could still be described by a British Prime Minister, Harold Macmillan, as 'an English farm in the Pacific'.[1]

By 1914, Auckland had developed into New Zealand's leading *entrepôt* and a major financial centre. Auckland's prosperity was intertwined with the economic health of the nation. Supply and demand linkages operated in both directions. Auckland produced goods and services that were consumed in other parts of New Zealand; Auckland, in turn, consumed many of the products of other regions. It also competed with other regions in product and factor markets. The New Zealand economy benefited from the presence of a dynamic and increasingly dominant metropolitan centre in the form of Auckland. At times, though, the Auckland economy may have been held back by the weaknesses in the national and international trading environments.

New Zealand economy: an overview

New Zealanders enjoyed some of the highest living standards in the world during the second half of the nineteenth century and the first half of the twentieth century. Gross domestic product (GDP) per capita continued to rise, with some interruptions, during the second half of the twentieth century, but New Zealand's rate of growth, although reasonable in absolute terms, was now sluggish in comparison with the rates achieved in other developed countries. Living standards in New Zealand were gradually overtaken by those in most Western European countries, and even in several countries in East Asia, including Japan and Singapore. New Zealand's GDP per capita in the early twenty-first century put it firmly in the bottom half of the OECD league table.

David Greasley and Les Oxley, the authors of several perceptive articles on New Zealand's long-run economic history, find that '[m]any elements of New Zealand's economic development since 1870 appear idiosyncratic'.[2] New Zealand's dismal long-term record of growth, and the protectionist stance it took during the mid-twentieth century, are more typical of Latin America experience than of Western Europe, Australia or Canada. Greasley and Oxley conclude that 'New Zealand emerges as an oddity'.[3] Angus Maddison, the leading commentator on long-run comparative economic performance, allocates New Zealand to a middle-income group of countries, which includes Czechoslovakia, Hungary, Portugal, Spain and the former USSR, despite the fact that in 1913 New Zealand was one of the richest countries in the globe in terms of income per capita.[4]

New Zealand's economic history since the mid-nineteenth century can be split into several periods. Until the First World War, the pastoral history reigned supreme, and conferred a high level of prosperity on the dominion. The interwar period saw international markets weaken. Governments began to intervene in the economy, with the intention of restoring its health. Between the Second World War and the mid-1980s, New Zealand was a highly regulated or 'insulated' economy. By the 1970s and the early 1980s, there was a growing body of evidence to suggest that this approach did not prevent crises or generate an acceptable level of economic growth. After 1984, there was a lurch back to something akin to the free market regime that had been abandoned in the 1930s.[5] An intriguing feature of New Zealand's economic history is the fact that both the interventionism of the mid-twentieth century and the deregulation of the late twentieth century rendered the country an outlier in comparison with other liberal democracies, including Australia and the United Kingdom.

TABLE 1: PER CAPITA GDP IN WESTERN OFFSHOOTS, 1840–2000
(1990 International Geary-Khamis dollars)

Year	USA	Australia	New Zealand	NZ as % of USA	NZ as % of Australia
1840	1,588	1,374	400	25	29
1900	4,091	4,013	4,298	105	107
1950	9,561	7,412	8,456	88	114
2000	28,129	21,540	16,010	57	74

Source: A. Maddison, *The World Economy: Historical Statistics*, OECD, Paris, 2003, pp. 85–7.

New Zealand is geographically and culturally closer to Australia than to any other developed country. Thus New Zealanders generally regard Australia as the most important international benchmark for wages, house prices and other economic phenomena. Although Australia was not a stellar performer in the international growth race until the 1990s, it managed to keep ahead of New Zealand for the bulk of the twentieth century. GDP per capita in New Zealand was consistently below that of Australia until the late 1930s. New Zealand did enjoy a brief ascendancy during the Second World War and the Korean War, but Australia was back in front by the 1960s and continued to widen its lead until the end of the millennium.[6] Strangely enough, the 1940s turn out to have been a sort of Golden Age for the New Zealand economy. During the 1940s, per capita incomes in New Zealand were in excess of those in many of the Australian states. By the end of the twentieth century, however, New Zealand had been overtaken by Victoria, New South Wales and Western Australia, and had more in common with such relatively poor states as Tasmania and Queensland.[7]

Macroeconomic and microeconomic reforms after 1984 did not lead to any measurable improvement in New Zealand's absolute or comparative economic performance – indeed quite the reverse – in the first few years. After the early 1990s, however, New Zealand did enter a phase of robust economic growth, although it is too early to say whether this will be sustained for long enough to restore it to the economic premier league.[8]

Of course, per capita income is only one measure of affluence. Although New Zealand ranked twenty-first in the OECD in terms of per capita GDP in 1998, it was ranked eleventh equal in household wealth, defined by indicators such as access to consumer durables, the number of bathrooms per dwelling, and so on. But it should be pointed out that the survey of household wealth on which these findings are based is a snapshot, and it is probable that even on this indicator New Zealand's relative position has deteriorated over time.[9]

We might also suggest that life in New Zealand has other compensations, although this may be less true of life in Auckland, which is more prone than some other parts of the country to problems (such as congestion) afflicting big cities all over the world. In short, the economies of Auckland and New Zealand have continued to grow, but they could – and possibly should – have done better.

Several explanations have been offered for New Zealand's relatively poor economic performance during the twentieth century. While the various explanations are not mutually exclusive, readers may prefer some to others. First, serious problems arose in the pastoral industry after the First World War. International commodity markets and prices were generally weak during the 1920s and 1930s. There was a strong recovery in demand in the 1940s and early 1950s, but after the early 1950s prices and returns were felt to be unsatisfactory, not least because of the discriminatory agricultural and commercial policies of the United States, the European Union countries and Japan. The primary industries that had brought prosperity to New Zealand in Victorian and Edwardian times were no longer able to drive the economy forward.

Attempts by the private sector, either with or without government encouragement, to diversify into the production of other commodities, including manufactures, were only partially successful. High labour costs and the small size of the domestic market were barriers to the efficient production of standardised labour-intensive goods (e.g., garments) and standardised capital-intensive goods (e.g., cars), but were not necessarily obstacles to specialisation in customised and skill-intensive manufactures. Regrettably, the policy environment was not conducive to the promotion of excellence in these branches of industry.

New Zealand introduced import and exchange controls in 1938 as an emergency response to a balance of payments crisis. Importing was constrained by the need to apply to the authorities for permission to use sterling and other currencies. Once in place, these controls became entrenched, and New Zealand began to exhibit a Latin American-style regime of trade restrictions. Protectionism was a recipe for a ramshackle industrial economy. After the Second World War, New Zealand manufactured a wide array of high-cost, low-quality industrial products. In the early postwar period, industrial development had been influenced by the continued short supply of goods from the United Kingdom and other countries. But there was also a strong emphasis on the assembly of imported kits and components, as, for example, in the car industry. Urban consumers, farmers and user industries paid the price of this approach, and would have liked the opportunity to buy cheaper imports. Only in the late 1980s was protectionism decisively rejected.

Auckland would have been a significant industrial centre under a more liberal regime. Even in countries that have a comparative advantage in primary products, economic development involves structural change.[10] Over time, the relative importance of industry, and then of services, expands. As a result of protectionism, however, Auckland was saddled with a less competitive and less focused industrial base than might otherwise have been the case. Insofar as protectionism encouraged industrial growth in many smaller centres around New Zealand, it may further have hindered the full development of Auckland as a manufacturing centre.

Geographical and geological factors also worked to New Zealand's disadvantage. It is no coincidence that Australia drew ahead of New Zealand in the 1960s, following the discovery of large mineral deposits for which there was a ready market in Japan. Staple theory – a Canadian contribution to economic thought – suggests that developing countries may industrialise successfully by processing their own primary products, instead of by exporting them in a raw, or almost raw, state. Aided by vast coal and mineral deposits, Canada became a significant industrial power during the twentieth century. Unfortunately for New Zealand, however, wool, meat and dairy produce offered few downstream linkages. Canada had a further advantage over Australia and New Zealand through its proximity to a huge market and source of capital and technology in the United States. Similarly, Ireland and Finland were in a position to capitalise on their closeness to the major European economies. But Australia and New Zealand were a long way from the world's economic centres, and it was difficult for their firms to establish contact with potential customers and collaborators, although they did have access to British capital. American-style institutions in the labour market, business, education and government were influential in Canada, whereas New Zealand and Australia continued to rely on, arguably inferior, British-style institutions. In management, for example, the British, Australians and New Zealanders were resistant to professional training, while in the area of labour relations they were often corporatist in approach.[11] A recent IMF study supports the thesis that isolation has been a major constraint on New Zealand's comparative economic performance over the last three decades.[12]

In summary, New Zealand faced several disadvantages in the twentieth century – trade barriers to its exports, a small local market, a lack of raw materials, and isolation. As we shall see, these problems were aggravated between the Second World War and the 1980s by the pursuit of misguided economic policies.

New Zealand's Golden Age

Timber, gum and grain were the foundations of Auckland's, as well as of New Zealand's trade in the 1840s. But the next wave of economic expansion, starting in the 1850s and 1860s, was underpinned by Yorkshire's insatiable demand for wool, and, for a relatively brief period, by discoveries of gold, particularly in Otago. Auckland was not a leading player in the first pastoral boom, and continued for some years to specialise in the timber trade, supplemented by gold from the Coromandel. Auckland did, however, become a key banking and financial centre, channelling capital to pastoralists in other parts of the country, through the Bank of New Zealand and other intermediaries.

With the introduction of refrigeration techniques in the 1880s, a second wave of agricultural expansion occurred, based on the export of meat and dairy products. Auckland's hinterland took a full part in this growth, providing further business for the port and other service industries. Cheap produce from the Antipodes found a ready market in the bellies of the British working class. But the full benefits of refrigeration were not realised for some years, since world prices were quite depressed between the mid-1870s and the mid-1890s. Following the long-awaited recovery in international commodity prices in the late 1890s, however, the New Zealand economy crossed into an era of opulence. The centre of gravity of the economy was shifting northwards, as more pasture land was sought, while conflict between white settlers, the government and Maori tribes subsided.[13] Landowners, including the rising number of relatively small proprietors, benefited disproportionately from the pre-1914 pastoral boom. Demand increased for the services supplied by the urban areas, although the rate of growth of real wages was sluggish.[14]

British capital, often filtered through Auckland's financial institutions, played a central role in New Zealand's economic development. Land was cheap initially, since it could be obtained very inexpensively and/or seized from Maori. But it was costly to clear and prepare the land for pastoral use, as well as to construct farm buildings, scouring mills, milking sheds, freezing works, and transport infrastructure, including railways, warehouses and port facilities. Pastoralists and the urban businesses servicing them also needed large amounts of working capital.

The City of London, the world's premier financial centre, was the obvious source of capital for both the private and the public sectors. Along with the rest of the Empire, New Zealand was regarded as a relatively safe outlet for British capital. The major banks operating in New Zealand (most of which were also active in Australia) all enjoyed close ties to the British financial establishment, as did many of the stock and station agents, which specialised in the provision of finance to the rural sector, and were amongst the major customers of the banks.[15] British capital was dominant in the shipping industry, and very important in the processing and marketing of meat and dairy produce.

James Belich highlights the 'recolonisation' of New Zealand by Britain in the late nineteenth century.[16] Refrigeration led to the intensification of New Zealand's economic relationship with the United Kingdom. Whereas New Zealand wool producers could export to many markets, Britain was the only major economy to persist with a policy of free trade in temperate foodstuffs. In view of New Zealand's reliance on British markets and British capital, it must be classified as a dependent economy, although it is important to note that, at least for Pakeha, the benefits of dependency greatly outweighed the costs.

A debate has emerged around the 'gentlemanly capitalism' thesis of Peter Cain and Tony Hopkins, who maintain that economic policy in the British Empire was subordinated to the City of London and the gentlemanly élite of the Home Counties. So far as New Zealand is concerned, however, Jim McAloon points out that business and farming leaders – and the same could be said of politicians – were in British terms essentially lower middle class. They acted in their own interests, and definitely did not regard themselves as agents of the City. While McAloon's assessment of the background of the New Zealand business class is persuasive, especially for the South Island (the focus of his own research), it remains the case that they were working in an economic environment in which the City possessed great structural power. To the extent that New Zealand required British capital, it had to play the City's game, which meant managing the economy in such a way that New Zealand would always be able to meet its external financial obligations.[17]

Interwar turmoil

The First World War saw robust demand for New Zealand's primary exports, there being considerable disruption of agriculture in Europe. Anticipating the continuation of strong export demand, New Zealand farmers invested in various improvements, and land exchanged hands at very high prices. The slump in international commodity markets in the early 1920s was unexpected, and set the scene for the next two decades. Farmers – especially those that had borrowed heavily to buy land at peak prices – began to struggle, and this state of affairs had repercussions for the service industries of the urban centres.[18]

New Zealand's economic performance was lacklustre during the 1920s. The early 1930s brought depression, but not on the massive scale experienced in Germany and the United States. It was easier in a country of farms and small businesses to adjust costs and prices after a demand shock than it was in a major industrial country, where oligopolies, cartels, and mass unions constrained flexibility. The less flexible the economy, the greater was the loss of production and jobs. Nevertheless, the experience of living through the Depression profoundly affected many New Zealanders and shaped their view of the international economy for decades to come. New Zealand's recovery from the Depression was spectacular, although in its later stages it was accompanied by a change in policy – an increase in protection – for which the economy would pay dearly.

The global economic downturn, starting in 1929–30, was transmitted to New Zealand by means of the collapse in commodity prices on the London market. Not only did demand fall, but supply increased, as world output continued to rise, and countries such as Holland and Denmark diverted food exports to Britain in the wake of the intensification of protection on the European continent. Farmers bore the brunt of the Depression in New Zealand. At the trough, in 1931–32, net farm income was negative.[19] Declining commodity prices increased the already onerous burden of servicing and repaying farm mortgages. The fall in rural incomes exerted a powerful ripple effect on the rest of the economy. Freezing works, woollen mills and dairy factories were all caught in the spiral of decline. Farmers had less to spend on locally made consumer goods, less to spend on services, and less to spend in the pub. Unemployment rose, and some of the urban jobless in Auckland and other centres drifted back to the family farm, where they were able to eke out some form of living. The burden of external debt, the overwhelming bulk of which was in sterling, rose dramatically relative to export receipts, but New Zealand did not come as close to default as Australia did. A protracted balance of payments crisis was avoided because the demand for imports fell sharply in response to the drop in incomes.[20]

Policy makers, both in New Zealand and overseas, had no reason to expect that the downturn in 1929–30 would develop into the worst slump in history. Brief recessions were commonplace. As tax and customs revenue began to fall, the government trimmed expenditure plans in the forlorn hope of balancing the budget. It was not until 1931 that the severity of the crisis was realised. In accordance with 'orthodox' economic doctrine, further cuts were made in public spending. The New Zealand government also intervened in the labour market, securing an order for an all-round reduction in wages. It cajoled and then forced the banks to reduce interest rates. Ministers sought to maintain confidence in New Zealand, and to restore prosperity by reducing the costs borne by farms and other businesses, including those in urban centres such

Men from an unemployed men's camp in Akatarawa improving the Akatarawa Road as part of a relief scheme during the Great Depression. ALEXANDER TURNBULL LIBRARY, NATIONAL LIBRARY OF NEW ZEALAND, 1/2-084131G.

as Auckland. At the same time, though, their policies resulted in a further weakening of aggregate demand.[21]

During 1931, the New Zealand pound (the external value of which was set by an oligopoly of trading banks) experienced a measure of depreciation against sterling, before stabilising at a new level. Farmers sold their produce on the London market and were paid in sterling, which they then converted into New Zealand pounds. Whenever the New Zealand pound depreciated against sterling, a boost was given to farmers' incomes. Depreciation also made domestic manufactures more competitive *vis-à-vis* imports. But there were offsetting effects. Imports became more expensive, leading to an increase in the cost of living, and higher costs for the industrial firms that assembled imported components and kits, or relied on imported capital goods. Support for a further, deliberate devaluation grew during 1932. Advocates of this policy argued that farmers had suffered disproportionately from the slump, and that the economic burden should be spread more evenly. They also maintained that devaluation would on balance aid recovery because of the multiplier effect of higher rural incomes. After considerable wrangling within Cabinet, the government compelled the banks to devalue by around 14 per cent in January 1933. Denmark retaliated, devaluing the krone and cutting the price of its dairy exports, thereby negating some of the benefits to many New Zealand dairy farmers. However, other exporters derived significant benefits.[22]

Devaluation led to a direct increase in the domestic money supply, as most farmers' receipts and deposits rose. The stimulatory effects of devaluation could have been reinforced by a further reduction in interest rates and a more adventurous bank lending policy, and by a less restrictive budgetary strategy, but both the banks and the government persisted in their cautious and restrictive approaches, and failed to take advantage of this opportunity. Apart from the Bank of New South Wales, all of the trading banks considered the devaluation to be unjustified, and believed that it would soon be reversed. They remained pessimistic about the prospects for business, and managed their affairs accordingly. Under a misconceived arrangement with the government (the Banks' Indemnity Act), the banks were able to invest 'surplus' sterling funds in 5 per cent Treasury bills, instead of extending more loans to the public. The Indemnity Act effectively put a 5 per cent floor under interest rates.[23]

Despite the banks' and the authorities' failure to make the most of devaluation, the positive effects of the rise in farmers' incomes percolated through the economy. Other factors were also starting to work towards economic recovery. First, commodity prices began to stabilise and pick up. Secondly, pastoral output and productivity were continuing to rise within New Zealand. Thirdly, the 1932 Ottawa Agreements on imperial trade consolidated New Zealand's position in the British market relative to foreign competitors such as Argentina, and prefigured an increase in the New Zealand tariff on non-empire manufactures.[24]

Greasley and Oxley argue that the establishment of the Reserve Bank of New Zealand in 1934 ushered in a further loosening of monetary conditions, which enabled New Zealand to achieve rapid economic growth by international standards in the second half of the 1930s.[25] But the establishment of a central bank did not in itself have an immediate impact. More important were two related actions by the authorities: the decision that the 1933 devaluation would hold in the medium term, and the abolition of the Banks' Indemnity Act. Revaluation might have necessitated further deflation. By removing this possibility, the authorities boosted confidence and encouraged households and firms to spend. Without the Indemnity Act to fall back on, banks were forced to seek out new loan business. Lending increased and interest rates fell.

In 1936, the new Labour Government nationalised the Reserve Bank and began to manipulate credit, instructing the central bank to create advances for the support of agricultural marketing and state housing schemes. Strong economic growth helped to stimulate industry in Auckland and other urban centres, as well as to generate renewed prosperity in the pastoral sector.

New Zealand's siege economy, 1938–1984

New Zealand was prosperous throughout the 1940s and the commodity boom during the Korean War at the start of the 1950s. Thereafter New Zealand experienced four decades of growth that, while perfectly acceptable by the standards of the 1920s, was sluggish in comparison with the growth of other developed economies. The second half of the twentieth century was the age of 'catch-up' growth. Whereas the gap in per capita real income between the world leader, the United States, and the nations of Western Europe, and East Asia was narrowing, New Zealand was actually falling further behind. In 1950 the level of per capita income in New Zealand was 88 per cent of the American level; in 2000 it was just 57 per cent.

Some of the reasons for New Zealand's comparatively poor economic performance have already been mentioned. International conditions were unpropitious for the pastoral sector after the early 1950s. Despite the aspirations of GATT (the General Agreement on Tariffs and Trade), the United States, Western Europe and Japan all restricted agricultural imports, especially of temperate foodstuffs, subsidised their own farmers and, in the case of the Americans and the Europeans, dumped their surpluses in third markets. The British market, which remained open until 1973 when the United Kingdom was absorbed into the European Economic Community, was too small to satisfy the needs of New Zealand importers. Moreover, even the British resorted to agricultural subsidies. Compared with the price of industrial goods, the price of agricultural produce was tending to weaken over the long term.[26] New Zealand's terms of trade (the price of exports divided by the price of imports) had risen strongly during the 1940s and the Korean War boom at the start of the 1950s. The terms of trade tended downwards between the early 1950s and mid-1970s.[27]

Anticipating further weakness in pastoral markets, and possibly the recurrence of global depression, policy makers in New Zealand devised a strategy in the 1940s that the economist Colin Simkin termed 'insulationism'.[28] Full employment was now the priority. Since the pastoral sector was unlikely to provide sufficient jobs for the growing population, industrial expansion was

An advertisement for a Frigidaire refrigerator, General Motors New Zealand Frigidaire Division, c. 1955. Import barriers induced many British, American and Australian multinationals to establish plants in New Zealand. ALEXANDER TURNBULL LIBRARY, NATIONAL LIBRARY OF NEW ZEALAND, EPH-A-HOUSEHOLD-1955-01.

desirable, notwithstanding the absence of economies of scale in such a small economy. Potentially unstable conditions in export markets, combined with the high levels of aggregate demand necessary to ensure full employment, were a formula for chronic balance of payments problems. In the eyes of policy makers, this state of affairs justified stringent and perhaps permanent controls over manufactured imports. New Zealand had begun to restrict imports in 1938–39, at a time of external difficulty. During the Second World War, domestic industry had expanded to supply goods that were no longer obtainable from Britain and other suppliers.[29] After 1945, it was deemed inexpedient to allow these industries to collapse. Import controls were retained, although their severity fluctuated according to circumstances.

Protection was a boon to manufacturers in cities such as Auckland, as well as in smaller towns. A highly diversified industrial structure developed in New Zealand, although the emphasis was on consumer goods not producer goods.

A view of Gracefield in Lower Hutt, showing General Motors and Will's Capstan factories in Bouverie Street, c. 1950. ALEXANDER TURNBULL LIBRARY, NATIONAL LIBRARY OF NEW ZEALAND, PACOLL-5927-43.

Competition was ineffectual, and firms were able to pass cost increases on to the consumer.[30] Import barriers induced many British, American and Australian multinationals to establish plants in New Zealand, not least in Auckland.[31] On the other hand, import controls were detrimental to the growth of Auckland's port and associated services.

John Gould and Brian Easton argue that the protected industrial economy was not all bad. It created jobs – New Zealand enjoyed full employment until the 1970s – and provided the economy with a stock of technical and managerial skills, even though these skills were not used effectively at the time.[32] A small minority of firms, led by Fisher & Paykel, did eventually transform themselves into internationally competitive manufacturers. On the whole, however, consumers and downstream firms were deprived of access to cheaper, and often better quality, imported goods during the protectionist era. New Zealand industry would have been more competitive, irrespective of the disadvantages that it faced (such as isolation), if trade had been more open, and firms had been under pressure to specialise in lucrative niches, as they were forced to do after 1984.

William Ball Sutch, 1907–1975, civil servant and advocate of New Zealand industrialisation, c. 1936. ALEXANDER TURNBULL LIBRARY, NATIONAL LIBRARY OF NEW ZEALAND, PACOLL-5469-013.

Rapid population growth also ensured that construction, in which Fletchers were the leaders, was one of the strongest industries in postwar New Zealand. After the Second World War, New Zealand's immigration policy started to become less exclusive, and the flow of migrants from continental Europe began to rise. Many European immigrants found work in Auckland factories and associated service industries. Polynesians followed in the 1960s, and substantial numbers of Maori migrated to the cities from the hinterland.

By the early 1960s, policy makers were becoming aware that New Zealand was falling behind in the race for greater prosperity. The British food market was under threat, as the Macmillan Government initiated what proved to be a lengthy campaign to secure membership of the protectionist European Economic Community. New Zealand began to look for other economic partners, the most obvious candidate being Australia.

In 1901, New Zealand had chosen not to join the new federation of Australian colonies. Non-participation in the Australian federation meant that New Zealand did not share in the benefits of the Australian common market. Fletchers, who were heavily involved in the Tasman pulp and paper complex (known as Murupara), were anxious to secure a trade agreement that would guarantee continued free access for their products into the Australian market.[33] After lengthy negotiations, a limited New Zealand Australia Free Trade Agreement (NAFTA) was signed in 1965. Although New Zealand manufacturers had lobbied successfully to retain some measure of protection against Australian imports, the Australians had few qualms about opening their own doors to New Zealand industrial products. The Australian market provided many Auckland and New Zealand manufacturers with their first experience of exporting. Industrial exports, particularly to Australia, grew rapidly from the late 1960s onwards, albeit from a low base.[34] On the other hand, the Australian market was very soft, since the Australian tariff against the rest of the world was relatively high. Success in Australia did not necessarily equate to competitiveness further afield. NAFTA was given renewed impetus by the Muldoon Government under the Closer Economic Relations (CER) agreement of 1983.

Although Robert Muldoon is often portrayed as an arch-protectionist, his motives were rather more complicated. Muldoon sometimes expressed a genuine interest in liberalising the import control system, but was constrained by opposition from political allies, including the Auckland manufacturers. Industrialists such as Sir Laurence Stevens, of Auckland Knitting Mills, foresaw dire consequences for their firms from import liberalisation.[35] Muldoon and his governments (1975–84) were overwhelmed by a group of interrelated economic crises, including two serious supply shocks (the oil crises), rising inflation and increasing unemployment. Muldoon responded with increasingly erratic macroeconomic policies and tighter economic regulations, which contributed to dramatic fluctuations in inflation and economic growth, culminating in the wage and price freeze of 1982–84. He also instituted the Think Big programme of large-scale investments, including the expansion of the New Zealand Steel plant at Glenbrook near Auckland,[36] and the Marsden Point oil refinery, with a view to attaining a durable improvement in the balance of payments. But Think Big failed – the projects selected were inadequately costed and inherently risky. In desperation, the government had taken a big punt. Whereas it was Muldoon's intention to stabilise the economy, his policies had quite the opposite effect.[37] There was increasing uncertainty in all areas of the economy. It became harder and harder for households and small businesses to borrow funds. New Zealand was coming to resemble a Latin American-style (or East European) economy.

New Zealand (and Auckland) underwent both extensive and intensive growth during the insulationist era. The achievements of these years cannot be completely dismissed, yet it is reasonable to argue that somewhat higher levels of growth and prosperity would have been attained if markets had been given more scope to fulfil their role of allocating resources.

Dismantling the regulated economy

The toppling of Muldoon in 1984, and the discrediting of his interventionist regime, created an opportunity for an economic policy revolution in New Zealand. Within a week the new Labour Government had virtually abolished all controls over interest rates. Financial markets were deregulated, and in March 1985 the New Zealand dollar was permitted to float. Other changes followed at a less hectic pace, including the corporatisation and sale of public sector trading organisations, and the reduction of border protection. But decisive reform of the labour market was delayed until the early 1990s.[38]

The Labour Government endeavoured to reinvigorate the New Zealand economy, of which Auckland was a key component. The Minister of Finance (1984–88) and architect of the reforms, Roger Douglas, was an Aucklander with strong business interests.[39] Douglas was a relatively new convert to free market policies. He had the good fortune to be in the right place at the right time when the Muldoon Government was defeated. Considering the failure of the insulated and regulated economy, many people were prepared to give Douglas's radical policies a chance. The transition to a market-driven economy did not go smoothly, but a clear improvement in economic performance was evident after the early 1990s.

Once credit rationing had ceased, there was a large increase in private-sector borrowing and a boom in asset prices. Numerous speculative investment and property companies were set up in the mid-1980s, especially in Auckland. New Zealand's banks, most of which lacked experience in managing risk in a deregulated environment, scrambled to lend to these companies in an effort not to miss out. Many of these speculative ventures turned sour, especially after the 1987 sharemarket crash, and the banks were forced to rein in their lending, to the detriment of sound as well as unsound borrowers.[40]

Tight monetary policy, combined with financial deregulation, was a recipe for soaring interest rates after 1984. The New Zealand dollar surged. Farmers bore the initial brunt of high interest rates and the high real exchange rate. Manufactured imports became more competitive, although the full impact of the new policy regime was not felt by import substitution industries until the late 1980s because of delays in trade liberalisation. In November 1988, however, the Manufacturers' Federation organised a seminar at Auckland

University, at which there was much criticism of certain economic policies perceived to be restraining growth and threatening jobs and businesses. There was widespread acceptance that some economic reform was overdue, but dismay at the government's supposedly extreme emphasis on tight monetary policy. Unfavourable comparisons were drawn between the recent economic performances of New Zealand and Australia.[41] The manufacturers, with the assistance of sympathetic academics, continued to lobby for a softening of policy during 1989, but under a Labour Government they no longer had much influence.[42]

During the second half of the 1980s, New Zealand started to turn to 'non-traditional' sources of immigrants, including Asia, who found Auckland a particularly convenient and congenial destination. But population growth in New Zealand continued to be driven overwhelmingly by natural increase rather than by permanent net flows of migrants. To a large extent, the new immigrants acted as replacements for New Zealanders departing in search of more lucrative jobs in Australia, Britain and the United States. The ethnic structure of New Zealand cities was changing and their culture was becoming more globalised, but the long-term economic impact of this process is harder to evaluate.[43]

The early 1990s saw an international recession, which was particularly painful for New Zealand firms because of the hopes raised by the post-1984 reforms. An economic recovery began towards the end of 1991, and, to the surprise of many, persisted for the remainder of the decade, punctuated by a brief recession in 1998 associated with a severe drought and the Asian financial crisis.[44] Confidence was gradually restored to the business sector. Large structural changes occurred in the economy during the years of deregulation. The contribution to economic activity of the service industries, especially of financial services and communications, grew relative to that of manufacturing. Some manufacturing industries, including chemicals and rubber, adapted reasonably well, but others contracted. By the mid-1990s, the manufacturing sector was much more export-minded than it had been before 1984. Many of the firms that went under had focused on the assembly of imported components and kits, an activity for which there was no need after the dismantling of protection.[45]

Some exceptional firms did, however, make the transition from import substitution to exporting. Fisher & Paykel, an Auckland company, was established in 1938 to import electrical appliances. It soon progressed to the assembly of appliances in collaboration with overseas partners. In the 1960s, Fisher & Paykel began to export whiteware, especially to Australia, and subsequently opened production facilities in that country. In 1978, the company's accumulated total of exports reached US$100 million. Fisher & Paykel also began to make appliances to its own designs, and to cultivate a niche at the upper end of the market in countries such as the United States. The company has since successfully diversified into medical technologies.[46] Unfortunately, Auckland and New Zealand have few companies of the calibre of Fisher & Paykel, and none to compare with, say, Nokia of Finland, although it could be argued that the Finns have put too many eggs in the one basket.[47]

Overall, the reforms of the 1980s and 1990s created a more competitive economy. New Zealand's economic decline relative to the rest of the OECD was halted, although it has not yet been reversed.[48] Over the 1990s, New Zealand enjoyed faster economic growth than either Germany or Japan, an outcome that would have been inconceivable in the 1980s. But Australia's economic performance was even better than New Zealand's until the turn of the millennium. Auckland still struggled to compete with the leading Australian cities as a business and cultural centre. A number of important New Zealand companies moved their headquarters to Australia, although Auckland was able to attract the headquarters of some businesses from Wellington and other smaller New Zealand centres.

Conclusion

The processing of grass into wool, meat, and dairy products, and the export of these commodities, principally to the United Kingdom, has been the 'core business' of the New Zealand economy over much of the past 150 years. Auckland has provided port facilities and financial and other services for many farmers. The city has also developed an economy of its own, based on the assembling and processing of imported components and materials. During the era of insulation, Auckland's manufacturing sector attained further growth, although its productivity remained low by international standards. More recently, Auckland has to some extent reverted to its original emphasis on services. New service industries, including tourism and export education, have started to thrive. Most international visitors make Auckland their point of entry to the rest of New Zealand.

The economic performance of New Zealand, especially since the Second World War, has been lacklustre, and it is too early to say whether the improvements since the early 1990s will be sustained. In the face of trade manipulation by countries in the northern hemisphere, the pastoral industries stuttered. The search for competitive new export industries was hampered

An early dairy-processing enterprise: making cheese at the Kaupokonui Dairy Company in Taranaki, c. 1920. ALEXANDER TURNBULL LIBRARY, NATIONAL LIBRARY OF NEW ZEALAND, PACOLL-6304-32.

for many years by extensive import controls. These controls raised costs throughout the economy. It is difficult to say how much Auckland would have gained in the long run, had governments in Wellington chosen to pursue somewhat less defensive policies between 1945 and 1984, but it does seem likely that the gap in prosperity between Auckland and Sydney or Melbourne would not have become as great as it is today.

Auckland and New Zealand could, and perhaps should, have done better during the twentieth century. The adoption of insulationism in the mid-twentieth century was an important policy error, as was New Zealand's earlier failure to join the Australian common market in 1901. The benefits of closer economic contact with New South Wales and Victoria would have afforded some compensation, albeit partial, for New Zealand's isolation from the rest of the world.[49]

CHAPTER TWO

Maori Enterprise: Ships and Flour Mills

HAZEL PETRIE

Economic historians have tended to avoid the history of Maori commercial endeavours because quantifiable data is in short supply concerning this topic. As economic historian Simon Ville wrote, 'very little evidence survives regarding Maori enterprise in coastal shipping or in other areas of the economy'.[1] However, by utilising the methods of the social historian, especially those developed in connection with other areas of historical endeavour that were once considered unknowable, such as women's history or 'history from below',[2] insight can be gained into the Maori contribution to the growth of early Auckland. In this case, Maori correspondence, waiata, Maori and English newspapers and government archives, as well as the writings of eighteenth- and nineteenth-century explorers, travellers and missionaries, provide glimpses of the motivations behind Maori economic endeavour, its extent and effects. Particularly important for the founding of a new colony were the Maori's communally organised wheat-growing, flour milling, and coastal shipping enterprises.

Maori attitudes to trade from the time of European contact
Although Auckland did not become a centre of Pakeha population until after

1840, Maori enthusiasm for commerce was evident wherever foreign ships visited from the time of the first European contact with this country. Within about thirty years of Captain James Cook's arrival, the potential market for Maori enterprise expanded from a purely domestic one restricted to a relatively small population to encompass Europe, Asia, North and South America, Australia and the wider Pacific. It was an opportunity Maori grasped quickly and actively.

When Cook and his crew were in New Zealand waters, Maori communities undertook large-scale fishing expeditions to take advantage of the trading opportunities the Pakeha presence offered. They also soon adopted new crops, such as white potatoes (*Solanum tuberosum*), to meet the demands of their new customers: the sealers, whalers and other Euro-American sailing ships that began to call at New Zealand harbours. Potatoes met a very ready market, being a particularly convenient and valuable source of vitamin C for the ships' crew who were at sea for long periods. By 1803, Maori plantations were such that potatoes could be purchased by the ton.[3] William Dalton, surgeon aboard the whaling ship *Phoenix*, which visited the Bay of Islands in 1824, compared the health of his crew with those of the *Francis*, to stress 'the absolute necessity of supplying . . . ships abundantly with potatoes'.[4] The New Zealanders' ability to meet all the needs of South Seas shipping became well known. Governor Philip King of New South Wales advised Earl Camden in April 1805 that Tuki Tahua and Ngahuruhuru, who had spent several months on Norfolk Island in 1793, had turned the seeds and other articles they were given to 'very beneficial account, not only for their own advantage, but also in supplying the whaling ships very liberally with potatoes and other productions'. King continued that:

> The many vessels that have put into the Bay of Islands and other parts of [the New Zealand] coast have never, as far as I have learn'd, had any altercation with the natives, but have received every kind office and assistance in procuring their wood and water, etc., at a very cheap rate in barter.[5]

The captain of a whaler that visited the Bay in April 1838 revealed how the variety of Maori trade goods had expanded, recording that his ship was surrounded by canoes loaded with potatoes, peaches, melons, grapes, fish, pigs and women.[6]

In order to broaden their knowledge of the outside world and the functioning of international trade, Maori needed to travel overseas themselves. This usually required little encouragement as individuals began joining whalers and other foreign vessels shortly after these appeared in New Zealand waters and became much sought after as crew.[7] As a result of these overseas travels, by the 1790s some Maori became more aware of and directly engaged in international trade. Late-eighteenth and early-nineteenth century journeys to the Pacific Islands, Australia, North and South America, Asia and Europe familiarised Maori with overseas markets, products and economic systems. Returning travellers not only taught their relatives and chiefs about the world beyond Polynesia, they also brought back innovations such as wheat cultivation and dairy farming. Ruatara was the first person to harvest a wheat crop in New Zealand and Rawiri Taiwhanga was the first to produce butter commercially.[8] The fact that Maori pioneered these enterprises before Europeans attests to their ability and willingness to seek out and master new technologies to enhance their economic position.

Tribal leaders were keen to pursue opportunities for export. In order to facilitate this, a number of them are known to have sent letters or gifts or travelled overseas to visit at least four British monarchs, four governors of New South Wales, and an unknown number of overseas merchants, with the aim of seeking diplomatic and trading alliances. This was a Maori response to the new environment, seeking to build relationships with leaders and communities perceived to have the greatest power internationally. The Northern tribes first developed relationships with the British Crown through visits to British Navy ships. Leading rangatira known to have made such direct contact include Ngati Maru's Te Horeta, Te Popoto's Te Taonui, Ngati Hao's Waka Nene and Patuone, and Titore Takiri of Te Moana i Pikopiko i Whiti.[9]

Maori eagerness to trade was remarked on by a number of observers. According to Duperrey, whose corvette, *La Coquille*, put into the Bay of Islands in 1824:

> Scarcely had the anchor touched bottom when from all directions canoes laden with natives came alongside. More than 400 New Zealanders climbed up on to the deck, where their curiosity gave rise to an unusual uproar. Toui, paramount chief of the Pa of Kawera [Kahuwera] and of the district in which we were about to stay, offered us his services and introduced his family to us, guaranteeing that we would never have cause to complain of the conduct of his fellow countrymen towards us. And indeed, during the whole stay we never felt any need to be on our guard. The natives came aboard daily unarmed, and accompanied us on our expeditions with great willingness.[10]

Robert Jarman, who reported a great many Maori in Sydney when he visited in 1833, described them generally as 'industrious, intelligent, bold, and enterprising'. He predicted that the size of their country, the productiveness of its soil, the spirit of its inhabitants, and its convenient situation for trade with Australia, Tahiti and Hawaii, would cause it to become 'a place of considerable importance'. Maori were certainly sought after as trading partners. Pigs and potatoes, introduced by Cook and others for the convenience of western seafarers, proved lucrative trade items, but indigenous products such as flax were also in demand. The peak year for the flax trade was 1831: 1182 tons being exported to Sydney, 800 tons of which had been contracted by the British Navy Board. Flax, hand-prepared by Maori, was particularly highly valued for making the rope so essential in the sailing ship era. According to Bishop Williams, Maori communities threw themselves so eagerly into the business that for several years the cultivation of crops and other occupations were very seriously neglected. Extractive industries such as sealing, whaling, flax cropping and timber felling rose and fell with the demands of an international economy. But the fluidity of Maori society and the limited capital investment required for profitable participation allowed Maori to adjust quickly. By 1833, timber had replaced flax as the Maori's greatest export earner. However, these trades were not sustainable in the long term, which may have encouraged an intensification of agricultural production.

In 1830, twenty-eight ships averaging 110 tons made fifty-six voyages between Sydney and New Zealand carrying Maori grown potatoes and milled grain. Although statistics vary greatly between sources, they all agree that 1831 saw a very healthy trade surplus. However, it must be remembered that Britain was not the Maori's primary customer prior to annexation. The early trade in sealskins was largely for the Chinese market, American ships outlasting those from Australia and Britain in this trade, and visiting whalers and trading ships also came increasingly from America. Other vessels came from France, Portugal, Germany, the Netherlands, Tahiti, Brazil, New South Wales and Tasmania. Spars were destined for India and China. In 1826 the *Sydney Gazette* reported that '[t]wenty sail of ships is no uncommon sight in the Bay of Islands'.[11]

While the Maori economy was flourishing, in the face of commercial success, Maori would soon appreciate the need for protection under international law. This became particularly clear in 1830, when the Hokianga-built ship *Sir George Murray*, with chiefs Patuone and Taonui on board, was seized in Sydney for not flying a national flag. Northern Maori were also concerned by rumours that France had designs on New Zealand, which threatened Maori sovereignty – fears that were heightened when the French vessel *La Favorite* arrived in October 1831. Consequently, in late 1831 a number of northern chiefs petitioned King William IV for an economic and defence alliance. Their address, which cited their sales of timber, flax, pork and potatoes to British traders and claimed that his Britain was the only one well disposed to them, was laid before a meeting of the New South Wales Executive Council on 22 December 1831.

Governor Darling and his successor, Major-General Sir Richard Bourke, stressed the importance of Maori trade to the colony of New South Wales and Great Britain. Bourke expressed eagerness to 'conciliate the good will of the Chiefs' and encourage the production of goods needed by Britain and New South Wales. Trade figures supplied by the Sydney Customs House, showing imports from New Zealand to that town with a declared value of £34,282 and exports to New Zealand valued at £30,760 between 1 January and 8 December 1831, were also laid before the Council. Irrespective of the economic significance of these figures in the context of the wider New South Wales economy, they were politically significant.[12] On the basis of these documents and representations made by missionaries and Sydney-based merchants, James Busby was appointed British Resident in 1833.

In March 1834, Busby convened a meeting of Maori chiefs to deal with the difficulties faced by Maori and European-owned shipping in international waters and problems with Sydney's customs regulations. The first New Zealand flag was selected on this occasion and, in the following year, a Declaration of Independence was signed by the Confederation of United Chiefs for the purpose of framing 'laws for the dispensation of justice, the preservation of peace and good order, and the regulation of trade'.

Maori were strengthening their alliance with Britain but staunchly maintained their autonomy and continued to seek economic opportunities in traditional ways. They were also outward looking. Maniapoto leaders Haupokia and Te Waru, for example, travelled to Sydney aboard a flax trader in 1830 hoping to entice a trader to their southern side of Kawhia Harbour. Their offer of abundant flax supplies, land, a house and a store for his agent enticed Joseph Montefiore to visit their area and establish two traders.[13] Like a number of other Sydney and Hobart merchants, Montefiore and Company placed agents throughout New Zealand, supplying them with trade goods to purchase prepared flax. But apart from communal initiatives to bring traders to New Zealand, individual Maori were engaged in the various Pacific trades of the day, from whaling to involvement in obtaining *bêche-de-mer* for the Chinese market.[14] Among these international entrepreneurs was a group of five Maori whalers who established trading operations at Ponape in the Caroline

Islands. This group had married local women and formed such a relationship with the indigenous people that, when they killed two rival European traders who had planned to kidnap their wives, they were placed under the protection of the local chief and guarded by a force of fifty.

Commerce between Maori and European required a greater degree of adjustment, but even the most fundamental of Maori cultural injunctions were flexible enough to facilitate interaction with those who did not share them. This is perhaps most evident in cases where non-Maori transgressed the fundamental code of tapu (ritual prohibition). Incidents such as touching the head of a chief, which may have resulted in death for another Maori, were often excused in the case of outsiders if commercial advantage was perceived to be gained from a more diplomatic resolution.

While some Maori entrepreneurs established businesses overseas and others met with kings, governors, and merchants, still others sought alliances with missionaries to enhance their economic opportunities. Reverend Samuel Marsden of the Church Missionary Society, resident in Sydney from 1794 to 1838, had taken a particular interest in the evangelisation of Maori. Bay of Islands leader Te Pahi had discussions with him on a visit to Sydney in late 1805 and early 1806, but plans to establish a Church Missionary Society station under his protection were foiled by the massacre of a ship's crew for which Te Pahi was, probably unjustly, held responsible.

Te Pahi's successor, Ruatara, who left New Zealand in 1805 as a crew member on a whaling ship, apparently hoping to meet Britain's King George III, spent some four years on various whalers, before eventually disembarking at Port Jackson where he spent about five months studying European agricultural techniques at Marsden's home in Parramatta. Marsden provided instruction to visitors in fish-curing, rope making, brick making, and agriculture, together with moral and religious lessons. When taken to see the process of weaving stockings on a loom, Ruatara remarked that Maori could do without hosiery, but they did want agricultural implements in order to produce their own bread. As early as 1814, Kendall reported from New Zealand that Maori were very fond of bread and keen for wheat to be established.[15] Traditional Maori cultigens could not necessarily guarantee continuity of supply, or a year-round carbohydrate staple so Ruatara was excited by the prospective advantages of wheat.[16]

However, Ruatara's vision went beyond the immediate food requirements of Maori to a potentially lucrative export opportunity. Because wheat was scarce at Port Jackson at the time, he decided that on his return to New Zealand he would cultivate surplus crops of wheat for export to Australia. This venture, he told Marsden, would enable him to buy hoes, axes, spades, tea and sugar, and enable New Zealand to become 'a great country'. Ruatara departed New South Wales with a quantity of seed wheat and tools as well as a mare, a cow and other livestock given to him by then Governor of New South Wales, Lachlan Macquarie, who was anxious to smooth the path of a proposed mission station in New Zealand. Unfortunately, Ruatara's attempts to popularise the crop among Maori communities were initially stymied by the lack of mills with which to grind the grain.[17]

In 1814, Ruatara seized the chance to offer protection to the first missionaries in New Zealand in order to take advantage of the economic benefits associated with their residence.[18] Sadly, he died very shortly after their arrival, but Hongi Hika took over the role of patron, staunchly defending missionaries and seamen alike against his own people when necessary, in the knowledge that a reputation for peace and security would encourage traders. However, Hongi was equally determined to contain their activities within his territory, which Marsden recognised when he visited the Hokianga Harbour on the west coast of Northland:

> The chiefs and priest . . . asked us if we had mentioned our coming to Shunghee [Hongi], for they feared the chiefs on the east side would not be pleased if any ship should visit them. I told them I had acquainted Shunghee with our intention, and he had sent his son to show us the way. They were much pleased at this information and remarked that, as we had come of our own accord, without invitation, the chiefs had no ground to be offended with them.[19]

Maintaining the commercial supremacy of one's own tribal area was of particular importance to Maori leaders. Titore sought to secure the benefits he had achieved for his homeport of Kororareka by hindering trade at nearby Whangaroa, which was under his tutelage. He appears to have done this by limiting the number of vessels trading at Whangaroa and, in 1834, by attempting to obstruct the loading of HMS *Buffalo*, a British naval vessel on a timber-buying trip, until he was given a part in the proceedings.[20] Anxious to establish an ongoing relationship with the British monarch, Titore wrote to King William IV offering to place a tapu on his timber and guaranteeing future supplies of spars for the British navy.[21] As a sign of good faith his letter was accompanied by a mere pounamu (a greenstone hand weapon) and two kakahu (chiefly garments). He was also careful to give a gift to the messenger. Captain Saddler, who would carry the letter and gifts to the king, received a bone flute and cloak pin, a greenstone mere and a hei tiki/hei matau. Titore, whose gifts were motivated by his desire to achieve a favoured position for his people in terms of a trading and friendship alliance, must have been gratified to receive a reply from King William, which was accompanied by a suit of armour.[22]

In 1840, the relationship between Maori and the British was further strengthened when over 500 Maori signed the Treaty of Waitangi, a formal alliance with Queen Victoria, under which Britain would have kawanatanga (governance: administration and law) of New Zealand and Maori retain their rangatiratanga (chieftainship). Maori understood the arrangement to be one of partnership, reciprocal obligation and mutual benefit, with the guarantee of rangatiratanga ensuring autonomy over their own affairs.

The fundamental importance of trade and commercial protection in this agreement was confirmed by Colenso's account of proceedings at Waitangi on 5 February 1840 in which he quoted the Ngai Tawake chief, Wai's questions to Hobson:

> To thee, O Governor! this. Will you remedy the selling, the exchanging, the cheating, the lying, the stealing of the whites? . . . The white gives us Natives a pound for a pig; but he gives a white four pounds for such a pig. Is that straight? The white man gives us a shilling for a basket of potatoes; but to a white he gives four shillings for a basket like that one of ours. Is that straight? . . . Wilt thou make dealing straight?

However, the economic benefits Northland Maori expected to flow from the Treaty with Britain were short-lived, as the imposition of customs duties encouraged shipping to divert to duty-free ports overseas, and local tribes were no longer permitted to levy anchorage fees on shipping.[23] The resulting decline in commercial activity affected both Maori and Pakeha traders. The Bay's two leading merchants, James Clendon and Gilbert Mair, both went out of business in 1842 and the once-prosperous town of Kororareka fell into decay.[24] The fortunes of the Pakeha traders paralleled those of Northland tribes who also suffered from the relocation of New Zealand's capital to Auckland in September 1840. Nga Puhi chief, Hone Heke, who protested the economic ill-effects of colonisation by chopping down the British flagstaff at Kororareka, turned to armed rebellion in 1845. Ngati Whatua and other groups near Auckland were now reaping the economic benefits of British settlement, but these would also be short-lived.

A drawing of Robertson's rope walk and Low and Motion's flour mill at Mechanics Bay
Auckland in 1845. The rope walk was supplied with flax prepared by Maori women and carried
there in large baskets – an 'ordinary man's load' apparently fetching about 8s 6d, which was
equivalent to about a week's wages for a male Pakeha worker at that time. ASHTON ALBUM,
AUCKLAND INSTITUTE AND MUSEUM.

The Maori role in the early Auckland economy

Ngati Whatua's 1840 invitation to New Zealand's first Governor, William
Hobson, to relocate New Zealand's capital in Auckland was politically as
well as commercially motivated, ensuring greater security for both the Maori
hosts and the British settlers as well as opportunities for the former to gain
economically from the influx of immigrants. It was a move that initially proved
fruitful for Maori throughout the region as well as for the infant colony more
generally.

When the first two immigrant ships, the *Duchess of Argyle* and the *Jane
Gifford*, arrived in Auckland from Scotland in October 1842, the town was
in the grip of a depression, and the arrival of so many poor, working-class
people was not appreciated by the likes of established merchant, John Logan
Campbell, who wrote that Auckland needed an influx of capitalists rather
than labourers.[25] However, because these settlers needed food, fuel and
housing, the immigration of British labourers and artisans was paralleled by
the immigration of Maori from the hinterland as nearby tribal groups acquired
rights to reside and cultivate in the Auckland area under the mana of local iwi.

The Maori hostelry built by Ngati Whatua at Mechanics Bay (in the foreground), photographed c. 1864. ALEXANDER TURNBULL LIBRARY, NATIONAL LIBRARY OF NEW ZEALAND, 1/2-036270.

Others came as 'guest workers' to learn agricultural skills or earn money for community projects in their home settlements.[26]

The rapidly increasing settler population and their demands for food resulted in increased agricultural production in the areas immediately adjacent to the new township, enormous quantities of produce coming to Auckland on foot or by canoe from further afield. Long-established Maori trails from the interior became cart roads; canoe landing-places, like the one at Te Rore, the river port of the upper Waipa district, became depots for trade with Auckland.[27] Flour and other produce was brought to Te Rore by bullock-drawn drays, then down the Waipa and Waikato rivers and on via Awaroa Stream to Waiuku, on the shores of the Manukau Harbour.[28] When Charles Abraham took this route in August 1855, he found over thirty canoes and more than 200 of their Maori occupants encamped at the portage on the Awaroa Stream with supplies of wheat for loading onto Waiuku carts for transportation to the Auckland market.[29] Hostelries were erected at Onehunga and on the Waitemata at Mechanics Bay to accommodate visiting Maori traders.

By the early 1850s, the Ngati Maru and Ngati Tama-Te-Ra leader, Taraia, was bringing parties of his people to Auckland once or twice a year in a fleet of forty waka taua (war canoes) and setting up a tent encampment on the beach from where they sold pigs, potatoes, wheat, maize, melons, onions, flax, firewood, poultry and various other goods.[30] The importance of canoe traffic generally was officially recognised by 1852 when official returns of canoe traffic began to be compiled. As the following table indicates, the value of goods brought to Auckland by canoe was increasing rapidly from 1852 to 1854, but began to decline from then on as Maori expanded their fleet of Western-style sailing ships.

TABLE 1: VALUE OF MAORI PRODUCE BROUGHT TO AUCKLAND BY CANOE, 1852–55

Year	Value
1852	£3,564 11s 6d
1853	£9,581 13s 6d
1854	£12,417 15s 4d
1885	£10,390 14s 3d

Source: *AJHR*, 1865, E No. 12, pp. 1–18.

As the European population of Auckland grew from about 1000 in 1841 to over 9000 by 1851, and about 15,335 by 1856, Maori agricultural production continued apace.[31] But whereas whalers and other visiting ships had wanted potatoes, settlers wanted a more varied and familiar diet. Wheat, being the

A view from the end of the wharf at the foot of Queen Street in 1852, showing Maori canoes and street traders. P. J. HOGAN HAND-COLOURED LITHOGRAPH, ALEXANDER TURNBULL LIBRARY, NATIONAL LIBRARY OF NEW ZEALAND, C-010-020.

staple food of the predominantly British immigrants, and increasingly of Maori themselves, became a particularly important commodity both for domestic consumption and for export to Australia. Large areas of Maori land were under cultivation in the Waikato and other areas, the financial success of their operations being bolstered not only by the needs of Auckland's burgeoning European population, but also by an expanding export market.[32] The discovery of gold in Victoria, Australia, in 1851, which caused a rapid increase in that state's population, saw the price of wheat in Melbourne rise from 4s 3d per bushel in October 1850 to 15s a bushel in October 1854, and flour from £10 10s to £35 during the same period.[33] In order to profit from these markets, Maori communities, especially those on the east coast of the North Island, increasingly found it economically prudent to take advantage of the greater efficiency of ships, especially schooners, to transport unprocessed wheat and other produce to Auckland.[34]

The rise of Maori ship ownership

There were a number of incentives for Maori to acquire their own ships. These included the greater carrying capacity of cutters and schooners and the seasonality of canoe passage. Missionary Richard Taylor recorded a time-consuming journey from the Waikato through the Mangatawhiri narrows when canoes had to be dragged a considerable distance before finally being abandoned for a walk of almost 2 kilometres across a swamp.[35] Reverend Buttle described a similar situation when a large party from Waipa set off for Auckland in January 1855. On this occasion, insufficient water in the tributary stream meant it took a whole month to reach the town by canoe. The return journey took yet another five months to complete because the travellers had to wait in town until enough rain had fallen to allow canoe passage home.[36]

Given the typically bush-covered and mountainous terrain of the New Zealand interior, developing an effective inland transport system was a costly and time-consuming process which government could not justify in these early, cash-strapped days.[37] Ships, on the other hand, were comparatively cheap to run and crews of two or three were a far less labour-intensive means of conveyance than the overland alternatives. The vessels typically purchased were of modest size and relatively shallow draught, particularly suited to the narrow creeks and inlets, and the many small harbours along the coast. These small sailing vessels, which have been referred to as 'the horses and carts of the first decades of settlement', became the main means of getting goods about the North Island coast.[38]

Another factor stimulating ship purchase was a growing appreciation among Maori producers more distant from Auckland that they were being disadvantaged by having to sell their goods through locally based traders rather than dealing directly with Auckland merchants. By the early 1840s, Maori in Northland, Auckland, the East Coast, the Bay of Plenty, Thames–Coromandel and elsewhere were buying Western-style sailing ships to trade directly with Auckland. Edward Shortland's comments concerning Bay of Plenty Maori were likely to have reflected a more widespread phenomenon:

> They have imbibed a suspicion of all European traders, they are aware that they have often been cheated and not knowing the real value of their property fear to ask too low a price for it and in their turn use every act to impose on Europeans.[39]

When Maori sold flax to locally based traders at the stated rate of £4 10s per ton, they were actually paid in trade goods such as blankets and clothing. But manufactured items had high margins added to them which made such deals unattractive from the Maori point of view – not to mention a narrow range of stock to choose from. Because they were well aware that they could get better prices for their production, and purchase manufactured goods more cheaply at Auckland, Maori communities attempted to ameliorate these disadvantages as best they could. Missionary Thomas Chapman, who returned to his station at Maketu in 1845 with a hundred shirts and some £15 worth of calico as trade goods, was told by his local patrons that they should not need to recompense him for the land carriage of these items because he was able to buy their potatoes 'so cheaply'.[40] Not surprisingly, local traders began to disappear from coastal settlements as Maori dispensed with the need for middlemen and conducted business on their own account.

The rise of Maori flour milling

Whereas coastal tribes could transport unprocessed wheat to Auckland's Waitemata Harbour by sea with relative ease, the situation for the inland tribes was different. Tribes such as those in the upper Waikato, where communications were far more difficult and therefore more expensive in terms of time and labour, were more inclined to build water-powered flour mills. As the *New Zealander* newspaper pointed out:

> . . . with the natives, as with the European settlers, a productive harvest of wheat is comparatively no benefit to the resident population, unless there are mills on the

spot, to convert it into flour. This very circumstance has much retarded the success of farmers in the neighbourhood of Auckland, where grain might be shipped to other ports; but such disadvantage would operate still more powerfully against the farmer in the interior, and indeed, in districts distant from the coast, and without any roads to the capital, would prevent altogether the cultivation of wheat.[41]

Increased production without any comparable improvement in overland transport systems did little to improve the standard of living for Maori communities. John Morgan, the missionary stationed at Otawhao in the upper Waikato, referred to the drawbacks of living in inland areas in 1846 when he wrote:

> [I]t is seldom, except on the coast, that a native possesses more than a blanket, and in the interior in order to procure this trifling article of clothing, they have generally to spend three or four weeks in performing a journey to Auckland, driving the pigs of a European trader.[42]

Processing wheat into flour at the point of production provided a cheaper home food supply, reduced the costs of transportation to Auckland, and added value to the crop. As a consequence, Maori communities built some twenty-six mills in the Waikato region between 1846 and 1860. The area became an important centre of flour production, which benefited Auckland by supplying incoming settlers and bolstering the port's export revenues.[43] Although New Zealand's exports continued to decline until 1849, George Grey explained to the Colonial Secretary, Earl Grey, that this was due to Maori turning their attention to the settler market for wheat and farm produce as the most profitable enterprise, adding that local consumption 'merely render[ed] the transaction so much more profitable for the country, as the cost of shipment and other charges [were] saved'.[44]

The first Maori-owned flour mill was built at Raoraokauere, near the Aotea Harbour and the site of Reverend Gideon Smales' 'Beechamdale' mission. This community had cultivated about a hundred acres of wheat over the previous two years, but the local rangatira decided that continued production would be profitable only if they invested in a water-powered mill to convert grain into flour. Having commissioned millwright Stewart McMullan to build one for £80, the owners did the earthworks, felled the timber, brought stones from Kawhia and cut them under McMullan's direction.[45] This mill began operation in 1846, but a lack of experience and, perhaps the quality of the stones, led to the latter being damaged beyond repair when the mill was allowed to continue running overlong.[46]

Following closely on the heels of the Aotea mill was the first of two flour mills to be built further inland, at Rangiaowhia on a branch of the Waipa River. This mill also started grinding in 1846. Costing £200, it was considerably more expensive than the Aotea mill. However, it utilised stones cut from Mt Eden scoria and was capable of grinding at a rate of six bushels per hour rather than the two bushels per hour ground at Aotea. By 1851, the mill was producing about 150 tons of flour, two-thirds of which was sent to the Auckland market. By this time, the owners had also built a brick oven from funds left over after paying the millwright for the mill construction.[47] They had engaged a Pakeha brick maker to make some 2700 bricks and, by 1853, were baking 400 loaves at a time.[48] Well before this, however, in January 1849, missionary Alfred Brown had recorded that the Maori who accompanied him from nearby Maungatautari 'had a large supply of wholesome, home-baked bread, for they have become of late on a very extensive scale, practical farmers, millers and bakers'.[49]

Maori contributions to the early Auckland economy

The 1840s and early 1850s have often been termed the Golden Age of Maori commerce but they were also something of a Golden Age for Auckland. As early as 1847, the *New Zealander* had warned that because of Maori production and their contributions to the development of the colony, Auckland had 'become one of the wealthiest colonial communities in the world' and that the inhabitants' taste for luxuries was as 'unsuited to the age of the settlement, as it [was] unfriendly to its interest and prospects'.[50] In the same issue, a correspondent calling himself 'The Voice of a Settler' claimed that Maori were Auckland's 'very life blood' and that, contrary to claims from others to the south, the region's large Maori population was a significant commercial reason for Auckland to remain the colony's capital.[51] His opinion was borne out over the subsequent nine years, during which time the economic fortunes of both Auckland and Maori rose and fell in tandem with each other.

'The Voice of a Settler' had hinted at the need for an association 'to encourage and promote the preparation of native produce for exportation'. During George Grey's first governorship in particular, under what was often termed his 'flour and sugar' policy, government-sponsored technical and financial assistance allowed Maori to develop wheat growing, flour milling, and shipping, as well as fostering the notion of a reciprocal partnership between Maori and the colonial government.

The growing importance of Maori shipping was implied in the Collector of Customs' 1849 request that forms for the entry and clearance of ships and license obligations be translated into Maori because of the considerable increase in Maori-owned vessels employed in the trade.[52] This was further indicated by George Grey's 1851 statement that 'the already considerable and increasing coasting trade' was 'chiefly carried on in vessels owned and manned by Maori' and the Wellington *Spectator*'s 1852 prediction that the coasting trade would soon be in Maori hands.[53] Francis Dart Fenton expressed similar views,[54] as did Richard Taylor who found the trade of Auckland to be 'perfectly surprising; the number of small coasters, most of which belong to the natives, and are laden with their produce, cannot fail striking the stranger who visits the port with astonishment'.[55]

A list of 118 Auckland-owned vessels of 10 tons or more employed in the coastal trade on 1 January 1853 revealed that the two largest were Maori-owned.[56] Some Maori shipowners engaged Auckland agents such as Charles Davis, William Smellie Grahame, E. King, Davies and Middlemas, and T. Russell; some also had other business relationships with these men concerning the financing of their vessels.

There is considerable evidence that Maori were a dominant force in the North Island coastal shipping industry by the early 1850s despite the fact that most of their vessels were neither registered nor licensed. Only fifty-eight vessels were officially registered as Maori-owned prior to 1860 but, by collating references from other sources, such as contemporary newspapers, missionary journals and government correspondence, over 160 additional vessels have already been identified as being Maori-owned before this date.[57] Because these references cannot be considered to be by any means comprehensive, it is almost certain that considerably more vessels were actually operating. One of many factors disguising the extent of Maori ship ownership is the fact that Maori ship purchases were typically made on an instalment basis and the government registers did not record changes of ownership until the final payment had been made. This often occurred some years after Maori had taken possession of the vessels and begun using them for trade.[58]

In addition to a low rate of registration, Maori activity in this industry has been further obscured by a low rate of reporting their arrivals and departures to the customs houses – a circumstance stressed by the *Southern Cross* in January 1852.[59] From that date, advertisements began to appear in the *Maori Messenger* informing shipowners that customs house forms were available from the Native Secretary's office. A copy of the bilingual form was published and the advertisement was supported by an editorial suggesting that an awareness of the extent of Auckland trade and goods supplied by Maori entrepreneurs would encourage whaling ships calling at more northern ports to travel to Auckland for reprovisioning.[60] But despite these exhortations, Maori were generally disinclined to cooperate with the demands of bureaucracy and many, perhaps most, Maori voyages seem to have gone unrecorded.

Maori shipping provided a vital means of communication between Auckland and more distant settlements for clergymen and their families, merchants and government officials. Contemporary missionary writings suggest that clergy of all denominations were very reliant on Maori shipowners for their own transportation, for sending and receiving mail, and for supplies such as food and building materials. Bishop Pompallier's complaint in an 1851 letter from Auckland to Father Moreau that: 'We have no other means of communication than the ships of the natives' was typical.[61] The value of Maori shipping to Pakeha trade is further underscored by Pakeha appeals for licences to use Maori-owned ships when government restrictions were put in place to prevent their being used to supply 'rebels' during times of war.[62]

Although it seems certain that only a small proportion of Maori trading vessels reported their arrivals and departures to the Customs House, the recorded inward and outward cargoes indicate that the owning communities were doing well economically and contributing significantly to the Auckland economy as purchasers of manufactured goods.

Maori came to Auckland to buy agricultural tools and ploughs, to engage millwrights and other trades people, and to purchase or commission the building of schooners, as well as to buy clothing, foodstuffs and household goods. William Brown and his partner, John Logan Campbell, were among those merchants who benefited from the availability of cheap Maori produce and from their custom. When merchants were struggling to keep afloat in 1843, Campbell had compared Auckland with another, now bankrupt settlement in Western Australia:

> But for the Native Population we would have been a *Swan River* long ago. They raise us cheap food which they sell us – they spend the money among us – it remains in the colony – it is equivalent to an export.[63]

Having made profits from 20 per cent to 75 per cent on blankets, Brown and Campbell eventually opened a retail shop catering specifically for the 'native trade'.[64] Perhaps it was awareness of these margins that led one of those who migrated to the Auckland area in the early 1840s, the Hokianga chief, Patuone, to set up his own country agent. This elderly man in the Volcanic Plateau area of the North Island sold blankets on Patuone's behalf and returned the takings to Auckland in pigs.[65]

Despite the fact that Pakeha merchants in Auckland benefited from having a wide pool of suppliers, Maori were not necessarily respected as good customers. Brown and Campbell, for example, on-sold a consignment of flour that was partly sour and partly maggoty to a baker who supplied bread to Maori customers in 1853.[66]

There is considerable evidence that, until 1856, Maori production was an important component of the colonial economy and, in particular, of the largest population centre, Auckland.[67] Notwithstanding the provisioning of new immigrants, the value of New Zealand's exports rose from £134,000 in 1849 to £336,000 in 1855 when agricultural produce accounted for half the total.[68] The estimated annual value of produce brought to Auckland by canoe (see Table 1) indicates the rapidly increasing significance of this trade to Maori agriculture. However, although it is clear that many, if not most, Maori-owned ships did not register their cargoes with the Customs House, the following table suggests that Maori were increasing their use of coastal shipping to convey their wheat to Auckland:

TABLE 2: WHEAT IMPORTS INTO AUCKLAND PER COASTAL SHIPPING, DECEMBER 1854 – SEPTEMBER 1856

Quarter	Total bushels	Total value (£)	Average value per bushel
Dec. 1854	21,920	13,700	12s 6d
Mar. 1855	13,518	6,759	10s
Jun. 1855	32,356	19,413	12s
Sep. 1855	24,854	15,533	12s 6d
Dec. 1855	11,500	6,900	12s
Mar. 1856	5,397	2,968	11s
Jun. 1856	23,202	7,540	6s 6d
Sep. 1856	28,331	10,624	7s 6d

Source: *Auckland Provincial Government Gazette*, 1855 and 1856.

The reduced quantities in the December 1855 and March 1856 quarters appear to be a response to the sudden drop in demand which was subsequently reflected in value. The table below, which also indicates increasing production – at least until 1855 – provides some indication of the increasing use of schooners over canoes for transporting produce:

TABLE 3: AUCKLAND IMPORTS OF SELECTED MAORI PRODUCE, 1852–56

Year	Vessel	Wheat (bushels)	Maize (bushels)	Potatoes (tons)
1852	Coastal vessels*	30,633	10,959	188
1852	Canoes	1,674	2,157	235
1853	Coastal vessels	37,541	14,556	850
1853	Canoes	2,454	4,139	282
1854	Coastal vessels	65,833	18,569	535
1854	Canoes*	3,715	1,123	94
1855	Coastal vessels	82,228	29,250	1,175
1855	Canoes	1,372	bags	1,398
1856	Coastal vessels*	56,930	7,873	279
1856	Canoes	3,557	774	125

*These figures are incomplete. The 1852 return for coastal vessels covers only the six months from July to December; the 1854 return excludes canoe traffic from April to June, and the coastal vessel return for 1856 excludes October to December.

The 1852 return for coastal vessels covers only the six months from July to December, the 1854 return excludes canoe traffic from April to June, and the coastal vessel return for 1856 excludes October to December.[69] Such statistical material as is available, together with comments in newspapers, parliamentary debates and government reports, supports the contention that Auckland's economic dominance, which dissolved by 1856, was driven by Maori commercial enterprise.[70] Available statistics are so incomplete that neither the precise proportion of Auckland's domestic food supply that was satisfied from Maori production, nor the proportion of their contribution to exports, can be easily determined.

What is clear is that most contemporary commentators believed that contribution to be substantial. However, a dramatic slump in the wheat, flour and produce market, which followed the end of the Victorian gold rush in early 1856, had particularly serious economic implications for Maori entrepreneurs. As these products also underpinned the success of Maori shipping, the effects of this slump were compounded by increasing competition from more capital-intensive steam ships, which were beyond the financial resources of Maori communities or small traders. The financial strains of heavy investment in flour mills and coastal vessels plunged many Maori communities into serious debt, and there is evidence that their indebtedness also had flow-on effects for Pakeha business people in the Auckland Province.[71] Despite this, any possibility of weathering these storms was made much more difficult by a concurrent hardening of settler attitudes towards the economic 'competition' allegedly posed by Maori commercial endeavours towards Pakeha business.

One observer perceived such attitudes behind precipitous land sales, which by leaving Auckland's Fort Street without access to the sea would render the Maori marketplace inaccessible to canoes. '[W]hat [could] be more absurd than thus to prevent the convenient access of those, on whom the Town of Auckland is so dependent for its daily supplies of food', he asked.[72] Within six years, however, settler interests were hampering Maori commerce in other ways. For example, council control of Auckland's native hostelry was urged on the basis that the town market would not prove an adequate source of revenue unless 'native hawkers' were suppressed.[73]

Similarly, while the arrival of Taraia's trading parties had been described by William Swainson, the first Attorney-General, as having 'the appearance of a fair' and their produce as meeting with 'a ready market' in 1853, a deterioration in the Pakeha–Maori relationship was exposed soon after. For example, when a Maori party arrived at Freemans Bay in 1855, the *Southern Cross* reported:

> Their arrival was soon construed into a suspicious incident, and rumours gained ground in course of yesterday that they were a war party, and that the canoes were filled with arms. We have taken a little trouble to arrive at the truth, and find that it is a fishing party from Waiheki [*sic*]. They are en route to Mahurangi, on a shark fishing expedition, and have called here merely for the purchase of necessaries.[74]

The arrival of a canoe-borne shopping expedition may now have been perceived as intimidating, but trading schooners, like other aspects of Maori commerce, were being subjected to greater regulation too. In the commercially difficult year of 1856, Native Secretary, Donald McLean, would urge stricter supervision over the Maori coasting trade to prevent 'the evils' that he considered were being 'so justly complained of'.[75]

Tensions rise

Tensions reached a critical point in 1858 when debates over the proportional value of Maori contributions to colonial revenues became especially heated and statistics were being compiled or interpreted to suit political agendas. Even Colonial Treasurer, C. W. Richmond, who tried rather desperately to 'entirely dispel exaggerated notions respecting the magnitude of the Maori contributions to the revenue', was forced to acknowledge that 'in years such as 1854 and 1855, when agricultural produce was at an extraordinarily high price', considerable advantage had 'been derived to the colonial revenue by the *balance of the Maori contributions remaining after defraying the expense of services for their special benefit*' (italics added).[76] His wording suggests that these expenses were deducted from the revenue he reported. Remarks by the Governor are appended to this memorandum to the effect that he saw no 'reasons to think the mode of calculation here adopted [by Richmond was] more correct than the estimate given in [his previous despatch] of 31 May 1858'. Donald McLean agreed that the Maori contribution had been downplayed:

> In enumerating the causes operating to make the contributions in the northern island exceed, per head, those of the southern provinces, the large native population is omitted. It cannot be doubted that the produce of native labour, and the exports they mainly contributed to furnish, were not without considerable influence in causing the excess of revenue. It is believed that double the amount set down by the Ministers as the Maori contribution to the Customs would not be an over-estimate of the revenue accruing through their means, exclusive of the land revenue.[77]

F. D. Bell, who had criticised previous government expenditure for Maori purposes, nonetheless acknowledged that loans for ships, flour mills and agricultural implements 'should be grudged the less from the consideration of their large contributions to the revenue, and their having no representation in [the] House'.[78]

Maori were contributing to Auckland's economic success not only as producers and customers, but also, increasingly, as merchants. Wheat-grower, Rutene Ahunuku, for example, established a monthly wheat market at Turanga in January 1853 for the benefit of Auckland shipowners.[79] Ahunuku later purchased his own vessel, the 32-ton schooner *Queen*, in partnership with Warihi Potini.[80] Te Hemara Tauhia of Ngati Rango took an equally 'hands on' approach to timber sales at Mahurangi, Northland, in the 1850s. He employed Pakeha sawyers and commissioned the building of the 20-ton *Duke of Wellington* to convey the timber to Auckland. Like many other chiefs, Te Hemara not only superintended sales and kept the accounts himself, he also captained the vessel.[81]

Maori assertiveness and commercial astuteness had not been expected and was increasingly resented as unwanted competition for Pakeha business people. David Rough, Auckland's first harbour master, published a narrative of his 1852 journey through parts of the North Island in which he frequently complained that Maori were unwilling to carry luggage for travellers who arrived at their villages unexpectedly. Rough made his perception of the place of Maori in the new order quite clear:

> As the New Zealanders are in habits of industry, aptitude to acquire a knowledge of European arts, and fondness for agriculture, different from most of the aboriginal inhabitants of other lands who have disappeared before the colonising progress of our race, it may be hoped that the noble efforts which are being made in their behalf may prove successful in completely civilizing them, and turning the force of character and intellect which they possess to perfecting a knowledge of such occupations as may render them serviceable to the colonists, *who will value and cherish them in proportion to their usefulness*.[82]

The end of an era

The summer of 1855–56 had seen a dramatic turnaround in the Maori economy, especially in the Auckland province, but evidence of Maori wealth while the high expectations of settlers remained largely unmet had already exacerbated political tensions. In 1854, for example, when the Pakeha farmers of Port Nicholson owned not a single plough, Wiremu Kingi's people at the Waitara River had thirty-five. They also had 20 pairs of harrows, 40 carts, 300 cattle, 150 horses, a small flotilla of sailing-boats, and a considerable amount of money.[83] Settlers on the one hand sought to benefit from trading in Maori produce, but on the other feared that supporting this commercial activity would increase Maori determination to withhold land from sale – an issue that had significant repercussions in Taranaki.

Increasing economic and political marginalisation and anxiety about their inability to stem the tide of immigration had dampened Maori enthusiasm for the settlement process and prompted the rise of Maori nationalism. Ngati Haua's Wiremu Tamihana proposed the unification of tribes under a Maori king who would have authority to implement a policy of withholding land from sale as a means of controlling and slowing the rate of settlement. Consequently, a number of tribal groups from the Waikato area installed Te Wherowhero as their King in a process completed with an anointing ceremony at the flour-milling settlement of Rangiaowhia in 1858 – the same year that the extent of the Maori contribution to colonial revenues became an especially contentious issue.

Ever anxious to engage in trade, Maori had anticipated that a reciprocal alliance with Britain would benefit both parties. However, the expectations of the new immigrants who arrived in the wake of the Treaty of Waitangi ultimately proved incompatible with Maori aspirations. Kingi was denounced for refusing to sell, and in 1860 war broke out in Taranaki, eventually spreading to the Waikato and East Coast. As punishment for alleged rebellion, a final total of 1,610,718 acres in the Waikato and the other Maori wheat-growing and flour-mill-owning areas of Taranaki, Tauranga and Opotiki were confiscated under the New Zealand Settlement Act of 1863.[84] Maori flour milling and shipping went into decline simultaneously and the 'golden age' for Maori business came to an end as New Zealand's wheat supplies now came increasingly from the South Island and steam ships gradually displaced sail.

CHAPTER THREE

Hobson to Hubbing: Change and Continuity in Auckland's Maritime History

GAVIN MCLEAN

The maritime history of Auckland since colonisation is a blend of change and continuity. While the changes are interesting and significant, the continuities are stronger, always grounded on the centrality of the port and of maritime commerce to the economic well-being of this great *entrepôt* city and of its ever-widening hinterland. For all but a few brief periods, Auckland has been the country's major seaport. For most of that time it has also been the centre of shipbuilding and ship repairing. Thanks to the Union Steam Ship Company, Otago dominated ship owning for most of the late nineteenth and the early twentieth centuries, but even so Auckland has always had plenty of shipowners and ship operators. A 'mosquito fleet' of harbour and intra-provincial traders has given its waterfront a distinctive bustle. And when New Zealand's shipping industry contracted sharply late last century, it consolidated on the Queen City. While local owners and operators have declined sharply since the late 1990s, most foreign lines have their principal offices in Auckland, along with the locally owned shipping agents, stevedores and other suppliers of specialist maritime services. And in an era when many lines are merging and talking of 'hubbing' (consolidating on fewer ports), it is significant that recently the

P&O Nedlloyd Europe container service, successor to the old Conference Lines service, cut its new 4100-container super-ships back to just three New Zealand ports: Port Chalmers, Napier and Auckland (under review in 2005).

This chapter will concentrate on commercial shipping, which, broadly defined, covers not only ship owning and ship operating, which dominate the literature, but also ship agency, ship surveying, ship broking, ship provedoring, shipbuilding, ship repair, and a variety of cargo and container-related activities.

The trades may be divided most conveniently into two categories. Deep-sea trades are those to Britain and Europe (predominant until recently), the Americas, and to Asia (now New Zealand's dominant sea lane). Short-sea trades are the Pacific Islands, trans-Tasman (now the second-busiest trade route) and the coastal and harbour trades. In the space available to it, this chapter will concentrate on these shorter routes, which have given Auckland its characteristic port profile.

It is convenient to break the story into three periods: 1840–1914, 1914–69 and 1969 to the present. The first is largely the story of the city's colonial period, a time in which Auckland's maritime trade was distinctive, more localised than that of the major southern ports. By 1914, Auckland, now stimulated by the completion of the North Island main trunk railway (1908) and by the development of the Waikato hinterland, had become New Zealand's largest city, taking a lead that widened as the century progressed. At about the same time the decline in trans-shipping via Melbourne and the completion of the Panama Canal also helped give Auckland an edge over the South Island ports, but not Wellington, which for most of this period handled about the same amount of business. The third period is from the late 1960s, an era dominated by technological change, local government reform and economic liberalisation.

A colonial port, 1840–1914

In 1840, when Lieutenant-Governor William Hobson moved his capital a day's sail from Russell to Auckland, the deep, sheltered Waitemata was one of the main drawcards.[1] The narrow isthmus had a second string to its bow, in the muddy little port of Onehunga on the Manukau, which provided convenient access to west coast and southern ports. For all its physical limitations, Onehunga is still used by coastal shipping.

In the 1840s, shipping was vital to the mere existence of Auckland. The first vessel to call at the new capital direct from Australia, William C. Daldy's

Ports were crucial for new settlements. John Johnson's October 1840 watercolour shows the ships Anna Watson *and* Platina *anchored off Auckland, where tents have sprung up and building timber is being stored. The tent closest to the shore belonged to Captain Rough, Auckland's first harbour master.* ALEXANDER TURNBULL LIBRARY, NATIONAL LIBRARY OF NEW ZEALAND, E-216-F-115.

schooner *Shamrock,* was a welcome sight with its twenty-seven passengers, livestock and cargo of bricks. Early traders landed what David Johnson described as 'the sort of things a good country store would stock': food, clothing, building materials, and kitchen and laundry items.[2] Ships and boats were also crucial simply for getting about, especially for those who settled on 'The Island', as the early inhabitants called Devonport.[3]

As Russell Stone's biography of John Logan Campbell shows, even the most lubberly of Auckland's early merchants lived and breathed shipping. Fortunes rose and fell with every consignment of goods landed and each deal struck. Winning the sole agency for H. H. Willis and Company, for example, was the making of Brown and Campbell's business partnership in the late 1840s.[4] A selling point of what are now called the Merchants' Houses on Princes Street was their views, which allowed occupants to watch the comings and goings on the harbour.

Although the Maori share of seaborne trade is dealt with more expressly in another chapter, it should be noted that Maori vessels were very important in the 1840s and well into the 1850s. They were mere minnows, but there were plenty of them. On 1 January 1853 the Auckland-owned fleet comprised 118 vessels of 10 tons or more, the largest being just 43 tons. Thirty-seven of those vessels, including the two largest, were Maori-owned.[5] Waka laden with produce – fish, fruit, pigs, potatoes and firewood – disgorged their contents at Commercial Bay, near Fore (now Fort) Street and Mechanics Bay (just below Stanley Street), and Maori hawked their wares in the town's muddy streets. In the first three months of 1853 the police constable charged with the difficult task of counting canoes, cargoes and crews estimated that 553 canoes crewed by 1758 men and 773 women weaved in amongst the Maori and European coastal traders and the eagerly-awaited migrant ships.[6]

Commercial shipping is the focus of this paper, but it should be noted in passing that the harbour, long prized by Aucklanders as a recreational asset, has always generated jobs and business opportunities, too. Typically, almost as soon as Hobson's men had raised the Union Flag on Point Britomart after signing the deed to buy the land from Ngati Whatua on 18 September 1840, they staged a regatta.[7] Ever since then, Aucklanders have loved messing about in boats, whether in the waka and whaleboats of the early colonial days or the fizz boats and 'plastic fantastics' of today. Catering for them has kept plenty of people in work, from the men who built the flatties, dinghies and yachts at traditional boatyards such as Baileys' and Logans', to today's super yacht builders, sail training schools, marina operators, chandlers, providores and equipment vendors.[8]

Auckland's trades were more diverse than those of other ports, if only because its northern location made it the natural gateway to the Pacific Islands, and often the only New Zealand port of call for the mail steamers running between Australasia and San Francisco and Vancouver. While migrant ships from Britain were always a welcome sight on the Waitemata, as former shipping reporter turned publisher Henry Brett showed in *White Wings*, most of the cargo traffic came from the brigs, schooners, ketches and cutters engaged in the short-sea trades. Auckland had its share of the United Kingdom, or 'Home' trade, but imports have usually been more important in Auckland than elsewhere. As late as 1892 Auckland ranked third by value in export ports, with just two-thirds the business of Lyttelton, and barely £100,000 more than Napier and Dunedin.[9]

In the colonial period, ship owning was often an adjunct to other commercial activities and not a specialised business on its own. Syndicates flourished thanks to the 64ths system. By dividing ownership into affordable units (64ths), it enabled people of comparatively modest means to invest in shipping. Many

The annual regatta is underway in the background in this 1864 photograph. Note the long thin wharf (Queen Street), which characterised the colonial Auckland waterfront. The Henderson and Spraggon shipyard is in the foreground. ALEXANDER TURNBULL LIBRARY, NATIONAL LIBRARY OF NEW ZEALAND, G-96100-1/2.

spread their risk across several ships. George Binney, an Auckland merchant, for example, owned shares in several small vessels in the 1870s – the *Meteor*, *Amaranth*, *Wild Duck*, *Fiery Cross*, *Atalanta*, *Lionel* and *Geelong* – often taking 16/64th or 32/64th.[10] Often, too, a ship's master took a stake in his own vessel; if all went well he bought more shares or invested in other ships.

There was a particularly strong connection between the timber industry and the Queen City. As Duncan Mackay showed, men with a shipping background played an important role in founding the timber industries.[11] The Circular Saw Line, the popular name adopted by Thomas Henderson and John Macfarlane's shipping business, further reinforced that point. This ambitious city firm milled timber, warehoused goods and ran an ever-changing fleet of sailing vessels (and later a few steamers) in the coastal and Pacific Islands trades until the early 1900s when it sold its ships to bigger players and took up ship agency work.[12] In this reduced form, Henderson and Macfarlane traded well into the twentieth century.

For many years a similar enterprise, the Craig family of timber and coal merchants, ran a fleet of mainly sailing craft across the Tasman and around the coast. The brainchild of Joseph James Craig, its shipping activities took off after 1886 when he inherited his father's general merchant and cartage contracting activities. Craig had fingers in many pies: he was a merchant in coal, shingle and cement; manufacturer of bricks, tiles and lime; a customs and forwarding agent; a carter (owning several hundred draught horses); and a shipowner.[13] He had dabbled in shipping for some time before moving to larger vessels, starting with a majority share in the 430-ton barque *Notero* in 1887. Other ships followed: the *Waitemata*, *Hazel Craig*, *Constance Craig*, *Jessie Craig*, *James Craig*, *Alexander Craig*, *Selwyn Craig*, *Marjorie Craig*, *Louise Craig*, and the *Joseph Craig*. Until the early 1900s, Craig himself was able to finance the purchase of these typically 20–30-year-old ships and to run them profitably enough in the trans-Tasman timber trade. But like Henderson and Macfarlane, Craig lacked the capital to re-equip his fleet as his old sailers wore out and as the increased efficiency of steamers became apparent. In 1910, he entered a joint venture with R. S. Lamb, A. C. Sexton and A. Guthrey of Sydney and the Union Steam Ship Company of Dunedin. Between 1910 and his death in 1916, Craig and his partners acquired four powerful new steamers, but he was now only a minor shareholder and the strings were pulled by the Union Company, which incorporated them into its fleet in the 1920s.

Steam investment was risky and usually unprofitable before the 1870s. An Auckland syndicate launched the country's first steamer, the *Governor Wynyard*, on Christmas Eve 1851, saved only by the timely arrival in town of an American whaler with boilermaking experience.[14] The ship quickly proved uneconomic for the trade and was sent across the Tasman to be sold. The first moderately successful Auckland steamer, the *William Denny*, traded under subsidy for three years from 1854. Ships and syndicates came and went in this period. The early steamers were handicapped by their single-action engines (which were inefficient and expensive to run) and by the small populations of the pre-gold rush era settlements, which made it difficult to keep their holds full. So they relied on generous public subsidies. The Auckland Steam Packet Company was established in 1861 but lasted only six years. Its successor, the Auckland Steamship Company, failed shortly afterwards.

The lead in steam shipping went south, first to Wellington, and then to Dunedin, where the Otago Steam Company and the Harbour Steam Company were succeeded in 1875 by the Union Steam Ship Company of New Zealand Ltd. Within a couple of years the Union Company dominated the coastal and the trans-Tasman steamer business. For anyone wanting to travel from Auckland to Dunedin in 1875, its 720-ton steamers *Hawea* and *Taupo* were the way to go, sailing regularly between Onehunga and Port Chalmers. These large, modern steamers transformed coastal passenger and cargo transport. Whereas travellers in 1859 would have thought themselves lucky to get from Auckland to Dunedin in fewer than fifteen days, twenty years later, by taking a Union Company steamer from Onehunga to Lyttelton and then transferring to a train at Christchurch, they could cut the time to five-and-a-half days; by taking a steamer from Onehunga to New Plymouth, the train from New Plymouth to Wellington, a steamer from the capital to Lyttelton and the train south, that journey time had fallen to just three days by 1898.[15]

In 1883, the Union Company commissioned the small, high-speed *Takapuna*, designed especially for a weekly service between Onehunga and Port Chalmers (soon shortened to Onehunga–Lyttelton). Union Company steamers also dominated Auckland's trans-Tasman services, but as the company's 'horseshoe route' connected Bluff, Dunedin, Lyttelton and Wellington with Australian ports, from late Victorian times these centres got the bigger, newer ships and Auckland had its own direct connection using smaller, older vessels.

Auckland's ports and coastal vessels were different, too. In the more populous and prosperous south the completion of the main trunk railway in 1878–9 culled many of the smaller outports. Auckland's hinterland was different. Here, a network of small river ports, beaches and ramshackle jetties served often closely spaced but nevertheless isolated small communities and farming settlers. It was a 'call at your farm service', mixing up people, mail and freight: goods and supplies in – timber, kauri gum and farm produce out. Later dubbed the 'mosquito fleet', these small steamers, sometimes also called 'rock-hoppers' by their skippers, and one- or two-masted sailing vessels operated free of competition from rail or road transport until well into the twentieth century.

Although a variety of ship types and shipowners serviced these intra-provincial routes, two in particular gave Auckland a distinctive character. The first was a ship type: the scow. Like the double-ended, wooden harbour ferry, the scow became one of the icons for the Queen City. The scow emerged during the 1870s, influenced, as early names such as *Lake Erie*, *Lake Superior*, *Lake St. Clair* and *Lake Michigan* suggest, by North American flat-bottomed sailing craft.[16] The scow answered frontier needs for a vessel that could carry heavy loads, take the battering that log cargoes gave, and could sit on the bottom when the tide went out. In 1873 an American mariner living at Matanaka, George Spencer, ordered the first scow – a punt-like, wide shallow box with a sharp(ish) end and a blunt end – from Omaha shipbuilder Septimus Meiklejohn. Cargo sat on her deck. According to the *Southern Cross*, 'the idea of building a vessel of this description is to enable the owners to run the vessel up the shallow creek, and take in her cargo direct from the mills, instead of having to lie off some distance, as is so frequently the case with cutters and schooners, and so save the lightering off by small punts'.[17]

*For almost a century the Northern Steamship Company's steamers, and the sailing scows
(one of each appears in this photograph), gave the Auckland shipping scene its distinctive flavour.
The company's head office (right, background) still survives.* ALEXANDER TURNBULL LIBRARY,
NATIONAL LIBRARY OF NEW ZEALAND, 34714-1/4.

At first treated with disdain, scows soon proved themselves. As with any
ship type, they evolved over time, gaining pointed bows and better lines from
the 1880s, taking on an almost respectable appearance. They crowded the
Waitemata. P. A. Eaddy, the first chronicler of the scows, recorded that 'Niccol
turned out scows from his yard like a small builder would turn out rowing
boats.'[18] Fully loaded, a deck scow 'resembled a logpile with a bow and sails'.[19]
About 130 were built. They proved tough, adaptable little ships and several
survived multiple sinkings or strandings. Along with logs, their other staple
cargo was sand and gravel for the building trade. For decades scows would
run hard up on a beach on the Coromandel, Mahurangi, Omaha or one of the
Gulf islands, and put a plank over the side while their crews wheelbarrowed
aboard 40 or 50 tonnes of sand and gravel before the next high tide lifted their
ship off the beach.

The second distinctive player was the Northern Steamship Company,
whose elegant brick offices still grace modern Quay Street.[20] As we saw, early

attempts by Aucklanders to form major steam ship companies met little success and the initiative passed to southern ventures. The Northern Company dated from 1881 when Captain Alexander McGregor persuaded several shipowners to consolidate their efforts. Northern Steam served the northern North Island, from Wanganui north on the west coast and from East Cape north on the east. Generally, it operated services that the Union Company did not want to run itself. The Northern Company almost went under in the recession of the mid-1880s, but accountant Charles Ranson took control in 1887, wrote down its capital from £150,000 to £108,000 three years later, and restored it to sound financial health. By the mid-1890s its fleet had grown to twenty vessels.[21]

The Northern Company was a regional institution, sending its small ships into every creek, beach, and estuary or bar harbour in the North where a paying cargo could be found. Its timetables adjusted to suit the tides and the settlers, for whom it brought in building supplies, fencing materials, groceries and took away their wool, gum, animals and timber. In the words of Johnson, 'passengers were woken, given ship's tea and biscuits and dropped off at jetties or helped overboard into dinghies. In the road-less and rail-less North the whistles and tall black-and-white funnels of the Northern Company's fleet meant that civilisation was at hand.'[22] Needless to say, its ships were not big. A ship like the *Paeroa*, built in 1891 by Charles Bailey, was just 91 tons and less than 30 metres long. In 1914, when the Union Company had ceased ordering ships of less than 1000 tons gross, only Northern's *Manaia* (1159 tons) topped this figure, while two others exceeded 500 tons: the *Ngapuhi* and the *Clansman*. It suited the Union Company for the Northern Company to run its little ships in these poor-paying trades and to these often shallow and hazardous ports. In any case, the Dunedinites kept the Aucklanders on a short leash through pooling, rates agreements and joint ownership of the United Repairing Company in Auckland.

The size of coastal shipping varied enormously between the ports. As Table 1 shows, the ships entering Auckland were far smaller than the ones using southern ports. Auckland also remained the last stronghold of sail. In 1914, 2226 sailing vessels were registered at Auckland; in contrast, there were just 19 at Wellington, 71 at Lyttelton and a mere nine at Dunedin.[23]

Much of the Auckland coastal fleet was locally built. In Victorian Auckland, the shipbuilders concentrated at the city end of St Marys Bay, where they built or repaired everything from cutters and yachts through to small coastal steamers. Auckland's yacht builders became legendary. In the 1870s, the Bailey and the Logan families established famous boatyards that turned out the elegant keelers that symbolised the city's economic boom of the 1890s and

TABLE 1: AVERAGE TONNAGE OF COASTAL ARRIVALS AT THE MAIN PORTS, 1881–1914

Port	1881	1914
Auckland	66	148
Wellington	186	827
Lyttelton	158	1,043
Dunedin/Port Chalmers	224	1,549

Source: Simon Ville, 'The Coastal Trade of New Zealand Prior to World War One', *New Zealand Journal of History*, 27(1), April, 1993, p. 82.

the early 1900s: boats such as the *Viking* of 1893, or the *Ariki* of 1904 which won closely followed matches here and in Australia.[24]

The less elegant scows, ketches, cutters and rock-hoppers stamped a distinctive mark on the late Victorian/Edwardian Auckland maritime scene, one vastly different to Dunedin, home of the Union Company. Auckland's shipowners were still mostly merchants, who ran ships as adjuncts to their other activities, or they were owner-operators of single craft. These small entrepreneurs often ran close to the wind financially and they used Auckland's inflated definition of 'river limits' – from the Waitemata to Great Barrier Island and from Whangarei to Thames – as a way of getting around award provisions.[25] In the 1880s, Auckland seafarers' pay rates generally lagged behind those of the southern ports. Under early manager Alexander McGregor, the Northern Company had paid its seamen lower wages and it resisted an eight-hour day for cargo work. The tough-talking McGregor embroiled Northern in several bitter disputes in the late 1880s, including one that provoked the Federated Seamen's Union to run chartered ships in opposition to it until the Union Company sorted out the dispute, largely in the union's favour.

Auckland unionists were always a worry to their southern colleagues. The Dunedin and Wellington unions brought Auckland seamen's wages into line with theirs in the late 1890s, but Auckland members capitulated quickly during the 1913 strike. With crew levels on vessels entering and leaving Auckland averaging thirteen compared to thirty-two in Wellington and forty-five in Otago, 'labour relations were likely to be more informal, which helped to protect local seamen from the contagion of militancy'.[26] According to one union official, Auckland seamen included some cow cockies in the off-season – 'their love for the Seamen's Union is similar to the weasel's regard for a chicken'.[27] Scab labour was more plentiful, the seafarers were more settled in their voyaging and, most probably, more likely to be older and married.

The Queen City's reign, 1914–69

For much of the late Victorian period, as James Belich suggests, it had been correct to talk about the Big Four centres. By 1901, the North Island's population had outstripped that of the South, and Auckland, which had reclaimed first place from Dunedin in 1886, was pulling away from the others. In 1915, greater Auckland had 118,000 people, followed by Christchurch (88,000), Wellington (75,000) and Dunedin (69,000).[28] The Big One was out on its own. By 1970, the numbers read 603,000, 301,000, 260,000 and 110,000, respectively.[29]

This growth placed pressure on the Auckland Harbour Board, formed in 1871, to keep up demand. Nature had been kind to the Waitemata, so the city found it relatively easy to match ship growth, which went from 1000 tons gross in the sail era to 4500–6000 tons by the late 1880s, and to include a few ships over 10,000 tons by the early 1900s. Providing wharves and sheds was a little more difficult. In its 1902 *Cyclopedia* entry, the Auckland Harbour Board said that 'the wharfage accommodation of the Auckland Harbour, if not all that might be desired, is exceedingly creditable'.[30] The problem has been keeping up with reclamation (the Auckland Harbour Board itself had reclaimed over 27 hectares by 1879), leading to inconveniently long wharves.[31] By the mid-1880s the port had developed two large wharves, Queen's and the Railway Wharves, to replace earlier and inadequate structures such as Wynyard Pier. These in turn would be re-decked and joined by other large structures as the demographic balance shifted in Auckland's favour. By 1900, the port had over 3000 metres of berthage, and could accommodate ships drawing 7.9 metres and was dredging down to 9.2 metres. Development and redevelopment work between Princes Wharf and Kings Wharf was completed between 1904 and 1924, giving the waterfront the broad shape it would retain until the 1960s.

The other main ports, Dunedin especially, first felt Auckland's growing dominance in the trans-Tasman trade. The deep-sea shipping companies had previously discharged some British cargo destined for New Zealand at Melbourne and had trans-shipped it through the southern centres, but from around the time of the First World War they shipped more of the freight direct to northern New Zealand ports.[32] Wellington also came under pressure from Auckland, but it stood up rather better. The capital replaced Dunedin as the country's major transhipment centre, and also became a more attractive direct-call port of call after lines such as the New Zealand Shipping Company rerouted their ships through the Panama Canal after 1915. By the interwar era, Dunedin had lost its trans-Tasman passenger connection and some of its direct overseas passenger trade. After the Second World War the majority of such passenger business went to Auckland and Wellington alone, with Auckland getting most.

TABLE 2: IMPORTS AND EXPORTS (BY VOLUME) HANDLED BY AUCKLAND, 1867–1980

	Auckland			Four main ports		
	Imports (%)	Exports (%)	All trade (%)	Imports (%)	Exports (%)	All trade (%)
1867	14.6	6.3	9.8	67.4	42.4	50.4
1881	20.0	13.5	16.9	84.7	78.6	79.7
1911	29.5	17.3	22.3	87.7	59.0	72.1
1930	38.4	22.1	33.8	95.5		90.5
1940	47.0	30.2	41.8			85.2
1950	43.9	34.4	41.5			88.2
1960	38.4	26.8	35.2			72.6
1970	25.5	18.6	22.9			40.9
1980	26.5	12.6	19.4	49.0	20.0	

Source: 'New Zealand Ports and Shipping Developments', in *New Zealand Official Yearbook 1974*, Government Printer, Wellington, 1974, p. 1066.

In the deep-sea cargo trades, the four main ports increased their share of the import/export business from the 1870s (when railway lines benefited the main ports and the larger secondary ports at the expense of the very minor ones) until the 1950s, when the opening of the Marsden Point oil terminal near Whangarei and the growth of exports of bulk cargoes, such as forest products or iron sands, brought a reverse in that trend. Nevertheless, as Table 2 shows, Auckland's share of the four-port total actually increased.

Wellington had become the main trans-shipment port and the capital also attracted a large manufacturing base. Nevertheless, Auckland's wharves were kept busy servicing Conference Lines freighters, which began switching over to oil propulsion from the mid-1920s. By the late 1930s, European-trade ships had standardised at between 8000 and 11,000 tons gross. There were a few notable exceptions, the New Zealand Shipping Company's R-class liners of 1929 (16,700 tons gross), and in 1939 Shaw Savill's liner *Dominion Monarch,* which topped the scales at over 27,000 tons. Postwar ships were only slightly bigger. The eight 14,000-ton dwt *Haparangi* class freighters built for the New Zealand Shipping/Federal were large cargo carriers.

In the postwar era, Auckland surged ahead, but, as Table 3 shows, its lead over Wellington became commanding only from the 1960s. Like the capital, there was an imbalance between imports and exports, which being bulkier, then as now tended to go out through the nearest provincial ports. At the port

The postwar transport revolution weeded out the remaining scows such as the Owhiti *and the* Jane Gifford, *seen here in January 1971. Little cargo went to the Union Company's big coastal roll-on roll-off ferries (rear, left); most was captured by road transport.* ALEXANDER TURNBULL LIBRARY, NATIONAL LIBRARY OF NEW ZEALAND, BERTHOLD COLLECTION, 25186-1/4.

itself, Bledisloe, Jellicoe and Freyberg wharves were developed between 1940 and 1962. Even so, Auckland suffered from a lack of adequate infrastructural investment. The Royal Commission of Inquiry into the Waterfront Industry, which sat between 1951 and 1952, considered the port 'unable to deal with the modern ship with its large cargoes', criticising 'inadequate and obsolete sheds, uneven floor surfaces, entrances to sheds cluttered up with cargo'.[33]

The Auckland mosquito fleet shrank after the war. A few scows were motorised and refitted by optimistic owners, who traded them in diminishing numbers into the 1960s. As roads improved, however, trucks took business away from the last elderly steamers, ketches and scows. Typical was the withdrawal of the little 41-ton motor vessel *Wairuru* from the Auckland–Clevedon run in 1947, her end hastened by the lifting of wartime controls on road transport.[34] In 1959, the opening of the Auckland Harbour Bridge killed much of the ferry traffic; although a few double-enders lingered on. All of the vehicular ferries and many of the passenger vessels were withdrawn, as were the sugar lighters that had plied between the Chelsea works and the city wharves. But there were also some gains in these years. In the 1960s, tugs made a revival. The Auckland Harbour Board invested in more powerful ship-handling tugs, but most of the new tugs and workboats were smaller and were privately owned by firms such as Blue Boats, Parrys, Winstones or McCallums, or by the Julian family, which in the 1950s formed Gulf Freighters, a joint venture with Winstones. In 1958, Gulf Freighters built the first large modern barge, the 500-tonne capacity *Waiwaka*, and the tug *Toiler* in Hong Kong.[35] They, and the other small craft, were kept busy feeding the city's construction sites and motorways with barge-loads of gravel, sand and glass sand from Northland or the Gulf.

Over the same period 'the coastal trade out of Auckland and Onehunga was increasingly oriented towards the South Island'[36] using a new generation of engines-aft motor coasters of 800–1200 tons. The Northern Company took the lead in this, extending its routes down to the South Island's east coast ports of Bluff, Dunedin, Oamaru, Timaru and Lyttelton, and even calling at Doubtful Sound during the Manapouri power project. The *Awanui*, delivered from a Hong Kong shipyard in 1962, was 1185 tons gross with modern bipod masts, but was already obsolescent before she hit the water.

The second revolution, 1969 on

The shipping revolution of the 1960s and the 1970s transformed not only ports and shipping, dooming even new ships like the *Awanui*, but also the entire transport infrastructure. As the nation's major port, Auckland faced some of the greatest challenges. Wellington had the worst reputation for congestion, but Auckland's faster growth and the layout of its elderly finger piers, hemmed in by the most valuable urban real estate in the country, made port planning particularly difficult. The average number of days spent on the New Zealand coast by a Conference Line vessel increased from 51.6 days in 1950 to 62.1 days in 1961; truly killing statistics when it is remembered that ships really only make money when they are underway.[37] Nevertheless, work commenced in the late 1960s on a common-user container terminal for the small East Coast North America trade: Fergusson Wharf (now Axis Fergusson).

European trade was dominant, yet there were delays caused by the British lines' indecision over containerisation; the target date of 1971 slipped to 1973 and then to 1975.[38] If it had been left to the Conference Lines, there probably would have been just two North Island cellular container terminals and one southern one, but political considerations led to Lyttelton being added to the list after a great deal of delay and controversy. The main Europe-trade container fleet switched to cellular container ships in 1975–77, marking the swiftest and most dramatic change to the fleets serving New Zealand's overseas trades. Household names disappeared into huge consortia with acronyms (ACTA

[Associated Container Transport Australia] and OCL [Overseas Container Lines]) to match the TEUs (twenty-equivalent units) their ships now carried. But the four-port concept proved shaky, partially undermined by trade diversification after Britain entered the European Economic Community.

From the 1980s, more and more multi-purpose ships able to handle containers and conventional cargoes paid direct calls to provincial ports. The Auckland Harbour Board found itself further developing other terminals – principally on the Bledisloe (now Axis Bledisloe), Jellicoe and Freyberg wharves – to service a widening range of multi-purpose ships. Even so, Auckland's increased share of overseas shipping arrivals is obvious when compared to the next busiest general cargo port, Wellington (see Table 3). As industry consolidated on Auckland and fled the capital, the distance opened up between the two ports.

In common with the worldwide trend, Auckland's seaborne passenger traffic collapsed under competition from aircraft. First to go were the short-sea ships. The last trans-Tasman liners stopped running in the early 1960s and Pacific Islands passenger-cargo liners left service a decade later. The deep-water passenger trades also went into steep decline. The New Zealand Shipping Company pulled out of the loss-making, strike-affected passenger business at the end of the 1960s. Shaw Savill & Albion made a valiant effort with the specialist passenger liners *Southern Cross* (1955) and *Northern Star* (1962), but by the mid-1970s it, too, had to withdraw, leaving minor operators to eke a few more years out of their elderly ships. For a while Princess Wharf saw little passenger traffic until the cruising boom, which got underway in the 1980s.

TABLE 3: OVERSEAS SHIPPING ARRIVALS, AUCKLAND AND WELLINGTON, 1929–89 (NET TONNES IN MILLIONS)

Year	Auckland	Wellington
1929	2.0	2.0
1939	2.7	2.4
1949	1.6	1.7
1959	3.6	2.7
1969	4.5	2.3
1979	7.5	4.0
1989	10.7	4.0

Source: Data from the *New Zealand Official Yearbook*, Government Print, Wellington, various years.

The short-sea trades also transformed themselves, initially with roll-on, roll-off (RORO) vessels rather than cellular container ships, the preference of the dominant Union Company. The company built its own RORO terminal for its coastal ROROs and trans-Tasman and coastal ROROs, and the Northern Company even planned a RORO service between Onehunga and the South Island. For a while it worked on the Tasman, the introduction of the ROROs cutting freights by 17 per cent in 1969. But the commissioning of four big RORO Cook Strait rail ferries by the Railways Department between 1962 and 1974 and its development of partnerships with freight forwarders undermined the coastal general cargo trades.[39] The Northern Company, increasingly dependent on bulk grain cargoes in its later years, withdrew from shipping in 1974 and was later wound up.

Ian McKay had taken the Holm Shipping Company's management to Auckland in the 1960s and had branched out into the Islands trade. But Holm, by then also managing the fleets of Richardson & Co., and the Canterbury Steam Shipping Co., for its Union Company masters, sold its fleet between 1972 and 1975, unable to compete with freight forwarders and the railways (which the Labour Government had subsidised). The Union Company withdrew even its new ROROs *Hawea* and *Wanaka*; by 1975, the only scheduled general cargo carrier running between Auckland and southern ports was the Shipping Corporation's *Coastal Trader*. Not all cargo had moved from sea to land transport. Cement, previously bagged and a mainstay of the scheduled services, was now moving by specialised bulk carriers, as was oil (until the pipeline from Marsden Point to Auckland was completed in 1983).

The period was one of contraction for the short-sea businesses, but it also stimulated a new wave of entrepreneurs. In 1973, Ian McKay, backed by Lauritzens and Fruit Shippers, established McKay Shipping, which also dabbled in the Islands trades as a vessel operator. So, too, did Reef Shipping, also fighting for a share of the Pacific trade recently vacated by the Union Company and the government, and now increasingly dominated by firms such as France's Sofrana Unilines and by the new regional carrier, the Pacific Forum Line. In the dizzying consolidation of principals, some local agencies went out of business and others diversified into other activities. But containerisation also spawned a range of service industries, such as container parks, container washing and container servicing businesses.

While not all late-twentieth-century lines were Auckland-based (South Pacific Shipping [SPS] operated from Christchurch, Strait Shipping from Wellington, and Pacifica Shipping is Dunedin-owned and run from Lyttelton), new firms were most likely to set up in the Queen City or to relocate there. In

Containers dominated Auckland's liner trades by the late 1980s when Tasman Express Line's trans-Tasman freighter Canterbury Express *passed the restored Ferry Building. TEL challenged the Union Company monopoly, but by the late 1990s all Australasian lines had been forced from the Tasman by foreign cross-traders.* PRIVATE COLLECTION, GAVIN MCLEAN.

1983, the biggest of them all, the Union Shipping Group, built an impressive twelve-storey tower block at 36 Quay Street and moved its head office there. In many ways the Union Company's shifts – from Dunedin to Wellington in 1921 and from Wellington to Auckland in 1983 – symbolised the long drift north that has been going on since the 1880s.

The most vibrant of the newcomers was Tasman Express Line Ltd. Owned equally by Refrigerated Freight Lines, McKay Shipping, Geo. H. Scales and Sydney-based Hetherington Kingsbury Ltd, Tasman ran an innovative two-ship service between Onehunga (later Auckland), Sydney, Melbourne, Lyttelton and Wellington. The National Government's deregulation of the coastal trade in 1994 had little impact on the Tasman, but the Maritime Union of Australia's decision to let foreign-crewed ships into the Tasman was crucial. By 1996, trans-Tasman freight rates (over \$3,000 a box in 1985) had fallen to \$1,000 or less in the crowded Auckland market, where big foreign-crewed cross-traders transited the Tasman often enough to meet most customers' needs. By 1998/99, local participation on the Tasman was over. SPS went bust; the Union Company sold its ships and Tasman Express sold its shipping business to P&O Nedlloyd. For a while the revived coastal general trade held up better, but in 2003/4, Pacifica's coastal general cargo trade to Onehunga and to Auckland fell from three small chartered container ships to just one.

Foreign penetration extended even to the 'mosquito fleet'. Sea-Tow, born out of the Parry Brothers' old tug and barge operation, was partly Australian-owned until 2004. It now operates four tugs and four barges (one capable of carrying over 7000 tonnes), ranging as far afield as Australia and the South Pacific. The ferry fleets have revived as the harbour bridge's arteries have clogged. Traffic gridlock, tourism and the desirability of living in places such as Waiheke Island have created work for a new generation of vessels. Fullers (substantially owned by Scottish transport operator Stagecoach) and Subritzky Shipping (taken over by Australian interests in 2004) run a network of large high-speed catamarans, mono-hulls and small RORO vessels, many as big as nineteenth-century Northern Company steamers. In 2004 Subritzky added two large catamarans, the *Seacat* and the *Island Navigator*, to a crowded Gulf.[40]

Many vessels are imported or constructed elsewhere, but these small ships have provided useful business for the Auckland shipbuilding and ship repairing industry, which shares market dominance with Whangarei's. During the Second World War, Auckland builders had built steel minesweepers and Fairmile antisubmarine launches for the navy, while at St Marys Bay a consortium had built tugs, powered lighters and a few small cargo vessels.[41] After the war, firms such as Steel Ships and Mason Brothers had kept shipbuilding going: Masons, in 1961, setting a New Zealand record with the construction of the 627-ton Stewart Island ferry *Wairua*. More recently the city's yacht designers and builders have come to the fore. The America's Cup challenges and local designers' innovative use of materials, such as fibreglass, have provided a platform for luxury yacht building and reconstruction. By the late 1990s, orders were flooding in from wealthy overseas clients for super yachts, some bigger than the Hauraki Gulf ferries. The buyers' cheque books seem almost limitless. In 2004, for example, Alloy Yachts delivered the 54-metre sloop *Tiara*, claimed to be the word's first privately owned sailing yacht with a helipad.[42] That year, another yard had an 85-metre long yacht on order. Auckland has the lion's share of this work, but other firms also turn out large craft at Whangarei, New Plymouth and Wellington.

Changes in the shipping sector have been sweeping. Computerisation and mechanisation have cut staff numbers ashore as severely as automation reduced 'manning' at sea. A Union Company trans-Tasman freighter of the

1960s had a crew of about twenty-six; by 1996, SPS's similar-sized container ships were being run by crews of eleven or twelve, and even that was too many to meet foreign-flag competition. Political changes have also been important. The reforming fourth Labour Government of 1984–90 abolished the New Zealand Ports Authority (which had controlled capital expenditure in the ports since the late 1960s) and then enacted two pivotal pieces of legislation: the Port Companies Act 1988 and the Waterfront Reform Act 1989.

The Port Companies Act abolished harbour boards, transferring their commercial activities to new publicly owned companies and their social and environmental responsibilities to regional councils. The port companies employed fewer staff than their predecessors, but the biggest staffing cuts were made to the watersiders. Under the Waterfront Reform Act 1989, the centralised Waterfront Industry Commission (the WIC) was scrapped; its critics argued that the productivity agreement it operated with employees, which effectively rewarded them according to the increase in tonnage handled, 'had the effect of seriously inhibiting investment in new cargo-handling equipment'.[43] Now stevedoring companies employed labour, not the WIC. In scenes sometimes of considerable bitterness, many men took redundancy (1381 at a total cost of $45 million);[44] and more would follow in micro-adjustments later on. Shipowners, on the other hand, began enjoying the benefits virtually overnight. In February 1990, Tasman Express's chief executive officer reported that FCL (full container loads) costs per TEU had dropped dramatically since October 1989 – from $350–$400 per box to $220 at Onehunga; between 1988/89 and 1990/91 turnaround time for his ships improved by 32 per cent.[45]

Handling rates and costs improved even further in the 1990s as the Employment Contracts Act ended demarcation, the agreements that had kept non-cellular ships out of the container terminals were overturned, and as the port company added more cranes to the port. In 1998, the Ports of Auckland Ltd chief executive, Geoff Vazey, reported that the average turnaround time for a container vessel at Fergusson Container Terminal had dropped from more than 38 hours in 1989 to 15.5 hours. 'And today we are handling double the number of containers per ship within those hours.'[46] In its last year of operation in 1988, the Auckland Harbour Board spent $100 million on handling 6.2 million tonnes of cargo. In 1997 the figures (for Ports of Auckland Ltd) were $85 million and 11.3 million tonnes.

The port's position has not always been easy. Until relatively recently there was little effective competition between ports. The political climate was not conducive to this and, in any case, high internal transport costs kept all but the most valuable and least bulky cargo effectively 'captive' to the nearest port.

That changed in the 1980s with the new political climate, with improvements to the land transport system (which made it cheaper to move non-bulk cargo internally) and with the success of the shipping container, which accommodated an increasing range of commodities, such as sawn timber or steel. Northland had grandly dreamed of being the country's sole container port in the 1960s, but twenty years later Auckland found itself under real pressure from the modern deepwater port at Mount Maunganui, whose hinterland had effectively been expanded by the completion of the Kaimai railway tunnel. In the 1980s and 1990s, several lines switched from Auckland to Mount Maunganui, where the harbour board built a container terminal at Sulphur Point. By 2003 it had four container cranes.

Competition had intensified when Tauranga set up a 'dry port', MetroPort, in the South Auckland industrial belt, after signing up ANZDL (Australia New Zealand Direct Line) as its first major customer. Shipping lines contracted to use MetroPort Auckland call at the Port of Tauranga where import cargo destined for Auckland is offloaded and railed to MetroPort for distribution to its final destination; Auckland-sourced export cargo is aggregated at MetroPort Auckland, railed to Tauranga and shipped out. In 2001 MetroPort Auckland went on to a seven-day-a-week service. FNZEL (FESCO New Zealand Express Line) established Tauranga as its sole North Island port of call for its fixed-day weekly service to the Far East. In 2004, MetroPort container slots were increased from 642 to 1390, and the lighting was enhanced to permit 24-hour-a-day operations.

Auckland remains the largest container port in the country. It handles 43 per cent of New Zealand's total container trade and 56 per cent of the North Island's container trade. It is the port with the most closely balanced import/ export ratios – imports are 57 per cent of its container traffic, exports 43 per cent.[47] Tauranga handles more export containers than Auckland, but, despite their rivalry, the ports cooperate when it suits them. In 2003 they were each shareholders in North Tugz, a marine servicing business set up by Ports of Auckland Ltd in 1999 to service Marsden Point. In 2005, as this book went to print, however, P&O Nedlloyd, the biggest container line servicing New Zealand – including Toll NZ (the national rail operator) and Fonterra (New Zealand's largest exporter) – was in the final stages of deciding whether to use Tauranga in preference to Auckland, something that could, in the words of the *Dominion Post*, 'remove Auckland's premier port status'.[48] Some high-value freight has been lost to Auckland International Airport (which by value is the country's second most important import/export 'port'), although the tonnage handled, about 80,000 tonnes, is miniscule compared to the sea ports.

The changing face of local shipping is also reflected in the people who work in the industry. Once a male bastion, shipping now employs many women. Men still predominate aboard ships, but ashore the reverse is often the case, especially in finance, customer services, and trade or line management positions. In 2004, two of McKay Shipping's five agency managers were women, as was the finance controller, and, like most city shipping businesses, the company has been hiring as many women as men for several years. Partly as a consequence, the rough, tough portside pubs have declined in numbers and these days a shipping lunch is as likely to happen in the Viaduct Basin cafés or at Takapuna.

Auckland's ship-owning and operating companies have declined, with the loss of Union Shipping, Tasman Express and others in the late 1990s. If naming rights to buildings mean anything, the sector's most visible presence now comes from the Pacific traders. Sofrana Unilines NZ Ltd, French-owned but New Zealand-registered, has been an Auckland institution since 1968. One truly local line, Reef Shipping, has also weathered the storms of the Islands trades. Reef operates small multipurpose ships in the Pacific and to the Chatham Islands and offers clients a range of agency services. The regionally-owned Pacific Forum Line is another successful operator.

The hulls that enter and leave the Waitemata are largely foreign-owned, but some of their slots may be locally controlled. Oceanbridge Shipping is an example of a twenty-first century shipping company that does not even own or charter a ship. Oceanbridge was founded in 1981 by Bill Speedy and made a name for itself a couple of years later by selling general cargo freight space aboard specialist trans-Tasman forest products carriers. Oceanbridge is what is known as an NVOCC (a non-vessel-owning common carrier), a business that contracts with shipowners to provide space to its clients at preferential rates. It also offers liner agency services. Based at Takapuna, Oceanbridge employs about sixty people. Customers can find most of the staff's names on the Oceanbridge website, and can log in to track their containers. Guaranteed sailing dates, fast ship turnaround, and computer tracking of cargo offer them a level of service that would have seemed unimaginable to those Victorian Auckland merchants, John Logan Campbell and William Brown, who scanned the Waitemata anxiously awaiting news of their cargo ordered twelve months earlier from 'Home'.

Conclusion

Auckland has had a long and distinctive maritime history. For most of the past 160 years it has been the country's busiest port – a port always in the public eye thanks to its location at the foot of Queen Street and other central city streets. The deep-sea general cargo trades have always been important to this city, particularly for imports as the city grew last century, but Auckland's short-sea trades have marked it out from New Zealand's other major ports. Auckland has always had the lion's share of New Zealand's trade with the Pacific Islands, and even today, when barges and catamarans have taken over from scows and wooden ferries, it has the country's only 'mosquito fleet' worth noting.

Indeed, the survival of these trades reinforces that fact that, despite all the changes to the ships, companies and to the waterfront itself, the continuities are more remarkable. When selecting the site for the city in 1840, Captain David Rough, Auckland's first harbour master, recalled the pleasure that Lieutenant Governor Hobson took in 'the report I was able to give of the anchorage and depth of water near the shore where I had taken soundings'.[49] The sea is no less crucial to Auckland in 2004, as Ports of Auckland Ltd finishes dredging the channel to 13 metres below chart datum to service a port that it estimates handles half the country's container trade and facilitates or sustains $10.6 billion worth of activity, 32 per cent of the Auckland regional economy – about 173,000 jobs.[50]

Financial Management Strategies in the Auckland Gas Company, 1862–1915

MICHAEL KEENAN

In the early 1970s the Auckland Gas Company stopped manufacturing gas for supply to the city of Auckland, which had been its principal activity for more than a century, and began to distribute natural gas sourced from the Kapuni and Maui gas fields. During the mid-1980s a series of acquisitions of the company's shares, which had been publicly traded for more than 120 years, resulted in the company becoming a wholly owned subsidiary of Welgas Holdings Ltd. The latter company controlled two other regional gas-supply companies and was itself a wholly owned subsidiary of Brierley Investments Ltd. In 1992 Welgas Holdings Ltd was renamed Enerco New Zealand Ltd by its parent company and floated on the sharemarket. 'Enerco Gas' was adopted as a generic brand for the subsidiary gas companies, and the Auckland Gas Company disappeared from the register of companies when it was renamed Enerco Ltd in 1997.

These events put an end to the technological function and corporate form of a business whose origins lay in the mid-nineteenth century and whose effects on the social and commercial life of Auckland during the rest of that century were far-reaching. In being the first to provide the city with a reticulated supply of energy, the company was a leader in the transformation of Auckland from a pioneering frontier settlement to a recognisably modern metropolis. When the company was formed, the 10,500 European inhabitants of Auckland had no means of artificial lighting other than candles and oil lamps, their food was cooked over open fires or on solid fuel ranges, and the motive power for their industry, if not their own labour or that of their horses, was wind, water or steam. Gas lighting, gas cooking ranges, and gas engines changed that.

The introduction of mains supply of gas in 1865 was decades in advance of the provision of other public utilities to the city. An adequate mains supply of water only began to be established after the Auckland City Council acquired the Western Springs in 1875. Prior to that date the population relied for its water supplies on rain-fed tanks, increasingly polluted public wells 'before which queues formed at 5 a.m. in any prolonged dry spell during the summer'[1] and, from 1866, a single 6-inch diameter pipe from the Domain Springs to the centre of the city. When this latter source was over-taxed during a drought in 1872, it was augmented with water piped from a privately-owned well in Khyber Pass Road through pipes obtained from the Auckland Gas Company.[2]

City streets were easily drawn on plans, but not so easily surveyed, formed and surfaced. Throughout the nineteenth century the best city streets consisted of crushed scoria spread on the beaten clay or earth. A newspaper reporting the first supply of gas described the street leading to the gas works as a 'rugged path'.[3] Queen Street, the city's main thoroughfare, was the first to be given an asphalt surface, but not until 1902.[4]

Mains supply of electricity was also a twentieth-century phenomenon. Some supply, of uncertain continuity and economic viability, became available in 1905 from spare capacity in the Auckland Tramway Company's generating plant, and in 1908 from the combined refuse and coal-fired generating plant in the Auckland City Council's Refuse Destructor. Supplies on a significant scale became available only with the commissioning of the City Council's Kings Wharf coal-fired station in 1912. By 1915 electricity consumers numbered 1818.[5] Between 1908 and 1915 the number of gas consumers rose from 16,716 to 27,914.[6]

Strategic financial management

The Auckland Gas Company was formed in 1862 with an authorised capital of £20,000 and began commercial operations three years later in works which had cost £23,200. Fifty years on, in 1915, the company had an authorised capital of £1 million and an investment in its works of £842,000.

The sustained financial management of that capital-intensive project in the dynamic social and economic environment of early Auckland required significant strategic acumen. The core meaning of strategy in this context is the pursuit of competitive advantage. In business, as in military and sporting contexts, strategic decisions and actions are aimed at establishing, maintaining and improving competitive advantage. Strategic management in business focuses on exploiting opportunities for, and countering threats to, competitive advantage in the various markets in which businesses compete. On the demand side, businesses compete against each other for the financial and non-financial resources required for their production, marketing and distribution operations. Decisions on such resource issues provide answers to two fundamental questions which any corporate demand side strategy has to address: What assets should the company invest in to maximise the shareholders' wealth? And how should those assets be financed to minimise the company's cost of capital?

The Auckland Gas Company's directors were committed to exploiting a new and relatively sophisticated technology, and in addressing the first of these questions they encountered at least one obstacle that was specific to their time and place. The assets required for the enterprise – i.e., the plant and equipment for manufacturing gas on a commercial scale, supplies of raw material (be that coal or kerosene), and the engineering expertise required for first establishing and then operating a city gas works – were not available in the immature and still thin resource markets of nineteenth century New Zealand. Markets in England and Australia had to be accessed to obtain these resources, and company agents had to be appointed in London and Sydney to investigate their availability.

Addressing the second resource question did not require the company directors to access overseas markets. But it did require them to operate in two different financial markets: the market for debt finance supplied by lenders, and the market for equity finance supplied by investors in the sharemarket. The focus in this chapter is on the directors' responses to the threats to, and opportunities for, the company's competitive advantage in those markets. The resulting financial management strategies were distinctive, and have a contemporary relevance in addition to their historical interest. They sustained the long-term success of a major infrastructure enterprise which, from its inception, was funded by investment from the private sector. That type of funding for that type of business was an innovation in its time, and more than a century later is still a rarity in the New Zealand economy.

Promoting the company

A small group of Auckland businessmen led by Frederick Whitaker promoted the Auckland Gas Company during the three months May to July 1862. Whitaker already had a reputation for combining entrepreneurial activity with his careers in the legal profession and in colonial politics.[7] Shortly after arriving in the Bay of Islands in 1840 Whitaker had become a director of the first colonially-based bank, the New Zealand Banking Company, and remained the controlling influence until the bank was wound up in 1845. Having moved to Auckland in 1841 he was, in the following year, an original signatory to the Roll of Barristers and Solicitors admitted to practise in New Zealand. The legal partnership of Whitaker and Russell, formed in 1861, gained the reputation of being the most successful in the colony and was a platform for the extension of Whitaker's political career.

In 1853 Whitaker had been appointed to the first Legislative Council established under the Constitution Act 1852, and served his first term as Premier (the equivalent of Prime Minister in colonial politics) in 1863–64. His role in the so-called 'Continuous Ministry' that governed the colony between 1869 and 1891, during which he served another term as Premier and a total of seven terms as Attorney-General, was described by a younger Parliamentarian, William Pember Reeves: 'The Premier of one year may be a subordinate Minister the next; or some subtle and persistent nature, like that of Sir Frederick Whitaker, might manage chiefs whom he appeared to follow, and be the guiding mind of parties which he did not profess to direct'.[8] In addition to these political and legal careers, and other business ventures, Whitaker was chairman of the board of directors of the Auckland Gas Company continuously from its formation in 1862 until his death in 1891.

The group promoting the company established contact with a civil engineer in Australia, A. K. Smith, who had overseen the establishment of a gas works in Melbourne, and invited him to Auckland to advise on establishing a gas works in that city. A public meeting was called for 8 July 1862 to hear Smith's report and to gauge support for a local gas company. Smith's proposal was for the supply of gas to twenty-one streets of Auckland from works with a production capacity of four times the estimate of initial consumption, and a mains system with a distribution capacity of eight times that estimate. In support of his offer to construct the works and mains system in less than four months for £16,000, Smith undertook either to invest £1,000 in shares in the company set up for the purpose or to manage the operations of the company and pay its shareholders an annual dividend of 12 per cent. Smith's proposal was not the only one the company promoters had obtained. A proposal from

Frederick Whitaker (1812–1891) promoted the Auckland Gas Company in 1862 and was chairman of directors until 1891. ALEXANDER TURNBULL LIBRARY, NATIONAL LIBRARY OF NEW ZEALAND, 1/2-089526.

parties in Sydney to construct works of smaller scale for less than £10,000 was mentioned at the meeting but not described in detail.

It was sufficient for the promoters' immediate purpose that the proposals provided favourable expert opinion on the technical feasibility and commercial viability of a gas supply to the city, and encouraged support for a public equity investment to fund such an undertaking. Whitaker applied his skills of legal advocacy to that end during the meeting. He relayed the advice he had received from Sydney and Melbourne that gas companies there were highly remunerative.

He gently exploited commercial rivalry between Auckland and Dunedin by dwelling on the fact that in Dunedin a gas company was in the process of being formed with public subscriptions for 3,000 £5 shares. A sharebroker in the audience, Osmund Lewis, helpfully volunteered the information that more than two-thirds of that £15,000 capital had been raised within a week, and that he believed there would be no difficulty in raising similar capital in Auckland. 'He had received communications from several individuals who were ready to come forward and take shares.'[9] Whitaker reminded his audience of the larger population and greater number of dwellings in Auckland than in Dunedin and suggested that £20,000 should be raised for the company in Auckland of which '£16,000 only would be required – the small surplus . . . being available for any extension of works that might be found necessary'. [10] When put to the meeting Whitaker's proposal 'that the formation of a company for the purpose of lighting the city of Auckland with gas be proceeded with'[11] was adopted unanimously, and a Provisional Committee was appointed to implement it.

Meeting two days later, on 10 July, the Provisional Committee resolved to incorporate the Auckland Gas Company Ltd under the Joint Stock Companies Act 1860 with an authorised capital of £20,000 in 4,000 shares of £5 each, and with power to borrow up to £8,000. The shares were to be offered for sale to the public, with 10s per share to be paid on allotment, and the remainder on calls not exceeding £1 per share and at intervals of not less than one month. Holding forty shares was to be necessary for election as a director. Notices of the formation of the company and of the public share offer appeared in the *Daily Southern Cross* from 12 July. The notices repeated the points made at the public meeting on 8 July about the highly remunerative nature of gas companies in Sydney and Melbourne, the feasibility of a local undertaking on the scale proposed by Smith, and his personal commitment to such an undertaking. As an additional inducement to investors, the company's proposed power to borrow up to half of the estimated costs of establishing the works was presented as a means of reducing the amount that they would be called on to pay.

The plan to fund construction of the works with an equal mix of debt and equity struck a balance between the respective advantages and disadvantages of the two types of finance. In general, debt finance is less costly than equity finance because lenders are exposed to less risk than shareholders and, consequently, require a lower rate of return. Factors reducing the risk of debt are the more or less restrictive terms that lenders may impose on a company in a loan contract. Such restrictions might include terms guaranteeing payment of interest and repayment of the principal, pledging specific assets as security for the debt, limiting the types of investment that the borrowed finance can be used for, restricting further borrowing by the company, and requiring the company to maintain a minimum level of profit relative to the interest expense. While these factors create a cost advantage for debt finance over equity finance, their restrictions on managerial action create strategic disadvantages.

Equity finance is generally free from such restrictions. For example, there is no legal obligation on a company to pay dividends to its shareholders or to repay their investment in the company's shares. Dividend payments are at the discretion of the company directors, and the return of shareholders' investments is dependent on their sale of the shares to other parties at negotiated prices. These factors, while increasing the risk to investors and the cost to the company, allow directors more scope for discretionary action in their financial management and thereby give equity finance a strategic advantage over debt finance. There are, of course, other factors which limit that scope: in general, the need to maintain investor confidence in the future prospects of the company. Poor returns over any extended period, in the form of inadequate dividends or depressed share prices, are likely to sap investor confidence and induce a self-perpetuating stagnation or decline in the company's performance as it encounters increasing difficulty in attracting capital for expansion and growth. However, the strategic advantage of equity, created by the greater scope for its discretionary management, offsets its cost disadvantage with respect to debt. In planning the capital structure of the Auckland Gas Company, its promoters were justified in trying to balance these respective advantages and disadvantages of the two types of finance.

The optimism that had been expressed at the public meeting by the sharebroker, Lewis, for the success of the share offer was borne out by the issue being oversubscribed. When the offer closed at noon on 23 July, applications for 4,806 shares had been received from 134 subscribers. The Provisional Committee, meeting later that afternoon to allot the shares, reserved 200 shares for Smith (in the event of the construction contract being awarded to him) and scaled the allotment of the remaining 3,800 shares to maximise both the number of shareholders and the number of shareholders who would be eligible for election as a director. Applications for less than forty shares were met in full, and those for more than forty shares were scaled down to between forty and one hundred shares.

Before registering the company, the members of the Provisional Committee present at the meeting (to whom a total of 720 shares were allotted) completed the formalities by signing the Memorandum of Association and adopting, with four minor amendments, the Articles of Association set out in Table B of the Schedule to the Joint Stock Companies Act.

Establishing the gas works

The urgency with which Whitaker and the Provisional Committee had moved to establish the company was strategically significant in pre-empting potential moves by other company promoters to establish a rival gas company in Auckland. The board of directors of the new company under Whitaker's chairmanship maintained that urgency. Meeting on 24 July, the day after the company was formed, the board authorised Whitaker to pay £1,000 for a site for the works on the shore of Brickfield Bay by the intersection of Nelson and Wyndham Streets.

At the board's next meeting on 5 August Whitaker tabled documents for the completed purchase at £800. Acquisition of plant for the works was also discussed at that meeting and a director, David Graham, was requested to gather information on the price of plant from England. An unsolicited application for the position of Works Engineer from a civil engineer in Dunedin was declined 'because the company is in communication with other persons'.[12] The reference was to correspondence that Whitaker was having with a business associate in Sydney, Robert Gilfillan, whom he had appointed to act as the company's agent in its future dealings with Smith.

> We desire to give you a discretion so far as may be sufficient to secure to us what we want, good gas works at a reasonable price.[13]

Concerned that Smith's estimate of costs was higher than the other estimate received, Whitaker asked Gilfillan to obtain a revised offer from Smith within two months. A triangular correspondence between the company, Gilfillan and Smith ensued until the directors decided, at a meeting on 24 October, to reject Smith's offer. A local engineer, Stewart, was commissioned to prepare new proposals for procuring plant from Australia or England. At an extraordinary general meeting of the company on 4 November, called to explain the rejection of Smith's offer and to consider Stewart's proposals, it was resolved to procure plant from England.

In December, the company appointed William Grahame[14] and John Morrison as its agents in London to purchase plant for the works, arrange its shipment to Auckland, and recruit an engineer to supervise its construction and commissioning. Writing to the company in April 1863, Grahame and Morrison reported that having confirmed the superiority of coal to kerosene for gas production they had purchased appropriate manufacturing plant for shipment to Auckland in the following July and had also appointed a civil engineer, J. N. Wark, as construction and works manager in Auckland.

Some parts for the plant, on their arrival in Auckland, were lost overboard while being unloaded from the ship and replacements had to be ordered from England. The arrival of Wark and his family, expected before the end of the year, was delayed until February 1864 'owing to the protracted passage made by the vessel'.[15]

Neither of these delays, however, extended the delay that was continuing to affect the preparation of the site on the shore of Brickfield Bay. Whitaker's explanation of that delay at the company's second annual general meeting in July 1864 that 'from the first they [the directors] have had much trouble and annoyance regarding this matter'[16] covered a series of managerial problems and technical difficulties.

It was, surprisingly, after that site had been purchased in August 1862 that the board decided to examine it more closely and ascertain 'whether a more eligible site may be found'.[17] Reports commissioned from the local engineer, Stewart, indicated that the site was the best of those available but was too small for its purpose. Stewart recommended extending it to an acre in area by reclaiming land from Brickfield Bay and retaining it with a seawall. Even though the board accepted that the additional cost would be recovered eventually in cost savings from being able to unload coal for the works directly from boats berthed at the seawall, rather than having to transport it by horse and cart from more distant wharves, Stewart's cost estimate of £1,800 encouraged the directors to consider alternatives. The purchase of a one-acre site in Stanley Street, owned by Whitaker, was considered in November but was not made.

The board's attention reverted to the Brickfield Bay site in December when a lower cost estimate of £1,440 for earthworks and a rough scoria seawall was received from another engineer, Sanderson. Although that offer was not accepted, the board committed itself to the concept of a seaward extension of the site and entered negotiations with the Provincial Council for a ground-lease on the land affected. Negotiations were protracted, and terms of the lease (for fifty years at £8 per year) were not agreed until April 1863. By then the onset of winter prevented a start on the not inconsiderable tasks of building the seawall and 'cutting down' the site. This last required excavating with pick and shovel the high ground to the south of the site and transferring the clay by wheelbarrow, or perhaps by horse-drawn dray, to the section of foreshore to be reclaimed.

Preparation of the site, following Stewart's original plan, could not begin until the spring, by which time the first shipment of components of plant for the works was due to arrive from England. Belatedly, it was discovered that the height of Stewart's planned seawall, to be built of dressed stone, would be inadequate and that necessary modifications would almost treble the original estimate of cost and raise the combined cost of the wall and earthworks to £3,330. Different contracts were let for the different projects. The initial contract for the seawall, let in October 1863 for 200 feet of the wall to be built in eight weeks, was for the minimum length necessary so that the directors could consider cheaper alternatives for the remainder. At the same time, a right of way over a neighbouring property owned by a Reverend Hamer was purchased to facilitate access to the site with supplies of cement and dressed stone.

Eight weeks on, in December, only 140 feet of the wall had been built and there was an estimate of a further six weeks to completion of the first stage. New contracts were let for extending the wall, but it was March 1864 before the work had progressed sufficiently for the directors to let the contract for levelling the site. The works manager, Wark, arriving in February, was unable to begin assembly and installation of the imported plant and turned to supervising the laying of mains in the streets to be supplied with gas. When the onset of winter again interrupted earthworks on the site, the delay was complicated by a landslip caused by the excavations endangering the Reverend Hamer's neighbouring property, and by the contractor responsible for levelling the site abandoning the project. The directors dealt with the first by buying the property for £1,000, and with the second by taking over the contract amidst threats to pursue its guarantors. It fell to Wark to supervise the completion of the site preparation. Stabilising the southern side of the site against further slips, sinking a well 145 feet deep to reach supplies of fresh water required for the works, and preventing seawater from seeping into the tanks for the two gasometers (each one of 50-feet diameter) were significant challenges. But before the end of 1864 the site was in sufficient order for the construction of buildings and the installation of the imported plant to begin. And by April 1865, almost three years after the formation of the company, the works were in commercial operation.[18]

As the costs mounted with the delays during that time, some shareholders of the company, including the directors, might have wondered at the wisdom of having rejected Smith's original offer to build the works in four months for £16,000. The accounts presented at the company's annual general meeting in July 1865 showed that the £23,200 total capitalised cost of the works comprised £1,800 for the property purchases, £3,850 for the seawall and site excavations, and £17,550 for the acquisition and construction of plant and equipment. Moreover, part of Smith's offer had been the option of an annual dividend for shareholders of 12 per cent, but three years on from the rejection of that offer shareholders had received no dividend and had no immediate prospect of receiving one. The amount and timing of the capital expenditure had played havoc with Whitaker's original plan to fund the works by raising £16,000 in equal amounts of debt and equity finance. If the plan to raise £8,000 equity by

The Auckland Gas Company's original works on the shore of Brickfield Bay in the late 1860s.
SPECIAL COLLECTIONS, AUCKLAND CITY LIBRARIES, 7-A11393.

calling only 40 per cent of the company's £20,000 subscribed capital had been an inducement made to investors to ensure the success of the public share offer, it had succeeded. But success in funding the remainder of the expenditure by borrowing £8,000 depended not only on the actual capital expenditure staying within plan, but also on the prompt start of a revenue stream to begin meeting debt-servicing costs. Neither of these conditions eventuated and, as the cost over-runs and project delays became apparent, the directors' decisions about how to continue raising additional finance faced an increasingly sharp dilemma. Making repeated calls on shareholders when there was only a distant prospect of any return on the investment risked shareholders' resistance, and the possibility that some might decide to cut their losses and forfeit their shares. Borrowing, on the other hand, was at best a temporary, short-term alternative, as without a revenue stream the debt could only be serviced from equity finance.

The dilemma was not so significant in the first year, as the main items of capital expenditure (£800 for the land purchase and £2,500 remitted to the London agents as an advance on the purchase of plant) were able to be funded by the £1,900 received from shareholders on the allotment of their shares and the same amount realised from a call of 10s per share made in December 1862. The dilemma sharpened in the second year as funding for a further £11,500 of capital expenditure was required to meet site preparation costs and drafts drawn on the company by its London agents to complete the purchase of the plant. A call of £1 per share made in October 1863 realised £3,800, but raised the called portion of issued capital to 40 per cent, the level that Whitaker had suggested would be the upper limit. In December the company secretary, Hugh Reid, advised that within a month the company's liabilities would be £4,000 and 'would dispose of all available funds'.[19] As calls on shareholders were made with one month's notice, the advice implied a suggestion to the board that another call would be timely. The directors decided 'it was not expedient to make a further call at present'[20] and instructed Reid to arrange credit with the Bank of New Zealand to meet two £1,000 drafts drawn on the company by Grahame and Morrison in London.

The respite was temporary. In early February 1864, the secretary advised that in March the company would have a deficit of £1,400. Having little option, the directors responded immediately with a call of 10s per share and followed one month later with another call of £1 per share. Some shareholders' resistance to those calls, which had raised the called portion of issued capital to 70 per cent, was apparent at the end of May when £506 10s of the £5,700 combined total of the two calls due in early March and mid-April (equal to 8.8 per cent) remained unpaid. The secretary was instructed to write to each shareholder in arrears with a demand for immediate payment of not only the call but also the penalty interest of 15 per cent p.a. which was provided for in the company's Articles of Association.

The directors, however, also read the message in the shareholders' unpaid calls. Needing to raise a further £2,300 by the end of May 'the propriety of making another call was discussed; but it was not considered advisable'.[21] Another temporary respite was bought with a loan of £2,300 for three months from the Bank of New Zealand. In late August when the loan was due for repayment, the directors had to choose between extending it or making a further call on shareholders: 'because of the high rate of interest charged by the Bank at present'[22] they chose to make a call of £1 per share. Reid, the hard-pressed secretary whose annual remuneration was determined and paid in arrears, requested and was granted three months' sick leave.

An estimate of costs and available funds to complete the works, prepared in October 1864 by Reid's temporary replacement, William Dunlop, showed that after allowing for the £1,900 remaining on call from shareholders, there was an unfunded requirement of almost £6,000. The option of meeting that requirement by raising more equity finance, either by creating more shares or by increasing the par value of the existing shares, was considered by the directors but rejected, possibly because of the increasing difficulty being experienced in realising the par value of the shares already issued. From the most recent call, £447 of the £3,800 due in September was still outstanding in October, representing an increase in the rate of calls overdue after one month from 8.8 per cent to 11.7 per cent. As before, the secretary was instructed to pursue the shareholders in arrears by demanding immediate payment of the call with interest and, also as before, the directors deferred making a further call.

Through October and November as construction of the works progressed, allowing more reliable forecasts to be made not only of their completion but also of a start to commercial production and the beginning of a revenue stream to meet debt-servicing costs, the option to borrow the extra finance required became more feasible. In December the board negotiated a loan of £6,000 from the Auckland Savings Bank with interest at 10 per cent p.a. and the principal to be drawn down progressively and secured by a mortgage over the company's property and plant. The final call on shareholders of 10s per share, deferred in October, was made at the end of March 1865 and pursued with the customary vigour. Twelve shareholders responsible for £140 10s calls in arrears at the end of June (including a deceased estate owing £50) were named and shamed on the balance sheet presented at the company's annual general meeting in July. The balance sheet also revealed the extent to which the directors had been forced to deviate from their original financial plan for the establishment of the works. Instead of equal amounts of equity and debt finance funding a capital investment of £16,000, the company's capital structure comprised £19,000 of equity and £6,000 of debt for a capital investment of £23,200 and working capital of £1,800.

First light

The first mains supply of gas on Saturday 15 April 1865 was an event of considerable public interest.

> Queen Street was thronged until an advanced hour of the evening, with moving crowds of gazers, who seemed never to weary of staring at the unwonted spectacle presented to them, while there were occasional 'rushes' into some of the other street[s], as the report spread of some particularly effective illumination, or of some establishment whose meter had come to grief, and left it in sudden and ignoble obscurity.[23]

In spite of teething problems (for example, the burners in the street lamps were too small to give the best light), the three daily newspapers, the *Daily Southern*

Cross, the *New Zealander* and the *New Zealand Herald* were unanimous in their praise of the event:

> As a beginning it was more than a success; and while we felicitate ourselves on the approach of that millennium when Queen-street will cease to be rendered impassable by the City Board, we congratulate the shareholders on the approach of the time when they may expect a dividend.[24]

Initial consumers were not numerous. In the preceding weeks the company had contracted with the City Board to service 100 public street lamps and had canvassed for private consumers. But when supply commenced, barely forty of the public lamps and only fifty-six private premises were connected to the mains. Most potential consumers, understandably, had been unwilling to incur the expense of installing service pipes and fittings before supplies became available. Three months later, however, Wark was able to report to the company's annual general meeting that after the first fortnight demand had begun to increase sharply, daily consumption had risen to 25,000 cubic feet, and the total supply to date, not including the public lamps, was 565,000 cubic feet.[25]

Expanding the capacity

In the company's first full financial year of operations, starting in 1865, 6.7 million cubic feet of gas were sold. Fifty years on, in the financial year 1915, more than 650 million cubic feet were sold. The hundred-fold increase in consumption over half a century was driven both by metropolitan population growth and by increasing per capita consumption. Population figures at the censuses taken in 1881, 1891, 1901 and 1911 rose from 32,389 through 51,287 and 67,226 to 102,676. In the same years, annual per capita consumption of gas (in cubic feet) rose from 1390 through 2073 and 3530 to 5530. Per capita consumption was boosted by the additional domestic and industrial uses of gas following the introduction of gas stoves and gas engines in 1879. By 1898, 2500 stoves and 174 engines had been installed; in the two years 1913 and 1914, the number of stoves installed rose by 3002 to 10,992.

The company's capacity to supply anticipated increases in demand was created in a series of interleaved extensions to its production and storage facilities. In 1878 a 7-acre site on the far shore of Freemans Bay from Brickfield Bay was purchased for the location of a 142,000 cubic feet gasometer. The new storage facility, imported, assembled and in use by 1880, made increases in

The Auckland Gas Company's works in the late 1870s, landlocked by harbour-front
reclamation and bounded by Nelson and Fanshawe Streets. SPECIAL COLLECTIONS,
AUCKLAND CITY LIBRARIES, 4-567.

production capacity at Brickfield Bay feasible. Additional retorts were built there and in operation by 1882. In 1885, another 520,000 cubic feet gasometer was completed at Freemans Bay, 'not before it was urgently required'.[26] The establishment of branch works at Devonport and Onehunga was also part of this first phase of capacity building, which was complete by 1886.

A second phase began in 1897 following the decision to relocate the main works from Brickfield Bay to Freemans Bay. When the old works were eventually de-commissioned in 1906, the new works had a daily production capacity of 1.5 million cubic feet. There was yet another gasometer (imported from the United States), which doubled the previous storage capacity, and a coal store of 8000 tons' capacity – when 6000 tons were sufficient for three winter months' production. Further extensions to the works in the next two years, on land adjoining the site, barely kept pace with demand.

By 1908, the daily production capacity of 2 million cubic feet was being fully utilised on occasions, and plans were made to start a programme in 1910 to expand daily production capacity to 10 million cubic feet. One-quarter of that capacity was available by 1911; in the winter of 1912, the highest single day's output was 2.41 million cubic feet.

Later that year work started on a new retort house whose first stage would add a further 1.5 million cubic feet of daily production capacity, and went along with the construction of a 2.3 million cubic feet gasometer on a site in

The Auckland Gas Company's new Beaumont Street works in 1912, viewed across Victoria Park reclaimed from Freemans Bay. SPECIAL COLLECTIONS, AUCKLAND CITY LIBRARIES, I-W961.

Beresford Street. The expected completion of both projects in 1913 prompted the chairman's remark at that year's annual general meeting that 'we await the demands of the dark days of winter with equanimity.'[27] Extensions to the network of mains, which had been continual since 1865, also accelerated during this latter phase of capacity expansion. The 128 miles of mains laid by 1897 had increased to 226 miles by 1907 ('an enormous mileage for our population')[28] and to 417 miles by 1915.

Financing the expansion

The financial strategy adopted to fund this expansion of the company's production and distribution capacity was remarkable for several reasons. It eschewed debt finance and relied on the ability to raise equity finance by offering shares for sale by public tender. The strategy remained effective for four decades after its implementation in 1875, being augmented rather than replaced in 1905 when the company raised its first public loan with an issue of debentures. And in origin, the strategy was born of a mixture of necessity and opportunism.

The necessity was created at the end of 1865 when the Auckland Savings Bank suddenly recalled £2,500 of the company's £6,000 term loan. The minutes of the directors' meeting recording the recall also noted that alternative finance for three months which had been arranged with the Bank of New Zealand was on the personal guarantee of the directors because 'it was difficult if not impossible to get anyone to advance money to the company on a second mortgage'.[29] The phlegmatic tone of the report is less remarkable given the early warning that the directors would have had of the Auckland Savings Bank's financial crisis. Whitaker acted as solicitor for the bank; another company director, Graham, was currently Vice President (equivalent to chief executive officer) of the bank, and three other company directors, Macffarlane, Ridings and Wilson, were trustees of the bank. In view of this inside knowledge, and influence, it is more remarkable that, even after the value of the securities that the bank needed to call was reduced from £28,245 to £9,670, the company remained on the list of the bank's customers who were informed that they 'may have the privilege of paying off one third in thirty days'.[30]

Within the three-month term of the loan from the Bank of New Zealand the directors had to effect a capital reconstruction of the company. Contracting more debt was not an option, but there were alternatives for raising extra equity. An issue of preference shares paying an annual dividend of 12.5 per cent was contemplated and rejected. The directors decided, instead, to create 2000 ordinary shares of £5 each and offer them to existing shareholders on the basis of one new share for every two already held. The new shares would be issued as fully paid up for the discounted price of £2 10s, with £1 5s payable on allotment and the balance on call at two months' notice. The offer, approved at an extraordinary general meeting in March, was to remain open until 20 April after which shares not taken up would be auctioned, or 'submitted to competition', at the reserve price of £2 10s. One hundred of the new shares were reserved in relation to the 200 original shares that had been reserved for Smith and were still unissued. Of the 1900 new shares available to shareholders, 1404 were taken up before the offer closed.

At the auction for the remaining 496 shares on 1 May, 'bidding was brisk, and they realised from £2/12/- to £3/6/6 per share'.[31] The proceeds from the sale of the new shares, and the collection of the last calls in arrears on the original shares, were used before the end of the financial year in June to repay both the overdraft and the temporary loan from the Bank of New Zealand. At the company's annual general meeting in July, Whitaker made it clear that the directors' priority in the forthcoming year would be to use trading profits and the amount still on call for the new shares to repay the balance of the loan from the Auckland Savings Bank. Shareholders, who were still waiting for their first dividend, were reassured that the directors would 'in all probability, be able to announce that the Shareholders will be entitled to a dividend'.[32] Whitaker kept his word on both points and, in doing so, created initial conditions for the 'no-debt-all-equity' financial management strategy of the future. After repayment of the loan from the Auckland Savings Bank, the company would never again be beholden to a bank for term finance. And the nominal dividend of 10 per cent announced for the year to June 1867 began an unbroken series of dividends underpinning the continual supply of equity finance.

The opportunity to launch the strategy was created by a continuing upward trend in the market price of the company's shares. From a low of £2 10s in April 1866, when the original shareholders were facing a potential loss of 50 per cent on their fully paid shares, the price rose to an average of almost £3 at auction at the beginning of May. Through the second half of the year, buoyed by the continued growth in the company's business and Whitaker's pledge of a dividend, the share price continued to rise through the £3 and £4 ranges, to reach the par value of £5 in January 1867. The nominal dividend of 10 per cent was maintained in the following year and shares began to be traded at a premium over their par value, finishing at £5 10s in December 1868. Increased nominal dividends of 12.5 per cent and 15 per cent were declared in July 1869 and July 1870, and the share price rose to £8 by December 1869 and to £8 10s by December 1870. By December 1872, in spite of a dividend reduced to 10 per cent, shares were being traded at £10 (that is, a premium of £5 over their £5 par value).

The market was tested at auction by the sales of the 300 unissued shares in two equal parcels in 1873 and 1874. The first sale realised £1,476 5s at an average premium of £4 16s per share; the second sale realised £1,500 at an average premium of £5 per share. The nominal dividend rate was back up to 15 per cent and the pieces were in place for the launch of the strategy in 1875.

The pretext was the need to raise equity finance to cover capital expenditure of £5,810 14s 5d that had occurred spasmodically since 1868 and had been met, as it occurred, out of profits and temporary loans. The directors created 4000 shares of £5 par value, increasing the company's authorised capital to £50,000, and announced their strategy at the annual general meeting in July 1875:

> To put the company's affairs into a proper position, the Directors propose therefore, to sell at the market price a sufficient number of the new shares [to raise £5,810 14s 5d] and, from time to time afterwards, to effect other sales to meet the expenses of the further additions and extensions that will be required.[33]

Only 588 shares had to be sold to raise the sum required, the average accepted tender price of £9 17s 10d representing a premium of £4 17s 10d per share.

By February 1882, all 4000 shares had been disposed of in like manner, in quantities ranging between 183 and 900 per year, at an average premium of £4 2s 11d per share, and realising a total premium of £16,587 on the £20,000 par value. The strategy was continued almost immediately with another tranche of 5000 £5 shares created in May 1882, increasing the company's authorised capital to £75,000. By June 1884, 4000 of those shares had been sold, realising a total premium of £14,947 on the £20,000 par value. The lower average premium of £3 14s 9d per share prompted the directors to make another share issue before all existing shares had been sold, on terms modified to maintain a significant premium on share capital.

In 1884, 35,000 £5 shares were created, increasing the company's authorised capital more than threefold to £250,000; 14,000 shares were to be offered to existing shareholders on a one-for-one basis at a premium of £2 10s per share. Unlike the previous offers which required shares to be paid for in full at the time of purchase, payment for shares taken up in this offer was to be on call with a proportionate part of the premium being payable with each call. The other 21,000 new shares, and any not taken up by existing shareholders, could be disposed of by public tender at the directors' discretion.

The offer was attractive to existing shareholders, enabling them to buy shares on terms that amounted to deferred payment, and at a premium of only 50 per cent when the current market premium was almost 75 per cent. Moreover, the trend in the nominal annual dividend rate over the decade had been upward, having tracked at 15 per cent from 1874, up through 16 per cent in 1881 to rest at 17 per cent from 1882; 12,911 of the 14,000 shares on offer were taken up immediately and by 1886, when a ten-year pause in the company's equity raising began, the shares had been called to 50 per cent of their price. Calls resumed in 1896 and the shares were fully paid up by 1902. Sales of unissued shares also resumed in 1896. In spite of a decline in the nominal annual dividend rate from 17 per cent in 1889 through 16 per cent in 1890 to rest back at 15 per cent from 1891, prices tendered for the shares included unprecedented premiums. From 1897 to 1907, 6831 shares were sold at an average price of £13 18s, representing an average premium of £8 18s or 178 per cent of par value.

The directors took advantage of this share price strength to double the authorised capital of the company to £500,000 in 1908 and re-run the previous scenario with the 50,000 new £5 shares. On this occasion, however, the shares were offered to existing shareholders on a one-for-one basis at a premium of £5 per share, not £2 10s as before; 34,133 of the 36,074 shares offered on these terms were taken up immediately, and with little effect on the company's share price.

Auckland Gas Company workers. When the gasometers were fairly full, there was time to take a break from shovelling coal. SPECIAL COLLECTIONS, AUCKLAND CITY LIBRARIES, 4-RIC112.

The 1306 shares sold by public tender in 1909 realised an average premium of £8 16s 3d per share.

The market premium on shares was boosted, proportionately, by increased liquidity in the market following a five-for-one share split at the end of 1909.[34] The average successful tenders for £1 shares in 1910 and 1911 were £3 4s and £3 6s, representing premiums of 220 per cent and 230 per cent per share. Thereafter, there were fewer sales of shares and calls on shares as the extensions to the company's facilities were completed and the need to raise more capital abated. The two further increases in the company's authorised capital before 1915 were for other reasons. In 1913, 250,000 £1 shares were created to make a one-for-one bonus issue to shareholders, paid for from the accumulated share premium. And in 1914, with the company's capital expenditure in excess of £750,000, the authorised capital was increased to £1 million by the creation of another 250,000 £1 shares because 'it was proper that the authorised share capital should exceed the capital expenditure of the company'.[35]

Conclusion

The Auckland Gas Company was presented with a variety of threats and opportunities in the financial markets in which it operated before the First World

War. The principal threat arose in the market for debt when the Auckland Savings Bank recalled part of its term loan in 1865, and the emergency re-financing was only possible on the personal guarantee of the directors. The company's subsequent exit and long-term absence from the market for debt was an effective strategic response by the directors to the general threat of the unreliability of that market, a response informed by their immediate experience of the Auckland Savings Bank's crisis and reinforced by subsequent crises in the banking industry.

The principal opportunity arose in the market for equity in the late 1860s as the company's shares began to be traded at prices above their par value. Creating and selling shares by public tender to capture the market premium was a strategic response that enabled the directors to reduce the company's cost of (all-equity) capital below the nominal rate of dividend. Nominal dividend rates, struck on the par value of shares, represented lower effective rates of return on shares that had been bought at a premium. Thus, in 1910 the nominal dividend rate of 18 per cent paid on £1 shares which had been bought for £3 represented a return to the shareholder, and a cost to the company, of only 6 per cent.

The disclosure of this strategy, whenever increases in the authorised capital of the company were made and, more frequently, at annual general meetings of the company, pre-empts the suggestion that the directors attempted to deceive shareholders by announcing dividends in nominal rather than effective rates. On the contrary, the frequent disclosure, and persistent success, of the strategy suggests that for directors and shareholders it was a mutually satisfactory arrangement.

CHAPTER FIVE

Guilt by Association:
Attempts at Domination of the Late-Nineteenth- and Early-Twentieth-Century Auckland Timber Trade

KENNETH E. JACKSON

The late-nineteenth-century business environment in Auckland reflected some of the general traits of New Zealand as a whole and some more particular aspects of its own. Exploitation of the natural resource base was as much part of the Auckland scene as it was of the national one. In addition the desire, where possible, to control markets and maximise returns on the part of individual enterprises was also part of the national business environment. Within the timber trade, Auckland presented the prospect of doing both of these. What follows is an examination of the attempt to control the lucrative export market for timber from late nineteenth-century New Zealand. This means focusing on: one timber, kauri (*Agathis australis*), which accounts for the overwhelming part of all timber exports; one area of New Zealand (the Auckland Province) where most of the kauri grew; and one city in Australia (Melbourne) where most of the timber went.

This chapter starts with a background account of the export industry context, followed by a consideration of the general policy context both for timber policy and attitudes to industrial associations. It then examines the structure of the industry at the time and the specific attempts to control the trade through associations, and considers the strategic goals of those attempting to do so. The conclusions are drawn at the end of this chapter that the reasons for the failure of the enterprise to control the market were as much the result of industrial structure and free competition as they were of policy and regulation. The overall conclusion would seem to be inescapably that this was rather more in the nature of an attempt to acquire wealth, than it was an attempt at wealth creation.

Late nineteenth-century timber exports

The share of timber by value in New Zealand's international trade figures diminished after a peak of over 30 per cent in 1853.[1] It was generally small in a relative sense, never much more than double figures in percentage terms. The domestic trade may well have been several times larger, but is difficult to estimate. The absolute quantity position for exports of timber is described in the following graph, which is based on the figures given by Bloomfield.[2]

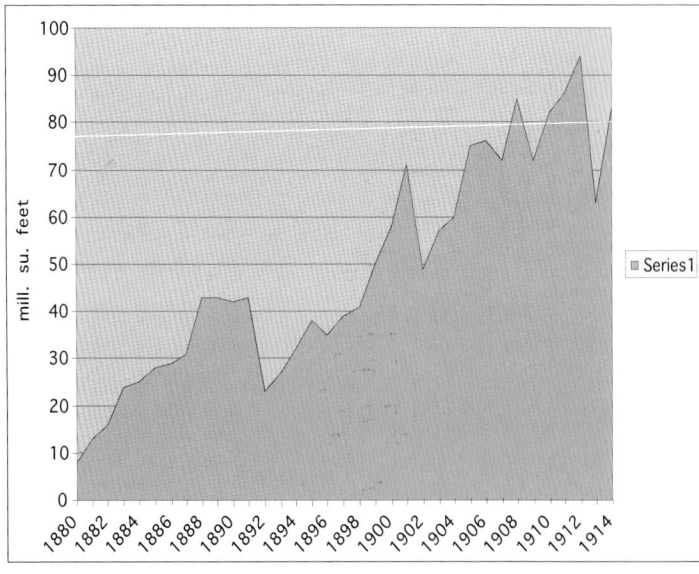

FIGURE 1: TIMBER EXPORTS

Kauri was a diminishing resource by the early twentieth century and some of the blame can arguably be laid at the door of the timber industry. Kauri accounted for only about one-half of 1 per cent of timber milled by the end of the First World War.[3] Sawmillers were good business operators and clearly were rent seekers, asking for government protection from imports and discouraging any ideas of conservation, including the proposal for an export tax noted in 1915.[4] The end of the graph coincides with a volume peak for exports, in 1914.[5]

The supply of export timber to meet the growth in demand by milling companies did have an influence on forest clearance, but only a very limited one. It can be argued that its impact on kauri was even more significant, but even there the clearances were pursued regardless of how much timber was being exported and how much was just burnt. Kauri timber was the main component of exports before 1914, with kahikatea being used for the specific purpose of packaging for butter and cheese, due to its non-tainting qualities.[6] Australia (and Melbourne especially) formed the basic market for exports of such timbers. In the interwar period the Imperial Government considered New Zealand as a potential source, but only briefly. Logistics prevented a fuller consideration of the issue. Essentially transport costs were too great an obstacle.

The British Reconstruction Committee report of 1917–18[7] effectively wrote New Zealand off, as well as other Empire sources such as India, South Africa and Australia. Only a few part shipments of relatively small amounts of kauri, rimu and totara ever made it onto the market in Britain in the 1920s.[8] In the nineteenth century, the traditional market, Australia, was the dominant customer, taking virtually all the timber exports. In the light of this, it is far from surprising that the biggest industrial combination ever to operate in the late nineteenth-century New Zealand timber industry, the Kauri Timber Company, had extensive financial, market and other links with Australia. It was ease of co-ordinated marketing arrangements that appealed most. After 1918, there were still some 98 per cent of exports by value heading across the Tasman.[9]

Late-nineteenth-century policy context

Timber had long been seen as an 'inexhaustible' resource and one whose cost of acquisition was essentially that of cutting and recovering standing timber, with various government policies and other institutional factors ensuring that more and more timber came on-stream as clearances continued.[10] Within the general aspects of the late nineteenth century attitude towards natural resources as immediate components of commercial activity, such an outcome was part of the overall desire to quarry the resource, to transform natural capital into physical capital. This was part of the expansionary power of the commercial process of the time. The securing of property rights to timber is here portrayed as part of a general attempt to secure the acquisition of a title to wealth, rather than wealth creation.

The early method of operation of the various small firms, who found themselves in a competitive situation in the early 1880s, is contrasted with the intent of the Kauri Timber Company to combine the Auckland producers and control the market. Contemporary attitudes to combinations and the failure of the promoters to successfully dominate the market, when analysed, reveal a general antagonism toward this collusive or monopoly control. However, this is not seen as the reason for the failure of the monopoly, which lies in the structure and context of the industry at this point in time. There are different dimensions of 'guilt' which were attempted to be placed on the activities of loggers and timber millers at this time, through their associations and their attempts to dominate the market, as well as those that were subsequently levelled at them by conservationists. The latter accusations of profligacy and destruction of the forest have some point, as do the former in the sense that they wished to control the trade. Circumstances are found to have prevented them from achieving their aim in the first case, just as there were greater forces at work in destroying the forests than the role of the sawmillers in the second case.

The timber trade in New Zealand was, by the end of the nineteenth century, one of the more significant sectors of the economy, both in terms of exports and of domestic activity. The exact amount of timber utilised within the country is difficult to determine with even general accuracy. As revealed in an earlier work,[11] timber was largely a by-product of land clearance and a substantial amount of standing timber was never utilised in any activity; it was burnt.

The timber that was used either as an input for various activities or for direct export, largely to Australia, was handled by a large number of companies all competing for custom. To be successful in the business required acumen and probably luck. The average size of most timber-milling businesses was relatively small by overseas standards, although they might appear large by local standards. Attempts to tip the market scales in favour of the entrepreneur appeared from time to time, and more particularly in the Auckland region where some of the larger operations were to be found.

Attempts to cartelise the industry and to exercise a degree of price control have some parallels with international efforts to control various commodities at other points in time and in other places. As with all international commodities but oil, the attempts to control the timber market in late nineteenth-century New Zealand all came to nought. This did not stop governments from looking to concern themselves with the perceived problem of collusion or association. The degree of competition and the ease of entry ensured the failure of such efforts rather more effectively than regulation, but the Royal Commission into Timber and Timber Prices of 1909 and the Cost of Living Commission in 1912 both investigated the dealings of the industry. The fact that the government itself was contributing to the problem through a lack of effective royalty payments for standing timber was usually overlooked. It was the rapacity of the businesses that was seen as threatening supplies and pushing up prices.

Regulation, forests and the quest for clearance

New Zealand regulation of forest clearance was minimal, and control was generally ineffective well into the twentieth century. The prevailing community ethos was one greatly in favour of clearance of land for agriculture and predominantly pastoral purposes. Trees grew best where soil fertility was highest. Even so, the dominant type of tree suggests that New Zealand was not blessed by nature in this respect: 'New Zealand forest soils appeared to be relatively nutrient-poor compared with those of the Northern Hemisphere.'[12] Climatic factors including abundant rainfall, rather than fertile soil, were a key part in pastoral success. The more fertile soils, albeit limited in quantity in New Zealand, were sought after for pastoral expansion. The physical difficulty of clearance was the main reason for the slowness of the process, rather than it being due to any great concern for retaining a sizeable stock of forest and operating forestry in a sustainable manner.

Early Conservators of Forests were not long-lasting. One drowned in the period before he took up office and another enjoyed only a short time in office before his post succumbed to budget cuts. All of this was symptomatic of the problem for those who wished to ensure the survival of the forest.

The New Zealand Forest Service emerged in the early 1920s at about the same moment that such bureaucratic structures were being established in many parts of the world. Within the Empire they were particularly encouraged or required as part of the Imperial Forest Conference's solution to the always imminent timber famine: a famine which incidentally was always around the corner, but never seemed to actually appear. Control over forest resources by government agencies was seen as the modern way. It had not been there before the First World War, apart from a few enthusiasts. The prevailing ethos was for clearance. As Condliffe quoted from the eloquent pen of L. Macintosh Ellis:

> The vital energies of the pioneer were concentrated on deforestation. Before axe and fire the virgin forests melted away . . . for ingrained in the settler from childhood was the tradition that the forest was his enemy . . . Indeed in time it came to pass that the forests were driven back to the uplands, to the mountainous hinterlands, to the cold morainal bogs; but the unreasoning habit of bush destruction had become a sort of religion . . . In the eyes of many the indigenous forest was so much garbage, to be swept out of existence.[13]

Eloquence may have exceeded reasoning on Ellis's part too, for a case can be made for some level of deforestation, even commercial extinction as rational, as has been investigated in the case of the New Zealand kauri forests.[14] For current purposes it is reasonable to assume that the role of clearance for settlement was already seen as the key factor rather than logging activity per se.

So, although the timber industry appeared set on a course of rapid cutting, its business decisions and any consequent impacts were largely the result of the institutional background they worked against. New Zealand could not be said to have been a conservation-conscious society in the late nineteenth century; the loggers were not the prime cause of the problem; rather agricultural expansion was. Any rise in pastoral produce prices increased the incentive to clear land, resulting in more timber being available for immediate cutting and reducing the likelihood of any conservation through increased price. Government policy hastened this process.

Participants in the 1896 Conference on Forestry correctly saw that too rapid a rate of depletion of the forest was occurring,[15] but wrongly attributed it to over-harvesting. Much, if not most, of the cleared timber was never harvested – it was burnt.[16] With such a large amount of standing timber available, particularly in the 1890s, it was only timber which was easily cut and close to market or transport that was likely to be milled. These factors determined the cost of timber supply to the mills, since the standing timber price all but approximated to zero. Nearly 14 per cent of the New Zealand land area was cleared in the 1890s; there was more standing timber than demand for it. With export quantities actually falling at the start of the decade, further burning was all but inevitable. The underlying approach to settlement was to aim at as rapid a method of clearance as possible, rather than to make the most of timber production opportunities. The details of the process have been fully outlined elsewhere.[17]

Entrepreneurial opportunities for sawmilling certainly existed, but there was a pattern of opportunistic and rapidly adaptive behaviour: as one species was worked out so others were substituted. There was a geographical spread of sources of timber supply over time, originating in the Auckland Province and kauri area, to elsewhere in the country into the major export mills, situated in Auckland. Government subsidies, infrastructure provision and the requirements of 'improvement leases' encouraged clearance.

Commercial regulation and sawmilling associations

Commercial, political and public views regarding the value or otherwise of associations to control the supply of goods to the market in the late nineteenth and early twentieth century were mixed, but generally antipathetic, except to those who sought the control. There were general feelings against combinations, pricing agreements, trusts and various other names for collusive activity amongst both politicians and the general public. In Auckland the operations of a brick trust – including the involvement of one of the later directors of the Kauri Timber Company 'combine' – met with general opposition, including from their customers, the builders. Attempting to control the market was as natural a function of business then as now. Various methods of doing this were tried in various sectors of activity in late-nineteenth-century Auckland. The travails and machinations of the Auckland Tramways and Electricity supply companies represent a case in point, under the globalised control of the British Electric Traction Company. (Or in the 1907 pamphleteer's phrase: 'the cosmopolitan gang of financial sharks' and their association with various members of the City Council.)[18] General attitudes saw monopoly as bad. The 1912 Commission on the Cost of Living was clear in its statement of the position:

> An isolated, highly protected and sparsely populated country like New Zealand, so far distant from the World's markets, especially lends itself to the manipulation of trusts and combines. It is a comparatively easy matter for a few wealthy individuals in any given industry or business to secure control of the output and by slightly raising prices, to levy secret taxation on the whole community.[19]

Efforts to combat private monopoly extended to the public ownership of infrastructural operations, including railways, posts and telecommunications, and electricity generation and supply. The threat of monopoly, and even more so the threat of foreign monopoly, was seen as great and to be avoided almost at any cost, in part to keep prices down.[20] Arguments that abnormal price rises were not threatened by efforts at association, made either by the promoters of associations at the time, or by later observers,[21] are not totally convincing.

Efforts to control and regulate were not so necessary in the case of timber. The efforts of the various firms in the industry to come to mutually advantageous trading arrangements in the Auckland area, as well as other areas later on, ultimately proved to be unsuccessful. This lack of success was not due to political or public opposition, which certainly existed, but rather to the underlying inability of the firms concerned to control the market. The structure and situation of the industry did not permit it to happen.

Structure of the industry

The larger firms accounted for most of the output for the New Zealand export trade and the overwhelming majority of these were to be found in the Auckland region. As Russell Stone has summarised so well: by 1881 over 90 per cent of timber exports by value were leaving through Auckland ports.[22] At this time the vast majority of these exports were of kauri.

The overall development of New Zealand's timber industry was one which passed through several organisational changes. It started in a rudimentary fashion, as did much of colonial industry. It was initially heavily reliant on manual labour. As it developed, some producers adopted more capital-intensive methods of production, from as early as the 1840s. Even by the later part of the century, however, the so-called 'drummers' still existed and operated with little capital. They could readily supply 10,000 super feet per week at short notice, but never much more than that even with longer notice.[23] The large-scale operations always faced some competition from such smaller operations.

Capital-intensive operations started with water-driven sawmills, followed by the increasing use of dams behind which logs could be stored and floated downstream, but in the early days only by destroying the dam itself. Trip gates set in dams later allowed more permanent structures. The introduction of steam power and refinements of equipment led to larger and larger scale operations, such that by the fourth quarter of the nineteenth century forestry was a major industrial sector in the New Zealand economy and the largest industry in the Auckland area. Within three or four decades of European settlement, the Auckland firms were leaders in the trend towards even larger-scale operations. The small drummer operations, however, continued and were always there at the margin to act as a constraint on their larger counterparts.

In general the Auckland establishments were among the largest in New Zealand, for which they attracted some unfavourable press: antagonism to monopolistic control and to a fear of foreign control had more part to play here than anything else. The major firms in Auckland, with their increasingly

Tops of planks of shut 'gate' are just showing as a dam (part of kauri timber operations) fills.
THOMAS E. SIMPSON, *KAURI TO RADIATA: ORIGIN AND EXPANSION OF THE TIMBER INDUSTRY OF NEW ZEALAND*,
HODDER AND STOUGHTON, AUCKLAND, 1973 (SOURCE: J. JACKSON).

large sawmills,[24] had by the latter part of the century overtaken the originally
larger South Island operations. The 1870s was a key period of change in this
regard.[25]

Four firms were said to be dominant in the Auckland trade by 1870:
Auckland Timber Company, C. A. Harris, Te Kopuru Sawmill Company,
and Union Steam Saw Moulding Sash and Door.[26] Dominance was not defined
in any 'control of market' sense, but rather in terms of number of employees. In
such terms the industry was the dominant manufacturing sector in Auckland
by the 1880s. Nationally, and in terms of processed product export receipts
specifically, it lagged behind meat freezing and tanning. Fluctuations occurred
in the numbers employed according to market conditions, but by the start of
the 1880s an average size per New Zealand mill was typically of the order
of twenty hands.[27] Within the New Zealand industrial context, they were
relatively large operations, but, as will be seen, not necessarily dominant in
terms of market power.

Attempts to associate and their outcomes

Large-scale and associated concerns were far from confined to the Auckland
timber industry in late-nineteenth-century New Zealand. The high capital costs
associated with meat freezing works led to that industry being dominated by
major players, such as Vesteys or by farmer-owned New Zealand cooperatives.

Association and attempts at 'orderly' marketing were the order of the day both in New Zealand and Great Britain. For the latter, some ninety-three major trust and combinations were reported as operating by the 1919 Committee on trusts,[28] and it was suggested this was likely to be an undercount.

The Royal Commission on the timber trade and timber prices in New Zealand, which was held in 1909, found the trade to have been thoroughly organised, as did the Cost of Living Commission of 1912.[29] This does not seem to totally equate with the Auckland experience. There were certainly attempts to control the trade, organisation was not missing, but success in these endeavours was. In 1888 there was an ambitious attempt to bring together several enterprises (some twenty-eight in all) forming the bulk of the kauri export millers situated in the Auckland region. Some names and locations of the companies and interests involved are included in Table 1, which is ultimately derived from Benita Carter's fine thesis of over thirty years ago.[30]

TABLE 1: KAURI TIMBER INTERESTS TAKEN OVER BY KAURI TIMBER COMPANY IN 1888

1.	Auckland Timber Co. Ltd.
2.	New Zealand Timber Co. Ltd.
3.	Union Steam Saw, Moulding, Sash and Door Co. Ltd.
4.	Te Kopuru Saw Mill Co., Kaipara (owner John Logan Campbell).
5.	Mercury Bay Saw Mill Co.
6.	David Blair and Son, Hikutaia, Thames River.
7.	Shortland Saw Mill (owner Stone & White).
8.	Jagger & Parker, Whananaki (Kaipara area).
9.	Sharpe & Ansenne, Mercury Bay.
10.	Pearce Lanigan, Ngunguru.
11.	Onehunga Saw Mill (owner F. P. Clarke), Waitakarei.
12.	John Wigmore, Whangaroa.
13.	Helensville Timber Co. Ltd.
14.	Coulthard Bros., Papakura.
15.	Hokianga Saw Mill Co, Ltd.
16.	Whitelaw and Day, Hikurangi (Whangarei area).
17.	Henry Brett, (Kaipara district).
18.	Port Fitzroy Timber Co. (Great Barrier Island).
19.	Bradley, Cairns, and Mander, Kaiwaka (Kaipara area).
20.	W. B. Jackson & Co. Ltd., Pupuki
21.	W. W. Jackson, Pupuki (Hokianga and Whangaroa).
22.	E. S. Dufaur, Auckland (held interest in both freehold and leasehold land in Kaipara district).
23.	Whangaroa Rafting Co., Whangaroa.
24.	Whangaroa Saw Mill Co., Whangaroa.
25.	William Meikle, Mercury Bay.
26.	J. Trounson.

Source: Based on Benita Carter, 'The Kauri Timber Company 1888–1914', M.A. thesis, University of Melbourne, 1972, p. 433. Taken from items in University of Auckland Archives Manuscript and Archives Collection 90/4 Inventory of the Records of KTC Auckland, compiled by Suzanne Loughlin (1991).

In the Auckland timber industry the pressure came on most heavily for association and collusion, in times of stagnant or falling demand and prices, with rising levels of spare capacity. Complaints of unfair practice and rank breaking by members also became common at such times. In fact this was part of the ultimate cause of failure of the efforts at combination. In addition to members trying to steal a march on others, there was also the inability of the association to prevent entry into the industry and to include every supplier in the group.

Trading difficulties from 1886 on saw a major effort to achieve a grouping of interests, culminating in the appearance of the Kauri Timber Company in 1888. This combination of some twenty-eight operations in the Auckland area had a significant element of Melbourne backing, with seventeen out of the twenty financial interests being based there and only one being New Zealand-based.[31] Melbourne's David Blair and Auckland Timber Company's George Holdship were the principal actors in this drama to utilise Melbourne money, principally sourced through Australian Steam Saw and Moulding Mills' John Sharpe, to reconstruct the Auckland kauri trade.[32] The Auckland trade was reliant upon the Melbourne market, and part of the plan was to control prices there as much as in New Zealand. While it might be anticipated that local opinion and politicians would be solely concerned with local effects rather than with what was happening in Melbourne, there was an inevitable onflow to local builders' costs from the strategy. There was also another aspect to the restraint of trade being attempted here.

Starting from April 1888, the Kauri syndicate was formed. The Kauri Timber Company (KTC) was floated on 7 July 1888, with 600,000 £2 shares. The prospectus claimed a virtual monopoly of the kauri forests in New Zealand currently alienated from the Crown and claimed that KTC owned most of the important sawmills.[33] The term 'virtual' and the term 'most' are important weasel words to note, because neither claim held up. Holdship, the managing director, promised the monopoly and thought the opposition non-existent.[34] This view was supported by a statement from Mr L. Nathan as a director that the monopoly would not be prejudicial to Auckland, with ruinous competition gone and systematic marketing introduced for the benefit of all.

Unfortunately for the enterprise, the opposition was very existent. Besides the ever-present 'drummers' talked of before, major mills including those of Leyland O'Brien (1888 or 1889), and Mitchellson Bros (1890) – the latter based on capital gained from a general store operation in Dargaville – appeared at about the same time that the Kauri Timber Company was set up. In addition, Mander and Bradley, who had sold out to KTC, later set up other mills.

Auckland Timber Company premises in Fanshawe Street, Auckland, before the Kauri Timber Company takeover in 1888. THOMAS E. SIMPSON, *KAURI TO RADIATA: ORIGIN AND EXPANSION OF THE TIMBER INDUSTRY OF NEW ZEALAND* (SOURCE: J. JACKSON).

Altogether some four major mills set up in Auckland after KTC had formed, with another four in the Kaipara.[35] There were few if any barriers to entry or exit, so that by early 1889 the Melbourne directors were already admitting that monopoly was impossible under present conditions.[36]

The switch in tactic was then to try to make the claimed monopoly of Crown timber effective by depriving the opposition of timber supplies and actively purchasing local supplies as they came on the market, land-banking their own stocks. Government regulation restricting amounts put up for use worked against this, and the actual supply was too great for the tactic to work. KTC was using more expensive timber than it might have, and the net result was not a crushing of the competition but rather a cash flow crisis for KTC and reduced profitability. Similar attempts to kill the opposition by placing timber on the Australian market regardless of price were unsuccessful, threatening KTC profits rather than the viability of the opposition.[37] Complete disaster was avoided, but it would seem only because of the booming demand in Melbourne, not the situation in Auckland. The quest for price rises was not achieved in the Auckland market, but it seems clear this was the intention, as it was to control prices in Melbourne. The opposition (such as Mitchellsons)

A kauri log broken down by vertical frame saw in the Kauri Timber Company Auckland Mill,
C. 1910. THOMAS E. SIMPSON, *KAURI TO RADIATA: ORIGIN AND EXPANSION OF THE TIMBER INDUSTRY OF NEW*
ZEALAND (SOURCE: MR PIERCE, MINISTRY OF TRANSPORT).

did play along at times, usually the good times. Price agreements between the
two existed in 1898 for markets in Melbourne, Sydney, Adelaide, Western
Australia and Queensland.[38] This and a further 1902 agreement for agreed
output quotas between them and the National Mortgage Co., and Trapp's
New Zealand Timber, were both short-lived. The normal situation was output
below capacity and widespread chiselling or 'disloyalty'.[39]

Other associations, such as the early twentieth century South Auckland Saw
Millers Association, found preventing entry into the industry impossible and
market dominance and control likewise impossible. KTC were again involved
through their link to the firm of Butler Bros. The minutes of the special board
meeting of 8 April 1913 include references to the control of selling operations
and placing of product on the various markets.[40] A general hope for some 20
per cent or so rise in prices was only ever forthcoming when the market price
was rising anyway. Auckland prices for sawn timber were not dramatically
different to those elsewhere, suggesting that control was never effectively
gained.

Some switch to using non-kauri species also appeared, with kahikatea
or white pine, and other timbers such as totara, matai and rimu. This was

symptomatic of an inability to control the market. The other timber types were first a substitute for kauri and later took over as kauri supplies diminished. If KTC had successfully pushed up kauri prices, substitute timbers would have been available. Despite continuing alliances, the KTC effort to control the Auckland industry, and with it kauri prices, never worked out.

The major New Zealand component of the initial strategy was to obtain a monopoly by combination. Their secondary strategy involved the acquisition of the land on which supplies of kauri were to be found, which were seen as coming into shorter and shorter supply. If this supply could be held back from the opposition by denying access to their competitors, the KTC combine could hopefully freeze the opposition out. Neither strategy worked.

Conclusion

With regard to the motives for combining, there was an assertion in the introduction that this was rather more in the nature of an attempt to acquire wealth than it was an attempt at wealth creation. This is part of the ambition of business to control the environment in which it operates and to maximise returns. If competition can be avoided, through agreements between producers or by knocking out the competition, then it is likely that a strategy to achieve this will be devised. The timber industry was no different in this respect than any other industry at the time. Shearer considered monopoly tendencies (some real some imagined) in flour milling and baking, in sugar and grocery supplies, in fishing, in the meat trade, milk distribution, in coal, shipping, cement, bricks, mineral oils and other areas.[41] It could also be said that in intent the nineteenth century was essentially no different from the modern era. The regulatory environment was quite different as were the social and political environments; the overall purpose of the business was to maximise returns.

What were the combiners guilty of? There were associations. Their ability to have an impact on the market was, however, less than was feared and far less than the members of the associations anticipated. That those involved are ultimately found not guilty of achieving wealth acquisition through monopoly had a great deal more to do with their inability to control the market than with their innocence of intent. Finding them not guilty does not equate to finding them innocent. They attempted to control the market, but largely they failed through their inability to restrict entry into their industry. New large entrants appeared, and there was re-entry by pre-existing small operators as business opportunities arose. Entry and exit costs were not sufficient to allow the monopoly to flourish. The ease of entry and exit with some producers coming and going with little capital commitment, and others using secondhand physical equipment from other industries and selling it afterwards to other industries, meant sunk costs were limited. Government policy also ensured a plentiful supply of timber until commercial extinction of kauri was just about achieved. All of these factors combined to ensure that the associations failed because of circumstances beyond their power to influence. They had less control of clearances and the market than they would have liked.

If not guilty of market control and raising prices, were the millers and loggers then guilty of the destruction of the forest? Again not guilty must be the finding. The attitude of the time to seek forest clearance for pastoral and agricultural output, together with enabling government policy, had more to do with this and resulted in probably more burning than use of the timber. The industry was compliant, if not complicit, but not the major perpetrator.

The industry role appears somewhat like that of an inanimate object, or like the equipment it used. Both the industry and the equipment it used were instrumental in assisting the clearance of the indigenous forest, but while the equipment was certainly incapable of guilt in terms of having any intention of malevolence, the human actors were not.

The timber association is found free of responsibility concerning the rate of clearance. Nor is it to be found guilty of actually controlling the market to any extent, or for any substantial period. It did, however, have every *intention* of achieving market control. Consequently, it is here found guilty on the third charge: that of conspiring and acting with the intention of acquiring a monopoly. The wealth was there, its conversion from its natural state to a commercial one involved a transformation rather than creation, and the acquisition of ownership and with it wealth was the main motivating force.

In conclusion, clearly many, if not most, in the industry saw wealth acquisition as the prime consideration, with any wealth creation being more akin to a happy accident than any intended outcome. It can be conjectured as to how common this state of affairs was across all industries. The answer is that it is likely that monopoly was sought by most, and that if it was achieved life was a great deal easier for the business concerned. How successful others may have been is a story yet to be told.

CHAPTER SIX

Making Space: Clusters and Districts in Auckland Manufacturing, 1889–1908

GORDON M. WINDER

Urban landscapes are layered by waves of investment in which the making of productive spaces is often catalytic for other developments. Aucklanders have built distinctive industrial places in waves of activity. Early projects created individual mills, works and yards throughout the region. Factories also clustered in identifiable districts: garments in the inner city; brick and pottery at New Lynn; freezing works at Westfield. A net retreat to city locations ensued after 1900 as manufacturing reoriented to domestic markets and took up reclaimed waterfront land. Only after 1945 did big, suburban industrial zones transform the geography of factories.

This chapter investigates the character of Auckland industrial spaces made and discarded by one wave of investment in the decades either side of 1900. There was an identifiable round of investment in Auckland's built environment between the end of the Long Depression and the hiatus occasioned by the First World War. Suburban residential development continued throughout the first half of the twentieth century and accelerated after 1950. But in the decades either side of 1900, as suburban villas multiplied, manufacturing retreated to inner-city locations. This net withdrawal to the inner city seems at odds with expectations. The purpose of this chapter is to understand this localisation of manufacturing in the inner city.

The chapter establishes the industrial and suburban context for this net withdrawal of manufacturing to the inner city. It uses data compiled from city business directories for 1889 and 1908 to get inside the inner city and map the spatial patterns of industrial investment before the round of investment evaporated with the First World War. It identifies a tendency towards the clustering of like establishments in particular parts of the city centre and argues that the 'retreat' involved a wave of investment in the inner city resulting in intensification of particular kinds of manufacturing activity. However, it also argues that Auckland's manufacturing complex and the urban area's pattern of growth are distinctive. Understanding this distinctive context for manufacturing development is vital to any account of the city's unexpected re-localisation of manufacturing activity in the inner city.

Auckland's suburban growth

Anyone familiar with North American patterns of suburbanisation will recognise the general pattern of Auckland's suburban residential growth of 1889–1908. The Auckland region experienced rapid suburbanisation of housing in an infilling process. The city's villas spread out but failed to engulf and join up the many existing and new ex-urban residential clusters.[1] This growth pattern conforms neatly to the periods dominated by 'centrifugal forces' identified by Carville Earle for US cities.[2] Almost all of Auckland's population growth of 1890–1908 was accommodated in the suburban boroughs and districts of the North Shore and isthmus (Table 1). As the region's population rocketed from 69,000 to 128,000, Auckland City grew only modestly. The City of Auckland housed the same population in 1890 as it did in 1882.[3] Residential development in Ponsonby lifted this score to 34,213 in 1904 and 42,748 in 1908, but growth rates were much higher in the suburbs.

Suburban growth coincided with investment in new transport infrastructure. After 1900 the urban area's horse-drawn omnibuses were replaced by a system of electric tramways under a new traction company franchise.[4] Ferries plied the Waitemata Harbour. Walking to work gave way to commuting, and the central business district's population was hollowed out as suburban residential growth dominated the period. But in Auckland's suburban expansion of 1890–1908, workers did not move to the suburbs to occupy residential districts vacated by the middle classes who had preceded them, as the Chicago School of sociology might have had us believe. They went seeking cheap housing constructed by speculative builders or by themselves on cheap, lightly regulated, and poorly serviced suburban land.[5]

TABLE 1: POPULATION OF CITY AND SUBURBS, 1890 AND 1908

	1890		1908	
	(No.)	(%)	(No.)	(%)
Auckland City*	30,860	44.6	42,748	33.3
Isthmus districts	22,199	32.1	54,963	42.9
North Shore Boroughs	2.910	4.2	9,113	7.1
Manukau County	11,595	16.7	13,480	10.5
Waitemata County	1,684	2.4	7,949	6.2
Auckland region	69,248		128,253	

* Auckland City as of the 1882 amalgamations comprised the City of 1871, plus Ponsonby, Karangahape, Newton and Grafton.
Source: *Statistics of New Zealand*

The surprise is that suburbanisation of manufacturing did not coincide with suburban residential growth. Under centrifugal forces 'bits and pieces of the city were flung far into the surrounding countryside and plopped down in an archipelago of suburban islands amid a rural sea'.[6] Industrial centres and residential areas were scattered 10–40 kilometres around US metropolitan centres. But in Auckland there was a net retreat of manufacturing from ex-urban locations into the inner city.[7] Godfrey Linge argues that industry was already dispersed across the region in 1890. It had initially concentrated around the port of Auckland to access imported materials, the local market and labour. Linge acknowledges early logging camps on the shores of the Manukau Harbour and in the Waitakere Ranges, but times the scattering of manufacturing activities 15–25 kilometres from the port in the period 1856–1900. Most of this ex-urban industrial activity comprised materials processing plants: sawmills, flour mills, flax mills, a paper mill, ship- and boatyards, brick works, tanneries, meat works, breweries, a cannery and a sugar refinery. Each mill attracted a cluster of workers' housing. Often the mill owners sought locations with water access, river discharge rights, or fresh water supplies. By 1890 the region's industry formed an archipelago of small resource-processing enterprises.

But from 1890, Auckland manufacturing investment concentrated on inner-city sites. For a part of the 1890s the region lost manufacturing employment, but, as Linge has shown, from 1901–30 industry engaged in 'a net *withdrawal* of industry from peripheral locations around Auckland'.[8] Partly, this was a matter of investment in new inner-city factories. The inner city was made more attractive to manufacturing through the supply of reclaimed waterfront land, and the reticulation of water, sewerage, telephone, electricity and gas services, the area being subject to considerable redevelopment in the period 1890–1910. By 1908, the Auckland Harbour Board's reclamation process was in full swing, electric trams linked city and suburbs, and investors jostled for inner-city sites for factories, workshops and yards. Access to the port remained crucial to manufacturers, partly because of the delays incurred in constructing rail links with other parts of the country.

In 1900, rail connections terminated at Helensville in the north and Rotorua to the south. Until lines linked with Wellington (1908) and Whangarei, Tauranga and New Plymouth in the 1920s, Auckland's hinterland comprised a coastal litter of wharves, hotels and stores all accessible from the port. Industrial activity was widely scattered within Auckland Province, with establishments spread among small towns like Thames and Dargaville; satellite industrial villages like Onehunga, Chelsea, Otahuhu and Avondale; beachfront boatyards like those at Whangaroa; and inner-city sites. The increased clustering of manufacturing in the inner city was also a result of the termination of some processing activities. Sawmillers ceased operations when they exhausted local timber supplies, but this did not apply to the City's waterfront mills which relied on logs rafted from many coastal locations. A number of ship- and boatyards closed as the province's shipbuilding industry adjusted to steam and steel ships built in Scottish and English yards, but employment in ship- and boat-building increased. Some ex-urban processing mills closed while others relocated to urban sites. Onehunga's port and industrial activity declined. Only Otahuhu, which attracted noxious industries, and New Lynn, which maintained a specialisation in brick and pottery using local clay, continued to prosper:

> Thus, many of the brick-works, sawmills, flour mills, boat building yards and other enterprises in the distant localities were closed, and their machinery was sold, or moved into the centre of town, or transferred to other parts of New Zealand.[9]

Suburban manufacturing development took on renewed force in the period 1931–56, but until then investment in manufacturing tended to focus on inner-city locations. The industrial establishments that dotted the isthmus were pulling up stakes as the villas spread out. This combination of suburban residential growth with a net withdrawal of manufacturing from the suburbs is unexpected. Generally suburban and ex-urban manufacturing sites remained in place as cities grew. This Auckland phenomenon deserves further attention. This is partly because of Linge's style of explanation, which focuses on the attractiveness of new inner-city infrastructure and a shift away from resource-processing to investments in making products for domestic consumption. It may pay to focus more attention on the distinctive character of Auckland region manufacturing and on the developments inside the central city in order to refine Linge's explanation.

Auckland's distinctive industrial complex

Auckland offered a distinctive context for manufacturing in terms of the scale of industrial activity, its geography within city and province, and the industrial specialisations pursued. Most research on nineteenth-century industrial districts has been on well developed industrial regions in Europe and North America.[10] Auckland does not stand up well in comparison with the industrial cities of these regions because of differences in scale and specialisation. Auckland was far removed from the large, specialised industrial cities of Western Europe or the North American manufacturing belt. If New Zealand's entire 1881 factory workforce of 18,000 hands had clustered in one city, this city would have ranked just ahead of Louisville, Kentucky (17,500), or Detroit (16,100) that year.[11] In fact only 1,100 workers or 17.6 per cent of Auckland Province factory workers resided in the Auckland urban area in 1896 – fewer than many satellite industrial towns of the North American manufacturing belt, let alone its metropolitan centres.[12] Moreover, European and North American industrial cities developed manufacturing specialisations as they participated in large, integrated economies. In contrast, the Auckland urban area retained a diversified industrial complex, mostly dedicated to export processing and the small domestic market.

Auckland was perhaps more akin to Pacific Rim towns like Vancouver than to the specialist industrial cities of North America. These cities had no more than one-fifth of their workforces in manufacturing in 1911, whereas Canada's industrial cities Toronto, Montreal, Hamilton and London all managed one-third to one-half.[13] But Auckland was also no Vancouver. By 1911 that city boasted nearly sixty sawmills and shingle mills and had 6000 of its 10,000-strong urban industrial workforce engaged in the wood products industry. Its population had rocketed from 14,000 in 1891 to 100,000 in 1911.

Australian cities also provided poor parallels. With 42,000 and 32,000 factory workers, respectively, in 1890, both Melbourne and Sydney were industrial giants next to Auckland. Each had well developed metals manufacturing sectors that were the leading employers in their industrial complexes.[14] Adelaide also had specialisations in flour-milling and agricultural implement manufacture that set it apart from Auckland. Perhaps Brisbane was the most similar. In 1890 it had a population of 88,000 to Auckland's 70,000. Like Auckland, Brisbane housed only a modest portion of its state's 16,000 industrial workers. Queensland factory workers were scattered in many coastal communities and heavily engaged in sugar mills and meat-processing works. Nevertheless, Auckland manufacturing remained small-scale and scattered by Australian urban standards.

TABLE 2: EMPLOYMENT IN MANUFACTURING, SELECTED INDUSTRIES, 1906

Industry	1906			Average Growth, 1890–1906 (%)	
	Auckland Province (hands)	New Zealand (hands)	Auckland location quotient*	Auckland Province	New Zealand
Printing	951	3,898	.94	3.6	3.2
Coachbuilding	315	1,465	.83	7.0	7.3
Shipbuilding	202	237	3.28	4.4	4.0
Clothing	591	1,914	1.19	1.2	3.0
Boot and shoe	728	2,206	1.27	1.2	0.8
Sawmills	3,618	9,111	1.53	16.2	11.2
Furniture	435	1,528	1.09	nd	nd
Saddlery	180	544	1.27	nd	nd
All manufacturing	14,657	56,359		4.8	5.5

* The location quotient is the industry's share of manufacturing employment rated against the industry's share of national manufacturing employment. Source: *Statistics of New Zealand*

The processing of natural resources dominated Auckland's provincial manufacturing complex in the 1880s and became even more important from 1890 to 1910. Sawmilling, flax milling and the processing of grain, meat and dairy products accounted for 30 per cent of provincial manufacturing employment in 1890; 38 per cent in 1906 (Table 2). Indeed this pattern was slightly more marked in Auckland Province than in New Zealand as a whole because of the strong growth in sawmilling and the relatively slow growth of the province's manufacturing complex overall, especially growth in urban-based industry like machinery and clothing manufacture. In 1890, Auckland Province had specialisations in shipbuilding, rope and twine making, and clothing (Table 2), but was poorly represented in machinery manufacture, meat processing, grain mills, and brick, tile and pottery making.

In 1906, Auckland's specialisations included lime and cement making, biscuit manufacture, sawmilling, gasworks, and soap and candle manufacture, as well as shipbuilding. But only sawmilling, flax milling and printing employed more than 900 workers.

The most substantial growth was recorded in sawmilling and brick, tile and pottery manufacture, industries closely associated with suburban construction, but ones that did not necessarily require inner-city sites. Some industries with obvious inner-city or suburban location requirements were not growing that fast. These included biscuit manufacture, bacon- and fish-curing plants, metalworking, printing, clothing, and leather products manufacture. Nevertheless, the shift towards production for domestic markets identified by Linge was underway.[15] Beverage, sauce and jam manufacture, including brewing, and coach building achieved above average employment growth.

Auckland's manufacturing spaces, like New Zealand's, were small. Many enterprises lacked capital, equipment or throughput. The mean Auckland Province factory employed fewer than seventeen workers in 1906, up from thirteen in 1890 (Table 3). Clothing factories, meat-freezing works, biscuit factories and sawmills tended to be the largest establishments, but even these were small to medium-sized enterprises by today's standards. In some of these industries prospects were not so good. Expansion of the frozen meat export trade was more modest in Auckland Province than elsewhere, partly because of slower development of pastoral land from forest and wetland. The rate at which kauri was being 'quarried' meant that sawmilling faced shortages of timber by the 1920s. However, in almost all sectors, the small scale of industrial activity allowed for low barriers to entry for new entrants. National corporations were rare in manufacturing even by 1920. Enterprises had opportunities for diverse networking relationships with other firms, the investment scene in the city and province was fluid, and there were high turnover rates as partnerships were formed and dissolved.

Auckland's downtown still had a mercantile city form around 1890 (Figure 1).[16] Mercantile cities were compact, with high residential densities. All activity clustered near the wharves because shipping provided the only reliable transport over long distance. Within the city, citizens relied on walking to get around and goods were moved by horse and cart. The dominant form of manufacturing organisation was the artisan shop, although *entrepôt* and commerce-serving industry was also present. Many people worked at their place of residence. Few establishments were of any size. The central area of the city might contain embryonic financial, administrative and carriage trade districts, and a specialised waterfront district, but otherwise it was

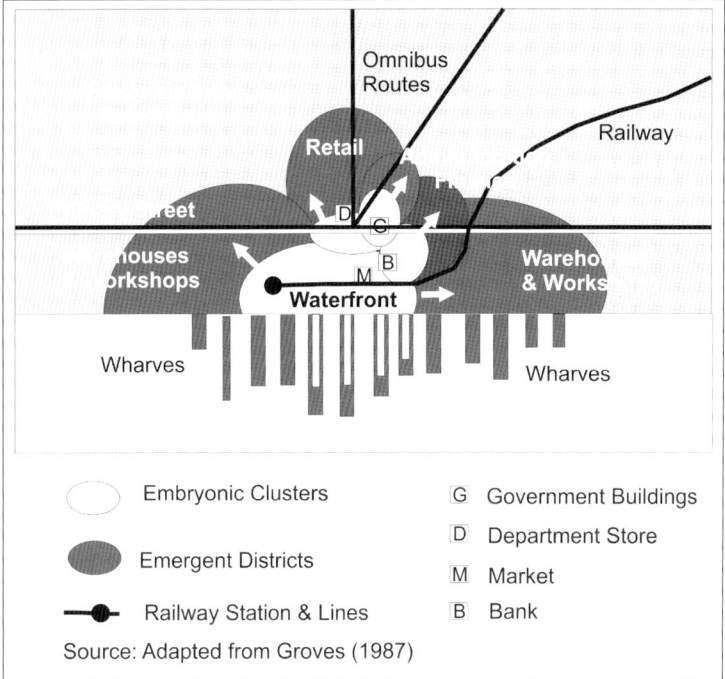

FIGURE 1: DOWNTOWN DISTRICTS EMERGE FROM THE MERCANTILE CITY

dominated by diverse streetscapes featuring artisans' workshops, residences and warehouses. As the city grew, it tended to develop expanding, specialised districts in the core. The commercial waterfront would be extended.

Noxious industries were placed on the edge of town. The upper and middle classes separated themselves out from the inner city. This was the dominant process in central Auckland in the period 1870–1914, and from 1890 it coincided with the suburban residential growth associated with centripetal forces. But the timing of these developments was out of synch with North American manufacturing-belt cities, which tended to develop distinct inner-city districts in the period 1830–70 and therefore before the introduction of electric tramways. In 1890, Auckland City was still a mercantile city with an emerging downtown.

When industrialisation did kick in, international experience shows distinct, specialised industrial districts emerged within city and suburb. Urban historical geographers have long identified diverse and distinct inner-city manufacturing districts emerging as part of this process.[17] Some of these proved long-lasting because of the inherent advantages of inner-city locations for the particular industrial activity.

TABLE 3: AVERAGE SIZE OF FACTORY, 1890 AND 1906

Industry	1890		1906	
	Auckland Province (hands)	New Zealand (hands)	Auckland Province (hands)	New Zealand (hands)
Beverages, sauces, jams	3.9	3.7	8.4	8.1
Biscuits	nd	nd	43.4	48.9
Grain Mills	5.8	3.9	23.0	7.0
Butter and cheese	3.9	3.6	5.6	5.6
Meat works	27.4	36.5	51.4	58.2
Other meat and fish	6.0	5.2	5.6	4.5
Tanning	16.3	11.5	18.7	13.5
Soap and candle	9.7	11.0	13.5	12.5
Machinery	4.0	14.7	4.4	9.9
Engineering	nd	nd	20.9	30.3
Iron and Brass	20.5	25.4	24.1	25.9
Tinware	nd	nd	7.1	8.8
Printing	20.1	18.1	20.2	16.3
Coachbuilding	8.3	6.6	8.3	8.0
Shipbuilding	5.0	3.9	10.6	7.9
Furniture	nd	nd	9.1	8.9
Sawmills	21.4	13.4	43.6	20.5
Clothing	49.4	67.9	84.4	83.2
Boot and Shoe	27.7	41.3	27.0	30.6
Saddlery	nd	nd	8.2	5.1
Gasworks	16.2	9.2	32.5	25.1
Lime and cement	nd	nd	27.7	14.0
Brick, Tile and Pottery	5.5	4.7	11.7	10.0
Flax mills	14.3	18.1	14.7	17.0
Rope and twine	12.5	9.3	14.0	19.5
All manufacturing	12.8	11.6	16.6	13.5

Printing tended to remain downtown because of its small-scale production establishments, long delays in developing high-speed, large-volume, automatic printing machines, and the advantages of face-to-face contacts in advertising, news and related businesses.[18] Garment districts also continued to occupy and develop inner-city sites, as did some specialised metals manufacturing.[19]

Industry also spawned many establishments outside the inner city. These ranged from suburban waterfront developments, through strings of rail-side industrial developments, to satellite industrial towns and villages.[20] Auckland did develop satellite industrial districts. Thames attracted iron and engineering works, including the Thames Iron Works (1869) and A. & G. Price (1871), which continued to operate its Onehunga works until 1874. Thames offered proximity to demand from gold-mine, sawmill and railroad establishments, as well as easy shipping from Auckland. Avondale sported brick and tile works and tanneries beginning with a first brick kiln in 1852. Onehunga's port sustained a separate industrial complex comprising a timber mill dating from 1842, a flour mill built in 1853, a woollen mill, shipyards and chemical works. Newmarket's railway workshops and the breweries in Khyber Pass located more production facilities beyond the old city line. Chelsea became home to the sugar works in 1884. Ex-urban Westfield developed a cluster of noxious industries as Hellaby, Auckland Farmers' Freezing Co-operative Ltd and the Auckland City abattoir (1903) all established works and fertiliser plants sprouted. However, this regional field of industrial sites remained underdeveloped by North American standards.[21] The industrial establishments remained small-scale, focused on resource-processing or housed *entrepôt* industry.

Thus, between 1890 and 1910, Auckland experienced a round of new investment, especially in inner-city factories and workshops; this should have been associated with an expansion of Auckland's central business district, and a decrease in its residential population along with suburban residential development. Perhaps identifiable industrial clusters developed within the central city area, but, equally, these may have been constrained by the distinctive timing and scale of Auckland's urban growth, and the small scale and peculiar specialisations of its manufacturing complex. The challenge is to establish just what patterns of inner-city manufacturing development took place.

Using directory data and selecting industries

The following analysis is based on a systematic reading of Cleave's Auckland city and suburban directories for 1889 and 1908. The directories present a great opportunity: the locations of factories can be associated with those of related retail, office, residential and warehouse spaces. The directory data has been compiled and sorted with this in mind. A listing of all establishments – whether workshops, mills, yards or factories associated with the industries under study – was compiled from each directory. In addition, all individuals associated with the industry – whether by trade, ownership or management – were registered in the same database. The data set was then sorted to remove double entries, and to identify the residences of proprietors and managers wherever possible.

Anyone trying to use business directories to establish systematic data and to discern aggregate patterns encounters problems. It is difficult to accurately identify and separate residences from workspaces, and retail, office, warehouse and production spaces. It is important to get this right, but it is a difficult task because of the small scale of most enterprises and the imprecision of the directory entries. The main source for confusion is the descriptions of trades used by the directories for individual tradespeople. For instance, some 'boot-makers' may have operated a workshop in their residence, while others worked in factories and yet others owned separate workshops or retail outlets, but in any one case the directories record only an individual, an address and a trade. Wherever an individual is associated with more than one location, one address is assumed to be a residence and the other a workshop.

Thus the directory data has been sorted to reveal three kinds of geographical information. Identifiable production, retail and warehouse sites were mapped by street address and by district. The residences of identifiable proprietors and managers were mapped by district. The residences (and potentially workshops) of workers associated with the industry were mapped by district. The region was treated as thirty separate districts. The city of Auckland as it stood in 1908 was divided into four constituent wards: City (comprising the old city boundary of 1871), Ponsonby, Grafton and Karangahape. The remaining districts were all suburban boroughs and roads districts of the time, all of which have subsequently been merged into Auckland, Waitakere or North Shore cities.

The changing classifications of skills and workers presented a second problem. For example, the directories showed that shipbuilding became a less important employer between 1889 and 1908. There were eighty-three ship- and boat-builders, shipwrights, ship carpenters and other boat-building tradespeople listed in 1889, but only thirty-three in 1908. In contrast, census figures for the province indicated a modest increase in the average size of shipyard (Table 3) and a 70 per cent increase in employment in the industry (Table 2). The discrepancy has probably resulted from inconsistent classification of tradespeople in the directory and shifts in employment within shipyards to include trades other than those involved in woodwork. It was decided not to use the directories to suggest changes in employment between directories unless trades were aggregated at the scale of industrial sectors.

Directory data has been analysed for just four industry groupings: wood products, clothing, leather products, and printing. Wood products were central to the provincial and city economies. Auckland was an exporter of wood products within New Zealand and overseas.[22] The province's mills experienced a 16.2 per cent average annual growth in employment 1890–1906 (Table 2). Shipbuilding was a specialisation for the province. Furniture manufacture, coach building, and blind, cork, veneer, sash and door, planing and moulding works all catered to the expanding construction and domestic markets. Timber merchants, ship- and boat-builders and sawmillers enjoyed prominent places on the city's waterfront. This was a substantial and diverse industry group and the directories can be used to isolate its components and their distinct geographic patterns within the city and suburbs.

In clothing, Auckland Province had a modest specialisation, and employed 600 workers in 1906 (Table 2). The industry employed many artisans who operated as dressmakers, tailors or hatters from their residences, but there were also some large factories. By 1906, the average provincial clothing factory employed eighty-four workers, many of them women. Most of the employment was urban, but the relative strength of artisan production, the pull of factory work to the suburbs and the clustering of factories and workshops near the inner-city retail district remains unclear.

Leather products also featured artisan and factory production for predominantly urban markets. Together, boot, shoe, saddle and harness production employed 900 Auckland province workers in 1906, albeit in relatively small shops: averaging twenty-seven workers in boots and shoes, and just eight in saddlery (Tables 2 and 3). This industry and its constituent parts offer comparison with clothing. Did leather products gravitate to distinct inner-city districts?

Printing was another substantial industry (there were 950 employees in the province in 1906), but printing should have been localised within the inner city. Printworks and print-related activities tended to stay downtown for face-to-face contacts with other professions and because of the modest size of establishments (an average of twenty employees in 1906). But printing sometimes struggled to keep inner-city premises in the face of competition from retail and office building investment. How did print shops nestle into the downtown fabric? Much of the answer lies in the competition for space printers experienced from other activities.

Wood products

Customs Street West was the centre of the timber trade in 1889. Timber merchants, shipbuilders and sawmills clustered along the commercial waterfront, their yards interspersed with metals engineering establishments, sail makers, carters, the occasional residence and warehouse, even the city's salt

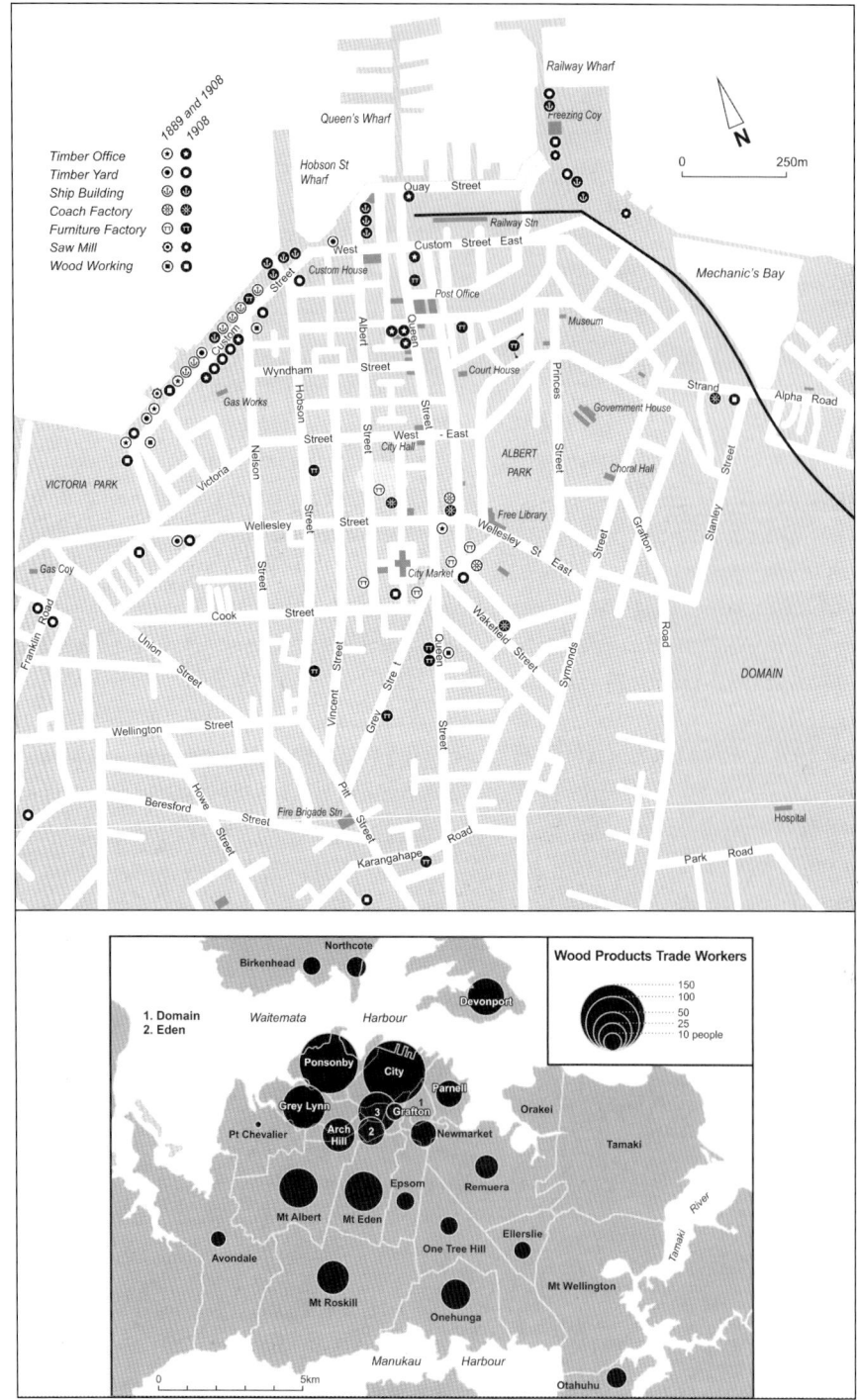

FIGURE 2: WOOD PRODUCTS

water baths. In contrast, the city's furniture manufacturers and coach builders clustered near Queen, Wellesley and Cook Streets. This pattern changed dramatically with investments in new plant and enterprise (Figure 2). By 1908, the timber trade activities had been spread to Mechanics Bay, while the furniture manufacturers took up new locations to the south and west of their existing ones, and the coach builders multiplied in city and suburb.

Shipbuilders reinvested in their yards and shifted to new locations within the City. Customs Street West was the centre of shipbuilding enterprise in 1889. Charles Bailey, Henderson and Spraggon, David Gouk, Sims and Brown, and J. W. Carr and Sons all had yards on Customs Street West, and Albert Willows operated there as a ship smith. Two further yards were located in Devonport. By 1908 several new yards and workshops catering to steam vessels appeared, including the Northern Steamship Co.'s workshop and the Seager Brothers' establishments at Hobson Street, and the Devonport Steam Ferry Co.'s yards and workshop in Devonport. The Auckland Harbour Board workshops and the Graving Dock, both on Customs Street West, were also new. Some yards on Customs Street West had changed hands. Charles Bailey was now involved in three separate establishments on the street. However, new yards were established on the new Railway Wharf reclamation. Here Logan Brothers, T. M. Lane and Son, and James Reid built yards. The overall result was a thorough reworking of the boat- and shipbuilding activities on the city wharves. This reinvestment also freed up space on Customs Street West for other activities.

The 1889 directory listed only Thomas Thwaites's sawmill on Custom Street West, a suburban mill on Mt Eden Road and the Onehunga Sawmilling Co.'s mill. Entries for sawyers, saw sharpeners and bush contractors implied that bush clearance was a continuing part of the ex-urban economy. By 1908, two new mills were listed in Mechanics Bay – D. Goldie's mill on the Railway Wharf and Leyland O'Brien Timber Co.'s King's Drive mill – and the Customs Street West mill was now in the hands of the Kauri Timber Co. Each of the three waterfront sawmills had sprouted associated yards, stables, workshops, box-manufacturing plants and offices, spread out along the waterfront with some offices located on Queen Street. Suburban mills continued to operate, but now at Onehunga and Grey Lynn.

Thus the inner-city sawmilling complex was intensified, and spread out along the waterfront. Partly, this was possible because of reclamation at Mechanics Bay. Partly, it was because of a freeing up of land on Customs Street West from other uses. Certainly it was related to the booming construction industry. Workers in the wood industries – carpenters, builders, furniture makers, shipwrights, coopers – were thoroughly suburban. Only 17 per cent resided within the City Ward. Many resided in far-flung suburbs rather than just in the immediate ring of districts around the City Ward (Figure 2). Indeed, the geography of wood trades workers listed in the 1908 directory neatly matched the distribution of population: 40 per cent in the City, 50 per cent in isthmus boroughs and districts, and 10 per cent in North Shore boroughs. The many builders, contractors and carpenters listed in the directories (823) stood witness to the important role of suburban house-building in the urban economy. It was to prosecute this activity that carpenters and builders took up residence in suburban districts, but it was to serve their activity that the sawmill complex on the waterfront was reorganised, under the watchful eyes of the string of timber merchants' offices in lower Queen Street, Customs Street West and Quay Street.

From their base east of Queen Street, the city's furniture manufacturers spread out south and west. Two investments stood apart. By expanding into adjacent buildings and taking over adjacent competitors, Tonson & Garlick organised a tight furniture complex comprising a Queen Street furnishings warehouse with Lorne Street workshop, factories and timber yard. Similarly, Smith and Caughey invested in an inner-city furniture factory just two blocks south of their department store on Queen Street. But these signs of retail investment in proximate factories cannot tell the whole story. A cluster of furniture and blind manufacturers emerged in Karangahape and Newton, and others were scattered through Ponsonby along with a sash and door company. Suburbanisation was the rule – unless a major retailer was backing the enterprise and looking to cluster shops together in the downtown. Furniture workshops and factories sprouted in Newton, Karangahape and Ponsonby.

The carriage factories occupied spaces on the eastern edge of the downtown, flanking Albert Park and, across it, the once 'high society' mansions of Princes and Symonds Streets. These were nevertheless small establishments. Some were also multi-locational enterprises within the city. William Cousins of Upper Symonds Street operated the Cousins and Atkins Ltd carriage factory on the Strand as well as the Cousins and Cousins Ltd coach factory and office on Lorne Street. But after 1889 new coach-building establishments proliferated in the suburbs. Organised by independent, trade-based entrepreneurs, coach-building enterprises diffused to the suburbs while retaining a few larger inner-city works.

The wood products industries told three different stories. One was of investment in new waterfront sites made possible by reclamation. Shipbuilding and sawmilling enterprises, with their associated timber yards and merchant offices and some affiliated woodworking establishments followed this pattern of investment. The second story spoke of suburbanisation of small-scale workshops. This was especially evident in carriage making. Coach and wagon shops emerged in several outlying suburbs and catered to the residential and commercial markets there. The third tale was one of establishments unable to cluster together but seeking locations on the edge of the central business district. In furniture and woodworking, existing enterprises maintained and expanded their operations on the edge of the central business district as and where they could. New entrants spread west into Freemans Bay and south towards Karangahape Road. The overall result was a strong cluster of works along the waterfront and a scatter of other establishments through the edges of the inner city.

Printing cluster

Those in the printing trades commuted to work (Figure 3). Only 13 per cent of those engaged in the printing trades resided in the City Ward in 1908, down from 29 per cent in 1889. Ponsonby had the single largest concentration of workers engaged in the printing business. Nevertheless, in 1908, Auckland City accounted for only 44 per cent of the ninety-one print trade workers listed in the directory, only slightly more than the City's 40 per cent share of the population.

Despite this suburbanisation of the workforce, printing establishments remained overwhelmingly concentrated in the central business district. The printing trades clustered together at the heart of the City's office district (Figure 3). The map perhaps underestimates the number of print shops and works, bookbinders, newspaper offices, and retail and wholesale stationers and booksellers. Another dozen printers resided in the central business district

In 1889 the City's printing enterprises were tightly clustered in Shortland, High and Lower Queen Streets and Vulcan Lane. The main news and publishing houses – Brett, Wilson and Horton, and Scott – had their offices and printworks in this area, close to the General Post Office and Reuters News Agency on Shortland Street. This location also placed print-related enterprises at the heart of the office district with its business clubs and legal, commercial, shipping, government and financial offices.

Nineteen years later, *Cleave's Directory* reported an expanded district, with twenty-one establishments that had not been present in 1889. Outliers featured beyond Wellesley Street: the Auckland Free Press took up a 'radical' position at a distance from the City's commercial hub. A cluster of printworks emerged

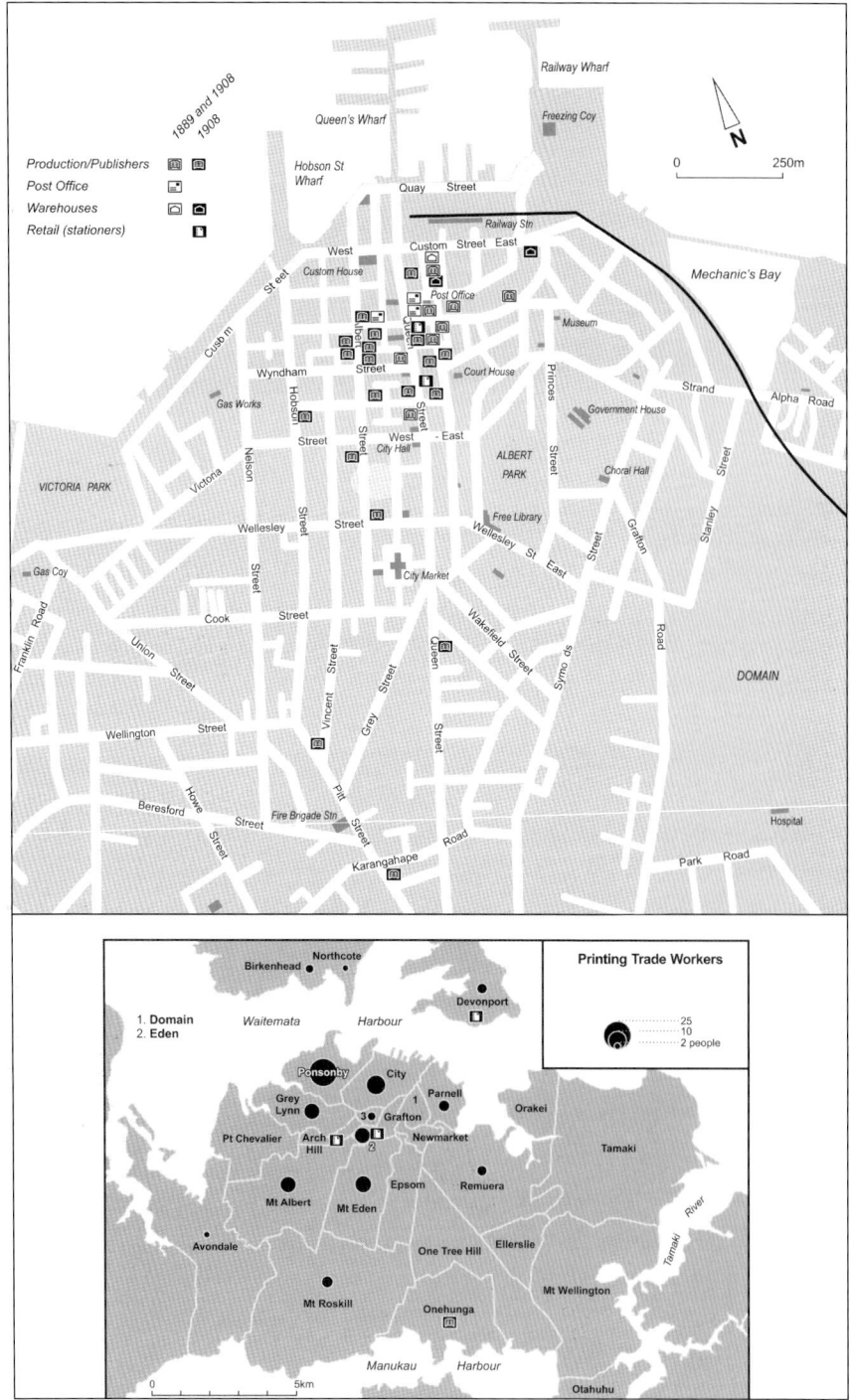

FIGURE 3: PRINTING

on Albert Street. Multi-locational operations featured among these enterprises. Upton and Co. established a bookbinding operation on Albert Street separate from its retail store on Queen Street. Both Wilson and Horton and Sport Printing operated separate printworks and offices. A few enterprises found locations just to the east of the 1889 cluster.

Generally, printing remained localised in the inner city, close to the expanding office district. Most of the new establishments were able to find premises in the mixed-use neighbourhood to the west of Queen Street. Printing, as expected, remained tightly clustered in the central business district.

Leather products

In contrast to printing, leather product manufacture was already dispersed into the suburbs in 1889 and downtown establishments were also scattered, with most shops located in streets away from the main retail complex on Queen Street. The City Ward housed six boot factories, nineteen boot-makers' shops, six saddlers' shops and one leather merchant's warehouse. Three other boot factories (Ponsonby, Newmarket and Parnell), thirteen boot-makers' shops, two saddlers' shops and a Newton leather merchant operated in the suburbs. There was little sign of clustering in either boot-making or saddle- and harness-making. In this industry, marked by small-scale of enterprise, clustering failed to take hold before 1890. Nevertheless, in 1889, 63 per cent of the urban area's 238 leather workers resided in the City of Auckland, 48 per cent in the City Ward.

There was enormous turnover among these enterprises in the 1889–1908 period. Only four of the 1889 boot, and saddle and harness establishments persisted in 1908: the Northern Boot and Shoe Manufacturing Co. factory in Hobson Street; the Trenwith Brothers' boot-making shop in Wakefield Street; J. Wiseman and Sons Ltd's horse collar factory in Hobson Street; and A. and G. Brook's boot-making shop, Newmarket. All of the other enterprises of 1908 were new. These included ten City Ward and twelve suburban boot-making establishments, and six saddle- and harness-making establishments in the City Ward. In addition, ten warehouses sprouted in the central business district operated by wholesale saddlers and leather merchants. Suburban production was prominent in Newmarket and Newton.

Leather industry workers were still more concentrated in the City of Auckland than the population as a whole (Figure 4). Where the City housed 40 per cent of the population, half of the 495 leather trades workers resided in Auckland City, and half of these were in the City Ward. The number of leather

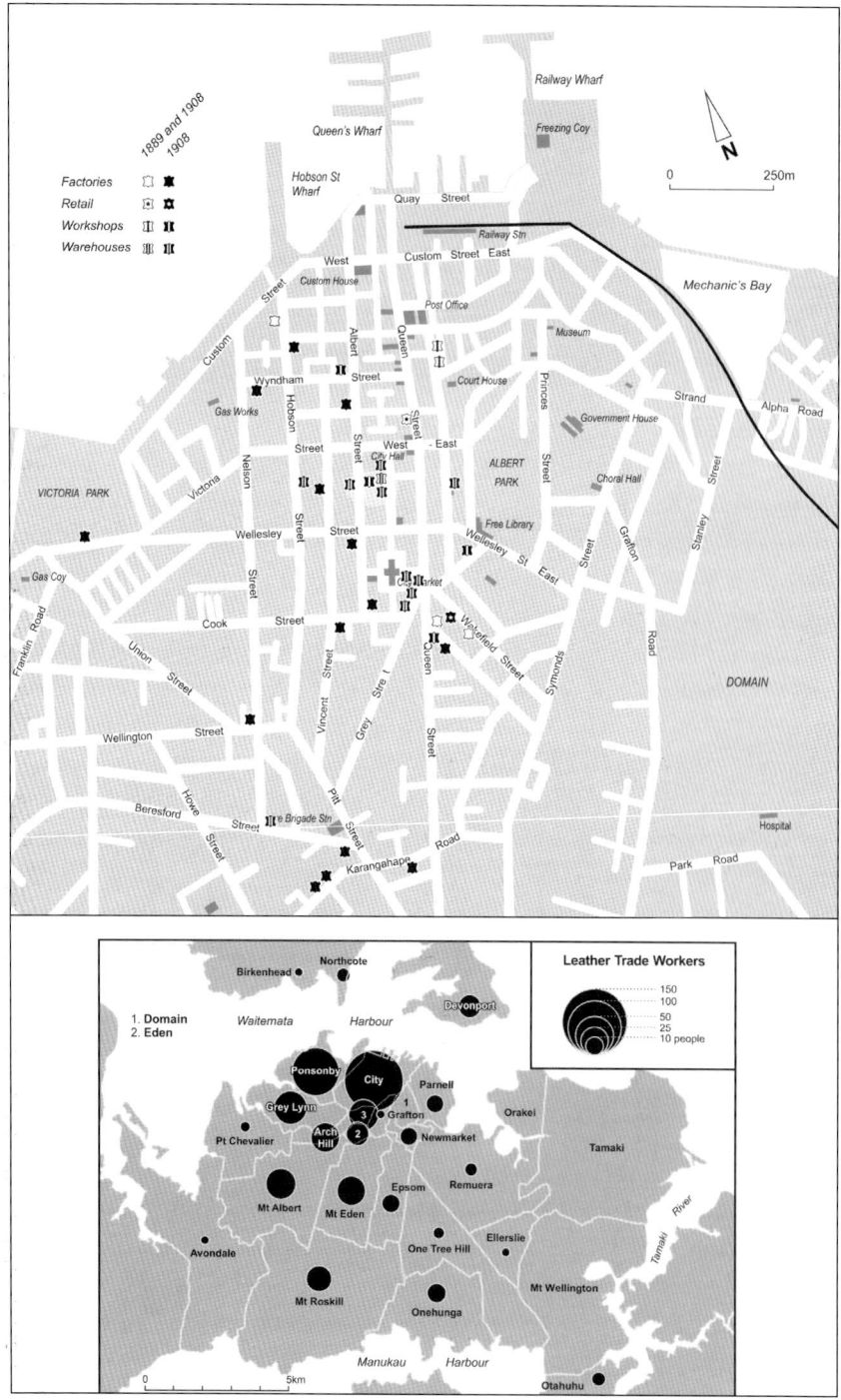

FIGURE 4: LEATHER PRODUCTS

workers in the City Ward had doubled since 1889, but growth in the rest of the City had been modest, and there had been an overall suburbanisation of workers.

There were now some signs of spatial clustering within the central business district (Figure 4). Wholesale saddlers and leather merchants clustered near the City Market, with another cluster on Elliott Street. Three saddle and harness workshops were located nearby – one on Elliott Street and others on Rutland and Alexandra Streets – but one occupied a site on the corner of Albert and Wyndham Streets. Most of the inner-city factories and workshops were engaged in boot production. Apart from two boot workshops on High Street, and outlying factories in Freemans Bay and southern Nelson Street, boot-making took place in factories scattered between Nelson and Albert Streets, and in nodes on Karangahape Road and Wakefield Street.

A round of investment transformed leather products manufacturing. It produced a new geography of inner-city and suburban production sites. New leather merchants' establishments keyed the industry in the central business district, and new production facilities sprouted in the mixed-use districts to the west of Queen Street. But suburban production developed at the same time. In this industry, investment came in the form of larger premises, more partnerships and companies. But it did not produce one tightly-knit industrial district.

Clothing

The city's clothing industry was closely confined to the City of Auckland. The residences of clothing workers were even less likely to be suburban than those of leather trades workers. In 1889, 66 per cent of the 254 clothing industry tradespeople resided in the City of Auckland, two-thirds of them in the City Ward. By 1908 there were only a few more of them listed in the City Ward than in 1889, but with Ponsonby the City Ward still made up 60 per cent of the 358 clothing tradespeople in the urban area. While almost half of the identifiable retail establishments were already located outside the City Ward in 1889, the same cannot be said for production establishments. There were just five clothing factories and nineteen tailors' and dressmakers' establishments in the City Ward, plus five tailors and dressmakers, an oil-skin manufacturer, and the Onehunga woollen mill in the suburbs. These 1889 patterns partly resulted from difficulties in distinguishing retailers from artisan producers and factory workers in the directory. At this time there were few factories, and many participants in the industry were artisan producers/retailers. They tended to locate in the mainly residential and mixed warehouse and workshop districts of the inner city and its immediately neighbouring districts.

There was a great deal of new activity in this industry to 1908, including signs of a shift from craft tailoring to the factory production of ready-to-wear garments in fourteen new factories. The City Ward boasted eleven of these factories in 1908, all of them located in new premises. Even Hallenstein Brothers Ltd moved its New Zealand Clothing Co. factory south on Queen Street to new premises. Three factories did spring up outside the City Ward. Macky, Logan, Caldwell and Co. operated factories in Eden Terrace and Grey Lynn in addition to their Graham Street factory in the inner city. One further suburban factory sprang up in Newton, but all of the other factories were located in the inner city and all were new.

Tailors and dressmakers also jockeyed for position in the inner city. Only four establishments could be found in the isthmus districts, two in Ponsonby and none on the North Shore. Newton now boasted eleven establishments and had emerged as a distinct node for artisan production of clothing in independent, small-scale shops. But there was also intense activity in the central business district where seventeen establishments, all located in new premises, lined up on or behind Queen Street. Every workshop establishment marked on Figure 5 either occupied new premises or involved new enterprises. Henry Possenniskie, tailor, moved from his 1889 premises on Shortland Street to workrooms in the new Victoria Arcade, 70 Queen Street. J. Davey and Sons moved their tailoring enterprise from Wakefield Street to Wellesley Street West. Both the Victoria and Strand Arcades were new and each housed production facilities and offices as well as retail clothing establishments among other activities. The Strand Arcade housed the offices of the Fenton Hat Fastener Syndicate and the Hibberd Pre-payment Machine Syndicate. There were even spaces for training workers in the top floors of Queen Street buildings. Workrooms, factories and related services clustered in the middle of the inner city.

The clustering of clothing manufacture in the inner city occurred for several reasons. In addition to the need to access the city's main labour market in the rag trade, and new infrastructure, manufacturers had their eyes on close proximity to the city's retail stores and warehouses. What emerged was an integrated fashion district rather than a straightforward manufacturing cluster. Production activity circled around the emerging retail district for clothing.

The prime retail positions were on Queen Street (Figure 5) between Victoria and Grey Streets, where the full gravitational effects of the Smith and Caughey, Milne and Choyce, and Rendell's department stores and the Strand Arcade

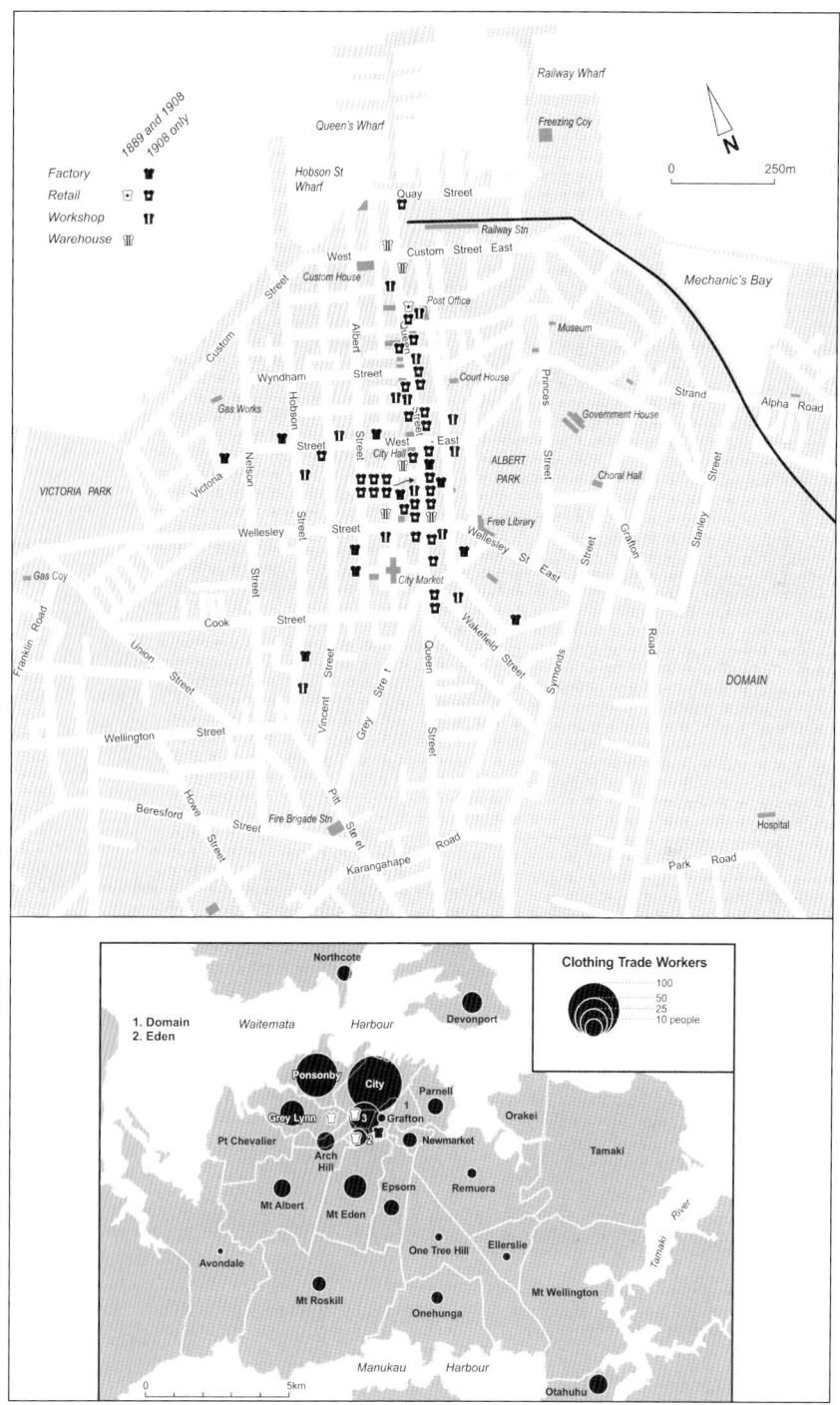

FIGURE 5: CLOTHING

were felt. North of Victoria Street the retailers specialised in menswear and some of the shops shared buildings predominantly devoted to office space. As retailers converged on middle Queen Street, the larger enterprises established new production facilities nearby, and independent workrooms and factories also converged on the neighbourhood. This was encouraged by some land developers whose new buildings offered spaces for workrooms. Together these agents created a fashion district comprising co-located production, warehouse and shop-front activities.

Conclusion

As the city's new villas and tramlines spread out across the isthmus, manufacturers staged a net withdrawal to the inner city. It seems that industry became less focused on resource processing as attention turned to production of building materials, furniture, clothing and footwear for domestic markets. Manufacturers were attracted by reclaimed waterfront land, and by new gas, sewerage, water and railroad infrastructure that could only be found in the inner city. Suburban rail sidings were thin on the ground and the movement of materials depended on horse-drawn conveyances and the port. Only in the inner city could manufacturers access the full potential of the urban labour market. For these reasons, suburban residential development was accompanied by a round of investment in production spaces in the inner city. This explanation, originally advanced by Linge, is not contested here, but it is argued that closer attention to Auckland's distinctive industrial complex and the patterns of factory development within the inner city reveals further insights into the peculiar combination of suburban residential development and investment in inner-city manufacturing in the period 1889–1908.

The small scale of Auckland manufacturing mattered. Few if any of the new establishments required large sites. There were few barriers to entry and many artisan producers continued to operate. Some artisan producers continued their operations in the downtown but now commuted from the suburbs. Land on the fringe of the central business district previously dedicated to boarding houses and residences was then taken up for industrial and commercial uses. Faced with a fragmented national market, Auckland industry looked to local market opportunities. Suburban construction dominated the urban economy. Some activities suburbanised, notably coach building, but there was little sign of investment in works for processing resources for export or national markets and no sign of such investments in new, large-scale suburban or ex-urban plants.

Instead investment went into industrial activity that could take advantage of inner-city locations and this is betrayed by the clustering of new activities in expanded specialised districts within the central business district. There was a resorting of industrial activity along the waterfront, partly made possible by reclamation work. This facilitated the proximate location of offices, mills, warehouses and yards for those engaged in the maritime and timber industries.

Some inner-city manufacturing was functionally or spatially associated with retailing or wholesaling. Smith and Caughey, Tonson and Garlick, L. D. Nathan and others invested in production facilities as they diversified their businesses. They looked to site their factories near their warehouses and retail stores and the city was small enough to permit this kind of clustering. Tailors' workrooms and garment lofts took up spaces behind and above Queen Street stores. So did furniture factories and carriage works. Printworks clustered together in the heart of the central business district. The Post Office's telegraph boys would not be winded as they connected the wider world to newspaper offices. Printers were readily at hand for lawyers, clerks, agents, brokers and retailers.

Indeed, the establishment of specialised inner-city districts was central to this pattern of development. A retail district had emerged keyed to department stores on middle Queen Street. Immediately to the north lay a modest office district, with an expanding and increasingly more specialised warehouse district on either side of lower Queen Street. None of these districts was a homogeneous space dedicated to only one set of economic activities, and none was particularly large, but there were identifiable clusters. Their presence and development fuelled the kinds of manufacturing investment that Auckland's inner city received. It was the small scale of Auckland city – so late in the piece – that made it feasible to locate production, sales, warehouse and office operations near each other. This was a walking city with horse-drawn omnibus transport in 1890 and only 70,000 people. Curiously, Auckland experienced mechanisation of its suburban commuter transport while it was still laid out as a mercantile city. Thus it was the tardy transition from a mercantile city core to a downtown of specialised retail, office, and warehouse and workshop districts that dominated the urban area's manufacturing scene from 1889 to 1908.

CHAPTER SEVEN

Stock and Station Agents and Wool Brokers

SIMON VILLE

The rapid expansion of wool production and export in Australia and New Zealand in the second half of the nineteenth century provided one of the earliest opportunities for business specialisation in the two embryonic colonial economies of Australasia.[1] The stock and station agent industry grew up in Australia from about the 1840s and in New Zealand from about the 1860s to provide a range of financial, marketing and technical services to pastoralists. In particular, these services included the provision of short- and long-term finance to farmers, either as the source of funds or as intermediaries for banks and other major lenders. Marketing wool included taking responsibility for consignment to sale in the London market, and, with the gradual relocation of the market, serving as brokers in the local auction system. Livestock and farm property was also auctioned by agents. Finally, agents provided advice on farming technology and the techniques of business management for small family farms. In some cases, particularly where farms were remotely located, agents also supplied a range of farming raw materials and household merchandise. In the course of the twentieth century, with the expansion and diversification of the New Zealand and Australian economies, agents diversified into new products, functions and markets, although rarely venturing beyond Australasia.[2]

This chapter will focus on the provision of these services in Auckland, the strategies of the key corporate players, and the business networks and industry linkages within the sector and to other parts of the Auckland corporate economy. While agents serviced the 'man on the land', they were an integral part of the emerging industrial and urban business élite in New Zealand. Led by their downtown head offices, they provided an essential conduit between country and town, and between primary, secondary and tertiary sectors. The imperative of this economic link between town and country was widely recognised, as Wright Stephenson observed in 1932: 'you must keep the grass growing in the country, or it will grow in the streets of your cities'.[3]

Pastoral agent services in the Auckland region

In Auckland, as elsewhere, strong synergies existed between the different pastoral services, which encouraged agents to offer a full line of services. Initial concentration on a particular function, such as wool broking or the conduct of livestock auctions, brought economies of scale, reputation and expertise. Diversification across pastoral services, though, provided economies of scope from using the same or similar physical assets, knowledge and customer information. Diversification produced information synergies through wider and more regular transactions with each farmer. Therefore, agents had greater client knowledge from which to make informed lending and marketing decisions, and this enabled closer monitoring. Thus, 'transactions costs' were reduced by increasing the amount of business with existing clients in an atmosphere of more complete information and enhanced trust.[4] These were important benefits for dealing with many small and remotely located family farms. Reputation and expertise in the pastoral industry were also extended. For the farmer, more business with a single intermediary reduced his transactions costs and increased the likelihood of positive externalities from this enriched relationship in the form of 'free' (zero-priced) services such as technical and business advice.[5]

Wool marketing

In the nineteenth century, most New Zealand wool was consigned for sale on the international wool market in London. As consignors, stock and station agents received the wool from the farmer, graded it, insured it, arranged for transportation to the port of shipment, and temporary storage there if warranted, its overseas shipment, and receipt by the foreign importer or selling

G. W. Binney and Sons were one of the leading Auckland stock and station agents and early wool brokers before the First World War. PHOTOGRAPH FROM J. C. IRVING, COURTESY OF FLETCHER CHALLENGE ARCHIVES, 4229P/1.

broker. Following the sale, the agent received payment and credited the farmer with his net receipts after deducting the consignment commission, handling charges incurred, and any agreed debt repayments. Consignors might also arrange for the wool to be scoured prior to shipment, although falling freight rates in the later nineteenth century and buyer preferences eroded this activity.[6] New Zealand Loan and Mercantile Agency (hereafter NZL&MA), whose close connection to the Auckland business community will be discussed below, was the largest consignor of New Zealand wool to London.

In the first half of the twentieth century, an increasing share of the clip was sold by auction in New Zealand before being shipped to its overseas buyer. A number of factors help explain this shift in the market's location, including the diversification of international demand and improved direct-shipping services to continental Europe, North America and Asia.[7] As local selling broker, the agent directly undertook more extensive handling processes. These began at the woolshed with the initial separation of the wool in each fleece into uniform quality by the company's sorter.[8] It was then pressed into bales, branded, weighed and dispatched to the agent's wool store. Here the wool was classed into uniform lots and carefully displayed so that it could be inspected by buyers prior to the sale. Agents took responsibility for printing and distributing catalogues as well as organising the sale itself.

TABLE 1: LOCAL AND OVERSEAS SALES OF NEW ZEALAND WOOL, 1891–1939

	Total exports	Local sales	Sales/Exports (%)
1895–1900	383,471	93,137	24
1901–10	424,206	158,069	37
1911–20	538,232	402,251	75
1921–30	640,633	465,997	73
1931–39	767,538	602,304	79

Source: *Australasian Insurance & Banking Record*; Dalgety's *Annual Wool Review*, various years.
Note: Bales, decennial averages.

Although Auckland has never been the leading wool-selling centre in New Zealand, it is believed to have been the location of the first public wool sale: in 1858, Alfred Buckland conducted a wool auction of about 250 bales from Messrs Henderson and Macfarlane's store on Queen's Wharf.[9] Wool auctions were modest and intermittent affairs in mid-nineteenth century New Zealand; however, more regular sales took place in Dunedin from the 1860s and Wellington by the 1870s. By the beginning of the twentieth century there were eight selling centres broadly spread through the country and located at major port cities. The main inter-regional shift in wool-broking business was away from the South Island towards the North Island with the relative decline of Christchurch and Dunedin and the expansion of Wellington and Auckland in the first half of the twentieth century. Some recovery in the share of the South Island cities has occurred in recent decades. These trends are reflected in the changing national share of Auckland, rising from 5 per cent in the first decade of the twentieth century to 17 per cent by the 1960s, and then dropping back slightly thereafter.

A major innovation around the end of the nineteenth century was joint selling by the various brokers in a central salesroom at each of the main centres. This reduced the sale costs for individual brokers by sharing overheads at a time when many were serving both the London and the New Zealand markets, and their desire to invest locally was constrained by uncertainty about the future market. Centralised sales also bolstered the number of buyers and sellers in the early years of thin volumes. The brokers drew lots to decide the selling order at the first auction of the year. From this, a system of rotation for the rest of the selling season could be mapped. The amount to be sold by each broker at each sale was also agreed. By 1887, wool sales were organised in a central salesroom in Dunedin.[10] The exact date of commencement of regular joint wool auctions at Auckland is not clear, but in 1906 three brokers auctioned 6742 bales of wool at Auckland.[11] By 1913, four brokers participated in a joint auction at Auckland Town Hall and this included the two enduring major players in the city, Dalgety and NZL&MA.[12] Data covering all of the wool sales in New Zealand for the year 1922/3 (July to June) illustrates how Auckland fitted into the national system. During this twelve-month period, there was a total of forty-seven auctions, of which four were held in Auckland, on 2 December, 12 February, 17 March and 2 June. The idea was to achieve a reasonable spread of time between each auction with some concentration during the main shearing period from November to March.[13]

TABLE 2: WOOL SALES AT AUCKLAND, 1906–80

	Bales	% of NZ total
1906–10	10,688	5
1911–20	34,929	9
1921–30	39,357	8
1931–40	69,083	11
1941–50	117,097	14
1951–60	154,415	15
1961–70	242,413	17
1971–80	178,415	13

Source: *Australasian Insurance & Banking Record*; Dalgety's *Annual Wool Review*, various years.
Note: Decennial averages.

Several observations can be made by analysing an excellent dataset of wool sales by individual brokers in Auckland covering most of the twentieth century. The number of wool brokers at any time was relatively small, no more than nine in any year and more commonly about six.[14] This partly reflected the relatively small market share held by Auckland, but also the fact that only the larger stock and station agents also served as wool brokers. They worked closely with many smaller rural firms whose farmer clients' wool they sold. Within this select group of agent-brokers there is a notable degree of concentration. The two-firm share fluctuated mostly within 0.4 and 0.6.[15] This reflected a distinction between firms with a national or international focus, most notably Dalgety, NZL&MA, National Mortgage & Agency Company (hereafter NMA) and Wright Stephenson, and the remainder, who were largely local or regional

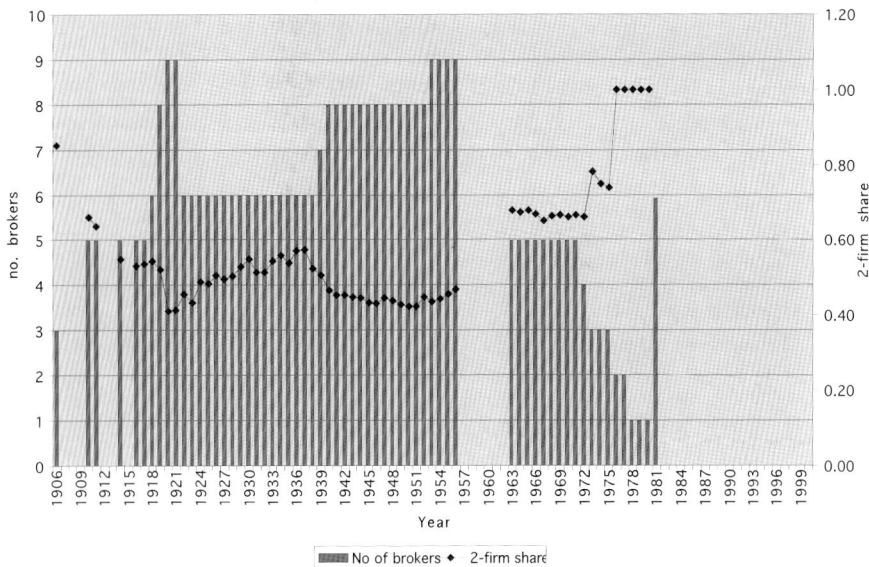

FIGURE 1: AUCKLAND WOOL BROKING: FIRM CONCENTRATION, 1906–80

in orientation, such as Alfred Buckland and Abraham & Williams, and were eventually absorbed into the larger companies. The resulting reduction in broker numbers lifted concentration levels in the second half of the century.

Wool auctions ceased at Auckland following a cost-reducing centralisation strategy in 1984, which located a single auction in each island: at Napier and Christchurch, respectively. Auckland now serves as one of eight aggregation centres, where brokers hold wool and from where samples are sent to the auction centre and a testing company. The introduction of Woolnet in 1999, an internet-based trading system for New Zealand wool, and attempts by the New Zealand Futures and Options Exchange to establish a wool futures market on the Sydney Futures Exchange (1988, 1991, 2004) are further evidence of the decline of the regional public physical wool market in New Zealand.[16]

Merchandise sales

While it deferred to Wellington, Hawke's Bay, Canterbury and Otago in terms of its share of the national wool market, Auckland was of especial significance to the stock and station agents for its merchandise business. The firms increasingly looked to centralise key functions within the organisation by the early twentieth century in order to yield scale economies and keep a closer control over branch activities. In this context, Auckland was favoured by most firms to handle their merchandise needs. This was because of its excellent international trade and shipping facilities and large and rapidly expanding population, which provided the opportunity for the firms to act as importing agents and supply the Auckland and then national markets.[17]

In this sense, the experience of NMA is instructive. While predominantly a South Island firm, it opened an export and import department at Auckland in 1919 in order to handle its trade flows through the port and co-ordinate the purchase of merchandise on behalf of all of the firm's branches. In the following years, the company monitored its Auckland activities closely. Some directors proposed closing down its presence in Auckland, but its general manager, G. R. Ritchie, argued that they were prepared to incur losses, 'for indirectly we consider that the agency is very vital to our other branches'. He additionally showed an awareness of the strategic importance of Auckland as a conduit into the international business environment and the probability of continued growth and diversification of the Auckland economy.[18] As will be indicated below, the agents sought to diversify away from the pastoral sector in line with the changing economic structure of New Zealand from the middle decades of the twentieth century.

In addition to general merchandise, the agents provided a range of inputs for farmers, particularly seeds and fertilisers. Much of New Zealand's manufacturing growth has been located in South Auckland, which has provided suitable external economies for fertiliser plants through localised access to a combination of cheap land, a suitable supply of labour, and ancillary and related industries. As part of the reparations payments arising from the First World War, New Zealand, Australia and the United Kingdom acquired the rights to the phosphate deposits of Nauru and the Ocean Islands. This gave New Zealand, with its phosphate-deficient soil, access to the highest grade phosphate (84 per cent) in the world. In response to this opportunity, Wright Stephenson established a fertiliser works at Otahuhu in South Auckland in 1920. Here it produced the Challenge brand of fertiliser for sale through its national network of branches. With the expansion of manufactured fertilisers, in 1924 the company erected a large superphosphate and sulphuric acid-making plant connected to their original fertiliser works.[19] In a similar fashion, Wright Stephenson expanded its interests in seed merchanting through the acquisition of the seed-retailing business of Auckland mayor J. H. Gunson in 1916. Wright Stephenson had operated in the wholesale seed trade, including the supply of Gunson, for some years; forward vertical integration had now brought them into retailing.

The industrial district of South Auckland provided the ideal location for the operation of Wright Stephenson's fertiliser works. PHOTOGRAPH FROM J. C. IRVING, COURTESY OF FLETCHER CHALLENGE ARCHIVES, 4003P/4.

Livestock auctions

Less is known about Auckland's role in the conduct of livestock auctions. In 1855, Alfred Buckland and Joseph Newman conducted livestock auctions in saleyards at Newmarket. Buckland continued these auctions on his own when the joint business dissolved in the following year, adding impressive large new premises at Haymarket in 1865 in the centre of the commercial district of Auckland. In 1909, he built the Westfield Saleyards with Dalgety and NZL&MA, indicating the breadth of stock and station activities now pursued by these three market leaders in Auckland. His livestock auctioneering business expanded further as he added new saleyards in several provincial towns, helped by the waterway systems and expansion of the rail network. These included Otahuhu, which was to become the location of Auckland's fat stock market.[20] When the New Zealand Livestock Auctioneers Association was established in the 1920s, the constituent association from Auckland was classified as 'large' along with about half of the other regional members, suggesting that livestock activities continued to be of importance in the area.[21]

Farmer finance

Finance has always been closely tied to the agents' other core businesses of wool and livestock marketing and merchandise sales. Providing financial support was one means of securing the loyalty of sheep farmers in the disposal of their clip. Indeed, agents were prepared merely to break even or endure losses on loans in order to yield valuable marketing commissions, which were the dominant source of earnings in most years. As NZL&MA explained in 1892: 'the two are necessarily very closely connected. You cannot carry on a mercantile agency business unless you are prepared to make advances upon produce.'[22] For South Island firms like NMA and Wright Stephenson, limited finance was initially provided to their embryonic Auckland business: in 1919, the Auckland branch's overdraft limit at Wright Stephenson was a relatively modest £10,000, well behind Wellington (£35,000), Dunedin (£26,000) and even Invercargill (£16,000).[23]

Initially, however, NZL&MA was a different company from the other large stock and station agents. Its emphasis at the start was upon mortgage lending in the Auckland province, drawing upon debenture funds sourced from London, rather than focusing on wool and livestock marketing in the South Island colonial farming communities. Besides funding farmers, it supported land developers in the Waikato and Thames Valley, and a range of local industries, including coal, railways and shipping, the latter two acknowledged as infrastructure industries of importance to the expansion of rural production. Further, it acted as financial intermediary and guarantor of capital and interest for a number of large mortgages granted by British financial institutions to Aucklanders; risky business probably not justified by the smallness of the commissions received.[24]

Stone has described NZL&MA as the second most important financial institution originating in nineteenth-century Auckland after the Bank of New Zealand (BNZ), and an institution with widespread interests and influence.[25] The two institutions worked closely together at first, NZL&MA often sharing premises and personnel with the bank and receiving customers through the bank. Thus, customers who held bank accounts or received short-term trade finance through the bank were introduced to NZL&MA for the purposes of longer-term lending on mortgage. However, in the late 1870s NZL&MA rapidly severed its management and premises ties with the BNZ, which it believed had put it at a disadvantage in the increasingly competitive rural finance market.[26] The reason for this opinion is not explained, but probably derived from NZL&MA's connections to Auckland's financial élite through the BNZ, which had begun to take on an unsavoury reputation around this time. Stone and Chappell have each noted that these close ties, which will be explained in more detail below, led to undue financial favours to members of this 'inner (or "limited") circle' that unravelled in the financial collapses in Auckland in the 1880s.[27] The full consequences of such relationships and the concentration on mortgage lending had an impact on NZL&MA during the difficult years of the 1890s when it was forced into a major financial restructure. While the opinion of nineteenth-century NZL&MA has been heavily tainted by the reconstruction and the damning account by Falconer Larkworthy, it achieved rapid expansion during its first twenty years to become one of the leading wool agency and finance institutions in New Zealand, paying generous profits to its shareholders.[28]

Business networks and industry linkages

One of the critical competitive advantages of the stock and station agent industry was its ability to develop close personal networks in country towns as a means of establishing and sustaining long-term business relations with farmers, and enhancing their knowledge of the area and its inhabitants. In essence, agents invested in the social capital of rural communities to build levels of trust, cooperation and reciprocity on which business relationships and networks could flourish.[29] As Ville and Fleming have shown, in New Zealand these networks helped agents to ration credit among pastoralists in an efficient manner through their knowledge of relative risk levels.[30] Agent networking was equally important in the broader business community by bringing the firm into close and regular contact with complementary service providers, such as banks, insurers and shipowners, along with producers of farming equipment and inputs. Agents networked through developing personal connections and more formal business relationships derived from transactions and ownership interests. Finally, intra-sector networking relationships among agents and the benefits they yielded should be mentioned.

Alfred Buckland was typical of the well-connected nineteenth-century Auckland entrepreneur. Besides operating his own business, he sat on the board of a number of prominent local public companies, including New Zealand Insurance, South British Fire and Marine Insurance Company of New Zealand, Kaipara Steamship Company Limited, and New Zealand Frozen Meat and Storage Company Limited. His weekly horse bazaar at the Haymarket became a general meeting place of town and country. His sporting interests provided further networking opportunities, including his presidency of the Auckland Racing Club and of the Auckland Agricultural and Pastoral Association. Buckland's grand Highwic residence in fashionable Epsom placed him among other business élites living in that suburb or in Remuera or Mt Eden by the late nineteenth century.[31]

Buckland remained on the fringe of the so-called 'limited circle' business élite of late nineteenth-century Auckland, mentioned in the previous section.

This group served as directors of many of the leading business institutions, particularly in finance, land development, agriculture and mining. Their accumulated expertise, reputation and influence doubtless brought many strategic benefits to the companies they served. Their familiarity with each other in addition fostered a high trust and low transaction cost environment.[32] These arrangements worked well in the expansive environment of mid-century but less so in the crisis-ridden 1880s and 1890s. No institution was as closely enmeshed with the limited circle as the NZL&MA – sixteen of the eighteen in the clique were directors of the company, more so even than the BNZ, many of whom borrowed from NZL&MA and entangled it with their own particular business interests. When members of the clique faced serious indebtedness or even bankruptcy in the 1880s, they looked to the 'friendly' companies under their control, such as NZL&MA, for favours. John Logan Campbell, for example, was provided with extended support at low rates of interest by NZL&MA and a guarantee to repay a large loan from Commercial Union Assurance Company of Britain, arranged by other 'limited circle' figures, Thomas Russell and Falconer Larkworthy. In a study of the Auckland-based New Zealand Frozen Meat and Storage Company, Stone illustrates how the collapse of this company can be traced back to such conflicts of interest within the clique. He concludes:

> in the light of the alarming balance sheet presented at the annual meeting of the Freezing Company in November 1885 ... the Loan Company would scarcely have acted like a benevolent society had not members of its Colonial Board figured so prominently in the proprietary of the ailing meat company.[33]

In addition to inter-industry cooperation and networking, agents, in spite of being fiercely competitive, recognised that there were circumstances where cooperation among themselves brought mutual benefits or, put formally, pareto-optimal outcomes. Cooperation was most extensive and ongoing where everyone stood to gain from lower costs and improved co-ordination. Since there was no need for secrecy on such matters, and the punity of transgressors was uncommon, the costs of cooperation were also minimal. Firms worked closely together in the provision of a market infrastructure for wool and livestock auctions, which included the development of procedural rules, and the negotiation of sale rosters. Cooperation to promote and defend the interests of the pastoral agent industry was also strong when it was under threat from a particular source or suffering economic hardship. Collectively, the agents could negotiate more effectively and cheaply with other peak bodies and major institutions such as governments, banks, wool buyers and graziers. The main vehicles of intra-industry cooperation were national associations of stock and station agents, wool brokers, and livestock auctioneers. While functionally distinguished in this manner, the major companies were represented in all three types of association. Local associations comprised federal membership of the national associations, which gives us some insight into the regional picture for Auckland, and its relationship with the other centres.

Inter-firm and inter-regional disagreements were played out and largely resolved here. In spite of Auckland's initial reluctance to join the New Zealand Woolbrokers Association (NZWBA) at its formation in 1907, generally harmonious relations subsequently existed between Auckland and the other local associations, which may reflect the dominance of each group by the major firms.[34] However, some regional nuances existed, reflecting different traditions, local practices and economic imperatives between areas and some element of internal and external competition among the majors.

When wool was consigned for sale in London, local agents had generally rebated part of their commission to the bank that provided short-term finance to the wool grower while the wool was in transit. With the gradual repatriation of the wool market to New Zealand in the twentieth century, Auckland agents were reluctant to continue this rebate given the much shorter period of finance, covering little more than the period of shearing. When the rebates were halted by NZWBA at Auckland's instigation in 1932, Wellington agents opposed this move, citing the loss of goodwill of local banks, 'who so largely finance the woolgrowers in this district'.[35] In a somewhat similar fashion, Auckland was keen to provide incentives to wool buyers for early payment, by offering interest rebates, a move opposed by most members of the NZWBA.[36]

Finally, differences periodically emerged over the national sales roster, each centre seeking regular, equally spaced auctions that minimised delays and warehousing costs. In 1925, for example, Auckland was said to be unhappy about the sales roster, 'not getting justice at the hands of the other members of the Association'.[37]

Strategies of the major firms

This section looks more closely at the major stock and station agents, some already identified by name at least, who were associated with Auckland, and traces their expansion, focusing on the role of Auckland in their strategies. Wool-broking figures provide an annual snapshot of the industry in Auckland.

TABLE 3: LIST OF ALL WOOL BROKERS AT AUCKLAND, 1906–80

Broker	Years
Abraham & Williams Ltd	1919–49
Auckland Farmers' Freezing Co-op.	1919–20
Auckland Farmers Union	1910–11, 1914
Binney, G. W. and Sons	1906–18
Buckland, A. and Sons	1906–56
Dalgety	1910–62
Dalgety-NZL	1963–75
East Co-op Freezing Co.	1919–21
Farmers Co-op Auction Co.	c. 1911–71
The Farmers – NK Wools	1972–77
Gisborne Farmers Co-op Co.	1921
National Mortgage & Agency	1970–72
Newton King	1939–71
N.Z. Co-op W. Market Assn Ltd	1940–c. 1956
NZL&MA	1906–62
N. Auckland Farmers Co-op	c. 1911–c. 1956
Vercoe & Co., G. W.	1953–c.1956
Westfield Freezing Co.	1918–21
Wiri Woolbrokers	1976–80
Wright Stephenson	1950–72
Wrightson-NMA	1973–75

Source: *Australasian Insurance & Banking Record*; Dalgety's *Annual Wool Review*, various years; National Library of New Zealand, New Zealand Woolbrokers Association, minutes, MSY 4133.
Note: Dates at which they are known to have sold wool at Auckland. Assumptions are made about missing years where possible.

Table 3 lists all of the firms who served as wool brokers in Auckland during 1906–80. As noted in an earlier section, these tended to be the larger stock and station agents who received the wool of smaller local firms in the province in addition to that of their own branches. Several firms participated in the auctions for only several years because their main interests lay elsewhere in another function or geographic area. Auckland Farmers' Freezing Co-operative, East Co-op Freezing Company, and Westfield Freezing Company each sold wool for several years at the end of the First World War. Gisborne Farmers Co-op sold a mere seventeen bales of wool in 1921. As part of the rationalisation of the industry after the First World War, Auckland Farmers Union merged with mail order firm Laidlaw Leeds in 1918 and subsequently moved into general wholesale and retail including the Farmers department store.[38] Most remaining firms were committed to the Auckland market, participating for longer periods. It was the waves of mergers and acquisitions that accounted for most of the turnover amongst them. Of particular note was the absorption of two local/regional firms: the complete acquisition of Abraham & Williams by Wright Stephenson in 1950 (a majority shareholding having been acquired in 1922) and the takeover of Alfred Buckland by NMA in 1957. Newton King merged with Farmers Co-op Auction Company to form Farmers–NK Wools in 1972 before ending up as part of Dalgety Crown in 1983.

Table 4 lists firms with 20 per cent or more market share. Dalgety is the dominant firm both in terms of its endurance within this group and the fact that it was the market leader in most years. NZL&MA, by contrast, declined in relative significance, dropping below the 20 per cent floor by the early 1940s and leaving Dalgety in an unassailable position until the entry of Wright Stephenson into the Auckland market in 1950 via Abraham & Williams. This is a story that is mirrored nationally and in Australia. Much of the explanation lies in Dalgety establishing a first-mover advantage in local wool sales and the excellence of its local management teams. NZL&MA, by contrast, was held back for a long while by divisions and disagreements between its London and colonial boards and the slowness of its branch expansion.[39] Wright Stephenson entered the market in 1950, and within five years had reached and maintained the 20 per cent threshold. NMA did not sell wool at Auckland until 1970 and failed to reach 20 per cent until after the merger with Wright Stephenson two years later.

TABLE 4: LIST OF WOOL BROKERS WITH 20%+ MARKET SHARE AT AUCKLAND

Broker	Years
Buckland, A. and Sons	1906–19
NZL&MA	1906–19, 1921, 1924, 1926–41
Dalgety	1917–20, 1922–62
Farmers Co-op Auction Co.	1923–24
Wright Stephenson	1955–56, 1963–72
Dalgety-NZL	1963–75
The Farmers – NK Wools	1972–77
Wrightson-NMA	1973–75
Wiri Woolbrokers	1976–80

Source: *Australasian Insurance & Banking Record*; Dalgety's *Annual Wool Review*, various years.
Note: Assumptions are made about missing years where possible.

National expansion was one of the key strategies developed by the companies that came to dominate the Auckland wool market. The geographic

Accurate wool-classing by stock and station agents was vital to their reputation and the success of auctions. This photograph shows wool undergoing an appraisal, c. 1967. COURTESY OF FLETCHER CHALLENGE ARCHIVES, 4003P/78.

growth of a firm is a strong indication of its industry leadership, providing it with the opportunity to control rights over widely distributed resources and strategic assets, and to exploit larger factor and product markets. In the case of the agents, this included greater leverage over the national wool auction system, stronger bargaining power in freight and farming input markets, and wider markets for their brands. Operationally, it provided greater locational flexibility, including the opportunity for some degree of regional specialisation. Thus, for example, Wright Stephenson could market its Challenge brand of seeds and fertilisers over a larger national market while locating production of these farming inputs at the preferred location of Auckland as discussed above. The preference of many firms for locating their expanding mercantile and non-farming business at Auckland was noted earlier. When Wright Stephenson diversified into the sale and servicing of vehicles during the interwar period, Auckland was the ideal site for importing them.[40]

It was observed earlier that NMA general manager G. R. Ritchie was aware of the prospective and strategic value of including operations at Auckland. Many of the agents had initially established on the South Island with the early growth of Otago and Canterbury wool output in the second half of the nineteenth century. By the early years of the twentieth century, the balance of pastoral production and the diversification of economic and industrial activity favoured the North Island.[41] Encouraged by infrastructure such as the opening of the Auckland Stock Market (1872) and the Auckland–Wellington rail link (1908), firms in many sectors began to expand their operations and in many cases relocate their head offices to Wellington or Auckland.

Wright Stephenson is an important example of this geographic shift. It established a district office at Auckland in 1908, a branch in 1916, acquired Gunson's seed business in the same year, a majority stake in Abraham & Williams in 1922, and set up its fertiliser plant in 1920. Wright Stephenson additionally relocated their head office from Dunedin to Wellington in 1918, noting 'the expansion of our business in the North Island made Dunedin too much at one end of our territory for effective control. We therefore follow the example of so many other businesses . . . and transferred our headquarters to Wellington.'[42]

NMA appear to have been slower to make the move in spite of their initial enthusiasm for conducting merchandising operations in Auckland and the establishment of a branch there by 1914. Most of their northward expansion waited until the mid-1950s and was accelerated by a series of acquisitions during that decade. Significantly, NMA only began wool brokerage at Auckland in 1970. The comments of the general manager in 1922 may have been indicative of their attitude. Opposing further expansion of their Auckland operations, he noted, 'Our hands are fairly full in the South Island . . . the position of the farmer is better in this Island than the North.'[43] What this means is not made clear. What seems likely is the opposition to a shift northwards from company directors originating from and wedded to the southern pastures.

Wright Stephenson faced similar opposition, but its conversion to a public company in 1906 provided the funds, strategic thinking, and accountability pressure to overcome conservative and vested interests.[44] NMA was established as a public company from the outset, but control remained vested in London, which, similar to the experiences of NZL&MA, may have curtailed their responsiveness to changing conditions locally.[45] The benefits of national expansion are reflected in a more than doubling of Wright Stephenson's share of the wool market in the first half of the century, while NMA's remained unchanged.[46] Dalgety established a national presence very early on, whereas NZL&MA took the opposite direction of expansion from NMA and Wright Stephenson, moving southwards from its Auckland head office and adding non-financial services.

*Wright Stephenson and
Co., Auckland Branch,
Albert Street, c. 1940.*
COURTESY FLETCHER
CHALLENGE ARCHIVES
4003P/57.

As firms expand, they have a range of strategic options governing their methods of growth; notably, internally through merger, or by inter-firm agreements. Each has its benefits and shortcomings. Internal growth provides full control over the development process and affords protection of proprietary knowledge. Mergers, on the other hand, can telescope the growth process and provide for cross-organisational fertilisation, but may prove expensive due to purchase premiums and may involve a protracted integration process. Inter-firm agreements enable firms to acquire expertise and yield synergies through only a partial surrender of corporate sovereignty and at a generally lower cost than merger or internal growth, but require constant attention to maintain the relationship.[47]

NMA relied on mergers in the postwar period, cognisant of the competitive disadvantage of a limited presence in Auckland and Wellington. These notably included Buckland in 1957, which gave the company a strong foothold in the Auckland region, and the minority of Hamilton-based G. W. Vercoe not already owned by Buckland in the following year.

Wright Stephenson and Co., Motor Division, Albert Street, Auckland, c. 1970.
COURTESY FLETCHER CHALLENGE ARCHIVES 4003P/23.

Wright Stephenson used all three methods, noting with great honesty in 1916 of their expansion at Auckland, 'We do not know of course whether just to buy up a seed business already in Auckland or to start out on our own.'[48] As was seen earlier, they opted for the acquisition of Gunson. Their progressive acquisition of Abraham & Williams was equally important for entry into the Auckland wool market, although operating under the acquired firm's name until full ownership was attained in 1950.[49] Internal growth was used in the establishment of the company's fertiliser works and the development of the Challenge brand. In 1927 the firm launched Challenge Phosphate Company, owned jointly with New Zealand Dairy Co-operative Company, to take over the Otahuhu works.[50] Inter-firm agreements with small local stock and station agents were also common.

Subsequent merger activity has made the industry highly concentrated in one or two hands. Dalgety and NZL&MA merged in 1963 and in turn joined forces with the group of companies known as Crown in 1983. Wright Stephenson and NMA merged in 1972 in a coming together of the two old southern rivals. Exploiting the powerful Wright Stephenson brand, they changed the company name to Challenge in 1975 before merging with Auckland building products firm Fletcher Holdings in 1980 and absorbing Dalgety Crown into the group in 1986. Fletcher Challenge, with its head office in the industrial heartland of South Auckland, became New Zealand's largest and most diverse company – a conglomerate worth NZ$80 million by 1980, with interests as diverse as pastoral agency, motor trading, merchanting, engineering, machinery, finance, fish processing, and property. In 1993, Wrightson was floated off by Fletcher Challenge and has since extended its primary industry services to include horticulture and forestry. In 2004 it was acquired by Rural Portfolio Investments.

Mention should also be made of the arrival of a similar Australian institution – leading stock and station agent turned conglomerate – Elders Pastoral in 1984, acquiring Allied Farmers Co-operative (the product of a 1972 merger of North Auckland Farmers Co-op and Farmers Auctioneering Company) and locating its head office in Auckland.

Conclusion

The development of the stock and station agent industry in Auckland reflected in many respects the broad growth of the industry throughout Australia and New Zealand from the second half of the nineteenth century. While serving rural communities, agents were a key part of the urban and industrial business élites, including that of Auckland.

Auckland's mix of rural services (broking, merchandise and finance), however, distinguished it from other major centres. The first public wool sale in New Zealand is thought to have taken place in Auckland in 1858. The excellent international trade and shipping facilities, international business connections, and rapid population growth caused agents to concentrate their merchandise business at Auckland as a conduit to international business networks. In addition, manufacturing style activities, such as fertiliser and seed production, were located in South Auckland to yield localised external economies of scale in this industrial area.

Strategic investments were made at Auckland from the early twentieth century, forward-looking firms being prepared to incur losses here in order to become established in the most rapidly growing region of the country. The relative experiences of Wright Stephenson and NMA suggest significant rents (or super profits) accrued to prime movers in the expansion northwards in the twentieth century. Exceptionally, NZL&MA began in Auckland and played a major role in financing the economic and industrial expansion of Auckland in the middle decades of the nineteenth century as well as being a leading stock and station agent. Subsequently, they were caught up in the financial crises and the allegedly duplicitous behaviour of the 'limited circle' clique, and lost ground in the twentieth century.

The incorporation of stock and station agents into large conglomerates in the 1980s and their subsequent floating off in the 1990s is reflected in the formation of Fletcher Challenge and Wrightson at Auckland. Viewed through the history of such companies, the stock and station agent industry has reflected, in miniature, the regional and sectoral shifts in the New Zealand economy over the past century and a half.

A 'Business to Business Relationship': The Origin and Development of Auckland Newspapers, 1841–2004

DIANA MORROW

In 1902, the *Cyclopedia of New Zealand* praised the *New Zealand Herald* and the *Auckland Star* as being among the best examples of the 'continued prosperity of Auckland firms'.[1] This description of Auckland's two major daily newspapers as well-established, thriving business enterprises was accurate, but notably uncommon. Contemporaries rarely described the press solely, or even primarily, as a business endeavour, as attention was more usually directed towards its social and political functions. The tendency to overlook the commercial aspects of the New Zealand press has proved persistent. By the early years of the twenty-first century, the history of newspapers as businesses has been left largely unexplored.[2] Equally, little critical attention has been paid to the symbiosis between newspaper content and business relationships. In order to fully understand how this country's 'fourth estate' has evolved and continues to function, its origins, commercial imperatives, and business relationships warrant more extensive examination.

This chapter surveys key developments in the growth and evolution of Auckland's press from its inception in 1841 to the present day. It focuses on the city's major weekly and then daily newspapers, highlighting the fact that these were, and still remain, business operations that depend on a close relationship with the business community. Auckland's major newspapers and Auckland businesses have grown up and prospered together in a 'business to business' relationship.[3] Even in their formative stage, when newspapers were a drain on proprietors' pockets and political agendas and ambitions appeared to predominate, local business interests played a seminal part in the struggles and ambitions of both the press and the colony as a whole.

Defiant dependence, 1841–1843

Between July 1841 and April 1843, the newspaper business in Auckland was dramatic and highly precarious. Although several papers were born, their lives were curtailed by a fierce struggle with the Crown Colony government. This conflict was the key factor determining newspaper mortality. As the settlement's only printing press was controlled by the official-military establishment, editors who cast a critical eye towards the ruling authorities did so at their peril. Embattled relations between the press and officialdom were not without precedent. In December 1840, the *New Zealand Advertiser and Bay of Islands Gazette*, edited by the intrepid and memorably named Reverend Barzillai Quaife, was repressed after only nine issues for being critical of the government.[4] When the capital moved to the Waitemata in September 1840, similar tensions quickly arose. Auckland's first newspaper, the *New Zealand Herald and Auckland Gazette*, began publication on 10 July 1841; like its northern counterpart, it was closed down by the government in less than a year.[5]

Contemporaries might well have predicted a much longer lifespan, as the *Herald* had appeared a hearty enough infant. Its parent company, the Auckland Newspaper General Printing Company, was one of the most considerable commercial ventures in the fledgling town. Capital amounting to £3,000 was raised for it, partly in Sydney. An expensive and sophisticated printing plant suitable for commercial printing and newspaper production was also acquired in New South Wales. Twenty shareholders were qualified to vote for five company trustees, four of whom were non-officials. At this early stage, the majority of trustees were non-officials, although half of the shareholders were officials, including some key members of the administration. Inevitably, the bulk of government printing was entrusted to the company.

Despite such links, the one shilling weekly was keen to establish from the outset that it would be conducted entirely upon independent principles. Its first editor, Charles Terry, a pioneer of the New Zealand flax-milling industry and a talented writer, was one of the five company trustees and a man seemingly well suited to the task ahead. By August 1841, however, only one of the five elected trustees remained a non-official, the company capital was exhausted, and more funds could not easily be obtained. This state of affairs can be partially explained by the small European population, which restricted the market for both newspaper readers and advertisers.[6] There was also frequently a general shortage of cash in the colony and many newspaper subscriptions were apparently left unpaid.[7] However, such factors should have been mitigated by a steady revenue source from government printing. Terry soon resigned to visit England. His successor, William Corbett, was openly critical of the administration's land policy, and was consequently summarily dismissed by the official majority of the trustees.[8]

The trustees then sought and found a new editor in New South Wales, offering a two-year contract to Dr Samuel McDonald Martin. The choice was somewhat surprising. Martin, a fiery Scot, already had a difficult relationship with the government, because his 2500-acre land claim on the Coromandel Peninsula in 1839 had been disallowed after New Zealand became a Crown Colony.[9] Land issues were a priority for Martin throughout his brief and stormy period of employment. He demanded full control of the paper when he took charge in January 1842, in the hope that through its pages he could effect a speedier settlement of land claims.

This hope proved groundless. When the Land Claims Bill was debated in the Legislative Council, Martin virulently criticised government land policies in the *Herald*. The government responded by ordering the Registrar of the Supreme Court to demand the manuscript from *Herald* printer John Moore, who duly yielded it. An enraged Martin then challenged the Registrar to a duel; when he refused, Martin denounced him as 'a coward and a blackguard'. He also accused Willoughby Shortland of attempting to bribe him to adopt a pro-government stance. The *Herald* trustees, most of whom were connected with official circles, were upset by Martin's vehement attacks, and instructed Moore not to print his copy without their authority. At this, the disgruntled editor disclaimed all responsibility for the policy of the newspaper. The company was dissolved and the plant sold to the government for £1,425. In May 1842, Martin successfully sued the trustees for the balance of salary owed, receiving £641.[10] Despite having begun so promisingly, the first *Herald* had not been a financial success. The fact that it folded, however, was due to conflict with the ruling authorities, who were intolerant of criticism.

Other Auckland newspapers in the early 1840s also experienced the mortal repercussions of using the government-owned press to criticise the government. For example, G. A. Eagar's *Chronicle and New Zealand Colonist*, a bi-weekly, began publication on 8 November 1841. Unlike the first *Herald*, this new paper did not have trustees who were linked to the administration. Nevertheless, in less than a year it was at loggerheads with the authorities and forced to suspend publication. Nor was political compliance any guarantee of longevity: the pro-government *Auckland Standard* lasted a mere six months, having attracted few readers. The *Auckland Times*, which first appeared in August 1842, had a somewhat longer run, due solely to the indomitable spirit of its editor and publisher, Henry Falwasser. When Administrator Willoughby Shortland refused to allow the government press to produce so critical a paper, Falwasser went to desperate and determined lengths, laboriously pulling copies through a mangle. After halting publication from April to November 1843, he eventually obtained better equipment and carried on valiantly producing the newspaper until his death in 1846.[11]

The fact that Auckland newspapers were short-lived and not particularly thriving enterprises in the July 1841–April 1843 period was, of course, not solely due to conflict with the authorities. As mentioned, the population of the settlement in the early 1840s was small, and there were only about a dozen merchant houses that advertised consistently in newspapers.[12] It was doubtless difficult to compete and succeed in so restricted a market. Nevertheless, it was the struggle for political independence and for an independent means of newspaper production that dominated these first tumultuous years. In the absence of any representative institutions, the press was the primary means of expressing settler discontent.

The already super-heated atmosphere was fuelled by personal rivalries, vendettas and petty disputes among newspaper proprietors and employees. Libellous insults, verbal threats, physical assault and even, on occasion, duels, all added to the heady mix. Most disputes involved individuals from rival papers. For example, *Herald* printer John Moore physically assaulted the *Auckland Chronicle*'s editor John Kitchen and was duly fined. Kitchen and Falwasser engaged in a protracted and all-too-typical slanging match in their respective publications: when the former contemptuously referred to 'Our Lady of the Mangle', Falwasser replied that Mr Kitchen's name was where he came from.[13] Other colourful incidents involved disgruntled readers. In 1844, Falwasser was called out for a duel by the eccentric Lieutenant Philpotts R. N. of H.M.S. *Hazard*, who was aggrieved at the *Times*'s account of operations against Hone Heke. Shots were exchanged on the site of what is now the Northern Club. Falwasser was said to have received a bullet through his coat-tail, while his antagonist lost a button.[14]

Business and politics, 1843–62

Although these sorts of dramas and rivalries continued for some time, the unsatisfactory dependence on the government press ended in April 1843. From this time, Auckland newspapers had an existence independent of the Crown Colony government, and managed to achieve considerable stability. It was somewhat ironic that the city's first long-standing newspaper, the *Southern Cross, New Zealand Guardian and Auckland, Thames and Bay of Islands Advertiser*, was edited by Samuel Martin, the passionately partisan former editor of the *Herald*. The irony was nicely compounded by the fact that Martin used the £641 awarded to him for breach of his former contract to travel to Sydney and purchase a printing press.

The *Southern Cross* made its first appearance on 22 April 1843. Subscriptions were 10s a quarter, and the advertising rate 3s per inch. Its motto *Luceo non uro* ('I enlighten but do not burn') was perhaps a signal of intent, announcing a new era of independence and endurance for the press.[15] The first edition certainly made a strong claim to be an independent voice for the settler community: 'In the conduct of this paper we shall be guided by two principles, truth and impartiality, throwing our lot in with our former friends, the public.'[16]

But both these avowals – of impartial independence and of speaking on behalf of the public at large – need to be critically assessed within the context of the times. Samuel Martin was a vociferous exponent of self-government and an activist on behalf of land claimants. The paper's founder, manager and proprietor, William Brown, was also a fervent campaigner for self-government and a vocal critic of Crown Colony government. Both men's antagonism was heightened by disgust at the self-interested speculation by officials in the first sales of city lots in April 1841. This antagonism was shared by Auckland's business community, of which Brown was a prominent member. With Dr John Logan Campbell, he presided over Brown and Campbell, one of the town's first and most prosperous commercial merchant houses.[17] Not surprisingly, advertisements for Brown and Campbell featured prominently in the pages of the *Southern Cross*: the enterprising merchants' newspaper and business interests effectively dovetailed, as did their political and economic agendas.

Brown and Campbell were pioneers of Auckland's business community, and their political stance was in many respects inextricably linked to for-warding that community's prosperity, power and status. Self-government, a more effective infrastructure in the form of port and road facilities, and the ability to acquire land and profit from land sales were all goals that would smooth the path of men of commerce like themselves. It was in fact this settler élite (sometimes referred to by contemporaries as 'the Senate' or 'the Clique') which comprised 'the public' for whom the *Southern Cross* was crusading.

When the first issue announced that 'Our every interest is necessarily involved in the prosperity of the Colony',[18] the proprietors were speaking no more than the truth. Owning and operating a newspaper provided not only a forum for their own political aims and views, but a means to facilitate, both through advertising and substantive articles and editorials, the progress of Auckland business interests. Thus the first edition of the paper contained articles designed to advocate Auckland as a 'field for Emigration and the investment of English capital'.[19] In future issues, the paper would often act as an advocate and vital spur to commercial endeavour. On 20 January 1852, for example, John Logan Campbell and four other Auckland businessmen, well aware of how gold had benefited Australian business activity, ran an advertisement offering a £100 reward for 'any one who shall first discover an available Gold Field in the Province of New Ulster'.[20] Within a very short time, an ex-Californian miner came forward declaring that he had discovered gold at Coromandel.[21]

Political goals and economic goals were inextricable in this early period, and self-government in the form of representative institutions was deemed the best means of advancing settler financial and property interests. Even though Brown and Martin were appointed to the Legislative Council in 1844, they remained fervently opposed to the government. The very issue of the *Southern Cross* which announced their appointments went on to describe the council as 'a mere mockery of the rights of the people'.[22]

Late in 1844, Brown and Martin both journeyed to Britain; the former went temporarily on business, but the latter did not return. In his partner's absence, Dr John Logan Campbell took over managing the *Southern Cross*. Finding that the paper was losing ground in the difficult economic climate precipitated by the New Zealand Wars, he suspended it from April 1845 to July 1847. Brown returned in 1847 and resumed publication. The advocacy of the paper doubtless assisted his burgeoning political career. He was again elected to the Legislative Council of New Ulster, and in 1854 to Parliament, representing Auckland City. Early in 1855, he was chosen for the powerful and prestigious position of Superintendent of the Province. However, family matters caused him to return permanently to Scotland in the same year. Brown nevertheless continued to play an important role in the *Southern Cross*, appointing a series of talented individuals to serve as editor.[23]

The next Auckland newspaper to achieve some stability emerged in 1845, during the *Southern Cross*'s temporary closure. John Williamson, the founder and proprietor of the new venture, believed that his then only competitor, the *Auckland Times*, was overly preoccupied with the demands of land claimants. A sympathetic advocate of Maori, Williamson was assisted by the Wesleyan Mission, which provided funding to purchase a press. By the time the *Southern Cross* recommenced publication in July 1847, the *New Zealander* was a well-established bi-weekly.[24]

Each of the city's major papers fought its own political corner. While the *Southern Cross* remained a vocal and ardent critic of Crown Colony government, the *New Zealander* was less confrontational. During Grey's period as governor, it defended both Grey and his policies. Williamson, originally a printer from Northern Ireland, played a prominent political role in New Zealand, and used the newspaper to espouse his political point of view. He was a member of the Auckland Provincial Council for twenty-two years, Superintendent of the province for three separate terms, and a member of Parliament from 1855 until 1875. The two newspapers were mouthpieces for the two main political groups in Auckland. Although both favoured self-government, the *New Zealander* accepted Grey's timetable for its introduction. After the elections of 1853, this political dichotomy continued, as individuals from each newspaper became active members of the government, with the assistance and support of their respective publications. The *Southern Cross* and the *New Zealander* were thus integral to the political process in Auckland, both before self-government and after its introduction. Each had its own rival factions, and the press was the primary forum for spirited political attack and defence, as well as a pool from which political candidates were drawn.[25]

The few newspapers that attempted to break out of this pattern of political allegiance in the late 1850s were short-lived. The *Examiner*, in its first edition on 11 December 1856, announced that it would aim at establishing 'an organ untrammelled by party ties'. It lasted four years, largely due to its proprietors' perseverance rather than public support. Similarly, the *Telegraph*, launched in September 1859, and the *Independent*, in October 1859, survived only five and three months, respectively.[26]

But even though the two major politically aligned papers endured, their longevity did not reflect any financial success as business enterprises. Fortunately, both were linked to successful printing establishments. William Brown's continued financial backing of the *Southern Cross* reputedly cost him £10,000. However, the General Printing Office, from which the *Southern Cross* was issued, earned a handsome profit. Similarly, John Williamson, who with William Chisholm Wilson ran the rival *New Zealander*, carried that newspaper on the back of their increasingly profitable general printing business.[27] In recognition of the paper's pro-government views, Williamson and Wilson soon became the Government Printers, and at the same time, expanded their non-government clientele. Their printing enterprise grew so large and successful that they constructed Auckland's first gas works at the rear of the printing office, in order to supply it with the necessary gas.[28] This measure was typical of their forward-thinking business acumen. Wilson, in particular, was attuned to the latest developments in print technology, introducing the first printing machine and the first news folding machine to the country, as well as importing a complete lithographic plant for the production of mining plans, show cards and labels.[29]

Neither the *New Zealander* nor the *Southern Cross* made money for their proprietors in this period, although it was likely that the papers' existence, and notably the various services they provided for the burgeoning business community, helped indirectly to bolster the profits of their respective printing businesses. Instead of being perceived as money-making propositions, newspapers were valued and maintained for their important social, commercial and political functions. They were deemed a vital and influential component of life in the new colony, despite the fact that they incurred considerable cost. However, the days of running a newspaper as an unprofitable adjunct to a profitable printing enterprise were numbered.

Profit and populism: daily papers for the masses, 1863–70

The 1860s and 1870s were a major turning point in the growth and evolution of the Auckland press. From being unprofitable, overtly politically aligned weeklies or bi-weeklies intent on furthering the political and/or economic aims and personal political ambitions of the city's social and economic élite, they were transformed into profitable mass dailies, aimed at a more diverse and expanding readership. Political allegiance by no means disappeared, as the new type of daily newspaper still possessed an obvious political stance. Links with the city's financial and commercial élite remained strong, reinforced through advertising relationships, editorials, business notices and market news, as well as supportive pro-business feature articles. What did disappear was the notion that a newspaper and newspaper ownership were primarily a means to furthering the political career of an editor or proprietor. The new type of newspaper proprietor was more entrepreneur than political activist. Wilson was the first and foremost example of this profit-minded breed.

The times were ripe for a more populist and profitable type of newspaper. Between 1863 and 1864, the population of Auckland town rose from 8000 to

12,500.[30] During the booming 1870s, the population of Auckland Province grew from about 60,000 to 95,000.[31] The pattern of migration in the 1860s and 1870s brought a predominantly working-class population to New Zealand, but they were an increasingly literate working class. These people began to form the bulk of newspaper readers. Auckland newspapers, which had previously been aimed at a more select minority, were transformed in the wake of this unprecedented population surge. Simultaneously, the combined technologies of the steam engine and cylindrical printing press made it suddenly possible to print enough copies of newspapers to reach and maintain higher circulations.[32] In the course of 1862, Auckland's two major papers, the *New Zealander* and the *Southern Cross*, changed from being relatively costly subscription publications aimed at a small élite to mass dailies. The switch to daily publication was accompanied by a price reduction: from 6d to 3d.[33] Both of those papers were, at the point of change, floundering financially. The former was nearing the end of its existence, although the latter would continue for another fourteen somewhat rocky and eventful years.

By contrast, the second *New Zealand Herald*, which confidently and with a commendable lack of superstition, commenced daily publication on Friday, 13 November 1863, was in fine financial fettle from the start. As proudly announced in the first issue, it was founded for financial rather than political profit: 'this journal will be conducted upon the straight-forward and intelligible principle of mutual benefit to patrons and proprietors'.[34] Proprietors William Chisholm Wilson and David Burns (who sold out to Wilson within a year) were veterans of the *New Zealander*. Late in 1863, Wilson dissolved his partnership with John Williamson, believing the *New Zealander*'s pro-Maori stance to be unpopular with the settler population and bad for the paper's future financial viability. This view proved correct. Williamson's *New Zealander* staggered on for another three years: following an office fire in May 1866, no attempt was made to revive it.[35]

Wilson, an experienced printer who had worked on the first *New Zealand Herald and Auckland Gazette* before serving as the practical manager of the *New Zealander*, began energetically setting up another newspaper and printing business immediately upon severing ties with Williamson. His aim was to create a daily that was more in keeping with public opinion, and more profit-oriented. He promptly lined up assurances from a range of businesses to advertise in the new newspaper. From the outset, the *Herald* thus had solid financial support in the form of advertising revenue from some of the key commercial and industrial enterprises in Auckland. Impressively, by the end of its first week of publication, Wilson had managed to secure the advertising

William Chisholm Wilson, who founded the New Zealand Herald *on 13 November 1863.* NEW ZEALAND HERALD, H280604.

support of 150 Auckland business firms.[36] His publication, unlike so many of its predecessors, was organised on sound financial lines.

The new paper was keen to portray itself as an independent proponent of public opinion which had 'no personal, political or party purpose to serve', one which would be 'the unflinching advocate of the true and legitimate interests of New Zealand and those of the province of Auckland as well'.[37] Yet despite this self-proclaimed independence from personal political or party allegiances, its stance was very much in keeping with the views of both a prominent political group and those of the city's commercial élite. Its bellicosity towards 'the native rebellion' mirrored the view of the majority of the city's capitalists: men such as W. T. Buckland, Samuel Jackson, Hugh Carleton, J. C. Firth, and W. C. Daldy.[38] This group's belief that Maori needed to be decisively defeated was accompanied by the notion that Maori land should come more freely into European hands. Espousing such views put the *Herald* firmly in the camp of the Fox–Whitaker Ministry of 1863–64. Often described as a 'war ministry', it was dominated by Auckland moneyed interests. Three of its key members, Reader Wood, Frederick Whitaker, and Thomas Russell were influential members of Auckland's business élite.[39]

Both at its inception and in the years to come, the *Herald*'s stance on most issues was very much in accord with that of Auckland's captains of commerce. As one historian has observed: 'The *Herald* . . . so often and so felicitously captured the local mood that its editorials might almost have been regarded as the business community thinking aloud in public.'[40] In its first issue, it announced the intention to promote and encourage capital development and business enterprise as a 'great colonial cause'.[41] Subsequent issues included regular weekly articles paying tribute to 'Our Manufacturers'. A reporter would tour through various Auckland factories and workplaces, describing the work processes, materials and finished product with relentless enthusiasm.[42]

In addition, the *Herald* provided a range of services specially designed to serve and inform the local business community. Most significantly, like its predecessors but on a more extensive scale, it offered advertising space. This not only provided revenue but was in turn a vital adjunct to many business endeavours: newspaper advertising was both a major ingredient in raising public awareness about a business and an important means by which many businesses achieved and increased financial profit. Overseas commercial links were also cultivated. In the first month of publication, the editor hastened to assure the merchant princes of the city that the new daily would 'be transmitted to all the principal building houses having mercantile intercourse with Auckland; also to shipping agents at various seaports of London, Liverpool, Leith, Bristol, Glasgow, Belfast, Dublin, Cork, etc.'[43] A free advertising sheet delivered on Tuesday, Thursday and Saturday would include a summary of business engagements and appointments, and chronicle the arrival and departure of shipping together with 'any other matter of immediate interest that may arise'.[44]

In addition to these various business-friendly features and services, the paper offered enough local, political and overseas news to satisfy Auckland's growing population. Increasingly from the 1870s, the *Herald* boasted a more diverse range of items concerned with cultural developments and leisure activities. Entertainment reviews, stories about fashion and gardening, as well as a 'Ladies Column', all helped to ensure a loyal readership from the expanding Auckland community. These sorts of items featured particularly prominently in the *Herald*'s Saturday supplement. In addition, the rural and suburban market was not neglected. From 1866, Wilson published a separate

Alfred George Horton joined forces with William and Joseph Wilson as a proprietor for the New Zealand Herald *in 1876.* NEW ZEALAND HERALD, H_HISTPERSHORTON.

Weekly Herald, Onehunga and Otahuhu Courier and General Country Advertiser, which in 1876 amalgamated with the *Weekly News*. From 1877 known as the *Auckland Weekly News*, this enduring and much-loved illustrated compendium was especially appreciated in news-hungry rural communities.[45]

The joining together of these two weeklies was part of a broader, very timely merger which took place in 1876. In that year, Alfred George Horton, a former proprietor of the *Thames Advertiser*, purchased the ailing *Southern Cross*.[46] A few weeks later, William Chisholm Wilson died, leaving the *Herald* in the capable hands of his two sons, Willam Scott Wilson and Joseph Liston Wilson. Rather than engage in competition with a potentially powerful rival, negotiations were opened for an amalgamation. The result was an enduring and profitable union of publishing expertise and acumen: the Wilson brothers and Horton entered into a partnership as owners of four papers, a daily and a weekly published from each office. On 1 January 1877, the *Southern Cross* was incorporated into the *New Zealand Herald* and the two weeklies were merged.[47]

The impact of this move was to strengthen even further the growing *Herald* publishing house. In addition to boasting a popular and financially viable Auckland daily with a loyal and extensive advertising clientele, it was now augmented by a popular, richly illustrated weekly.

The *Herald*'s political stance and editorial perspective on economic matters had from the outset fitted hand in glove with the local business community. Now the printing and publishing business began to flourish even more rapidly than it had done previously, as Horton brought a range of talents to the partnership. An experienced printer, editor, reporter and newspaper proprietor, he was particularly interested in the technological side of the printing industry, undertaking several trips abroad to keep abreast of the latest developments. As a result, the *Herald* consistently led in technical improvements. It acquired New Zealand's first rotary press in 1883, a web machine in 1887, linotypes in 1898, and in 1909 was the first paper to adopt classification of wanted advertisements.

Horton's interest in technology also led him to take a prominent part in founding the United Press Association in 1879.[48] This body ensured that each newspaper's local news was made available, forming a pool of national news upon which all New Zealand papers could draw. International news was also supplied by the association, thus ending the competition between rival papers to monopolise telegraph cables.[49]

Competition between newspapers had become particularly intense by the time the United Press Association was formed. An impressive number of papers were launched in New Zealand in the late nineteenth century, most notably in the period from 1860–79.[50] Auckland in the late 1860s and early 1870s was a particularly fertile place for new newspapers, largely because prospective proprietors were encouraged by the expanding population. Unlike the *Herald*, however, most of these new ventures were fairly short-lived. The *Auckland Evening Post*, for example, began in November 1867 and ended shortly thereafter; the *Auckland Free Press*, a penny daily, lasted only six weeks; the *Morning News* began and ended in 1871; and the *Auckland Daily News* (1869), a throw-back to the old style newspaper as political advocate, lasted as long as it took to get Judge Gillies elected Provincial Superintendent. The *Auckland and Thames Leader* was published from 1869 until 1870; the *Morning Advertiser* appeared in 1870, but ceased publication the same year; while the *Evening News* endured from 1867 until 1871.[51] As the twentieth century progressed, it became harder and harder for aspiring newspapers to compete with established dailies such as the *Herald*. Technological advances increased the reach of the larger papers, while plant and production costs became prohibitive.[52]

A Herald *printer at work, when producing a newspaper was a more mechanical and labour-intensive process than it is today.* NEW ZEALAND HERALD, H_051103.

But in 1870, one great and enduring rival for the *Herald* successfully took root in Auckland. William Tyrone Ferrar, a young man employed on the commercial staff of the *Evening News*, believed there was a market for another evening paper with a different political perspective. He enlisted George McCullough Reed, recently arrived from Victoria, as a partner and editor. The first edition of their new venture, the *Evening Star*, appeared on 8 January 1870. Although it started off well, Reed and Ferrar were conscious of the need to acquire both more capital and a more experienced collaborator. They were fortunate to attract the interest of an outstanding and resourceful news reporter, Henry Brett, currently employed by the *Herald*. The move was both beneficial and astute, for in so doing they forestalled Brett's attempts to purchase the rival *Evening News*. Instead, in March 1870, he purchased a one-third interest in the *Evening Star*. By the end of 1871, Ferrar had sold out to Reed. Brett and Reed then purchased the *Evening News*, incorporating it with the *Star*.[53]

The *Evening Star* (from 1874 the *Auckland Evening Star*, and from 1887 the *Auckland Star*) was a major supporter of the developing liberal perspective, and later an advocate for the Liberal Party. Originally the *Star*'s motto was simply 'Press Onward', but in 1871 it employed the following verse:

> For the cause that lacks assistance
> For the wrong that needs resistance,
> For the future in the distance
> And the good that we can do.[54]

The new paper's message and tone hit a chord with Aucklanders. From the outset, the *Star* enjoyed considerable financial success: originally only four pages, it was so well patronised by advertisers that its news columns were restricted. From a circulation of 2700 in 1872 it had reached 4700 by 1875.[55] By 1879, it had increased its size several times, and a Saturday supplement introduced in 1875 proved extremely popular. By 1898, the *Auckland Star* boasted the highest circulation of any daily in the country.[56]

Henry Brett, who became sole proprietor in 1876 when he purchased Reed's share for £4,000, proudly presided over this success story. He appointed as editor Thomson Wilson Leys, a strong Liberal in politics, who had joined the *Star*'s staff as a sub-editor after serving an apprenticeship on the *Southern Cross*. In 1889, the talented and capable Leys became Brett's partner in the business, which grew to include a number of other publications, most notably the *New Zealand Graphic* (1890) as well as a number of popular guidebooks and almanacs. In 1900, Brett and Leys formed the Brett Printing and Publishing Company.[57]

Aspects of the *Star*'s operations in its early years have a particular charm and vitality, largely due to Brett's energy, innovation and enthusiasm. A former pair-oar champion of England's south coast, Brett had more than proved his worth in the rowing race to board ships at the harbour entrance and scoop the latest news. As proprietor of the *Star*, he took a keen interest in this competition, and acquired several boats especially designed for the purpose. When news by telegraph began in the early 1870s, he was also an adept participant in the competitive game of monopolising the telegraph and thus delaying access to rival newspapers. Extended biblical extracts were frequently telegraphed, a practise that continued until regulations spoiled the fun by forbidding the transmission of messages over 200 words.[58]

Brett also pioneered the colourful practise of using pigeons to carry news. In 1873, during a contest for the provincial superintendency, the *Star* knew the

Thomson Wilson Leys and Henry Brett, whose talents and business acumen helped to make the Auckland Star *the most popular newspaper in New Zealand by 1898.* T. W. LEYS, ALEXANDER TURNBULL LIBRARY, HERMAN JOHN SCHMIDT COLLECTION, PACOLL-3059, 1/1-001452; HENRY BRETT, AUCKLAND CITY LIBRARY, A 12295.

election results before its rivals courtesy of the birds. Pigeons were also used in 1875 when Sir George Grey delivered an important speech at Thames. The *Star* and the *Thames Advertiser* pooled their report, which filled a full page. This was photographed and sent to Auckland by pigeon post. The photographs were then deciphered through a strong magnifying glass, rewritten and handed to the *Star*'s compositors. Pigeons continued to be used into the 1890s, particularly for results of race meetings.[59]

Expansion and concentration: a family affair, 1870–1923

With the establishment of the *Auckland Star* in 1870, Auckland's press enjoyed a long and relatively settled Golden Age. For many decades to come, residents could choose from a conservative morning paper or a more liberal evening one. In some respects, this pattern resembled the previous dual reign of the conservative business-minded *Southern Cross* and the reforming *New Zealander*. However, there were substantial differences, most importantly a more profit-minded business ethos and the changed role and aims of the proprietors. Although neither the *Herald* nor the *Star* had relinquished a political stance, their respective proprietors no longer used the papers to pursue personal political careers. Both sets of proprietors were keen to establish and run their newspapers as profitable enterprises, and their target readership was no longer just the Auckland élite, but the broader community.

The new-style mass dailies enjoyed a 'business to business' relationship with the city's business community.[60] They shared with that community an incentive to provide a popular high-quality newspaper that would attract as large a readership as possible. As purchasers of newspaper advertising space, businesses were conscious that greater circulation meant greater exposure and higher impact. The ability to attract and retain advertising revenue from the business community was at the same time the mainstay of the newspaper's financial success.[61] The papers in turn offered several other services to business. For example, in addition to regular business news, from around 1880s onwards they published prospectuses of businesses being formed. This offered the public the opportunity to invest in these concerns by buying shares, a service that helped to draw together the business and broader communities.[62]

This 'business to business' relationship between the two major daily newspapers and Auckland's business community was strengthened by the fact that both sets of proprietors were themselves talented and astute businessmen, with diverse and extensive business interests. Alfred George Horton, for example, not only presided over a flourishing newspaper and publishing enterprise, but also had interests in the Bank of New Zealand, New Zealand Insurance, and the Bank of New Zealand Estates Company.[63] William Wilson was a director of the Bank of New Zealand, the New Zealand Insurance Company, the Northern Shipping Company, the Accident Assurance Company, the Northern Boot Company, and the Riverhead paper mill.[64] Henry Brett, in addition to his publishing interests, was a director of the Auckland Savings Bank and of the Kauri Timber Company.[65] T. W. Leys had interests in the *Napier Daily Telegraph*, the Northern Roller Milling Company, and the Auckland Gas Company.[66]

As well as these business interests, the founding proprietors of the *Herald* and the *Star* were high-profile public men, who engaged in a range of philanthropic and community-minded projects. Brett was Mayor of Auckland for one year (1877) and served on the City Council in 1877–78, although this reflected his status and influence rather than any broader political ambition. A supporter of the Ballance and Seddon administrations, he declined a seat in the Legislative Council in 1899, and twice declined a knighthood before finally accepting in 1926. He made generous gifts to Auckland University College and to the Auckland Art Gallery, among others. Leys also declined two offers of a seat on the Legislative Council, and was involved in numerous civic and community affairs. His most generous legacy was the establishment of the Leys Institute in Ponsonby, a project initiated by a bequest from his brother William and further endowed by Leys himself.[67] William Scott Wilson was a generous supporter of the Young Men's Christian Association, while Joseph Liston Wilson's 1902 obituary described him as 'a zealous worker in many religious and social movements claiming for their aim the spiritual and moral advance of their fellow creatures'.[68]

Auckland was thus fortunate to have newspaper proprietors of this calibre, who combined business acumen with community-mindedness. It was also fortunate for the fate of both the *Herald* and the *Star* that their descendants and successors proved able to maintain a high standard of business capability and foresight. Although one or two competitors momentarily appeared on the horizon, these two venerable dailies dominated the Auckland newspaper market, operating within a cosy duopoly that would prove surprisingly durable. Technological expansion and concentration aided the growth and increasing prosperity of their considerable publishing interests, which remained under family control for remarkably long periods of time.

In 1900, the Brett Printing and Publishing Company was registered as the publishers of the *Auckland Star*, the *Graphic*, the *New Zealand Farmer* and several other publications. In 1920, a public issue was made of £100,000 in shares and stocks in the company, the proprietors retaining £150,000 of the total capital of £250,000.[69] Brett and Leys remained managing directors until their deaths in 1927 and 1924, respectively. W. Cecil Leys, after serving in the First World War, was appointed editor of the *Star* in 1926, and managing editor in 1927. Shortly before he died in 1950, his son T. Hilton Leys was appointed managing director. In 1929, the directors of Brett Printing and Publishing founded New Zealand Newspapers Ltd, after purchasing the *Lyttelton Times* and the *Christchurch Star*. W. Cecil Leys was one of the new company's five directors. When G. H. Reed returned from Australia in 1927 and started a rival evening paper, the *Auckland Sun*, competition was fierce but short-lived, as the *Star* bought out Reed in 1930.[70] Brett and Leys thus controlled an expanding and increasingly sophisticated publishing empire until their deaths in the 1920s, while Leys' descendants continued to play an important role until well into the twentieth century.

The Wilson and Horton families followed the same pattern of expanding their publishing interests and buying up attractive publications, but retained an even tighter family control throughout the process. In 1903, although death removed the three partners W. S. Wilson, J. L. Wilson and A. G. Horton, the management of Wilson and Horton devolved upon Henry Horton, son of A. G. Horton, and W. R. Wilson, son of W. S. Wilson. At different times, other sons and descendants of the original partners were associated with them in running the business. By the early twentieth century, they presided over a thriving commercial printing establishment as well as a healthy stable of newspaper and magazine publications. In 1913, they bought the *New Zealand Graphic* from Brett Publishing and incorporated it with the *Weekly News*. When the *New Zealand Herald* and other Wilson and Horton interests were made into a company, Wilson and Horton Ltd, in 1925 the business had a capital of £650,000. Although a public company, transfer of shares was restricted to relatives of the original partners, the whole of the issued capital was still held by descendants of the original families, and all company directors were members of the Wilson and Horton families. It was not until November 1961 that the first open public share issue took place.[71]

Politics and pride: advertising achievements, 1923–63

Through the twentieth century, the *Herald* and the *Auckland Star* continued along much the same course as they had set at the outset. They remained competitive, but with the understanding that the *Herald* was the established morning paper and the *Star* the established evening paper. Although the *Star*'s political association with the Liberal party waned with the fortunes of that party, it remained to the left of the conservative *Herald*. This political stance should not be exaggerated, however. Neither of Auckland's mass dailies ever supported the labour movement. Both took a dim view of strikes and were indignantly opposed to phenomena such as riots by the unemployed. As press historian Patrick Day has observed: 'Labour newspapers in Auckland, as in New Zealand, faced the insuperable opposition of the entrenched press. Their philosophy was deemed antithetical to the essentially pro-business orientation of the press.'[72]

But if Auckland's mass daily newspapers did not embrace the cause of labour, they prided themselves on their ongoing contribution to the economic and cultural progress of the city, on their own progressive record as business enterprises, and on their congenial longstanding relationship with the Auckland businesses which provided advertising revenue. This pride is nowhere more apparent than in the various commemorative issues that have appeared over the years. The *Herald*'s 13 November 1923 edition, for example, celebrated sixty successful years under the headline 'Beautiful and Progressive Auckland'. Articles paid glowingly emotive tributes to Auckland's economic buoyancy and to the *Herald*'s role in recording key events and bolstering the city's strong sense of community. Praise was also directed toward the paper's longstanding advertisers, many of whom, such as the Bank of New Zealand, the Auckland Gas Company, and New Zealand Insurance, had advertised in the first 1863 issue.[73]

The *Auckland Star*'s diamond jubilee edition of 7 May 1930 was similarly brimming with parochial pride and fervent praise for the *Star*'s part in fostering the 'almost unbelievable' progress of the city. Tributes were paid to Brett and Leys, and to the paper's origins as a pro-Grey 'red-blooded organism with any amount of ginger'.[74] The paper's financial reporting was also commended, and, like the *Herald*, the *Star* paid tribute to its longstanding advertisers. Some of those advertisers responded in kind by placing their own laudatory messages. The department store Milne and Choyce, for example, effused: 'We have grown up together in intimate business relationship, and it would be remiss upon our part did we not take the opportunity of publicly expressing our appreciation of services rendered through the medium of your paper.'[75]

In the prosperous economic climate that prevailed following the Second World War, Auckland firms advertised more extensively in the two major dailies than ever before. On 29 November 1958, the *Herald* ran an article proudly announcing that the department store Farmers had purchased four record-breaking pages of adverts to highlight its Christmas goods: 'This is the largest single advertisement which has appeared in the New Zealand Herald and, we believe, is the largest single advertisement ever to be published in any newspaper in New Zealand.'[76] On 1 August 1960, it could boast another advertising first, when the number of classified ads placed in the *Herald* in one day represented a record for any New Zealand newspaper.[77]

In common with the many Auckland merchants who purchased advertising space, the *Herald* was a keen critic of import licensing. In 1959, Labour politicians began to express increasing concerns about the paper's conservative political bias. One referred to it as a 'literary cyclops', adding that a Labour MP would 'have to drive a rocket to the moon to get a small headline in the Herald'.[78] Prime Minister Walter Nash also spoke out against this perceived bias: 'On behalf of the Government and of the people of New Zealand as a whole—I do ask for fair and balanced comment from our newspapers. Let them justify their long-claimed position as the watchdog of the public.'[79]

Yet the idea of the press as an independent watchdog had arguably always been more apparent than real; certainly in Auckland the mass dailies had clearly espoused a political stance from the outset. This did not, however, impair their ability to provide a range of social and political functions. Watchdogs had always been one-eyed but nevertheless fulfilled a range of functions, from reporting local and international news, to providing a range of commendable community services and initiatives, such as scholarships and educational programmes, sports competitions and events, literary and cultural activities, charity drives, philanthropic donations, and much more. Improvements in layout legibility and design, plus an increase in popular lifestyle features, all helped to keep their circulations healthy and their advertising revenue buoyant in the early 1960s.

There was no lack of public confidence in the *Herald* as a successful business enterprise. When Wilson and Horton issued its first public share issue in November 1961, the response was overwhelming and the shares heavily oversubscribed.[80] In addition to having become a vast and flourishing commercial printing and publishing business, Wilson and Horton's flagship newspaper extolled itself as a great Auckland icon. In the special *Herald* centennial record issue of 13 November 1963, the paper proudly claimed credit not just for recording Auckland's progress, but for actively fostering it. Advertising was recognised as having played a significant part in promoting the city's seemingly inexorable progress. Indeed, a follow-up article a day later pursued this theme, hailing advertising as one of the two great purposes of the press:

> A daily newspaper serves two purposes – to present the news and to provide a shop window for the display of goods and services. The one function is complementary to the other. In one hundred years of uninterrupted daily publishing the Herald has enjoyed the advertising support of virtually every local and national business of importance in the country.[81]

The author went on to expand on advertising's indispensable benefits: by bringing products of industry to the notice of readers, it enlarged the markets available for the sale of goods and services, and by promoting greater production helped to lower the unit cost of consumer goods. The following day, the paper included an account of a cocktail party held in Farmers lounge to celebrate the *Herald* centenary. Among the 450 guests were representatives from eighteen Auckland firms that had advertised in the first 13 November 1863 edition.[82]

Foreign ownership and deregulation, 1965–2004

This intimate relationship with the business community, coupled with a perceived bias towards National, were by the late 1960s and early 1970s however, provoking more criticism from writers such as Michael Bassett and Gordon Parry.[83] When in 1965, Keith Holyoake's National Government passed the News Media Ownership Act precluding foreign ownership of New Zealand newspapers, Labour party members were prominent among those opposed to the Bill. This was largely because they hoped foreign ownership of even one newspaper might prove an antidote to the complacency and uniform political conservatism of the New Zealand press.[84]

Media commentators were also, from the late 1960s onwards, remarking on the steady decline in the number of New Zealand dailies and the concentration of ownership by a few large and influential publishing concerns. Concentration advanced a bit further in 1972, with the formation of Independent News Ltd. This company's origins were in the Wellington Publishing Company, formed in 1906. In 1964, just prior to the News Media Ownership Act, Rupert Murdoch had acquired a 30 per cent interest in that company. In 1970, it successfully took over Truth New Zealand Ltd, and in 1971 acquired Independent Publishers Ltd, which owned the *Waikato Times*. After purchasing Blundell Brothers Ltd, the publishers of Wellington's *Evening Post* in 1972, it changed its name to INL.[85] By 1973, New Zealand News (which had its origins in Brett Publishing) controlled the *Auckland Star*, the *Christchurch Star*, the *New Zealand Woman's Weekly*, *New Zealand Home Journal* and *New Zealand Farmer*. Wilson and Horton also owned several other publications in addition to the *Herald*, producing an estimated 30–40 per cent of all printed matter in New Zealand by the early 1970s.[86]

Following the demise of the News Media Ownership Act in 1975, international media conglomerates quickly came to dominate the New Zealand mediascape. With no cross-media ownership regulations and no prohibitions on vertical and horizontal ownership, by the late 1980s the country boasted the most deregulated media market in the world.[87] Auckland newspapers experienced several key developments in the wake of these changes. The most crucial were the rise and fall of the *Auckland Sun* in 1987; the resulting sale of New Zealand News to INL in 1989; the demise of the *Auckland Star* in 1991; and the sale of Wilson and Horton Limited to Independent News and Media of Dublin in 1996.

By the early 1980s, the *Auckland Star* was suffering a declining readership, a trend experienced by evening papers around the globe.[88] New Zealand News, which owned the paper, launched the *Auckland Sun* in an attempt to challenge the *Herald*'s longstanding dominance of the morning market. The *Herald* responded by increasing its size and improving conditions for advertisers. The *Sun* sank; its demise led to New Zealand News incurring considerable financial losses and selling off their publishing interests. Their Taranaki and Auckland titles were bought by INL, while Wilson and Horton bought their Hawke's Bay and South Island titles.[89]

Despite many valiant attempts by staff to increase circulation, the *Star* continued to flounder. In 1991, after losing $8 million in the previous financial year, INL closed the paper down, thus terminating a 127-year run.[90] In the poignant and apologetic final issue of 16 August 1991, publisher Alan Hitchens lamented the fact that, despite extensive restructuring, the hoped-for levels of circulation and advertising had not eventuated. He primarily blamed the depressed state of the New Zealand economy for the paper's failure, a factor also stressed by INL managing director Mike Robson in another 'farewell' article.[91] The *Sunday Star*, established in 1986, was not affected by the *Auckland Star*'s closure.

Although the *Herald* emerged in a monopoly position, it too was experiencing falling circulation. 'Granny Herald', described by one commentator as 'the bulletin board of the Auckland establishment',[92] was perceived by many as somewhat stodgy and complacent. This complacency was shaken in November 1994, however, by a surprise raid in which Brierley Investments acquired a 29 per cent stake of Wilson and Horton Ltd. In May 1995, Irish media magnate Dr Tony O'Reilly's Independent News and Media of Dublin purchased that stake. By early 1996, the Wilson and Horton families sold their remaining shares in Wilson and Horton Ltd, to interests associated with O'Reilly, thus ending 133 years of family involvement in the company. By 1998, O'Reilly had 100 per cent control of Wilson and Horton Ltd.[93]

Since these developments, the *Herald* has undergone extensive restructuring and redevelopment. This has included launching a greatly expanded business section, changes in indexing and design format and expansion of the weekend (Saturday) edition.[94] To this day, it continues to enjoy primacy of place as Auckland's sole daily.[95]

Conclusion

The Auckland press has thus moved a long way from its origins. In the 1840s and 1850s, although unprofitable, newspapers played a key part in the political struggle. They were owned by locally based proprietors, either individuals or joint partners, who frequently had strong links to or were themselves part of the local commercial élite. The newspapers' function as a 'shop-window' for Auckland enterprises and advertisers further ensured an intimate relationship with the business community. Newspapers in this period operated not just as a means of advocating particular policies, but also as a stepping stone for the political careers of editors, proprietors and reporters alike. Political and economic agendas were largely inextricable. As a business, newspapers were a financial liability, and those that survived did so on the back of their proprietors' flourishing printing enterprises.

From 1863, with the establishment of the second *New Zealand Herald*, the city had its first newspaper run on sound business and organisational lines. It still espoused a particular political perspective, but the proprietors and employees no longer perceived the paper as a means to their own political advancement. Moreover, from the early 1860s, weekly newspapers were transformed into dailies aimed at a broader readership. The establishment of the *Auckland Star* in 1870 inaugurated a long and prosperous Golden Age, during which Aucklanders could choose from a conservative morning paper or a liberal evening one. The founding proprietors of these venerable dailies were astute businessmen, who maintained close relations with advertisers and kept pace with advancing technology. For many decades, they held close family control over what grew to be successful and extensive publishing enterprises, gradually acquiring a stable of newspapers and magazines through concentration, acquisition and merger.

The last decades of the twentieth century saw several key transformations in the Auckland newspaper scene, most notably the relaxation of restrictions on foreign media ownership in 1975. In some respects, foreign ownership has not apparently radically altered the local newspaper scene: there are important and obvious continuities. As in previous times, Auckland's sole surviving daily newspaper continues to engage with local, national and international business interests as a provider of services. It still maintains strong, mutually beneficial relationships with both the business and the broader communities.

Yet both foreign ownership and the deregulated media environment have brought significant change. In the past, the city's newspapers were an integral part of the local and national business communities, whereas the *Herald* now forms part of a network of global ownership and control. Auckland's daily newspaper is not, as was for so long the case, owned by people who are themselves prominent members of the local business community and who have interlocking and overlapping links to its many components.

The *Herald* still faces no local competitors for the Auckland daily newspaper market. It is, however, subject to the prime demand of profit generation.

Despite the idea of the press as a 'fourth estate', a newspaper is ultimately a business that needs to remain solvent by attracting readers and advertising revenue. This commercial imperative, as has been shown, is by no means a new phenomenon. But as several contemporary media commentators and critics have suggested, it has arguably assumed a more prominent role in New Zealand's deregulated multinational media industry. The degree to which newspapers in Auckland, and in New Zealand as a whole, have recently undergone a process of 'tabloidisation' has attracted critical comment, as has the degree to which public relations firms have colonised the business pages.[96] The somewhat uneasy relationship between theories about the press's role as a watchdog of liberal democratic society and the nature and impact of its business and commercial relationships is a subject that warrants ongoing critical observation and scholarly analysis.

CHAPTER NINE

Retail Innovation and the Farmers Trading Company: Auckland's Big Store

IAN HUNTER

This chapter examines the retail and management innovations wrought by one of the most significant firms in the Auckland retail sector by the mid-twentieth century, the Farmers Trading Company. Surveying the history of the firm between 1909 and 1930, it examines how through innovative merchandising, promotion and the adoption of American-style management practices the firm was able to successfully enter a market that was already replete with established firms. Largely through the distinctive management style of the firm's founder, Robert Laidlaw, the head office Hobson Street store developed an iconic status among Aucklanders, reinforced by its prominent position on the city skyline.

The chapter begins with a brief survey of the main trends in retailing over the period. It reviews the different types of retail structures in operation in the colony, and considers how changes in these structures paralleled those occurring in more developed economies, such as the United Kingdom and the United States. The firm of Laidlaw Leeds (later to become the Farmers Trading Company) is then profiled: commencing as a mail-order operation, the firm moved into retail sales after the First World War, and then into branch ownership. Overall, the experiences of Robert Laidlaw and Farmers Trading

Company are illustrative of the process of economic development in capitalist economies, whereby entrepreneurs break existing patterns and market structures using innovation and, in so doing, create wealth.

New Zealand retailing – background

In all its numerous manifestations – the stand-alone store, the general store, the emporium, the arcade, the department store – retailing was central to the development of the colonial economy. The earliest form of mercantile arrangement had been the trading post. From the 1830s onwards, traders established these mercantile outposts at a number of locations around New Zealand. One of the most popular was Kororareka (modern-day Russell) in the north. Here, promoters such as Gilbert Mair, who established a trading station at Te Wahapu, three miles south of Kororareka, and Samuel Stephenson, the son of a London shipowner, who opened a trading station at nearby Okiato, located substantial enterprises for the benefit of whalers and shipping.[1] The numbers of vessels frequenting these spots were large. Early accounts suggest twenty or thirty at a time could be at anchor, some for months on end while their crews refitted and restocked.[2] To facilitate this process, traders brought in goods from many points on the globe: American tobacco, Irish butter, English cheeses and ales, Jamaican rum, salt from Liverpool, sugar from Mauritius, calico and cloth by the yard, cross-cut saws, spades, tents, tea, rice, blankets, cutlery, flour, soap, ironmongery, even two- and six-roomed homes. At Kororareka, some locals, like John Montefiore aboard *Tuscan*, traded from their store-ships berthed offshore; while in the bay, auction marts and merchants established themselves along the waterfront, competing for the lucrative trade in ship-supply.

In July 1840, David Nathan took out the largest advertisement to date in the *New Zealand Advertiser and Bay of Islands Gazette*, to advise the residents of Kororareka of the opening of his Sydney Store retailing ready-made clothing, blankets, sheeting, cutlery, crockery and spirits, direct from wholesale houses in Sydney and Hobart. The ambitious Nathan did not remain in Kororareka, but followed the movement of population and enterprise southwards, venturing to the new capital, Auckland, in 1841. And it was here, with a location that was destined to become a determined centre for enterprise, that possibilities arose for more permanent and varied types of retail activity.

Quite aptly, the city retail district concentrated in the suitably named Commercial Bay. Wooden shops with tin and shingle roofs lined the bay and edged their way up Shortland Crescent. Within just over a year, the population had increased to about 3000, and demanded, among their other necessities of life, increasing amounts of retail goods. Shops were not of a uniform character: one in three, remarked John Graham on his short stay in 1842, was a grog shop.[3] While the predominance of the liquor trade would subside, one characteristic that did not (nor would it in any of the main cities that developed around New Zealand) was for retail stores to be concentrated in the central hub of the city.

Between the 1840s and the 1880s, retailing in New Zealand advanced out of sheer need. With a population which at times expanded by 27 per cent per year,[4] the need for mercantile goods and retail services was acute. Although historians and economists have cited wool, whale oil, timber and gold as important in New Zealand's early years as a colony, the importation of textiles, clothing, tea, sugar, drapery and hardware consistently outweighed any of the efforts toward exporting. Between 1854 and 1864, imports were on average 130 per cent greater than exports, and drapery items were the largest single class of goods in this account. In 1880, for example, imports of apparel, drapery and woollens constituted 18 per cent of imports by value; by 1910, this figure had dropped to 10 per cent, although it still represented a sizeable proportion of economic activity. To put these figures in perspective, imports of textile goods in 1910 at £17 million were just slightly less than the value of butter exported that year from the thriving dairy industry.[5] Aside from clothing items, sugar, tea and spirits also featured heavily in the import account. In fact, it was not until the 1930s that the imports of hardware and ironmongery exceeded New Zealand's imports of sugar. The explanation for this is in itself revealing of the structure of New Zealand retail industry in the late nineteenth and early twentieth century as well as of patterns of consumption. By 1891, postal directories listed over 1100 bakers and confectioners across the colony, catering for consumers who clearly enjoyed the sweeter things of life in large amounts. Confectioner and family grocer Charles Laurie is but one example, yet his two-storey factory in Manukau Road used 150 tons of sugar annually in the manufacture and retail of marmalades, biscuits, jams, preserves, lozenges, candied peel (importing skins and limes direct from Genoa) and comfits.

In rural communities, country stores and general merchants serviced farming communities and outposts with a broad range of stock, while also acting as suppliers of credit, estate agents, auctioneers and postmasters. But the country storeowner in these instances was more than just a purveyor of goods; many were what David Hamer has described as 'town-boosters'. These boosters – influential town patriarchs, usually with extensive business connections – were able to direct and influence the development of a town, playing a central position in the motions of everyday life. Without him, and it was typically 'him', rural communities and isolated outposts would have languished.[6]

In the growing centres of Auckland, Wellington, Christchurch, Dunedin, Nelson and Invercargill, more sophisticated retail offerings could be sustained. Consequently, by the latter part of the nineteenth century, retailing in larger centres in New Zealand and Australia had a distinctively cosmopolitan appearance. Shoppers in Melbourne, Auckland or Dunedin could be assured that what they might purchase in Oxford Street, London, they could also purchase in their respective main shopping districts. In Dunedin, for example, Princes Street was home to the mercantile trade. Customers had a wide choice: Brown Ewing and Co. marketed the latest all-wool flannel produced locally by the Kaikorai Woollen Factory; Herbert Haynes and Co. retailed specialty products like Canadian tweeds, Japanese silks, Grecian cords and French merinos. Other retailers, such as Kirkpatrick, Glendining and Co., Thomson Strang and Co., and Mollison, Duthie and Co., sold a wide range of imported cloth, hats, jackets and shirts. The English firm Arthur Briscoe and Co. stocked a wide range of goods: stoves, fencing wire, table lamps, baths, flower vases, cricket bats and ice pitchers. Their wholesale premises in Princes Street contained 2000 manufacturers' catalogues. With branches in Britain, Australia and New Zealand, Briscoe and Co. (like some shipping, banking and insurance firms) was a nineteenth-century version of the multinational firm.[7]

Such was the dominance of the textile trade in the colony that other main centres also had clusters of large drapery firms. In Wellington, for example, Kirkcaldie & Stains sold a complete range of imported drapery, jackets, silks, millinery, underclothing, curtains, sheets, quilts, shirts and lace. So, too, did S. W. Alcorn, T. J. Steele, Wilson and Richardson (all on Lambton Quay), McDowell Brothers, opposite the Bank of New Zealand, and James Smith in Cuba Street.

How this industry functioned was crucial to understanding the development of the New Zealand retail environment: substantial firms were at both ends of the retail supply chain, with a cluster of large firms dominating wholesale supply of goods to the retail industry. Most, such as Sargood Son & Ewing, Ross & Glendining and, in Auckland, Archibald, Clark & Son, combined importation and distribution with local manufacture, often in textiles or footwear. Archibald, Clark & Son, for example, commenced operations in 1850, and by 1900 had over 500 staff across its Shortland Street warehouse and Grey Lynn shirt factory. Equally, Auckland warehouseman and manufacturers Macky, Logan, Steen and Co. had started in 1882, and by 1900 boasted over 200 staff and was successfully manufacturing the Cambridge brand of shirts and clothing as well as sustaining a London office for home buying. By 1900, the Dunedin firm of Ross & Glendining had approximately 300 staff in their warehouses situated in Wellington, Christchurch, Dunedin, Invercargill and Napier, which were in turn supported by the woollen mill at Roslyn, a clothing factory in Dunedin city, a farm at Lauder station, and head office – the overall organisation totalling around 1000 staff.[8]

The wholesale grocery trade repeated this industry structure. By 1891, there were 198 grocers and tea dealers across Auckland and suburbs, combining a range of produce and grocery items in their retail offerings. W. & J. Peet, for example, commenced business in Karangahape Rd in 1884, selling butter, cheese, bacon, maize and wheat. The shop hoarding emphasised Peet's position as a cash grocer, and with ten staff, four horses and two vans Peet made daily deliveries throughout Auckland town and country. Peet, and other grocers like him, were serviced by the dominant grocery warehouse in Auckland, L. D. Nathan and Co. Having grown considerably from its early beginnings in the Bay of Islands, the Auckland firm, now run by Lawrence David Nathan and Nathan Alfred Nathan, operated a warehouse in Shortland Street, with a tea warehouse and produce store in Customs Street – as well as a sizeable kauri gum business.

The large size of these wholesaling and manufacturing firms is instructive for two reasons. First, to run such enterprises required significant and determined attention to management, for these were not small undertakings by the standards of any developed nation at the time; secondly, had the retail trade itself not been buoyant, such an extensive wholesale industry would have floundered. But it did not.

Changes to this retail structure emerged from the latter part of the nineteenth century throughout the world with the development of the chain store. With its emphasis on selling a narrow range of lines, combined with distinctive store appearance and branch network, multiple retailing had commenced in Britain in the 1850s. By the 1870s, it had established itself in the men's clothing trade and the grocery trade before spreading out to other types of retailing. Grocer Thomas Lipton, for example, opened his first store in Glasgow in 1872, retailing tea and dairy produce, and by 1890 had over seventy branches in London.[9] In the United States, tea and tobacco stores pursued chain store structures in similar fashion. In New Zealand, there was one standout pioneer who seized upon this retail innovation: the Jewish merchant, Bendix Hallenstein.

Born in Brunswick, Germany, in 1835, Bendix Hallenstein followed his brothers to the Australian goldfields and together opened their first mercantile store in Victoria. In 1863, with the decline in the gold trade, Hallenstein moved to New Zealand and opened a general store in Invercargill, before settling in Queenstown. By the early 1870s, and aged in his mid-thirties, Hallenstein had managed to extend his general store business to branches at Arrowtown, Lawrence and Cromwell. Hallenstein then put in place plans to construct an ambitious purpose-built clothing factory in Dunedin to ensure consistent supply to his general stores. Overreaching himself, in 1875 he was forced to sell the factory to the National Insurance Company for £11,700, promptly leasing it back for the annual rate of £700. At this point, Hallenstein made his foray into chain stores. Like Lipton, Hallenstein economised on scarce capital by leasing premises. Taking over the lease of a retail store in the centre of Dunedin, he began retailing discount clothing, adding further branches in Christchurch and Timaru in 1876. The following year, 1877, he added branches in Oamaru and Greymouth, and Wellington in the North Island. By 1879, three years into his retail business, Hallenstein had added further branches in Auckland, Napier, Ashburton, Wanganui, Invercargill, Nelson, New Plymouth and Thames. This pace of expansion continued; by 1900, Hallenstein had expanded his operation to thirty-six branch stores throughout New Zealand, while his clothing factory employed 350 staff, producing 2500 garments per week on eighty sewing machines.[10]

Other retail promoters followed Hallenstein's lead in chain-store development. One well-known example is the Christchurch booksellers, printers and publishers Whitcombe and Tombs. Commencing in 1882, the partnership of George Whitcombe and George Tombs expanded steadily. In 1894, the company extended to Wellington, purchasing the business of Lyon and Blair, which gave them access to the North Island. By this stage, the firm had already opened a London office to streamline purchasing. In 1903, a Melbourne office was opened, where the son of George Whitcombe, Bertie Whitcombe, was appointed manager of the Melbourne office to assist with the company's expanding Australian trade. Having tried to enter the Auckland market for a number of years, the firm did so successfully in 1916, by acquiring the bookselling and stationery business of Upton and Co., and constructed a purpose-built printing works and retail premises on the corner of Queen and Durham Streets in Auckland.[11] Other branches then followed in Invercargill, Timaru, Lower Hutt, Hamilton and Hastings, supported by printing facilities in Auckland, Wellington and Dunedin.

Other chain-store retailers who began business in the nineteenth century included shoe retailer Robert Hannah, who commenced in Wellington in 1874, also supported by his own factory. The butchers R. and W. Hellaby ran a chain of stores in addition to their meat-processing plants, as did Wellington butcher

James Gear. Cycle manufacture and sales, too, figured among chain stores as early promoters in the trade. Robert Murie, for example, established his Invercargill cycle-manufacturing business in Invercargill in 1893, producing the Phoenix brand cycle.[12] Being the first to a region allowed the promoter to expand, and soon Murie had a chain of seven stores throughout Otago and Southland. Similar was Auckland businessman and colonial cycling champion, E. Reynolds, who commenced his cycle-manufacturing business in Auckland in 1895. Within a few years Reynolds had branches in Wellington, New Plymouth and Palmerston North. However, the largest cycle firm in the colony was based in Christchurch, Oates, Lowry and Co.[13] Commencing in 1880, Nicholas Oates and Alexander Lowry operated the Zealandia Cycle Works, producing branded bicycles of the same name. By the late 1800s, they had established branches in Napier and Ashburton along with a two-storey Christchurch factory and a staff of forty.

Interestingly, one international company also figured among New Zealand chain stores. The Singer Manufacturing Company opened their first store in New Zealand in 1883, and by 1906 had fourteen branches.

As New Zealand cities expanded, economies of scale became increasingly important in the retail industry. The department store, which had started as a retail form with the opening of Paris's Bon Marché in 1869, was firmly part of the New Zealand commercial landscape by the early 1900s. On a scale beyond the emporium or larger general store, the department store not only offered a wider variety of goods under one roof, it offered customers a distinct shopping experience, with specialist departments, bold merchandising and ample refreshments.[14]

The oldest of the Auckland department stores was Milne and Choyce. Starting in 1867, sisters Mary and Charlotte Milne purchased an existing millinery and drapery shop on the corner of Wyndham and Albert Streets at a cost of £281. By 1874, they had moved to larger premises on Queen Street, and in 1876 (after Charlotte Milne married Henry Choyce) the firm became known as Milne and Choyce. The business gradually extended the goods it stocked to include millinery, straw goods, jackets, waterproofs, drapery, haberdashery and underclothing. In 1901, Milne and Choyce became a public company, by which stage it employed over 140 people in its four-storey premises on the corner of Queen and Wellesley Streets. In 1909, the firm moved to the central Queen Street premises that it would occupy for the next sixty years. Determined to stay abreast of changes in fashion, the Milne sisters, like their other competitor, Smith and Caughey's, made regular buying trips to the United Kingdom and Europe.[15]

Smith and Caughey's, which had originally commenced trade as Smith's Cheap Drapery Warehouse on Queen Street in 1880, accentuated the kinds of characteristics seen in these large and growing drapery stores. Founded by Marianne Smith, the firm pursued a strategy of high turnover through low margins. In 1882, Andrew Caughey joined the firm and the name was changed to Smith and Caughey's. Like other Auckland merchants, Smith and Caughey found they could forge ahead and expand their enterprise despite the recessionary trend in the 1880s. By 1884, the firm was already able to move to the more expensive western side of Queen Street; clothes and drapery – like foodstuffs in the 1930s – proving a resilient consumer item. Rendells, too, commenced in Karangahape Road in 1882, and was within a short walk of Court Brothers, originally established in 1886. The Court brothers themselves, George and Frederick, had two stores by 1889, when they were joined by a third brother, John. In 1902, the brothers dissolved their partnership, and John took over the firm's two Queen Street stores while George continued with the renamed George Courts in Karangahape Rd. In 1910, and still expanding, John Court took over premises on the corner of Queen Street and Victoria Street East, in what would become known as one of Auckland's landmark department stores. McKenzies (starting in 1910 in Dunedin) and Woolworths, perhaps better classified as variety stores, were both later entrants. By 1933, the Sydney-based Woolworths company (unrelated to the American F. W. Woolworth) had twenty-three stores in Australia and eight in New Zealand.[16]

As Auckland's suburbs expanded in the years after the First World War, village-type shopping experiences followed. Mirroring a pattern of suburban development in Australia, urban 'high streets' developed offering a staple mix of retail offerings – butcher, baker, draper, fruiterer, chemist, newsagent, estate agent, confectioner, hair dresser, bank – to growing suburbs. Often such groups of stores were located at main road intersections, tram termini, or along the suburban main streets. The main street 'strip' shopping of Mt Eden, Mt Roskill, Pt Chevalier and Mt Albert was repeated throughout the city. Although a lingering reminder of an earlier pattern of colonial life, some retailers – butcher, baker, grocer, chemist, milk vendor, ice vendor – still took their carts up the city streets, calling on consumers in their homes. For a more intensive, and arguably better, shopping experience, the consumer ventured to the central city. And it was in the cities that the larger emporiums, chain stores and, more importantly, department stores held a firm grip.

The question arises: How could a newcomer, Robert Laidlaw, manage to establish a foothold in the already arguably full, Auckland mercantile sector? Even the youngest of his competitors, the Court brothers, had been in the

Robert Laidlaw in 1912. LAIDLAW LEEDS CATALOGUE 1912, LAIDLAW FAMILY, PRIVATE COLLECTION.

industry for over twenty years by the time Laidlaw started. Nor was the market static at the time Laidlaw started his firm. For example, in the year Laidlaw commenced his mail-order catalogue, Milne and Choyce moved into their showcase Queen Street store which had just been purchased at a cost of £50,000, and in the following year, John Courts expanded into his central Queen Street site. Moreover, by 1909, Hallenstein's D.I.C., as well as Smith and Caughey's, both had limited mail-order operations.

Anyone commencing an enterprise under such conditions, with the aim of becoming the greatest business in the Southern hemisphere, must have seemed errant, if not foolhardy. Yet, the case of Laidlaw illustrates the veracity of Schumpeterian-style 'creative destruction', whereby larger, more established firms with the advantages of capital, products, size and longevity remain vulnerable to innovation – especially that of the small firm – which penetrates the market with new products, new processes, new ways of conducting trade that larger enterprises, hampered by size and structure, are not able to adequately counter.[17]

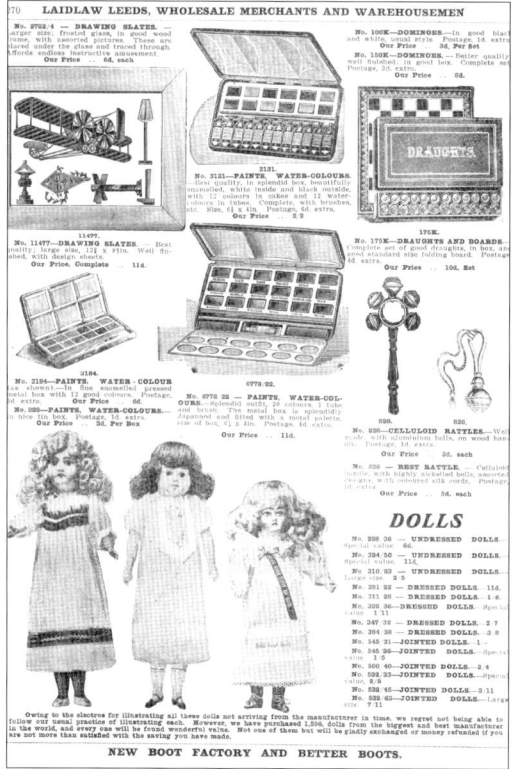

The Laidlaw Leeds Catalogue, toys section, 1912. LAIDLAW FAMILY, PRIVATE COLLECTION.

Beginnings of the Farmers Trading Company

In 1886, the Laidlaw family emigrated from Scotland to Dunedin in the South Island of New Zealand. Robert Laidlaw, the eldest son in the family, was a year old. His father, Robert Laidlaw snr (the son of a Scottish knitting-mill entrepreneur), had travelled to the colony without significant capital, but with the hope of a more prosperous future away from the constraints of inheritance strategies that would see him working for his elder brother. Initially, he established a small hosiery business; in 1896, he commenced a hardware store in partnership with a fellow Scot, Presbyterian John Gray.

In 1901, at the age of sixteen, Robert Laidlaw left school and commenced work in his father's hardware firm, Laidlaw and Gray. Receiving no privilege as the founder's son, he worked fifty-four hours per week, first as cash boy, then as salesman. Three years later, when his father sold his share of the business to his partner, John Gray, and left on an extended tour of England and Europe, Robert Laidlaw chose to remain in New Zealand and was promoted to senior wholesale traveller. In 1905, a colleague gave him a copy of American business magazine *System*, and then, later that same year, Laidlaw himself stumbled on a Montgomery Ward mail-order catalogue while staying in a country hotel. Together, these publications inspired him to pursue a business venture in mail-order selling, something he commenced planning for immediately.[18]

In 1907, Laidlaw followed his family to Auckland, where they settled; Laidlaw continued working as a travelling hardware salesman, this time for the Queen Street firm of Wingate & Co. While touring country districts, he discussed the possibility of a mail-order firm with farmers and the rural population. Receiving positive feedback, he resigned his position at the end of 1908 and commenced work on his first mail-order catalogue.[19] In the following months, he visited wholesalers, importers and manufacturers in Auckland's port district, agreeing terms and drafting the first catalogue.

From his previous experience in the wholesale of hardware and general merchandise, Laidlaw knew which goods were the fastest-moving stock items in a country store: these he used as loss leaders to attract custom, designing an aggressive marketing push around the sale of tea, watches, sewing machines, work wear, baking powder, luggage trunks and writing paper, at prices sometimes one-third of his competition. However, Laidlaw also went to some effort in his first catalogue to educate country customers as to the reasons why product pricing at their local country stores could not compare with his own price advantages, as this excerpt from a watch advertisement illustrates:

> To educate the Farmer of New Zealand to the real value of goods is part of our business. This watch costs us 2/6 landed (and we will forfeit 500 pounds to the Auckland hospital board if you can prove this to be an untrue statement). We add 5d profit, which pays our expenses and leaves us a small profit, and sell this watch to you at 2/11. As a further proof that the statements above are true we are willing to accept an order for any number of up to 10,000 of these watches at this price.[20]

From the outset, Laidlaw's venture strategically avoided the area of trade where he would have encountered the greatest opposition: the city department stores. The policy of Laidlaw Leeds was to sell only to those outside a 10-mile radius of the Auckland central post office. This had a two-pronged effect: it endeared him to country customers who saw this as a business being run solely for their benefit and, secondly, it effectively signalled to the big city stores that Laidlaw was not poaching their customers.

Eight months after leaving his previous employment, his first catalogue was ready; 118 pages long, it contained over 2000 items – beds, bicycles, hardware, lace, drapery, crockery, paint, stoves and furniture. Laidlaw also arranged to have a house brand of tea packaged under the brand name 'Rival'. His method of business was to take orders for cash, and then visit wholesalers and merchants to purchase goods on the day of order and despatch to the customer. However, realising that this required a considerable act of faith by customers to send in money to an unknown firm, Laidlaw adopted a money-back guarantee similar to that used by Montgomery Ward, and in addition received a financial reference from the previous Under Secretary of Justice, C. J. A. Haselden:

> You need have no misgivings about sending your cash in advance to Messrs. Laidlaw Leeds and Co., Mail Order Merchants, Auckland, as, from intimate knowledge, I know them to be an honourable and financial firm. I further believe they will carry out in every detail their written guarantee to refund your money in full if you are not more than satisfied with their wonderful value.[21]

Aided by his brother Jack, Laidlaw compiled lists of several thousand potential customers from rural postal directories. These prospects were mailed letters prior to the opening of the firm, inviting them to apply for a catalogue – if they would agree to use it. Fortunately, enough replied positively, and Laidlaw was able to send out 2500 catalogues. The business, named Laidlaw Leeds, (a play on the word 'leads') opened 1 October 1909. Trade in the first month amounted to £380 and increased steadily over the coming months, forcing Laidlaw to shift premises. By September 1910, sales were £3,000 per month and, to accommodate his stockholdings and 120 staff, Laidlaw had to again move to larger premises, this time a four-storey warehouse. For the first year of trading, Laidlaw showed a net profit of almost £1,000 on sales of £16,862; 14,000 copies of the second catalogue were printed to meet market demand.[22] It seemed quickly apparent, that despite the misgivings of some parts of Auckland's business community, Laidlaw's innovations had found a resonance with country customers.

There are strong economic explanations for Laidlaw's early success. In the first years of the new century, the New Zealand economy experienced an export-led economic recovery. Between 1887 and 1930 there were only four years when the colony experienced a negative balance of trade. Commencing in 1882, the processing of primary products for export markets – frozen meat, cheese and butter – developed significantly. Capital accumulated rapidly in these new industries, as more producers entered and production expanded.[23] However, while farm communities themselves benefited from increased spending power, prices remained high as rural communities remained isolated from larger markets. In a bid to counter high-input prices, farmers formed supplier cooperatives but with only limited success and market penetration. While stock and station agents expanded the range of merchandise offered to the farming community, the local storeowner, offering goods on credit to farmers, remained a central figure in the New Zealand rural economy.[24]

Furthermore, the rudimentary transportation and communication infrastructure meant that rural communities were isolated from larger populations and worked as their own micro-markets. This peculiarity of New Zealand's economic development supported an excessive duplication of small manufacturers and retailers, which was progressively eroded with merger and acquisition waves from the 1920s onwards.[25] The increasing popularity of road transportation and the more effective utilisation of the New Zealand rail network following the completion of the main trunk line in 1908 between Auckland and Wellington (extended to Whangarei in 1925 and the Bay of Plenty in 1928) assisted this change. Coastal shipping services remained an important part of the transportation infrastructure.[26] Any person establishing a mail-order firm in New Zealand in the early twentieth century was well-served by these improvements.

Per capita income increased significantly from the late 1880s onwards, more than doubling by the First World War. In particular, the purchasing power of the lower-middle classes in the latter part of the nineteenth century had increased considerably. The wives of small business owners and professionals found that they had money to spare to spend on a few luxuries, where half a century earlier the family budget would have been consumed with housekeeping necessities and foodstuffs.[27] Newly found affluence among customers was something that the large department stores catered for admirably. Price was clearly displayed on tickets, and choice was not limited to the few pieces that the cabinetmaker might have display in his speciality store, but selection could be made from a wide number of makes and models.

Given these forces, Laidlaw's venture into mail-order merchandise – offering rural communities a wider range of products than customers would have enjoyed at local outlets and at a more competitive price – was well timed. Using the relatively efficient postal service, combining carriage by cart, train or boat, he was well-placed to gain first-mover advantage in mail-order merchandising and offer the existing competition significant challenge. However, environmental factors by themselves do not effectively account for the success that Laidlaw enjoyed, for these were the same factors enjoyed by his competitors. Yet, those players were not able to extinguish his ability to gain a foothold and ultimately dominate the market. To explain this, we must look beyond economic determinism, which suggests that political and social structures are shaped by their economic environment, to the actions of the entrepreneur, who forcibly championed an innovation-led business strategy in the firm.

Innovation-led advance

In his second catalogue, Laidlaw moved to add further innovation in his marketing, introducing the Laidlaw Leeds Cooperative Workers League – a reward scheme for customers who induced others to do business with the mail-order firm. By affixing stickers to their orders and those of their friends, customers were eligible for prizes allocated every two months. A sizeable prize pool was offered: £900 of musical instruments, bicycles, silverware, saddles and jewellery. An annual prize of £150 was also offered. The market responded enthusiastically; sales in the first month of the competition tripled. By the end of the second year of trade, Laidlaw's firm had a turnover of £95,749 with a net profit of approximately £6,000. To manage the expansion in trade, Laidlaw, like the wholesale warehouses mentioned at the start of this chapter, departmentalised his organisation along functional and product lines. Family management remained strong in the firm. Laidlaw assumed the general manager role, while his brothers Arthur Laidlaw and Jack Laidlaw managed the drapery and despatch departments, respectively. By the time of the third catalogue, Laidlaw had increased his range of items to over 5500, with 28,000 copies of the catalogue distributed to customers.

The strategies soon bore tangible results. The rural community, known for its suspicion toward city interests, responded enthusiastically to Laidlaw's personal approach. By October 1912, he had received over 2300 letters from customers complementing his pricing, products and packaging, and he published three pages of them in the October 1912 catalogue. To further challenge his critics, he offered a cash prize of £1,000 if anyone could prove any of the letters false.

In 1911, two years after the founding of his company, Laidlaw published the first issue of his company magazine *The Optimist*. At sixteen pages long, each edition was edited by Laidlaw until March 1929. The magazine was a further measure to reinforce the kind of company culture that Laidlaw wanted to create. He used it for staff communication, but primarily to convey his thoughts on business, character, life and society. Much of its content was in keeping with its title: optimistic and motivational in content and language, with editorial, poems, quotations and biographical sketches of business and political figures, such as Abraham Lincoln, John Wanamaker, Selfridge, Thomas Edison, Marshall Field, Westinghouse and J. C. Penney.

The Farmers furniture department in 1912. LAIDLAW LEEDS CATALOGUE, LAIDLAW FAMILY, PRIVATE COLLECTION.

Laidlaw also used the magazine to transmit to the staff aspects of his Christian religious belief, in particular, those aspects related to business practice.[28] Making the most of opportunity when it presented itself was something that Laidlaw emphasised on many occasions. Such mini-sermons could be read two ways: exhortations to pursue opportunity and warnings against the perils of slothfulness and laxity.

> Lack of success is not caused by a dearth of opportunities. Men grow their opportunities, but they fail to harvest the crop. Every day has its own particular kind of fruit of opportunity, which must be gathered on that day or never. Opportunity beckons ability. She stands with open arms. She offers prizes for effort and development. Train yourself – don't envy success. It comes with constructive work . . . The world has always been full of opportunities. It exists everywhere for those who, with hands, eyes, brains, and ears are seeking to render service that serves.[29]

Laidlaw supported this kind of rhetoric with practical management action. In April 1912, with monthly sales of £16,000, he conducted the first mass

The free trolleybus to Farmers, early 1960s. LAIDLAW FAMILY, PRIVATE COLLECTION.

meeting of the firm to discuss efficiency.[30] Further meetings were held to discuss the elimination of waste, expense reduction, and a time-and-motion study. In addition, order-processing time was measured, breakages recorded, and suggestion boxes used to encourage further improvements in service.[31] While these measures had obvious benefits to his customers, Laidlaw also conceived of service as carrying with it an implicit duty of care. As a result, he ceased selling cigarettes when research from America pointed to harmful effects among school children, and deleted shoddy or unreliable goods from his product lines.

In addition, he promoted social activities regularly in the firm, including picnics to islands in Auckland's harbour, musical evenings, sports days, team competitions against other Auckland business houses, debating teams, a marching team, an athletic club and a girls' social club. In what we consider today as aspects of the Quality of Working Life movement (QWL),[32] Laidlaw explicitly designed work areas to be airy and well-lit by natural light. The inspiration behind such efforts was not his alone. Since 1905 he had been a regular subscriber to *System: The Magazine of Business*, and later to *Efficiency Magazine*, *Casson's Magazine* and *The Business Philosopher*. Early issues of *System* carried features on the innovations present at industrial installations such as Port Sunlight and Bourneville; the kinds of activities that Laidlaw undertook in the manner of staff welfare work, and later employee co-partnership, were replications of what had occurred in these plants.

Auckland and the 'Big Store'

Realising he needed to secure purpose-built premises to permit the further expansion of the firm, in 1913 Laidlaw purchased a site away from the main retail thoroughfare on the rise of Hobson Street and constructed a six-storey mail order warehouse at a total cost of £38,000. In the new building, he made further improvements to aid efficiency and staff welfare: he constructed a staff dining-room, supplying meals at cost, encouraged social clubs within the firm (not unlike other Auckland firms at the time), and purposely designed the building to maximise natural light. Labour-saving devices were also installed so as to increase staff efficiency and office mechanisation: dictaphones, comptometers, electric elevators for grocery produce, automatic weighing machines and steam cleaners.

To sustain such an approach required an attention to management that other Auckland firms would not pursue for over forty years. Applying the concepts and techniques of scientific management and American-style business efficiency methods, Laidlaw practised systemisation. He used card-index systems to monitor customer accounts and stock levels, undertook ratio analysis of his account books, measured work outputs, benchmarked against leading overseas mail-order houses such as Montgomery Ward and Sears, Roebuck, and had a rigorous programme of planned business method improvements, paying staff for suggestions (a practice the D.I.C. only implemented in the 1960s). In addition, applying management accounting techniques he had learned from American business journals, Laidlaw measured his working expenses on a daily, weekly and monthly basis. He put his executives through A. F. Sheldon's management training course in America, by correspondence, and subsidised the cost of the course to other interested staff.[33] The benefits of such a concerted effort toward improved business systems and management efficiency were clear. By 1913, only four years after starting his firm, Laidlaw had already exceeded the sales of the city's oldest department store – in 1913, sales at Milne and Choyce were £149,571; Laidlaw's were £202,142.[34]

Amalgamation

In 1918, Laidlaw sold his business in a reverse takeover of the Farmers Union Trading Company, a smaller farmers' cooperative. Laidlaw assumed the general manager's role over the combined businesses, and was himself the largest shareholder with 70 per cent of the paid-up capital of the firm. The new firm was called the Farmers Trading Company. The year following the takeover, Laidlaw commenced an expansion programme purchasing nineteen country stores, thereby countering a merger of nine farmers' cooperatives.[35] In 1920, with twenty-nine branch stores, a boot factory, a furniture factory, and a saddle-manufacturing plant, as well as annual sales around £1 million, the Hobson Street store was open to the public for the first time.

As a postwar recession took hold in Auckland, the opening of the store to retail custom was fortuitous. The company, like others in Auckland at the time, had to move significant amounts of stock on a depressed market. However, getting customers up the hill from Queen Street, the main shopping Mecca of Auckland's population, to the more distant Hobson Street proved problematic. In characteristic fashion, Laidlaw's innovation was to convert a store truck into a bus to carry customers between the two locations free of charge. It was not an instant success, yet partly drawn by the recently opened children's playground on the roof of the Hobson Street store, and the lure of the 'Big Store' itself, 4000 shoppers used the Farmers Free Bus on Christmas Eve 1922. The firm continued its expansion throughout the 1920s, and by 1930 had forty-five branch stores, around 1000 employees, and an annual turnover of £1.4 million.

By this time, a culture of innovation was endemic at the Farmers Trading Company. The firm was the first in New Zealand to institute widespread hire purchase over consumer items in 1924, and, as car ownership increased in Auckland, Laidlaw's response in 1930 was to open the first free customer car park in Australasia. In November 1934, while waging a war with Auckland department stores Milne and Choyce and George Courts over who could stage the most spectacular Christmas promotion, Laidlaw commenced his first Santa Parade.

For the next fifty years, these innovations, which had so successfully allowed a new firm to enter the market, became part of everyday life for Aucklanders: the trip to Farmers on a Friday night to pay hire-purchase accounts; a ride on the Farmers Free Bus; dining in the top-floor tearooms; Hector the parrot; the red neon Farmers sign flashing across Auckland; the pedal cars on the roof-top playground; the Farmers Santa Parade; and the 79-foot-tall Santa beckoning customers with his chubby pink finger – all part of the allure of the Big Store.

The Farmers Santa Parade in the 1960s. LAIDLAW FAMILY, PRIVATE COLLECTION.

Conclusion

Innovation was not new among Auckland retailers, and that Laidlaw used aggressive marketing or promotion to assist the establishment of his business enterprise is, at first glance, not particularly noteworthy. Milne and Choyce were heavy discounters to begin with, as were Smith and Caughey's – both using aggressive pricing strategies to entice custom. High turnover with low margins was also a strategy evident in Hallenstein's approach to business expansion.

What is unique to Laidlaw in terms of business strategy was that he entered the market not with a single innovation, but with a three-pronged attack. His was a new firm, distributing goods through a new channel (exclusive mail-order business) and using new business processes to run the firm. Such a multi-layered approach to entering the market had taken considerable planning: Laidlaw purposely researched and planned the organisation and its eventual systems for four years before commencing his enterprise. American mail-order books had been consulted, form letter volumes used to write customer letters, and card-index systems designed (again from American business magazines) with which to monitor stock, purchases and customer databases.

However, what is equally clear is that while innovation enabled the firm to successfully enter an already full marketplace, over the longer term, changing market conditions required further adaptation and management action. In the decades after the Second World War, the pace of social and economic change quickened in New Zealand. The government policy of protectionism, commenced as a temporary measure in December 1938 to stave off a foreign-exchange crisis, had become cemented, with import and export licensing controlling the flow of goods. Department stores, which had once prided themselves on providing customers with an up-to-date range of goods from all over the globe, increasingly had to look to local manufacturers. Some felt that, while the quality had perhaps not diminished, the choice certainly had, and at a time when consumers were becoming more fashion-conscious.

In the early 1960s, with increasing rates of car ownership, and growing urbanisation, mall shopping emerged as an attractive pull for retailers and consumers alike. Auckland malls were established in LynnMall (1964), Pakuranga (1965), Southmall (1967) and St Lukes (1969) in rapid fashion. The effect on central-city trade was noticeable. The cost of extensive renovation and redevelopment in cental-city locations was prohibitive, and the modern malls, with easy parking and convenient access for consumers, pulled customers away from the central city. Equally threatening for the department stores was the growth of smaller speciality stores selling high-fashion items. Appealing especially to women consumers, these single-store and small multiple chains were highly specialised and quick to respond to changes in fashion. Some, such as Lilly Freeman, were supported by their own small manufacturing enterprises; a familiar combination in retailing strategy for over a century.

With lower overheads, both in terms of staff numbers and rent charges, speciality stores and mall shopping chipped away at the market share of the larger stores. The glamour destinations of Queen Street and Karangahape Road, which were at the centre of the city's retail trade, lost some of their appeal to a younger, more fashion-conscious customer. In response, retailers like the Farmers Trading Company became anchor tenants in mall initiatives. Those who remained in the main streets suffered. A similar pattern occurred in other centres. In Christchurch, the central city's signature shop, J. Ballantyne & Co., also had to face the competition produced by the move to shopping malls. Company historian, Gordon Ogilvie, observed that malls established during the 1960s and 1970s at Bishopdale, Riccarton, Northlands, Barrington, Hornby, Merivale and New Brighton had the effect of 'sucking much of the life out of Christchurch's commercial heartland'.[36] It was a claim that some might equally have made of Auckland as the glamour department stores closed their doors in the 1980s.

By 1984, when the Farmers Trading Company celebrated its seventy-fifth anniversary, it was the country's largest department store chain, employing

3769 people across its stores and factories, with a turnover of $337 million. However, within two years, the firm was taken over by sharemarket raider, Chase Corporation. In 1990, Chase Corporation, itself a casualty of the 1987 sharemarket crash, was placed under statutory management. The Farmers Trading Company – after selling off its blue-chip properties, substantially investing in inventory management, and passing through several owners – now has another family as its owner, the Norman family, descendants of entrepreneur James Pascoe. It remains to be seen if this family, with its own particular style and culture, will infuse this old Auckland firm with a further lease of innovation. Oddly, it may not be an option for the new owners.

The Austrian-born economist, Joseph Schumpeter, argued that discontinuous and explosive change – abrupt shifts in markets, technology and industrial structures – was not uncharacteristic of economic progress, rather it was the central trait of the capitalist economic system. As Robert Laidlaw demonstrated a century ago, the aggressive small firm is more than capable of driving a wedge through the armour of even the most established firm in a disturbingly brief space of time. Laidlaw will not be the last; it is the process of innovation-led economic advance.

Ross & Glendining and the Clothing, Footwear and Textile Industries in New Zealand, 1938–1966: A Case of Strategic and Management Failure

S. R. H. JONES

Ross & Glendining Ltd was the largest domestically owned manufacturing enterprise in New Zealand at the beginning of the Second World War. Established in Dunedin in 1862 by two Scottish drapers, John Ross and Robert Glendining, the business was originally a general one that both imported and retailed soft goods. As the market expanded, the partners quickly sold their retailing operation to concentrate on the importation and wholesaling of clothing, textile piece goods and footwear. Converted to a limited liability company in 1900, by 1939 the firm distributed goods through a countrywide network of wholesale warehouses. Although Ross & Glendining regarded themselves primarily as importers and warehousemen, the development of manufacturing in New Zealand obliged the firm to become increasingly involved in the production and distribution of colonial-made goods.

Backwards integration first occurred in 1879 when the firm commenced manufacturing woollen goods at its newly erected Roslyn Woollen Mills on the outskirts of Dunedin. The product mix rapidly expanded thereafter, with hosiery, knitwear and worsted goods being produced at the mills while a clothing factory was established in the city. Further expansion took place around the turn of the century when straw and felt hat-making, boot manufacturing, and gown and mantle factories were opened. All goods were distributed through the warehouses, there being no direct contact between the retailer and the company's mills and factories. The warehouses also continued to import and distribute those items not yet produced in New Zealand, as well as buy in from local manufacturers. (See Chart 1.)

At the beginning of the Second World War, the majority of the firm's labour force of around 2000 was employed in Dunedin, considerable numbers being employed at its woollen and worsted mills and in the clothing and footwear factories in the centre of the city. The firm also owned clothing factories in Auckland, the rapid growth of northern markets together with lower wage costs encouraging Ross & Glendining to open shirt, clothing and underwear factories in the city after the First World War. Rationalisation in the 1930s saw the further relocation of production from Dunedin to Auckland, a process that was to continue into the 1960s.

Ross & Glendining thrived during the late 1930s and throughout the 1940s. Profits and turnover increased almost fourfold between 1938 and 1951, notwithstanding government restrictions placed on the importation of machinery, raw materials and finished goods and the imposition of price controls. Thereafter progress was modest, turnover slowly increasing from £4.4 million in 1951 to £6.3 million in 1961, while profits declined. In 1963 a loss of £4,250 was recorded. This reversal in fortunes was reflected in the share price, which fell from around 30s in the early 1950s to 10s a decade later. With net tangible assets of at least 21s 6d, the firm represented an attractive takeover target. In 1966 the inevitable occurred when it was acquired by U.E.B. Ltd in a cash and share deal equivalent to 12s 9d for each ordinary share.

The difficulties encountered by Ross & Glendining from 1951 onwards were partly a reflection of the fact that the traditional business model they employed, in which both their manufactured and imported goods were sold wholesale through their warehouses, was no longer relevant. Instead, retailers in New Zealand now tended to buy goods either directly from overseas manufacturers or from the myriad of domestic manufacturers that had sprung up following the introduction of import licensing in 1938. Such manufacturers, quick to copy the latest overseas fashions, often specialised in the production of a limited range of goods. Without the heavy overheads of a warehouse network, they were able to sell to selected outlets at a highly competitive price.

While the changing nature of the market for clothing, footwear and textiles undoubtedly made life difficult for Ross & Glendining, the poor performance of the firm was largely due to the failure of management to recognise and react to those changes. For them the wholesale warehouses were sacrosanct, and the notion that alternative modes of distribution might prove more effective was difficult to grasp. When they finally did permit their mill and factories to sell directly to their customers, the time it took both to roll out the new strategy and to develop the organisational structures necessary to implement that strategy resulted in heavy losses. These failings were to lead to the demise of a once-great New Zealand enterprise.

The introduction of import licensing in 1938

The election of the Labour Government in 1935 and the subsequent reflation of the economy saw prosperity return to the manufacturing sector in New Zealand. Like many other manufacturers, Ross & Glendining both refurbished and added to capacity in the late 1930s, modernising their woollen and worsted mills, extending their clothing and boot-making factories in Dunedin, and increasing output in Auckland.

The rapid expansion of the economy and the increase in imports for both production and consumption soon led to increasing deficits on New Zealand's current account. When export prices began to decline in the second half of 1938, a full-blown foreign-exchange crisis ensued, the true extent of the situation only becoming evident after the re-election of the Labour Government in November of that year. A system of foreign-exchange controls was immediately put in place, with importers being obliged to apply to the government both for import licences and the foreign exchange with which to conduct their purchases. Licence quotas were granted to firms on the basis of what they had imported in 1938. Although licensing was intended to be temporary, it formed the basis of industrial protection for many years to come.[1]

The new regime of licensing and controls necessarily made life more complicated for Ross & Glendining. Not only was the firm dependent on imports for those warehouse goods that it did not make itself, but both the factories and Roslyn Mills were reliant on overseas suppliers for raw materials, semi-finished goods, and machinery. Reliance on imported materials was particularly great in Auckland where cotton cloth, silk, canvas, artificial silk, buttons and thread were imported for use in the shirt, denim, coat and cover factories. Fortunately, with a long history of importation, the firm was able to secure licences up to the value of around 80 per cent of their total requirements.

Despite the inconvenience and loss of time involved in applying for import licences and foreign exchange, Ross & Glendining do not appear to

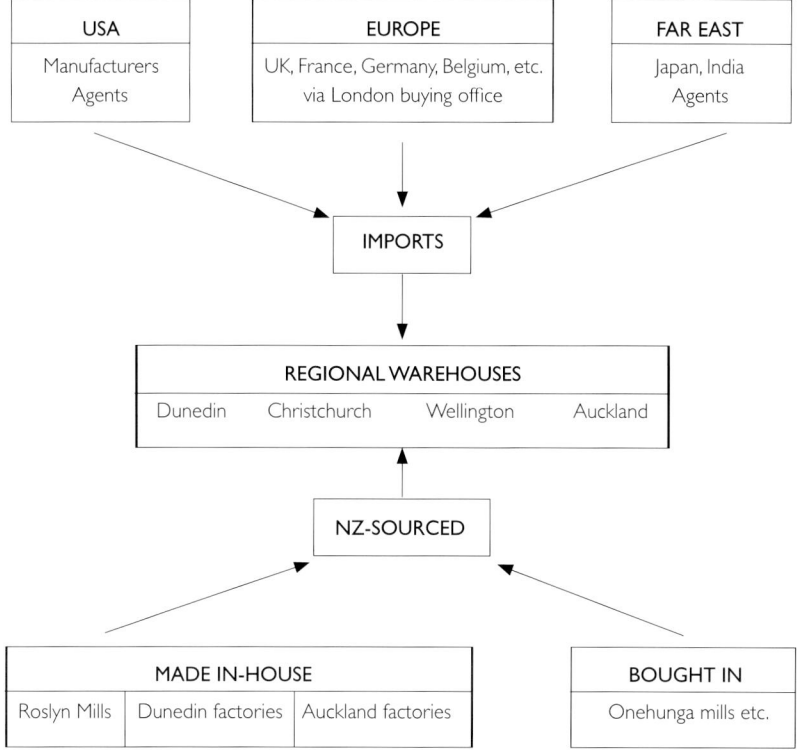

CHART 1: SOURCES OF WAREHOUSE GOODS

have suffered unduly from the introduction of controls. By dint of securing generous allocations and running down stocks, both the warehouses and factories recovered and even managed to increase returns in 1939. The de facto protection afforded by import licensing did, however, result in an increase in domestic competition, for a number of small clothing factories were set up to make goods that had previously been imported. In the short run, the emergence of these minnows seems to have passed unnoticed. Management in Dunedin actually contracted with one small Auckland maker, Childswear Ltd, to supply them with children's clothing.

By the outbreak of the Second World War in September 1939, Ross & Glendining were trading profitably. All manufacturing units were reported to be fully employed, the only problem being a shortage of labour.[2] These shortages appear to have been particularly acute in the South Island where competitors Lane, Walker, Rudkin & Co. set up branch factories on the West Coast to secure labour.[3]

War and peace

The New Zealand economy in wartime was characterised by price control, wage stabilisation, import licensing, rationing and shortages of materials and labour. Despite these restrictions on supply and demand, the value of goods sold by Ross & Glendining between 1939 and 1945 increased by 80 per cent to over £2.3 million. This was partly due to the performance of the company's manufacturing units, which were able to keep the warehouses relatively well supplied. Thus over the war years the output of the factories rose by 70 per cent to £590,796, while that of Roslyn Mills, heavily engaged in supplying the army with khaki cloth and blankets, rose by just under 70 per cent to £300,028.[4] This represented a significant real increase in production given that wholesale prices of locally produced goods increased by only about 25 per cent throughout the war.[5]

The bulk of the increase in production initially came from the factories in Auckland where output soared from £149,254 in the year ending July 1939 to £214,496 in the year to July 1941. Denim production, which was probably destined for the forces, accounted for more than half of this increase. During the course of 1940, Auckland operations were also boosted by the transfer of the underwear manufacturing unit, together with its invaluable import licences, from Dunedin. Why this should have occurred is unclear, although a shortage of labour seems to have been the most likely cause.

Shortage of space was the greatest problem in Auckland, the growth in existing activities plus the transfer of the underwear factory resulting in increasing congestion at the Greys Avenue factory. By the end of 1940, it had been built out to the limits of the existing section; in 1941 the site next door was purchased to allow expansion to continue.[6]

The other major departure in Auckland was for Ross & Glendining to acquire capacity for the mass production of clothing for children and teenagers. Previous attempts to manufacture for this market had been unsuccessful due to difficulties in procuring supplies and stiff competition from imports. In 1939, Ross & Glendining placed its first orders with Childswear Ltd, which had opened a small factory in Albert Street in the centre of Auckland. Ably managed by its owner, Dove Meyer Robinson, a future mayor of Auckland, output grew rapidly, the number of largely female employees at the factory growing from 6 to 126 over the space of two years.

To meet growing demand, the bulk of which came from the Dunedin firm, Childswear Ltd rapidly adopted modern mass-production methods. In 1941, Ross & Glendining decided to become more involved in the Auckland concern, providing working capital and paying £3,475 for a small parcel of shares, with an option for outright purchase in future.[7] In return, it obtained exclusive rights to the clothing produced. The arrangement benefited both parties. Employment at the Albert Street clothing factory increased to around 250 over the next two years, while Roslyn Mills found a steady outlet for types of cloth used mainly in school clothing. Output data no longer exists, but Childswear undoubtedly played a vital role in keeping the warehouses stocked with goods greatly in demand.[8]

The rapid expansion of clothing, footwear and textiles production in New Zealand ground to a halt in 1942 as spare capacity was used up and restrictions on the importation of raw materials and machinery began to bite. Employment also fell, notwithstanding the best efforts of the Director of Manpower to direct labour to the factories and mills.[9] The mills and factories owned by Ross & Glendining did not escape the check in production, the Auckland clothing factories finding it particularly difficult to maintain output throughout 1942 and 1943. A destructive fire in the Wellesley Street factory in 1944 also hampered production.[10]

The shortage of clothing led to the introduction of rationing in May 1942, individual firms being left to see that each retail customer received their 'fair share'.[11] To ensure the efficient use of resources, the New Zealand Standards Institute prepared standard specifications for many items of the sort that were manufactured in Auckland, including shirts and pyjamas, outerwear, and women's and girls' underwear. This, unfortunately, did little to curb the shortages. Frustrated members of the Hawkes' Bay branch of the Association of Retailers suggested that the Minister be petitioned to allow pyjama cloth to be released in the piece, thereby allowing people to make up pyjamas at home.[12]

Frustration was not confined to retailers and consumers; the difficulties faced by manufacturers in landing licensed goods, plus the near impossibility of getting licences for goods they did not habitually produce, made it hard for manufacturers to meet demands. In 1941, for example, Ross & Glendining informed their London office that their clothing factory was not interested in manufacturing army chevrons and badges as they did not possess the necessary licences.[13] Greater enterprise, it seems, existed in the underwear factory. When told by London that knicker elastic was virtually unprocurable, attention was drawn to the fact that a U.K. trade magazine had pointed out that elastic was absolutely essential for the manufacture of bloomers for the army. In any event, the plant wished to be sent examples of underwear in the latest styles and kept up to date with trimmings and machines used in their manufacture.[14]

The demands from the armed forces began to ease off during the course of 1943, leaving more blankets, clothing and footwear for civilian use. As winter approached, Ross & Glendining felt able to advertise that increasing supplies of piece goods, underwear and outerwear would now be available to their customers.[15] A year later, advertisements appeared in *The New Zealand Draper* featuring 'Childswear Children', inviting retailers to apply to the nearest branch warehouse for supplies of clothing for 'tots, toddlers and teens'.[16] How plentiful these supplies were is unclear, but it seems likely that the inability to charge remunerative prices due to price control meant that some lines were discontinued.

To compensate manufacturers for the high cost of some imported inputs, a system of subsidies was introduced late in 1944 which applied to the production of lower and middle qualities of flannel and cotton shirts, working trousers, and boys' and men's pyjamas.[17] While Childswear Ltd and the Dunedin factories may have benefited from these initiatives, output at the Auckland factories declined during the final year of the war.[18]

The end of the war did not see the return to a free market economy; rather, it saw a commitment by the Labour Government to economic insulation, resulting in the maintenance of price controls, import licensing and restricted access to foreign exchange. The strong growth in the economy due to the expansion of primary exports nevertheless meant that imports were allowed to rise – imports of apparel, textiles, fibres and yarns doubling between 1946 and 1947.[19] Careful selection of the items imported ensured that domestic manufacturers benefited from freer access to inputs, yet remained protected from foreign competition.

The major problem facing most manufacturers in the postwar years was not shortages of machinery or raw materials, although they remained serious, but shortages of labour.[20] Labour, especially female labour, started to drift away from the mills and factories even before the end of the war, the return of overseas servicemen from 1943 onwards seeing many young women leave work to get married. Ross & Glendining were particularly badly affected, the numbers directly employed by the firm falling from 2319 to 1493 between 1941 and 1948, 500 less than the pre-war peak.[21] Roslyn Mills, which employed over 950 men and women in 1943, was over 300 women short by 1948, with absolutely no prospect of filling vacancies in a town where the female vacancy rate stood at over 20 per cent of those employed.[22]

Shortages of labour were not quite so acute in Auckland where the female vacancy rate was about half that of Dunedin.[23] Even so, the labour situation in the city was sufficiently bad to encourage the firm to relocate its rapidly expanding underwear factory to the township of Henderson on the outskirts of Auckland. Opened in January 1948 and situated close to the railway station, the new factory was able to draw on the growing population of West Auckland for the female labour that made up the bulk of its workforce. Childswear Ltd also began to look further afield for labour, establishing cut, make and trim operations in Whangarei and Te Awamutu.[24]

By the end of the 1940s, it is clear that Ross & Glendining had been able to halt the decline in their manufacturing operations and expand output once more. Between 1946 and 1950, the output of the Dunedin factories increased by around a quarter to just over £511,000, all units showing a profit. In Auckland, the picture appears to have been less inspiring, for while output increased to over £300,000 during this period, this was largely due to contributions from the clothing and underwear factories. The shirt and millinery factories, located at Greys Avenue, seem neither to have increased output nor contributed much in the way of profits. Childswear Ltd on the other hand, continued to make progress, employing over 400 hands by the early 1950s.[25]

The warehouses benefited from the growth in production, but it is evident that a significant proportion of the goods they sold were still bought in. Many of the better quality and more fashionable goods were purchased by the London office although dealing with the licensing authorities was proving to be a bureaucratic nightmare.[26] Special applications had to be made for purchases over and above the basic import licences, granted in 1938, while the annual announcement of the import schedule, which specified the quantities of goods that might be imported in the following year, was usually made too late for orders to be placed in time.[27] Price controls, too, made it difficult for the firm to respond to the demands of the marketplace. Every time a new item was introduced or a price increase was proposed, detailed costings for each item, no matter how small, had to be included in a submission to the Price Tribunal for approval.

The 1940s, nevertheless, represented an Indian summer for Ross & Glendining. The turnover of the warehouses grew steadily throughout the war years, expanding more rapidly towards the end of the decade as parity with sterling was re-established and import restrictions eased. Profits, too, were substantial, the company being able to pay a dividend of 8 per cent in 1950 and transfer £94,000 of undistributed profits to the general reserve.[28] The fat years were not to last much longer. Relaxation of import controls by the newly elected National Government, together with changes in the trading environment, made it far harder to earn profits in the ensuing decade.

Branding and the challenges of fashion

The difficulties encountered by Ross & Glendining in operating within a highly regulated economy were insufficient to prevent turnover and profits from increasing again in the year to July 1951. This was due in no small measure to the Korean War, the outbreak of which led to a surge in commodity prices between 1949 and 1951.[29] A sharp increase in the price of wool and other inputs necessarily raised the firm's manufacturing costs, especially at Roslyn Mills, but it also resulted in increases in per capita incomes that encouraged customers in New Zealand to buy more. Late in 1950, therefore, additional capital was raised both to finance larger stocks and to further increase manufacturing capacity. The issue of 356,250 shares at £1 each raised the total issued capital of the firm to £950,000.[30]

The ease with which the company was able to ride out the subsequent downswing of 1951, occasioned by a combination of falling export prices and the watersiders' strike, seems to have persuaded the elderly chairman, J. Sutherland Ross, and his fellow directors that the business remained fundamentally sound.[31] Yet the fact that profits remained depressed over the next few years, notwithstanding an increase in turnover, should have alerted

FIGURE 1: TURNOVER AND PROFITS FOR ROSS & GLENDINING LTD, 1938–1965

them to the fact that all was not well. To their credit, they identified problems with mill management and enlisted the assistance of Sydney management consultants W. D. Scott & Co. to help sort out their problems. What they did not recognise, however, was that the traditional business model, in which the warehouses played a central role in the distribution of goods manufactured in-house and bought in, was no longer viable. Instead, they chose to blame external conditions, especially the relaxation of import controls from 1950 onwards, for the difficulties they encountered.[32]

There is little doubt that the company was adversely affected by the relaxation of import controls. Greater freedom to import clothing, footwear and textiles encouraged the more substantial New Zealand retailers to circumvent the wholesale warehouses and order directly from overseas suppliers. This development had an even greater impact on the warehouse business than an earlier phase of direct importation in the 1920s. Transportation improvements, including increased car ownership, also encouraged country customers to shop at the larger retail establishments in principal cities for sought-after importations of high-fashion goods.[33]

The principal threat to a warehouse-based trade, however, came from the growth in the number of individual clothing manufacturers who had flourished under the system of import controls. These relatively small, flexible firms developed their own direct-selling and distribution units, the vertical integration of manufacturing and selling doing away with the double-handling that the warehouse/factory system entailed. Unit costs were also lower by virtue of the fact that individual clothing manufacturers were not burdened with the huge overhead costs of supporting a network of warehouses with their large and varied stocks, numerous travellers, and expensive inner-city sites.[34]

The warehouses found that it was difficult to compete with individual manufacturers, not only on the basis of price but also in terms of the products on offer. Rather than compete across the board, the newcomers chose to specialise, especially in better quality, high-fashion garments that appealed to increasingly affluent New Zealanders. As the market expanded, so the number of small manufacturers grew, each tending to produce just a few lines, often in the latest materials, such as rayon and nylon.[35] In contrast, the garments produced by Ross & Glendining's own factories tended to hark back to the years of austerity in the 1940s being rather staid and old-fashioned.

The failure to produce modern and up-to-date goods was partly due to the unwillingness of the board to re-equip the mills and factories with the latest machinery after the war. But the main problem appears to have been that the factory managers had little incentive to keep in touch with latest fashions, the warehouses being expected to sell all that they produced. This 'production' rather than 'sales' orientation of the company led to considerable friction between the factories and the warehouse buyers. Despite repeated complaints, little changed. As a consequence, the warehouses found themselves dealing in basic products that yielded too low a margin to offset their high overheads.[36]

Faced with growing competition, Ross & Glendining resorted to increased advertising. The value of advertising had long been recognised by the firm, a department being set up in 1949 to take over responsibility for advertising and promotion from the chairman.[37] By 1952, considerable progress had been made in differentiating the products of some of the newer factories. Regent, Footeeze and Cathedral were the principal brands being manufactured at the recently acquired Christchurch footwear factory, while Mimosa lingerie and Ranelagh interlock underwear were among the ranges produced in Henderson.[38]

The advertising budget supporting these and other brands rose sharply in the early 1950s until by 1954 it stood at over £41,000, rather more than the after-tax profit earned in the preceding year.[39] Yet by itself greater advertising was insufficient to make up for overpriced and poorly styled goods, especially as individual manufacturers were able to offer retailers exclusive dealing rights and dedicated advertising. Ross & Glendining's warehouses, committed to a general trade, were unable to offer this type of support.[40]

Reorganisation and diversification

The attachment by Ross & Glendining to selling through warehouses during the 1950s doubtless had a lot to do with the origins of the firm as warehousemen. The long-serving chairman, Sutherland Ross, the former general manager, A.W. Jeavons, and a number of the other directors (none of whom were young) had spent their formative years working in the warehouses. The appointment in 1955 of the university-trained and former company secretary E. O. Hunter as general manager thus represented a break with tradition. At the suggestion of management consultants W. D. Scott & Co., Hunter had spent time in Australia studying the relationships between warehouses and drapers. Once back home, he began to cast a critical eye over his company's operations.[41]

The continued inability to compete was at first attributed to problems within the factories. During the course of 1955 a change of management was instituted at both the Auckland shirt factory and the Dunedin clothing factory, the latter plant also being reorganised. The workings of the poorly performing gown and mantle factories were also investigated. In 1956 it was decided to close both these units, transferring the production of the more fashionable ranges from Dunedin to Childswear Ltd in Auckland. The board believed that this would not only save on distribution costs, but also enable the firm to keep in touch with the growing and more sophisticated market in the north. Additional warehouse and factory space was purchased in the centre of Auckland in Wakefield and Lorne Streets, the latter being a three-storey reinforced-concrete building intended to provide storage facilities for the rapidly expanding Auckland market.[42]

Greater control was also exercised over key suppliers. In 1955 the company completed the acquisition of Clifton Knitwear, the bulk of the shares having been purchased the previous year. This firm, located at Sumner, had been supplying Ross & Glendining with fully fashioned knitwear since the late 1940s but, by the early 1950s, was experiencing production problems. The change of ownership enabled new manufacturing procedures and improvements in merchandising methods to take place. By 1956, the subsidiary was trading profitably.[43]

In addition to improving factory performance, Hunter made attempts to compete with the local production of fashion items by manufacturing well-known overseas brands under licence. Following an approach by John B. Stetson of America in 1955, Stetson hats were soon in production at the company's Dunedin hat factory. Other licensing agreements were to follow, including arrangements to manufacture Sax Altman trousers, Osti lingerie, Country Club shirts, Town Talk neckwear and Anthony Squire suits.[44]

The responsibility for manufacturing the suits, and ultimately the shirts and neckwear too, was handed to a subsidiary, J. A. Wilkinson & Son of Frankton Junction, acquired in 1957. The new firm, renamed International Style Co. Ltd, was to manufacture and merchandise Anthony Squire suits and other garments, much along the lines of many other successful vertically organised clothing manufacturers in New Zealand.[45]

The commencement of operations could not have happened at a worse time. A balance of payments crisis towards the end of 1957 saw the newly elected Labour Government raise taxes and reintroduce import controls, the latter making it difficult for International Style to import vital raw materials. Having invested heavily in both plant and promotion, the inability to run at anywhere near full capacity entailed heavy losses.[46] Worse was to follow when, in 1958, a fire broke out at the Frankton factory, completely destroying plant and equipment. Production was resumed and output increased, notwithstanding staffing problems. By 1960, the subsidiary was manufacturing and merchandising a number of well-received, high-class menswear products throughout New Zealand.[47]

The movement to direct-selling among subsidiaries continued in 1960 when Dove Meyer Robinson, increasingly active in politics, decided to sell the remainder of his shares in Childswear Ltd to Ross & Glendining. On taking over full control of Childswear, the Dunedin firm found it necessary 'to carry out a complete overhaul of the management, the general staff, and production planning, and integrate this operation with our parent company'. The opportunity was also taken to develop the capacity to engage in direct sales to customers, all products having previously passed through the warehouses.[48]

The attempt to 'outspecialise the specialists' continued in 1961 with the acquisition of R. W. Saunders Ltd of Christchurch. This firm, which produced the Adrian and Lisbet ranges of lingerie, was regarded as 'a perfect example of a completely vertical unit selling all of its goods to a limited number of retail accounts'.[49] During the course of 1963, both the Henderson underwear factory and Regent Footwear of Christchurch were invited by Hunter to adopt the Saunders model and submit plans to transform themselves into vertically organised units. It was intended that in future they should engage in direct-selling, progressively reducing their reliance on the warehouses.[50]

Warehouses: the end of an era

Although Hunter quickly realised that the old method of doing business was doomed, it is evident that he opted for evolutionary change rather than the immediate abandonment of the warehouse model. Whether this was because he believed that evolutionary change was less likely to damage the company, or because there was a lack of senior management to help him push through the changes, is not clear. What is clear, however, is that he found it difficult to persuade other members of the board that direct-selling was the way of the future. Thus, when he proposed that Roslyn Mills be allowed to experiment with direct-selling to outside customers, his proposal met with considerable resistance from the board. Eventually he pushed the measure through and, in September 1956, Garth Ledgard Ltd of Auckland was appointed as selling agent for the mills. In Hunter's own words 'the scheme was an outstanding success from the outset', paving the way for the adoption of direct-selling by International Style and, a little later, by other manufacturing units too.[51]

Hunter initially made few changes to the way in which warehouses operated, contenting himself with introducing a more rational bonus system and streamlining the ordering process through the adoption of central-buying. The latter, he felt, should economise on stockholding, reduce the quantities of fashion items that had to be written down at the end of each season, and provide greater guidance for the factories. He was also hopeful that concentration of buying in the hands of a few, well-qualified buyers would overcome the lack of high-quality specialist buyers in the warehouses.[52]

Hunter's assumption of the role of vice-chairman and managing director in 1958 encouraged him to embark on more far-reaching changes, especially as the effects of reintroduced import controls were now beginning to bite. After 'a complete survey of warehouses and selling staff', he gradually began to restructure the business so that the warehouses would ultimately be transformed from selling agencies to regional depots that provided display facilities and distributed goods on behalf of the factories.[53]

The first task was to strip out some of the overhead costs that burdened the company. Sub-branches at New Plymouth, Wanganui, Napier and Invercargill were closed and staff retired, laid-off or relocated, saving some £80,000–£90,000 over the course of a year.[54] Shortly afterwards, a special indent division and bulk store was opened in Dunedin to handle all forward orders for factories in the region. Indent divisions and bulk stores were subsequently opened in Christchurch and Auckland. A direct-sales division was also established to assist manufacturing units to sell directly to large buying groups.[55] Finally, in 1962, warehousing and manufacturing in the Auckland province was established as a separate entity, reporting directly to the board.[56]

Whether more fashionable items could be sold effectively through large divisions was not entirely clear. To handle some of the leading lines, two separate merchandising units were established in 1958 to sell to specialist stores. With a showroom in Auckland, Fleur Fashions was to promote and sell the newly acquired Osti range of lingerie, millinery and other ladies' fashion underwear manufactured in Henderson. The second company, Sacony (N.Z.) Ltd, was established to distribute dresses made under licence with designs and materials supplied from New York. The reintroduction of import licences made importation increasingly difficult, and it appears that creations with more local input were manufactured.[57]

To support the sale of fashion items, showrooms were opened in each of the four remaining warehouses. In 1960, the first Dominion-wide fashion show was held, when 'frocks, sportswear, lingerie, college-wear, kiddies-wear and menswear were all modelled in one grand display'.[58] The lack of focus probably did not help Sacony (N.Z.) Ltd, the agreement with the American brand owners being terminated in the following year. Fleur Fashions, after initially struggling, was transferred to R. W. Saunders, the lingerie manufacturer acquired in 1961. Henceforth the Christchurch subsidiary was to produce and merchandise the Osti range, along with its own Adrian and Lisbet ranges.[59]

A new unit, Fashion House, was created in Auckland to handle direct sales of other locally produced fashion goods to major customers.[60]

The major problem that Hunter faced in restructuring Ross & Glendining was how to maintain profitability of the warehouses while at the same time progressively transferring a major part of their business to the manufacturing units. Providing a role for the warehouses both as bulk stores and regional showrooms helped to preserve revenues: stripping out costs through closures and streamlining operations also made a contribution to profits.

In spite of these measures, the warehouses were unable to overcome the loss of high margin business, the situation being rendered much worse by the reintroduction of import controls in 1957. Between 1955 and 1962 the value of warehouse importations from London fell from £1,075,000 to £263,000 per annum. As their total sales over the same period fell from just over £5 million to around £4 million, the loss of £812,000 of high-margin business proved to be absolutely critical. Warehouse profits-before-tax plunged from almost £159,000 to £8,308, a small return on the £1.75 million funds employed by the warehouses.[61]

The shareholders doubtless regarded the decline in warehouse profits as unfortunate – but acceptable – as long as the decline was offset by profits earned by the mill, factories and manufacturing subsidiaries. Until the middle of 1962 this tended to be the case; the performance of Ross & Glendining even showed an improvement from the mid-1950s. But when, in 1963, losses of £156,000 at International Style and the recently acquired House of Sportscraft were uncovered, there was widespread concern both among shareholders and in the financial press.

The loss, unfortunately, was uncovered shortly after the announcement of preliminary results reporting modest profits of around £150,000. Hunter, a poor communicator, made matters even worse by not immediately issuing a profits warning. He then compounded his error when, at the annual general meeting in November, he simply treated the losses as exceptional items, focusing instead on operating profits for the year. When pressed, he reluctantly conceded that an overall loss of £4,245 had been made although by this stage he had lost the confidence of the shareholders. As the board had already suggested that the overstretched Hunter should take extended leave, it was perhaps inevitable that the meeting should vote for him to step down as chairman and managing director. He was subsequently dismissed by the board.

Closures and restructuring

The removal of Hunter at this juncture was probably not in the best interests of a company in transition. He had worked hard to develop new strategies since his appointment and, following a wide-ranging operational survey in conjunction with W. D. Scott & Co., was just about to announce plans for a radical restructuring. His proposals envisaged that Ross & Glendining adopt a modern, multi-divisional structure so that more effective control might be exercised over the enterprise in future.

The key elements of Hunter's proposals included a head office to assume strategic functions, exercise financial control, and oversee production, marketing and personnel. There were to be six operating divisions: a textile division that embraced Roslyn Mills and Clifton Knitwear; divisions concerned with footwear, menswear, womenswear and possibly schoolwear production; and a wholesale division that conducted a much-reduced warehouse business (see Chart 2).[62]

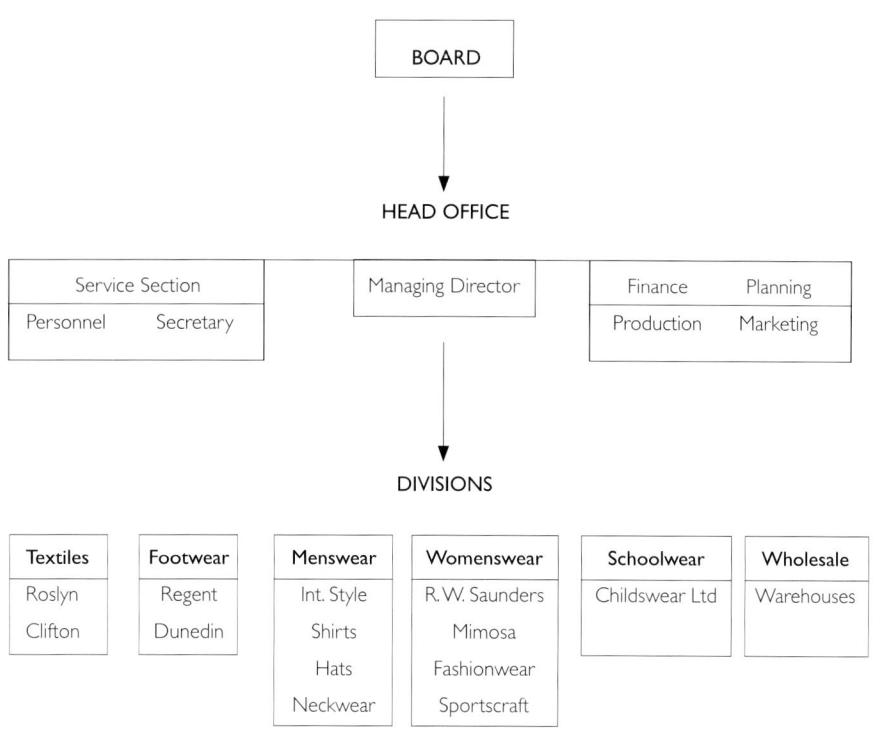

CHART 2: PROPOSED ORGANISATIONAL STRUCTURE, 1963

At the unit level, a number of the inner-city factories were to be closed and the buildings disposed of, including the Dunedin factories in High Street and Stafford Street, and the Greys Avenue and Albert Street factories in Auckland. Where appropriate, production was to be relocated in modern buildings in the suburbs, with the units selling direct to their customers. Most of the warehouse departments were to be closed, with just four merchandising departments retained at each centre. These were to handle manchester, piece goods, millinery and haberdashery, much of which was still imported. There would be now little use for the vast Wellington warehouse, and this was to be sold as smaller, leased premises would be used instead. Overall, it was anticipated that smaller stocks and the disposal of properties would reduce total funds employed from just over £5 million to just under £4 million.[63]

The general manager, Neil Sinclair, had been closely involved in drawing up the restructuring plans. Following Hunter's somewhat acrimonious departure, Sinclair was able to persuade the reconstituted board and its new chairman, B. E. Woodhams, to proceed with divisionalisation. A head office with staff support was established much as Hunter had envisaged, senior management being strengthened by the establishment of an executive committee that met weekly. There were only five operating divisions, however, the notion of a schoolwear division having been abandoned. There was also a far bigger role for the warehouses than Hunter planned, for not only were they involved in the merchandising of children's clothing, but significant quantities of underwear, dresses and outerwear as well. Suits and trousers remained the responsibility of a still quasi-independent International Style.[64]

During the course of 1964 the rationalisation of manufacturing units began to take place. The Dunedin footwear factory was closed, much as Hunter had planned. Production was moved to Christchurch, where a modern new building housed the Regent Footwear Division. In Auckland, the Greys Avenue factory was sold and shirt manufacturing was transferred to a new unit in Panmure. It was to operate as part of the menswear division, along with the clothing factory in Sale Street, which now manufactured sports jackets, waterproof coats and industrial clothing. International Style continued to manufacture and merchandise suits and trousers. [65]

The womenswear division, with headquarters at Fashion House in Albert Street, had responsibility for childswear and teenswear productions, Henderson lingerie, and dresses produced in the Albert Street factory. Women's garments were also manufactured in Panmure, where some of the Sportscraft and new Hi-Fi range of coats and dresses were made. Cut, make and trim operations were continued at the former Childswear plant in Whangarei. The aim of the division was to offer the increasingly affluent consumer fashionionable goods at reasonable prices. Rather confusingly, R. W. Saunders Ltd was to remain an independent entity manufacturing and selling Osti and other lingerie brands.[66]

The main change to occur during the year was undoubtedly the transfer of head office from Dunedin to Auckland. The chairman, 'Bunny' Woodhams, conscious of the animosity that this might generate, assured shareholders at the annual general meeting in November that this was already proving beneficial. He continued:

> A general should be where the fighting is thickest and with 70 percent of our business being done in the North Island—and 40 percent in Auckland province— that's where our top management belongs. Our roots will always be in Dunedin but we are no longer a Dunedin company—we're a New Zealand company. Controlling the company from Dunedin would be like trying to drive a motor car from the back seat.[67]

To take shareholders along with him and to keep the staff both informed and involved, a group magazine, *R & G Reporter*, was to be published six times a year.[68]

Woodhams, a former Waikato retailer, city councillor and professional director, was without doubt a better communicator than the somewhat remote Hunter.[69] Nevertheless, in spite of his optimistic tone, the financial message he had for the shareholders at the 1964 meeting was far from encouraging. Net profit after tax was no larger than that of 1963; if exceptional losses of the preceding year were excluded, while the dividend was cut from 6 per cent to 3.5 per cent. Morever, the troubled International Style Co. Ltd was 'still not out of the woods'; interruption of production during the relocation of the footwear plants had adversely affected profits; Clifton Knitwear only returned nominal profits; and Fleur Millinery was to cease activities. Worse still, distribution and inventory costs at the wholesale division, with its still extensive warehouse system, constituted a major problem. On a brighter note, the action for damages taken against the company by the former managing director, E. O. Hunter, had been settled out of court.[70]

The second year of Woodhams' chairmanship saw additional closures, disposals and further restructuring. By July 1965, a small Auckland tie workroom had been disposed of, and the waterproof and industrial clothing factory in Sale Street had been closed, some production being transferred to Dunedin. In Christchurch, the Regent footwear division was sold off as a going concern. The diffuse womenswear division, with headquarters in a factory that Hunter would have sold and operating in a way that Hunter would have regarded as sub-optimal, became a candidate for further restructuring when it returned a loss for the year. A veil was drawn over the activities of the wholesale division although subsequent events suggest that a loss was incurred there also.

If closures and restructuring were intended to reduce expenses, then they certainly succeeded, but only at the cost of reduced sales. As a result, net profit after tax fell back again, a dividend of 3.5 per cent being paid for the year.[71]

In spite of the gloom, Woodhams was still able to present good news at the annual general meeting in November 1965. Ross & Glendining, in association with the Australian textile group Osti Holdings, were about to embark on a fresh strategic initiative by entering the warp-knitting field. A joint company was to be formed, Amtex Ltd, and a new plant was to be erected on land recently acquired on the Rosebank Road industrial estate in West Auckland. The plant was to be capable of producing both synthetic and natural cloths for the garment industry.[72]

Shareholders were also aware, courtesy of the *R & G Reporter*, that the company was continuing to attempt to breathe life into one of the Department of Industry and Commerce's pet schemes, notably a New Zealand plant capable of spinning woollen tops for export. Woodhams was extremely enthusiastic about such a development, rather more enthusiastic than a number of technical experts in the woollen industry who some years earlier had pointed out the pitfalls faced in marketing such products on the other side of the world. Institutional memories, it seems, can be rather short, for executives spent considerable time overseas in 1965 investigating new markets.[73]

The positive message at the annual general meeting and upbeat articles in the *R & G Reporter* could not hide the fact that much work still needed to be done to turn the company round. Shortly after the annual general meeting in November, it was announced that the group was 'continuing its development to full divisional control'. This entailed the elimination of the menswear division, with the wholesale division merchandising Auckland-manufactured shirts and Dunedin-made clothing, while International Style continued to manufacture and market suits and trousers. The wholesale division was itself rationalised, being reduced to two major distribution centres, one in Auckland and the other in Christchurch. The Dunedin and Wellington warehouses were to be replaced by sales and stock service offices.[74]

Capitulation

Encouraging noises were made early in 1966 about the launch of new product ranges by Ross & Glendining and television advertising for increasingly popular Aotea knitting wool.[75] The market, however, was beginning to lose faith in Woodhams' ability to resuscitate the company. Its shares began to slide, falling from an average of around 10s in the preceding two years to a low of 6s 6d in March. Given that the net tangible asset backing per share was in the region of 21s 6d, it was perhaps inevitable that a takeover bid would soon be forthcoming in New Zealand's increasingly active stock market.[76]

On 2 April 1966, a letter was received from the United Empire Box Company Co. Ltd (U.E.B.), indicating that it wished to bid for the company.[77] The original offer from U.E.B., a packaging company that had already begun to diversify into the textile industry, turned out to be not particularly generous, being a straightforward exchange of shares. After procrastination by the directors of Ross & Glendining, the offer was raised to one U.E.B. 5s share plus 3s in cash, an offer that was ultimately worth around 12s 9d in view of the market value of each U.E.B. share.

A half-hearted attempted was made by Woodhams and the board to extract a better offer, but to little avail. Their lack of stomach for a fight was evident in the letter subsequently sent to shareholders. While admitting 'acceptance of the takeover offer would give the United Empire Box Company Limited control of net shareholders funds at present market values of about £4,000,000 for a price of less than £2,500,000', they were very cautious about the future prospects for Ross & Glendining. They concluded that if 75 per cent of the shareholders were prepared to accept the offer, they too would sell their shares.[78]

The failure of the board either to extract greater value or reject the offer outright is somewhat surprising. By their own conservative estimates, the asset backing of the shares in January 1966 was worth at least £3.9 million simply at book values, and that ignored the value of the mills, factories and their brands as going concerns.[79] One informed correspondent suggested that the market value of the newly equipped Roslyn Mills, still pre-eminent in New Zealand, was by itself worth £3 million. Even had the board broken up the firm themselves, they would have realised more than what was on offer from U.E.B.[80]

Not all board members were convinced that Ross & Glendining should allow itself to be taken over. D. I. Ross, the resident director in Dunedin, was privately of the view that the company had now turned the corner.[81] U.E.B., however, was one of the favourite growth stocks in New Zealand in the 1960s, and its performance was well known to the board, especially to newly appointed Dr G. A. Lau, a well-known corporate financier who had previous connections with U.E.B..[82] Given the potential for both earnings and capital growth with U.E.B., and having received carefully phrased assurances concerning the future of Ross & Glendining and its staff, it seems that the board felt there was little point in engaging in a long and arduous defence of their company. With the board offering tacit support for the bid, shareholders overwhelmingly voted to accept the offer from U.E.B.

Ross & Glendining was absorbed into the U.E.B. Group during the course of June 1966. Almost immediately a process of asset-stripping began. Retail customers soon received a notice that warehouse activities were being discontinued, and by the end of September 1966 the entire stocks of the wholesale division had been sold off. Aotea wools, rugs, blankets, underwear and knitwear continued to be supplied by Roslyn Mills, which formed part of the new U.E.B. woollen division.[83] The factory units were also progressively sold off, until by 1968 only Roslyn Mills was left in production. This, too, was destined to be sold off, a merger between Roslyn Mills and the much smaller Mosgiel Woollen Mills taking place in 1969.[84]

Conclusion

The demise of Ross & Glendining, after more than a century of enterprise and innovation, occurred in a decade which first saw large-scale mergers and acquisitions take place in New Zealand.[85] Merger activity, it has been suggested, is a reflection of the fact that capital markets are behaving efficiently, with management in charge of failing firms being replaced by those capable of using the assets more effectively. Whether the dismemberment of Ross & Glendining, with the loss of considerable tacit as well as technical knowledge, represented a more efficient use of assets is debatable.

What is clear from this study, however, is that from the late 1940s the shareholders of Ross & Glendining Ltd were poorly served by their directors and senior managers. Conservative and slow to change, they left the firm poorly placed to compete with vigorous new entrants to the clothing, footwear and textile industries. Conventional wisdom might argue that such conservatism was the product of protection and price controls, the ability to compete being dulled by state intervention designed to support New Zealand industry. Yet other firms, both large and small, were only too willing to compete, their management teams seemingly immune to a business environment that supposedly sapped entrepreneurial drive.

A more plausible explanation for the managerial failings of Ross & Glendining Ltd was that it was still essentially a family firm, with the elderly

John Sutherland Ross lacking the drive and ability of his father. Both he and members of his board had been trained in the company's warehouses to which they appeared to have an irrational attachment. When a change in strategy was finally implemented, the failure to create an organisational structure capable of monitoring a complex and dispersed business allowed inefficient unit managers to remain in place far too long. Had the problems of the firm been properly addressed in the 1950s, it may well have adapted and survived. By the 1960s, with consolidation the order of the day in New Zealand industry, it was too late.

CHAPTER ELEVEN

From Local to Global:
Auckland Accounting Partnerships

RACHEL F. MORLEY

The expansion of manufacturing, and retail activities in Auckland was accompanied by the development and growth of accounting partnerships in a manner distinctive from legal, medical or other professional service firms. Accounting partnerships mimicked characteristics of their clients more closely than did other professional service firms, growing from local offices to nationwide groupings, and then adopting international affiliations. In particular, the past forty years in the history of accounting partnerships in Auckland have shown a loss of local identifiers, the adoption of international firm names, and partners having to fight to survive in partnerships with dwindling partner numbers and rationalisation of branches. During this period, partnerships have also shifted from organisations based on principles of collectivism and collegiality to firms that have all the characteristics of corporations, usually described as managed professional bureaucracies.[1] The more recent study by Brock, Powell and Hinings further divides partnerships into three co-existing archetypes: the traditional professional partnership, the global corporate professional network (typified by the Big 8), and the intermediate form, the 'Star' form, with stable size and specialisation in particular types of accounting services.[2]

In this chapter, the focus is on accounting firms in Auckland which moved from the traditional professional partnership to a global corporate professional network. To illustrate this transformation, two particular case studies are provided. The first is the merger between the Auckland firms of Clark Menzies with McCulloch Butler and Spence; the second, when the Auckland partners in the firm of Lawrence Anderson Buddle joined Deloittes. These two cases illustrate the fierce competition between accounting partnerships to gain dominance and reputation in the Auckland business sphere while at the same time strengthening international affiliations with naming rights. However, an outcome from the adoption of international names was that firms in New Zealand were then subject to mergers dictated by their transatlantic offices. These mergers were a major cost to New Zealand partners, both in business clients and in the personal costs of partnership redundancies.[3]

It is not a claim of this study that accounting partnerships have demonstrated any fundamental characteristics unique to Auckland. However, Auckland business history has seen the rise of the service industries and retail sectors, relative to the manufacturing and primary industries, as an important contributor to its growth and development, and accounting firms are one of these service industries. Looking back to the early twentieth century, the business environment in Auckland was no different from elsewhere in New Zealand.

Early practising accountants in Auckland

One hundred years ago a businessman walking down Shortland Street and up Queen Street would have been provided with a choice of eighteen or so accountants or bookkeepers. Not as many as in Dunedin or the gold rush regions, but a good selection; include in this chartered accountants from England, members of the New Zealand Accountants and Auditors Association (Auckland-based)[4] or the Incorporated Institute of Accountants of New Zealand (Wellington-based).[5] A few 1904 names are recognisable, such as Henry Gilfillan; Cooke & Buddle at 76 Victoria Arcade; and Alexander Grierson in the Government Insurance Building on Queen Street. At the same time, Watkins and Hull, later to have offices at 47 Custom Street,[6] can be observed to have established their Wellington office.

Forty years later, the 1942 *Business Directory* showed A. & J. Grierson & Browne at 99 Queen Street, later to merge into McCulloch Menzies; and Hutchison Elliffe and Cameron at 2 Durham Street. Clark Menzies were now in Wellington[7], at 102 Featherston Street, shortly to expand to 18 High Street,

Auckland, and to play a key role in one firm on which this study focuses.

A very early issue of *The Accountants Journal*, the official organ of the New Zealand Society of Accountants, provided a discussion by J. O. McKinsey in 1925 concerning 'Modern Tendencies in Accounting Practice'.[8] He described the major growth in public accounting firms after 1896 in the United States, when large corporations were appealing for capital from lenders and shareholders. Their need for credible information provided an additional supply of work for the accountant; the other came with the income tax changes during the First World War. This situation was paralleled in New Zealand with the new company promotions, as documented for the period 1880–85 by Stone.[9]

One major change was the status of the financial controllers within companies, with administration, budgeting and statistical analysis becoming more important in company management. On the other hand, the accountant in public practice increasingly provided tax advice and assisted in preparing initial public offering statements. McKinsey noted the growth in small accounting partnerships as benefiting client relationships in a manner which was not possible for large firms. Personal contact between a partner and their client was resulting in more small partnerships, rather than the large firms getting bigger to service this market. The history of these four firms shows a steady pattern of partners repeatedly leaving large firms, especially to 'spin-off' firms, reflecting McKinsey's prediction of the benefits of providing client services in smaller firms. However, small firms do not often remain as small firms, as the next section illustrates.

Auckland firms in the 1970s

Mergers in the 1970s laid the foundations for affiliations to the Big 8 accounting firms. The mergers enabled otherwise small firms to gain a larger number of partners and a national spread of offices, while remaining under the maximum number of partners permitted by the New Zealand Society of Accountants. It was typical in the early 1970s that firm names continued to recognise founders of accounting firms. Some examples of this are when Buddle and Company merged with Anderson and Co. (Dunedin), Lawrence Godfrey and Co. (Christchurch), and Cook and Co. (Wellington), to form Lawrence Anderson Buddle. Another firm with local names was Kendon, Mills, Muldoon and Browne, which later merged with Cox Arcus to become Kendon Cox. It was then renamed K.M.G. Kendons, recognising its affiliation to Klynveld Main Goerdeler, a major European player.

The history of Peat Marwick can be seen, first, in the combining of: Burtt McGillivray & Mann; Morris Duncan Gyllies; and Pattrick Feil. These three firms merged in 1972 to form Morris Pattrick & Co. Secondly, in 1971 Gilfillan Gentles & Steen merged with Pickles, Perkins & Hadlee to form Gilfillan, Gentles, Pickles & Perkins[10]. This firm became Gilfillan & Co. after the merger with Bowden Bass & Cox (Wellington). A merger with Morris Pattrick & Co. resulted in Gilfillan Morris & Co., the firm affiliated to, and then adopting the name of, Peat Marwick Mitchell & Co.

Lastly, Wilkinson Christmas & Steen, Stewart Beckett & Co., Henry Kember & Son, Dymock MacShane & Co., and W. F. & R. J. Nankervis all merged to form Wilkinson Nankervis & Stewart in 1970; this merged with Wilberfoss & Co. in 1976 to become Wilkinson Wilberfoss, the firm affiliated to, and then adopting the name of, Arthur Young. Some of these firms already had an affiliation offshore by 1970. Others were slow off the block and did not get the opportunity to be the preferred providers for the biggest of the Big 8 names. Table 1 describes some of the early connections, and subsequent linkages, in the international affiliation events.

This study examines the history of Deloitte Touche Tohmatsu in particular. The history of that firm can be traced from the founding of the firm of Hutchison Elliffe Cameron & Co., by George W. Hutchison. He was Mayor of Auckland 1931–35, and President of the New Zealand Society of Accountants. Mr H. Y. Cameron joined Mr J. M. Elliffe and Geo. W. Hutchison in a partnership in 1923. J. M. Elliffe was Secretary of the Auckland Branch of the New Zealand Society of Accountants for twenty-eight years, and President 1931–32.[11] Hutchison Elliffe Cameron & Co. much later merged with Rowley Gill Davies & Co. (Wellington) and Jameson, Son & Anderson (Christchurch) to form the national firm of Hutchison Elliffe Davies Anderson & Co. in 1967. It was the link with Rowley Gill Davies & Co. that brought the international affiliation with Deloitte Plender Griffith & Co. in the United Kingdom to the merger table.

The 1971 merger to form Hutchison Hull was a merger between Watkins Hull Wheeler & Johnston, Hutchison Elliffe Davies, Anderson & Co.[12] and W. C. Reid & Sons (Dunedin).[13] Hutchison Hull then strengthened the affiliation to Deloitte Haskins & Sells, taking that name in 1983.

In addition to the use of local identifiers with long-established names in accounting partnership, a second characteristic of these firms up to the mid-1980s was that they were quintessential partnership organisations, not organisations based on corporate hierarchies. Income was most often shared within members of the partnership at the local level,[14] although Wilkinson

Wilberfoss, and Barr Burgess and Stewart, had nationally integrated systems of income allocation. However, all firms were based on democratic organisation, and partners adhered to the principle that they had a responsibility to future partners to leave the partnership in a better state than it was when they joined. They were also committed to staying in the partnership all their working lives; as one partner remembered, 'when you became partner your next dream was your retirement function, like there was nothing in between'.[15]

TABLE 1: EARLY CONNECTIONS

Overseas firm	New Zealand firm	Notes
Arthur Young & Co. Pannell Kerr Foster	Wilberfoss Harden Daniel & Co. Wilkinson Nankervis & Stewart	Merged and became Wilkinson Wilberfoss, and then Arthur Young in 1983
Whinney Murray & Co.; Ernst & Whinney	Hunt Duthie & Co.	
Coopers & Lybrand	Barr Burgess & Stewart	
Deloitte Haskins & Sells	Hutchison Hull & Co	
Horwath & Horwath Touche Ross & Co.	McCulloch Butler & Spence Clark Menzies	Merged in 1979 to form McCulloch Menzies; became Touche Ross & Co. in 1984; of the 85 partners only 21 went to the newly-formed DRT
Peat Marwick Mitchell Klynveld Main Goerdeler	Gilfillan & Co. Morris Pattrick & Co.	Merged in 1977 to become Gilfillan Morris & Co.; became Peat Marwick Mitchell & Co. in 1983
Price Waterhouse & Co.	Price Waterhouse & Co.	Unique in using an international name in New Zealand before 1982, because they had the name before a restriction on the use of international names was instituted
Thompson McClintock in United Kingdom, Main Lafrentz in United States	Cox Arcus Kendon Mills Muldoon & Browne	Merged with other firms to form Kendon Cox & Co. in 1980; K.M.G. Kendons (45 partners) split up in 1986/87 It was affiliated to K.M.G. after the Pattrick–Gilfillan merger, but lost affiliation after KMG*–Peat Marwick Mitchell transatlantic merger
Alexander Grant Tansley Witt	Cook & Co. Lawrence Godfrey & Co.	Split in 1979 between Hunt Duthie and Lawrence Anderson & Buddle
Mann Judd Hancock Woodward & Neil (Sydney)	Buddle & Co. Anderson & Co.	Lawrence Anderson Buddle (1980); 42 partners in 1986 and disintegrated in 1986/87. L.A.B. was in a correspondent relationship with Arthur Andersen until the Auckland partners left to go to Deloittes

* Klynveld Kraayenhof & Co. in Holland, the biggest firm in the Netherlands, and Deutsche Treuhand-Gesellschaft in Germany joined up with Turquand Barton Mayhew – as it then was – in London. Main Lafrentz merged with Hurdman and Cranstoun, and became Main Hurdman in New York, and then merged to become K.M.G. which was Klynveld Main Goerdeler.

The third distinguishing characteristic of accounting firms in the 1970s was that they had small numbers of partners and thus tended to specialise in different areas of services offered to the public. In contrast, the conglomerations of large firms in the 1990s were not only characterised by being large enough to support specialists, but also offered largely the same range of services as all the other Big 8. One point of difference between firms, even early on, was the degree to which they offered services for businesses facing insolvency or receivership. This proved to be key to survival and growth in the aftermath of the 1987 sharemarket crash in New Zealand. Although many partnerships lost a large number of audit clients, those with a developed insolvency specialisation were able to gain more business from that activity which, in part, compensated for the loss of income from auditing activities in the immediate post-1987 crash years.

Evolution and internationalism: two case studies

Why was there a change in the accounting firms from this point? Apart from the effect of the 1987 crash, there were four other major influences on the evolution of the firm. One was the move to service multinational enterprises by offering international audit services by globalised firms. Second, increasing consulting activities and risk management advice being undertaken by the firms. Third, the need for increasing capital to invest in large IT systems within the firms; and, last, the effect of the granting of approval by the New Zealand Society of Accountants in 1983 to allow international firm names.

The impact of these influences on New Zealand firms was that the large firms sought to take international firms' names, to retain large audit clients with the associated opportunities for consulting activities, and to keep at the top of the 'league table'. Reputation as being the largest firm was valuable, combined with having a strong international reputation. This was a two-edged sword: not only did the firms in New Zealand collapse when their American firms collapsed, as in the case of Arthur Andersen, but also they were then subject to directives to mergers from transatlantic imperatives. In order to illustrate these changes in accounting firms after the 1970s, this study now looks in detail at two particular events that epitomise problems in the transition from such local firms to the current state of the 'Big 4'.[16]

The merger of Clark Menzies with McCulloch Butler & Spence in 1979

McCulloch Butler & Spence, on the East Coast of the North Island, had a major audit client: Wattie Industries (producer of canned fruit and tomato sauce). Watties was shifting its head office from 'the fruit bowl of New Zealand' (Hawke's Bay) to Auckland. McCulloch Butler & Spence thus needed to provide a stronger Auckland base. Although they could have strengthened their Auckland office with transfers of staff from the East Coast region of New Zealand, they decided instead to merge with Clark Menzies, which had offices in Auckland, Wellington and Christchurch. Previously, the international link from McCulloch Butler & Spence had been to Horwath and Horwath; but they dropped this affiliation after the merger with Clark Menzies, as Clark Menzies already had a connection to Touche Ross & Co. The new firm was called McCulloch Menzies, dropping the Scottish pronunciation of 'Menzies'.

Parties from both sides do not remember it as being a successful merger. A former partner of the Clarke Menzies recalled differences largely due to the perception that partners from Auckland thought that they deserved more money than the others. There were also natural jealousies that emerged. Two former partners from the McCulloch Butler & Spence side recalled that they just 'got it wrong'; weakening the firm by 'developing a strategy that people would tell you was strengthening it. Because we strengthened the size, we strengthened the numbers, we strengthened the resource, but we weakened the culture and we weakened the expertise.' Another partner remembered a very clear feeling of 'an us and a them. There was McCullochs, and there was Clark Menzies; and there was definitely a friction between the two.' The East Coast group, the offices in Hastings, Gisborne, Napier, Waipawa and Wairoa, was very close and worked very well together. That didn't happen to the same extent after the Clark Menzies merger.

An indication of the failure of this merger to integrate sufficiently is provided in the debate within the firm concerning income allocation. McCulloch Menzies was attempting to develop a nationally acceptable method of profit allocation, with a distinction between regional and metropolitan offices. Although financial integration is considered to strengthen partnership cultures, the McCulloch Menzies system had not had the opportunity to mature to a point where it could unify the partners. Undoubtedly part of the delay in reaching agreement concerned the differences between the culture of Clarke Menzies and McCulloch Butler & Spence. Both had some weaknesses, there was no particularly strong leadership acceptable to both parties, and neither appeared to sufficiently respect its new merging partner, as noted in the above comments.

McCulloch Menzies then adopted the name of Touche Ross & Co. in 1984. Mergers with smaller firms continued. In 1985 five partners joined from the

Auckland firm of Grierson A. & J. Goodare Gibson & Co.,[17] and four of the five partners from Markham and Partners (Rotorua). But underlying problems remained. When they merged with Deloitte Haskins & Sells in 1989, they were not the stronger party to the merger. Many former Touche partners lost their jobs in the new large national organisation. In the Auckland office of McCulloch Menzies there were nine partners in 1981; ten years later none of these were in the firm of Deloitte Touche Tohmatsu. Table 2 provides data on partnership destinations nationwide three years after the merger.

TABLE 2: PARTNERSHIP DESTINATIONS THREE YEARS AFTER THE MERGER

	Touche Ross & Co.	Deloitte Haskins & Sells	Deloitte Touche Tohmatsu
Partners in 1989	83	66	149
Moving to other Big 8:			
K.P.M.G.*	-13		-13
C. & L.		-2	-2
E.Y.	-1		-1
To spin-off firms**	-24	-6	-30
To small firms	-10	-3	-13
To sole practice	-7		-7
Unable to trace after exit or retiring	-14	-10	-24
Moving to industry	-1	-1	-2
New partners admitted			10
No. of those leaving after merger			-1
Partners in 1993	13	44	66

* Nine of the thirteen who went to K.P.M.G. were in Gisborne.
** The spin-off firms from Touche Ross & Co. included Beattie Rickman in Hamilton, Silks in Wanganui, Tarrant Cotter in Wairoa, Iles Casey in Rotorua, Cottam Cave Evetts & Fah in New Plymouth, and Richardson Epplett & Pnrs in Hastings.

The merger of the Auckland office of Lawrence Anderson Buddle with Deloitte Haskins & Sells in 1987

The second event illustrating the importance of international affiliations can be observed in the movement of the Auckland office of Lawrence Anderson Buddle to Deloitte Haskins & Sells. The failure of Lawrence Anderson Buddle to gain a formal affiliation with name adoption of Arthur Andersen sowed the seeds of Lawrence Anderson Buddle's disintegration. The Auckland partners were unhappy that Arthur Andersen was not prepared to formalise the affiliation. In Auckland, Lawrence Anderson Buddle partners recalled that they had concerns about the unwillingness of Arthur Andersen to 'embrace' the New Zealand firm nationally. They were uncomfortable about staying on this representative basis; knowing they either had to get closer or change their representation. Their options were to seek to become the Arthur Andersen representative alone or to withdraw and seek an alternative association. The latter course was preferred, and the Auckland partners unexpectedly announced to the other offices that they were leaving and joining Deloittes Haskins & Sells.

From the other end of the country there was alarm at the loss of the Auckland office. It was variously described as 'unforgivable the way it was done' and 'a midnight coup'. Without an Auckland office the association with Arthur Andersen was no longer tenable, because Arthur Andersen wanted the representation in Auckland and Wellington, and were not really interested in Christchurch and Dunedin. The three other major urban branches were invited to join Deloittes with the Auckland office, but 'the feeling was so strong that we'd been betrayed that nobody was even interested in joining in with them'. Eventually, seventeen Lawrence Anderson Buddle partners from outside of Auckland went to Price Waterhouse, and this merger fitted very well for many of the partners.

This was one of the few occasions that partnership movements drew media attention; the *New Zealand Herald* noted on 15 September 1987 that the combined staff of 275 in the Auckland office of Deloitte Touche Tohmatsu after this event included twenty-one partners.[18] This suggests a relatively 'lean' organisation in terms of partner/staff ratios. Arthur Andersen then affiliated to a small firm (McLeod Lodjkine & Assoc.) in Auckland of five partners, all ex-Peat Marwick, and this gradually grew in the 1990s to have offices in the main centres.

These two cameos have been used to illustrate changes in accounting firms in Auckland after the large national firms were formed in the 1970s.

Major developments and their implications

There were three major changes in professional accounting firms in Auckland. Each of these had important implications for the partners, their clients, and the accelerating processes of globalisation of business activities and audit requirements.

First, the processes of internationalisation of firms led to structural changes in the accounting firms, moving away from partnership systems to complex hierarchies. This change has been well documented in the study by Rose and

Hinings,[19] which examined how global client demands were driving changes in the large accounting firms. The processes of internationalisation were followed by the necessity to comply with merger decisions. These decisions were principally driven by the need to maximise synergies or efficiencies in transatlantic business, but had the result of rupturing firms in Australia and New Zealand, as already described.

A second development was the loss of local identifiers: the predecessor firms of Deloitte Haskins & Sells and Touche Ross & Co. in New Zealand had been keen to adopt international names. These names brought the audit business of multinational clients, status, and the expertise and training the international connections provided. It was recognised that young staff benefited from working in the firms' London or US offices, to gain experience and take advantage of networking opportunities. However, an international merger event dictated by the US head office brought about a forced merger, without some of the Touche Ross & Co. audit clients in Australia or the Deloitte Haskins & Sells UK audit clients providing additional business after the merger.[20] The firms were now locked into a mega-merger that resulted in the disintegration of Touche Ross & Co. and, with it, the old well-established partnerships of McCulloch Butler & Spence, and Clark Menzies.[21]

Thirdly, there was the loss of the partnership model, with the shift to the professional service firm. One partner remembered that before the late 1980s he would have regarded his peers in the other accounting firms as his professional colleagues, not really as competitors. However, more recently the position is entirely different: 'We are much more competitive. The marketplace is much, much tougher. We do go and try and pinch other people's clients off them, whereas we never used to do that. You know, it used to be unprofessional to do that, it's no longer unprofessional to do that.' The situation is now much more competitive *vis-à-vis* other firms, other professional firms. It is acknowledged that 'in most ways it's for the better, it's only those of us who have been around quite a while who quite liked the more collegial sort of atmosphere'.[22] Another also found that 'the challenge wasn't to beat the enemy out in the marketplace, it was almost to get ahead of one's fellow partner . . . The post-crash period meant that the stabilisation of the pecking order was aggravated by the reduction in business generally.'

This reinforces the principle that partnership events cannot be understood on the assumption that partners are unified in their aspirations and commitment. In a study by Morris and Empson,[23] the experiences in two (unnamed) accounting firms are described, and it is noted how incentives and cooperative behaviour were enshrined within the culture of the firms. The authors also suggest that when firms are restructured through merger and international reorganisations, the later success of the firms partly depends on the management of knowledge transfers in the changing cultures of more hierarchical firms, and on the processes of knowledge transfer which may be aggravated by a lack of collegiality between partners.

The results of this study promote consideration of the extent to which the strength of an organisation relates to income allocation and financial integration of the partnership. A survey had been undertaken prior to the interviews for this project. In that survey, some responses to the question concerning 'the most significant factors in firm survival' identified financial integration as important to the firms' strength.[24] However, Deloittes did not have an integrated financial income allocation model, although Wellington and Auckland were one profit pool after 1990. Therefore, its strength during the Deloitte/Touche merger was not primarily derived from financial integration. In contrast, Touche Ross & Co. was attempting to develop a nationally acceptable system of profit allocation, with a distinction between regional and metropolitan offices in the allocation. While it was in the initial years of implementing a model, the Deloitte/Touche merger was proposed. Although financial integration may strengthen partnership cultures, for Touche Ross & Co. their system had not matured sufficiently. There are also hidden factors that can decimate a firm with little or no publicity, such as internal theft and out-of-court legal settlements in liability cases.[25] Touche Ross & Co. had problems with internal control, and/or defalcation of client funds, in at least four offices in the North Island in the 1980s.

Conclusion

It was acknowledged at the start of this study that, among professions, accounting firms in particular mimicked characteristics of their clients, moving from local firms to national firms to being part of multinational enterprises. Auckland accounting firms became part of national networks to audit their clients, and then international alliances were formed as Australian or other overseas enterprises absorbed their audit clients. The impact can be clearly observed from the analysis of partner numbers and partner movements in this study. Audit NZ also gained senior staff from the diaspora of Big 8 partners in the 1980s.

A more recent impact, not documented in this study, was the effect of the PriceWaterhouse/Coopers and Lybrand merger on partners in Auckland, and the effect of the collapse of Arthur Andersen in the United States on their partners in New Zealand, most of whom transferred to Ernst & Young. The movement of partners is like the top tenth of an iceberg; many staff below partner level moved with the Arthur Andersen partners to Ernst & Young, resulting in a sudden dearth of immediate employment opportunities for young graduates while the firms adjusted their staff numbers. The moderate increase in business from this shift was not commensurate with staff numbers, while the audits of surviving clients previously undertaken by Arthur Andersen worldwide were spread over the remaining Big 4 accounting firms.

Is bigger better? Perhaps yes, for the multinational clients, who depend on the reputation of auditors to ascribe confidence to their financial reports. But for the partner, the answer must be no for all but a few of the survivors; partners may well make more money over their working life in smaller, more stable firms. One partner commented that he would rather retire early than have to face another merger in his career. Firms other than the Big 8 continue to undertake audits of listed companies.[26]

So what does this tell us about Auckland business history? Auckland is the magnet for constant population movements from the Pacific, from Asia, and from other parts of New Zealand, and as the labour and consumer markets expand, it attracts businesses which expand in, or shift to, Auckland. Thus, first, the regular movement of head offices of companies, such as Watties, to Auckland has had a significant impact on their auditors. To keep the audit, the accounting firms have had to follow suit. Secondly, once an international affiliation had been forged, it is undoubtedly clear that the international affiliation was made or lost on the strength of the Auckland office. One major shift in the power of different urban branches was the swing of the pendulum between 1970 and 2000. In 1970, the majority of revenues for national accounting firms was derived from the Wellington offices of the large firms servicing clients such as banks, insurance companies and other head offices of national firms; by 2000, this had shifted to Auckland.

Adaptive behaviour by firms can be best understood if firms are not treated as one entity, but as a cluster of individuals competing between each other as well as competing with other firms. The value of a proprietary view over an entity perspective is rarely documented in organisational histories, and this study makes a contribution to the development of such an approach. In particular, the firm histories themselves have often glossed over the costs and downsides of expansion and mergers. These histories and stories of the survival and disintegration of accounting firms can be seen as closely related to both the role of Auckland and the role of international globalisation in New Zealand business history.

Auckland Business, 1841–2004:
Myth and Reality

RUSSELL STONE

A keynote address given at the New Zealand Business History Conference 2004,
'Enterprise in Distant Lands: Studies of South Pacific Business Development'

Auckland's exceptionalism

Auckland's reputation can be attributed to two, often related phenomena: the extraordinary growth of the city, and its commercial and entrepreneurial character. But before discussing these issues, I want to make a brief impressionistic comment on Auckland's unpopularity today. Outsiders are often irked by the way that Aucklanders, perhaps because their city is so big and so self-contained, tend to regard the rest of the country – as Australians are supposed to look on New Zealand – with benign indifference. In addition, what perhaps makes Auckland unappealing to the rest of New Zealand is that, unlike so-called 'old money' in Dunedin, much Auckland money is *new* money. Many Aucklanders who now make the Rich List have made their *entrée* in the past thirty years, giving rise to the perception of *nouveau riche* brashness as setting the tone of the city as a whole.

However that may be, people from abroad to whom I have spoken in recent years have told me that Auckland is by no means alone in the unpopularity stakes, that the distrust of the big city is not unique to New Zealand. In small-town Pennsylvania, for example, Pittsburgh is looked on as an oppressive presence. Or again, staying with the United States, the voting patterns of Republican-leaning small-town dwellers of the Mid-west during the 2004 presidential elections clearly demonstrated that New York, the 'Big Apple', by abandoning the moral values of the American heartland, had become an alien metropolis.[1]

A couple of years ago I read that it is mistaken to regard the great cultural divide in Canada as lying between the Francophone Canadians, the Quebeçois, and the English-speaking population. The writer asserted that what unites most of the provinces in this loose federation, ever prone to fly apart, is a shared dislike of Ontario, and particularly of its capital Toronto. Canadian historians to whom I have since spoken have told me this oversimplifies a complex situation. But they concede that there is a perception of Toronto among the Canadians who *don't* live there that it is too big, too commercialised and too arrogant. Is it Toronto or is it Auckland they are talking about?

But my concern is not with Auckland's unpopularity, but with what one might describe as its *exceptionalism.* Because outsiders have surely been right in seeing it as different, as a place apart. It was so before white settlers came to Auckland. The isthmus, on which metropolitan Auckland now stands, Maori called Tamaki-makau-rau, a maiden of such attractions that a hundred lovers contended for her. For its indigenous inhabitants, Tamaki had great natural advantages: its isthmus location and convenient portages, both so valuable in a canoe-borne society, its fish-rich harbours and fertile volcanic soils in combination enabling the isthmus to support many people. In that sense, heavily populated Tamaki-makau-rau prefigured the Pakeha Auckland that was to be.

Auckland as capital, 1840–1865

Whereas the gifts of nature set Maori Tamaki apart, for Pakeha the exceptionalism of Auckland is rooted in the commercial and entrepreneurial character that appeared at the time of its very foundation. The New Zealand Company settlements in Wellington and Nelson could claim some lofty self-justifying community ideal in their foundation, later embellished in the case of Dunedin and Christchurch by religious overtones. Auckland could never claim so high a purpose. It was a 'proclamation town', the creation of the governor Captain Hobson, an artificial settlement. Outside the official and armed services establishment, the leaders of the settlement were, from the word go, businessmen. They called themselves gentlemen of fortune. Settlers to the south referred to them as landsharks and speculators, men with an eye for the main chance. So, there was from the very beginning a particularity, something distinctive about Auckland. And clinging to this 'otherness' was the whiff of disrepute. The frenzied speculative bidding in April 1841 at Auckland's first Crown land auction for town sections seemed to confirm in the minds of southern settlers the dubious commercial tone of the new capital.

In fact most white settlers throughout the whole of New Zealand in the early days were anxious to take part in what Professor Gary Hawke once called the 'gigantic land lottery'.[2] Well-to-do settlers were aware from what had happened in Sydney and Adelaide that a royal road to wealth for men with capital was to buy cheap land early in the life of a settlement and to see property rise dramatically in value over time as the community grew up around it. But in pioneer Auckland, the attempt to reap a harvest of capital gains by speculating in land became so naked and so well developed a characteristic that it gave rise to the southern jibe that Auckland settlers seemed more interested in trading in land than in actually farming it. Government officials in Auckland itself, in fact, first made that charge. In June 1844, the Colonial Secretary, Dr Andrew Sinclair, complained in the Legislative Council that many of Auckland's first settlers were men who would rather speculate in land or merchandise 'than produce anything from the soil'.[3]

After eight years, Auckland's population lifted to over 9000, making it easily the largest settlement in the early colony. Facile explanations soon arose, generally denigratory. Critics accused the capital town of being a parasite, battening upon government expenditure and the commissariat needs of the armed forces stationed there.[4] One can easily understand why the locals turned to commerce. Pastoralism had quickly emerged as the mainstream of New Zealand's economic development, and it remained so for the rest of the nineteenth century and beyond. Lacking accessible pastoral land, and having (as the first censuses revealed)[5] so few sheep and cattle, Auckland lay on the margin of this mainstream. Nevertheless, the town was developing a more solid economic base than southern critics allowed.

The capitalists of the town turned to trade, exploiting (as Hobson predicted they would) Auckland's isthmus location as the natural point of convergence of vital South Seas trade routes. It is significant that in the 1864 census fifty-five Auckland citizens designated their occupation as 'merchants'.[6] As an *entrepôt*, Auckland began to draw its life from water-borne traffic, became a commercial centre through which imported goods streamed, some to be repackaged and transhipped elsewhere.

Looking at the story of Auckland business from the perspective of the later nineteenth century, it must not be imagined that continuing commercial success was the simple and inevitable consequence of Auckland's fortunate geographical location. The enterprise of its merchants, working in tandem with the far-sighted development of the infrastructure of the ports of Auckland on the Waitemata and Manukau Harbours, first by the provincial council, and (after 1871) by the harbour board, were vital contributors to Auckland's mercantile growth.

Nevertheless, in the later 1850s Auckland began steadily to lose ground to the southern provinces. As the 1864 census demonstrated, the rise of pastoralism and the discovery of gold in Canterbury and Otago had shifted the colony's demographic centre of gravity to the south. With two-thirds of the Parliament's votes in the hands of representatives of the South Island provinces, there was a certain inevitability about the shift of the capital to Wellington in 1865, much to the gratification of the settlers there.

From capital city to city of capital

With the General Assembly permanently relocated in Wellington, prominent Auckland businessmen, convinced that their town's proper business was business, began progressively to withdraw from central politics. That was why Auckland members of the General Assembly later in the century tended to be, so to speak, members of the City's Second XV. That leading Aucklanders should have chosen to fulfil themselves in the commercial rather than in the political arena is a distinctive characteristic of the city's business élite that has been apparent right through to modern times.

Quick to withdraw from politics after the shift of government in 1865 were a number of business leaders like Thomas Russell, John Logan Campbell, Robert Graham and Josiah Clifton Firth. An important exception was Frederick Whitaker, who with Thomas Russell in 1861 had founded what has become today's top-tier law firm of Bell Gully Buddle & Weir. Although perennially reluctant over the next twenty-six years to take his leave of Auckland, Frederick Whitaker had nevertheless dutifully turned up in Wellington, either unofficially as a lobbyist, or officially as a member of the Assembly. His brief, in either capacity, was to defend the interests of his firm and those of the Auckland commercial community of which he had become undisputed spokesman in Wellington.

That he should have done so is revealing. Thomas Buddle, a junior partner in the firm of Whitaker & Russell, in 1875 wrote to Thomas Russell (by now resident in England) informing him that Whitaker had been obliged to steel himself to going to the parliamentary session of that year. Whitaker (Buddle reported):

> . . . was a long time making up his mind to go, said he hated Wellington, hated travelling in the Steamers, hated being away from home & above all hated 'lobbying' and having to ask favours of noodles. However there seemed to be so many things demanding his attention & which without his presence would go wrong he felt that he was obliged to go to Wellington and I think he was right. The Shortland Saw Mill leases wanted him there, so did Piako,[7] Hunghunga,[8] Bay of Islands [Coal Company] Tramway,[9] the Bank of New Zealand, & to say nothing of the Abolition of the Provinces.[10]

The Auckland business community vehemently opposed the abolition of the provinces, fearing that the centralisation of governmental decision-making in Wellington could interfere with Auckland's economic development in an era of pork barrel politics, when public works and much else depended to a great extent on political influence and string pulling.

Auckland's business leaders, just like Whitaker, notwithstanding their reluctance to enter the political arena, and this is the case right through to the present day, have, just the same, never made the mistake of underestimating the need for a personal relationship with their political masters. Although this networking has been greatly facilitated in recent years by air travel and the use of email, major Auckland firms still maintain a Wellington presence in order to lobby and keep up personal contacts with politicians and members of the senior bureaucracy.[11] It is interesting to note how over the past decade politicians like Jim McLay, Jenny Shipley, Ruth Richardson and Doug Graham (among others) have been recruited to serve on the boards of public companies, and New Zealand-style quangos, primarily because of their previously established political connections. It is significant that, in 2004, the Auckland businessman Mike Williams was on five boards with a transport and energy emphasis, those two great concerns of the city, appointments which, he admitted, were not unconnected to his being president of the Labour Party 'with direct channels to [the present] Government'.[12]

Nevertheless, the need either to have a Wellington office, or to use professional lobbyists resident there to cosy up to policy makers in the so-called corridors of power (and this was noticeably the norm during the years of import licensing and exchange control, between 1938 and the mid-1980s), has fallen away dramatically in modern times. The retreat from government intervention in business activities initiated by Roger Douglas as Finance Minister of the fourth Labour Government, and continued by other politicians in the years since, has consolidated the trend. Some say that the outward manifestation of this ideological change in the world of business has been the continued shift of corporate head offices to Auckland and the 'downsizing' of the Wellington arm of the big two-city law partnerships such as Russell McVeagh Mackenzie Bartleet.

Back to 1865. While the loss of the seat of government to Wellington was a blow to the pride of Aucklanders, it little checked the progress of the northern city, and by reinforcing the entrepreneurial character of Auckland actually contributed to the city's emerging commercial dominance. To understand why, one must recognise the metamorphosis that Auckland passed through during its first fifty years. What began as a capital city became transformed into a city of capital. As we have seen, lacking pastoral resources to exploit, Auckland capitalists responded to economic reality, as they saw it, by striking out in new directions to create colony-wide financial institutions, such as the New Zealand Insurance Company in 1859,[13] the South British Insurance Company in 1872,[14] the Bank of New Zealand in 1861, the New Zealand Loan & Mercantile Agency Company Limited (NZL&MA) in 1865.

In floating the Auckland bank the promoters made a patriotic pitch for the support of investors in other provinces.[15] They promised that unlike foreign (i.e., Australian) banks such as the Union and the Bank of New South Wales that were already operating in the colony, the BNZ would have lending policies determined by New Zealand's own financial needs, uninfluenced as heretofore by the ebb and flow of Australia's business fortunes.[16]

This same group of mid-nineteenth-century Auckland businessmen was also responsible for setting up the heavily capitalised timber companies that milled the province's highly prized kauri resources, exporting them not only to the expanding southern provinces but also to overseas markets particularly in Australia. By these means, financial and industrial, Auckland entrepreneurs were able to break free from the shackles of a narrow provincial economy during the expansionist 1870s and early 1880s and thereby take advantage of the city building and pastoral development in the South Island and elsewhere.

A modern parallel may serve to illustrate. The rapidly growing money-earning industry working for today's economy is tourism.[17] The favoured destination for overseas visitors is obviously the South Island. That's where the clean and green image is actualised, that's where you have spectacular scenery and winter sports. Yet Auckland as the international point of entry and departure benefits as well, as does Rotorua through its proximity to Auckland. And it is often overlooked how many service industries operating in the scenic region, of which Queenstown is the epicentre, have an Auckland commercial base.

Back to the heady expansionist years of the nineteenth-century Vogel boom. When in the early 1880s these boom times evaporated, first in the South Island and then progressively further north, the expansion of Auckland (the city but not the province) to the mystification of overseas visitors seemed to carry on with a sustained impetus, a dynamism all of its own. The explanation surely is that the unusual surge of population in city and suburbs taking place during the late 1870s and early 1880s provided an ever-larger consumer market for goods and services. The city council and harbour board, and private firms and public companies, responded confidently to this growth, often continuing to borrow from abroad to meet the demands of the city's enlarged population. This explains why, by the time the expansionist bubble in the north finally burst in 1886, the population of Auckland's city and suburbs had risen to 57,048, as compared with 30,952, the previous census figure registered five years before.[18] It is interesting to note that, a hundred years later, Auckland, once again the destination of many of the people either moving there from within New Zealand or immigrating from abroad, fed on its own growth in precisely the same way.

The notorious 'Limited Circle'

The stagnation in Auckland business in 1887, and the collapse of rural land and timber companies, in turn, precipitated a banking crisis that imperilled the BNZ and its 'barnacle', the associated loan company, the New Zealand Loan and Mercantile Agency Company. While it is true that the crisis affected the whole colony, it had its greatest impact on Auckland, vaunted city of finance. The BNZ came under particular attack in 1887 when its shares, hitherto imagined by stakeholders to be blue chip, had a catastrophic fall in value, wiping out the greater part of the life savings of a number of investors. Furious shareholders set up an independent audit committee, which in due time provided them, in the person of the bank's directors, with whipping boys on whom they could vent their fury. Since a number of these delinquent directors were themselves mammoth borrowers, with loans inadequately secured on overvalued collateral, southern newspapers, and critics throughout the whole colony, were able, with some justice, to revive the canard of predatory Auckland speculators hunting as a pack. The directors of a number of Auckland's banking institutions, land and timber companies were accused of having played chuck farthing with the savings of southern capitalists, using the tricks and dodges of insider trading in a desperate attempt to save their own financial skins. Few of Auckland's first financial élite (stigmatised at the time as the 'Limited Circle') survived.[19] But what did survive was the city's disrepute for shady financial practices.

And the scandalous overtones attached to this BNZ crisis just would not go away. The continued fall, over a number of years, in the price of the bank's shares, the constant need for restructuring the bank, the shifting of its head office, the obligation of the Liberal Government in 1894 to underwrite it lest it fall, and finally an investigation into its affairs in 1895–96 kept the errant Auckland bank directors, for ever and a day, it seemed, in the public eye. But the crisis ultimately passed.

A new economy and leadership

Auckland, its shady reputation notwithstanding and under a new business leadership, was able to share in the general upswing of prosperity that set in for the colony after 1895 when refrigerated ocean transport transformed New Zealand into a kind of distant farmyard of the United Kingdom. Indeed, by the twentieth century, Auckland had developed its own regional economy, which on the surface, at least, seemed to make it more akin to the rest of New Zealand. This was a time when the port of Auckland emerged as the transport node for a newly productive hinterland that the province had hitherto lacked. No longer was it logical to refer to that province as a tadpole entity – all urban head and no productive body to speak of. One thinks here of the new farming districts like those in the Waikato, the Waipa, the Upper Thames Valley and the Bay of Plenty; Northland's rural development was to come somewhat later.

But at the same time another and countervailing change was working away silently to accentuate the otherness of the city. As we have seen, after the 1881 census the population of the Auckland urban area experienced a rate of growth that was easily the most rapid in New Zealand, a growth that met with little check in the twentieth century. The city of Auckland quite outstripped in size its one-time southern rivals such as Dunedin, in whose shadow Auckland had stood in days gone by. Between 1881 and 1945, when the population of New Zealand as a whole trebled, that of the Auckland urban area multiplied tenfold. This trend became even more marked after 1945, and continues to the present day. According to the 2001 census, 29 per cent of the New Zealand population lived in Auckland, compared with only 14 per cent in 1936.[20]

The 1996 census recorded that the aggregated population of the four cities making up the Auckland conurbation had reached a total of one million, a figure considerably in excess of that for the whole of the South Island. Significantly, Auckland's inter-censal rate of growth was 50 per cent greater than that of its nearest statistical rival, Christchurch. Heavy overseas immigration, much of it from the Pacific and Asia, has also changed the ethnic character of the city. The most recent census has emphasised the proportion of Auckland residents born overseas (one-third), of whom a substantial proportion are of non-European stock. One has only to walk down Queen Street to appreciate the ethnic and cultural diversity of the city.

But it is Auckland's size, not its multicultural character, that has continued to set it apart from the other New Zealand cities. The annoyance of Heartland New Zealand at the worsening transport problems generated by Auckland's extraordinary growth was strikingly demonstrated in 2002, when the Government floated the idea of a levy of 5 cents a litre on petrol to finance motorway construction that would ease traffic congestion in Auckland. Here I should like to cite a letter to the editor of the *Herald* written on 2 March 2002 by a citizen of Feilding. Headed 'Auckland killing rest of the country', the letter began with the remark that 'New Zealand is quickly evolving into a country of haves in Auckland and have-nots outside Auckland.'[21] Later it went on to say that 'For political reasons Helen Clark's Auckland Labour Party seems bent on killing the rest of the country where most of the nation's earnings are generated, even if the paper shuffling goes on in Auckland.' The old charge made against the commercial community of Auckland pops up once more: 'They toil not neither do they spin, yet Solomon in all his glory was not arrayed like these counters of beans and shufflers of paper in their towers of mirror glass.'

Graeme Hunt, former editor of the *National Business Review* and author of the authoritative publication, *The Rich List: Wealth and Enterprise in New Zealand*, is in no doubt that the Auckland region, which he defines as lying between Pukekohe and Wellsford, in fact more than pulls its weight. In a recent issue of the periodical *Metro,* Hunt estimated that the Auckland conurbation 'accounts for at least 40 percent of national GST activity'. He then went on to observe that whereas 'the region's population estimated at 1,290,800 in June 2003, accounts for 32.2 percent, or just under a third of the nation's inhabitants, its net GST activity is eight percentage points higher'.[22]

Nor is the growth of Auckland to be looked on as an aberration, peculiar to itself. Although registering the largest numerical increase, the growth of that city is simply emblematic of the rapid population increase and economic development taking place in the northern portion of the North Island from which, to be sure, the city benefits. The projections of the government statistician for the period 1996–2021 are for a growth rate in the four northernmost regions – Northland, Auckland, Waikato and the Bay of Plenty – of about a third, with the Tauranga area experiencing a growth rate considerably in excess of that of the Auckland urban area.[23] And this despite the expectation that by 2021 Auckland would 'be home to 33 percent of all New Zealanders, up from 28 percent in 1996'.[24] When discussing the implications of the 2001 census, the government statistician reminded us that in spite of its 'continued reliance on agricultural exports' New Zealand has become one of the most highly urbanised societies of the Western world. In 2001, 86 per cent of New Zealanders resided in urban areas, a slightly lower figure than the United Kingdom (90 per cent), but higher than Australia (85 per cent), Japan (79 per cent), the United States (77 per cent) and Europe (75 per cent).[25] Heartland New Zealand, it seems, is where an ever-diminishing minority of the population lives.

Growth after 1945

There are in fact sound economic reasons that explain why Auckland has grown so markedly since 1945. Auckland has become *the* commercial centre of the Dominion. As regional economies have tended to give way to a national economy, Auckland's predominance as an *entrepôt* has been reinforced. Consider these modern developments. Contemporary Auckland more than any other centre lies at the interface of the national and international economies. It has become the main point of entry of overseas capital in a 24-hour trading world. The containerisation of cargoes funnelled through the Fergusson Wharf complex, and the exponential increase in airfreighting at Mangere airport, have strengthened its position as an *entrepôt* at the expense of regional ports. The 1996 census ranked ports according to the values of cargoes loaded and unloaded in New Zealand in this order: first, Ports of Auckland – $8.4 billion; second, Auckland International airport – $7 billion (the Airport Company shares reached a record high on the stock exchange in 2004); third, Tauranga – $3.5 billion;[26] and fourth, Christchurch – $3.4 billion.

Auckland has now become the country's greatest industrial centre, having benefited disproportionately from the growth of manufacturing that has taken place in New Zealand since 1945. Because industries in New Zealand tend to be market-driven, and with Greater Auckland providing the greatest concentration of consumers of goods and services in the country, fresh industries have tended to establish themselves there, while existing southern industries have been increasingly drawn to the north.

Further, in what has been called the post-industrial age, it is inevitable that an increasing number of New Zealand workers should be involved in service industries: education, the professions, tourism, health, financial and commercial services, supermarkets, real estate agencies (which multiply like rabbits in this city), local government, restaurants, producers of junk mail and the like. Auckland has an unusual number of people engaged in a wide variety of urban service industries, as the 2500 pages of Auckland's *Yellow Pages* will attest. This is unusual for New Zealand, but not for the outside world, where increasing numbers entering the service sector is a well-established phenomenon.

But Auckland's growth in almost all of these activities has been at the expense of other ports, towns and cities. Industries have shifted north, company headquarters and people too. In the words of the Bible: 'For he that hath, to him shall be given: and he that hath not, from him shall be taken even that which he hath' (Mark 4: 25). Cold comfort to the rest of New Zealand. Even more so when one considers that Auckland's population growth and economic dominance are likely to continue. Better to speak of these developments as being for the most part irresistible and inevitable. Nor are they scandalous. Curiously enough, Michael Cullen and Helen Clark have reminded the rest of New Zealand during Labour's second term of government that non-Aucklanders have a vested interest in Auckland's economic well-being, since that is so often a barometer of the state of the national economy. And it does, indeed, seem to be the case that when Auckland catches a cold the rest of the country sneezes. That this saying has become a truism and therefore a cliché does not make it any the less true.

Terminus or staging port?

But isn't this picture of Auckland's dominance itself undergoing modification in the early twenty-first century? Let's begin with demographics. The *New Zealand Official Yearbook* has noted that the relative rise and fall of regional populations within our country has been mainly determined by the 'traffic' of a national community who throughout its 160-year history has proved to be unusually mobile. It has been the received wisdom that Auckland was the final destination of most of those on the move in New Zealand. Yet is this not itself a myth? Over one million Kiwis now live and work abroad; of these, 600,000 reside in Australia. Shouldn't we now start looking at Auckland not as the terminus but simply a staging post in what has become an accelerating trans-Tasman drift of so many ambitious and well-qualified New Zealanders?

And isn't this demographic shift symptomatic of a trans-Tasman corporate drift as well? Banks, breweries, newspapers, television and broadcast radio stations, travel agencies, energy companies, supermarket chains, oil exploration outfits, and a number of seemingly local concerns, while still flaunting their incontestably New Zealand brand names and having their putative headquarters in Auckland, are now owned by overseas capital, with increasing control in Australia, Asia and elsewhere. The recent sale of Auckland-based DB Breweries is symptomatic of the process. A successful takeover from what the press described as its 'Singapore-based parent Asia Pacific Breweries' soon proved not to be the end of the trail, because the Singaporean company was, in turn, owned by the multinational Heineken.[27]

Murray Weatherston, an Auckland financial consultant, well-known as a national radio broadcaster on investment affairs, recently said that 'a frequently occurring feature of this westward drift is that often the Auckland office becomes the branch office of an Australian firm that is in the process of moving its activities north-west to Singapore or China or Malaysia, or Vietnam'. He considers that coincident with the continuing shift of head offices to Auckland is the emerging reality that 'there is less autonomous decision-making here as Auckland corporates increasingly report to their offshore masters'. Or again, a recent *Metro* article has persuasively argued that this trans-Tasman corporate drift explains why it has come about that some of Auckland's top-tier legal firms are establishing branch offices in Australia or (as the author puts it) 'cuddling up' to legal 'heavy hitters' there, because increasingly that is where the action is.[28]

But will these facts supplant the old myths? Will the rest of the country now begin to accept that Auckland is not, after all, too big for its boots?[29] Will Heartland New Zealand begin to say 'Come back Auckland, all is forgiven'? That seems unlikely: for Janet and John Citizen, myths are as seductive as they are stubbornly long-lived.

I am reminded of the classic western film produced by John Ford in 1962, *The Man who Shot Liberty Valence*. In this film a tenderfoot lawyer, James Stewart, becomes a hero when he shoots the local bad man, played by Lee Marvin. But the shot that killed that 'no-good varmint' was really fired by a hardened old gunslinger John Wayne, friend and protector of James Stewart. The lawyer, who in later years becomes a senator, is conscience-stricken, believing that he has killed a man. Wayne, on the other hand, driven by the imperative of the West that 'A man's gotta do what a man's gotta do', has no such qualms of conscience. Inevitably the point is raised: 'Shouldn't the truth of the matter be told and the myth buried?' Then John Ford, whose worldview pervades the whole film, has a newspaper reporter refusing to record what really happened. 'When the legend becomes fact', the journalist declares, you 'print the legend'. Implicit in this declaration is the belief that, as a general rule, people prefer the entrenched legend (the myth) to reality. I expect that, for most non-Aucklanders, the myth of the crassly commercial city of the north is so well established that that's what they will continue to believe. So the myth of Auckland has become the fact. Most Aucklanders have learned to accept that.

But should New Zealand's business historians continue to do so? Or is the cost too great? Roland Barthes, the great French critic, once wrote: 'Myth deprives the object of which it speaks of all of its history.' This is a point well worth pondering.

NOTES

INTRODUCTION A WELCOME RENAISSANCE: BUSINESS HISTORY IN NEW ZEALAND

1   Terence Hodgson, *The Heart of Colonial Auckland, 1865–1910*, Auckland, Random Century, 1992, p. 103.

2   Alfred D. Chandler Jnr, *Strategy and Structure*, MIT Press, Cambridge (Mass.), 1962.

CHAPTER ONE AUCKLAND BUSINESS: THE NATIONAL AND INTERNATIONAL CONTEXT

1   H. Macmillan, *At the End of the Day 1961–1963*, Macmillan, London, 1973, p. 349.

2   D. Greasley and L. Oxley, 'Outside the Club: New Zealand's Economic Growth, 1870–1993', *International Review of Applied Economics*, 14(2), 1999, p. 175.

3   *Ibid.*, p. 190.

4   A. Maddison, *Dynamic Forces in Capitalist Development*, Oxford University Press, Oxford, 1991.

5   M. McKinnon, *Treasury: 160 Years of the New Zealand Treasury*, Auckland University Press in association with the Ministry of Culture and Heritage, Auckland, 2003.

6   D. Greasley and L. Oxley, 'Growing Apart? Australia and New Zealand Growth Experiences, 1870–1993', *New Zealand Economic Papers*, 33(2), 1999, pp. 1–14.

7   P. A. Cashin, 'Real GDP in the Seven Colonies of Australasia: 1861–1991', *Review of Income and Wealth*, 41(1), 1995, pp. 19–39.

8   D. Galt, 'New Zealand's Economic Growth', New Zealand Treasury Working Paper No. 00/09, 2000; B. Buckle and N. McLellan, 'The Growth Race at the OECD Stadium', *Competition and Regulation Times*, 11, 2003, pp. 1–2, 12; B. Buckle and N. McLellan, 'Skill and Stamina Win the Growth Race at the OECD Stadium', *Competition and Regulation Times*, 13, 2004, pp. 8–10.

9   A. Grimes, 'Why are New Zealanders so Wealthy?', *Competition and Regulation Times*, 9, 2002, pp. 4–5. It should be mentioned that this figure is far from definitive. It covers only a certain type of household and ignores financial wealth and debt.

10 C. A. Blyth (ed.), *The Future of Manufacturing in New Zealand,* Oxford University Press, London, 1964.

11 For further amplification on this point, see J. Singleton and P. L. Robertson, *Economic Relations Between Britain and Australasia 1945–1970*, Palgrave, Basingstoke, 2002, ch. 1; D. Greasley and L. Oxley, 'A Tale of Two Dominions: Comparing the Macroeconomic Records of Australia and Canada Since 1870', *Economic History Review*, 51(2), 1998, pp. 294–318; D Greasley and L. Oxley, 'Outside the Club: New Zealand's Economic Growth, 1870–1993', *International Review of Applied Economics*, 14(2), 2000, pp. 173–93; B. Schedvin, 'Staples and Regions of the Pax Britannica', *Economic History Review*, 43(4), 1990, pp. 533–59; G. R. Hawke, *The Making of New Zealand: An Economic History*, Cambridge University Press, Cambridge, 1985; S. R. H. Jones, 'Government Policy and Industry Structure in New Zealand, 1900–1970', *Australian Economic History Review*, 39(3), 1999, pp. 191–212; D. Mabbett, *Trade, Employment and Welfare: A Comparative Study of Trade and Labour Market Policies in Sweden and New Zealand, 1880–1980*, Clarendon Press, Oxford, 1995; B. Easton, *In Stormy Seas: The Post-War New Zealand Economy*, University of Otago Press, Dunedin, 1997.

12 International Monetary Fund, *New Zealand: Selected Issues*, Country Report No. 04/127, IMF, Washington D.C., 2004.

13 J. B. Condliffe, *New Zealand in the Making*, George Allen & Unwin, London, 1930.

14 D. Greasley and L. Oxley, 'Globalization and Real Wages in New Zealand 1873–1913', *Explorations in Economic History*, 41(1), 2004, pp. 26–47.

15   Hawke, *The Making of New Zealand, op. cit.*; G. R.
      Hawke, *The Thoroughbred Among Banks in New
      Zealand*, vol. 1, National Bank of New Zealand,
      Wellington, 1997; S. Ville, *The Rural Entrepreneurs:
      A History of the Stock and Station Agent Industry in
      Australia and New Zealand*, Cambridge University
      Press, Cambridge, 2000; S. Ville and G. Fleming,
      'The Nature and Structure of Trade–Financial
      Networks: Evidence from the New Zealand
      Pastoral Sector', *Business History*, 42(1), 2000,
      pp. 41–58.

16   J. Belich, *Paradise Reforged: A History of the New
      Zealanders from the 1880s to the Year 2000*, Penguin,
      Auckland, 2001.

17   P. J. Cain and A. G. Hopkins, *British Imperialism:
      Innovation and Expansion, 1688–1914*, Longman,
      London, 2003; A. G. Hopkins, 'Gentlemanly
      Capitalism in New Zealand', *Australian Economic
      History Review*, 43(3) 2003, pp. 287–97; J. McAloon,
      'Gentlemanly Capitalism and Settler Capitalists:
      Imperialism, Dependent Development and
      Colonial Wealth in the South Island of New
      Zealand', *Australian Economic History Review*,
      42(2), 2002, pp. 204–23; J. McAloon., 'Gentlemen,
      Capitalists and Settlers: A Brief Response',
      Australian Economic History Review, 43(3), 2003,
      pp. 298–304.

18   G. Fleming, 'Agricultural Support Policies in a
      Small Open Economy: New Zealand in the 1920s',
      Economic History Review, 52(2), 1999, pp. 334–54.

19   G. Fleming, 'Economists and Mortgage Relief in
      New Zealand in the 1930s', *Australian Economic
      History Review*, 37(1), 1997, p. 66.

20   J. Singleton, 'New Zealand: Devaluation without a
      Balance of Payments Crisis', in T. Balderston (ed.),
      *The World Economy and National Economies in the
      Interwar Slump*, Palgrave, Basingstoke, 2003, pp.
      172–90; T. Endres and K. Jackson, 'Policy Responses
      to the Crisis: Australasia in the 1930s', in W. R.
      Garside (ed.), *Capitalism in Crisis: International
      Responses to the Great Depression*, Pinter, London,
      1993; Hawke, *The Making of New Zealand, op. cit.*,
      chs 7–8; G. R. Hawke, 'Depression and Recovery in
      New Zealand', in R. G. Gregory and N. G. Butlin
      (eds), *Recovery from the Depression: Australia and the
      World Economy in the 1930s*, Cambridge University
      Press, Cambridge, 1988.

21   T. Endres, 'The Development of Economists' Policy
      Advice in New Zealand, 1930–4: With Particular
      Reference to Belshaw's Contribution', *Australian
      Economic History Review*, 30(1), 1990, pp. 64–78; T.
      Endres, 'The Economics of Wages and Wage Policy
      in the Depression and Recovery Period: Distinctive
      Elements in the New Zealand Debate', *New Zealand
      Journal of Industrial Relations*, 15, 1990, pp. 1–18; G.
      Fleming, 'Keynes, Purchasing Power Parity and
      Exchange Rate Policy in New Zealand During the

      1930s Depression', *New Zealand Economic Papers*, 31,
      1997, pp. 1–14.

22   Hawke, 'Recovery from Depression', *op. cit.*;
      Singleton, 'New Zealand: Devaluation', *op. cit.*; C. P.
      Kindleberger, 'Competitive Currency Depreciation
      Between Denmark and New Zealand', *Harvard
      Business Review*, 12, 1934, pp. 416–26.

23   D. Greasley and L. Oxley, 'Regime Shift and Fast
      Recovery on the Periphery: New Zealand in the
      1930s', *Economic History Review*, 55(4), 2002, pp.
      697–720.

24   I. M. Drummond, *Imperial Economic Policy
      1917–1939*, George Allen & Unwin, London, 1974;
      F. Capie, 'Australian and New Zealand Competition
      in the British Market 1920–39', *Australian Economic
      History Review*, 18(1), 1978, pp. 46–63.

25   Greasley and Oxley, 'Regime Shift', *op. cit.*

26   Singleton and Robertson, *Economic Relations, op.
      cit.*; C. Nixon and J. Yeabsley, *New Zealand's Trade
      Policy Odyssey: Ottawa, Via Marrakech, And On*,
      New Zealand Institute of Economic Research,
      Wellington, 2002.

27   Easton, *In Stormy Seas, op. cit.*, pp. 75–7.

28   C. G. H. Simkin, 'Insulationism and the Problem of
      Economic Stability', *Economic Record*, 22(1), 1946,
      pp. 50–65.

29   B. V. T. Baker, *The New Zealand People at War:
      War Economy*, Department of Internal Affairs,
      Wellington, 1973.

30   Hawke, *The Making of New Zealand, op. cit.*, ch. 13.

31   R. S. Deane, *Foreign Investment in New Zealand
      Manufacturing*, Sweet & Maxwell, Wellington, 1970.

32   J. D. Gould, *The Rake's Progress: The New Zealand
      Economy Since 1945*, Hodder & Stoughton,
      Auckland, 1982; Easton, *In Stormy Seas, op. cit.*

33   M. W. Guest and J. Singleton, 'The Murupara
      Project and Industrial Development in New
      Zealand 1945–65', *Australian Economic History
      Review*, 39(1), 1999, pp. 52–71.

34   S. Brownie and P. Dalziel, 'Shift-Share Analyses of
      New Zealand Exports, 1970–1984', *New Zealand
      Economic Papers*, 27(2), 1993, pp. 233–49.

35   B. Gustafson, *His Way: A Biography of Robert
      Muldoon*, Auckland University Press, Auckland,
      2000, pp. 276–7.

36   B. Easton, *The Nationbuilders*, Auckland University
      Press, Auckland, 2001.

37   M. Bassett, *The State in New Zealand 1840–1984*,
      Auckland University Press, Auckland, 1998, pp.
      352–75

38   B. Silverstone, A. Bollard and R. Lattimore (eds), *A
      Study of Economic Reform: The Case of New Zealand*,
      Elsevier, Amsterdam, 1996; L. Evans, A. Grimes and
      B. Wilkinson with D. Teece, 'Economic Reform in
      New Zealand 1984–95: The Pursuit of Efficiency',
      Journal of Economic Literature, 34(4), 1996, pp.
      1856–1902; Easton, *In Stormy Seas, op. cit.*; P. Dalziel

and R. Lattimore, *The New Zealand Macroeconomy: A Briefing on the Reforms and their Legacy*, (4th edn), Oxford University Press, South Melbourne, 2001; P. Dalziel, 'New Zealand's Economic Reforms: An Assessment', *Review of Political Economy*, 14(2), 2002, pp. 31–46.

39 R. Douglas and L. Callan, *Toward Prosperity: People and Politics in the 1980s: A Personal View*, David Bateman, Auckland, 1987.

40 Holmes argues that the National Bank succeeded in containing risk during the early years of the deregulated era, in stark contrast to the Bank of New Zealand and some other institutions. Sir Frank Holmes, *The Thoroughbred Among Banks in New Zealand*, vol. 3, National Bank of New Zealand, Wellington, 2003.

41 University of Auckland, 'Monetary Policy Seminar, November 22, 1988, Consensus of Views', Auckland, 1988.

42 D. Sheppard *et al.*, 'The Recent Conduct of Monetary Policy in New Zealand. The Theory and the Evidence', a discussion paper prepared for debate by New Zealand economists at the request of the New Zealand Manufacturers Federation Inc., 1989.

43 R. D. Bedford *et al*, 'The Globalization of Migration in New Zealand', *New Zealand Population Review*, 28(1), 2002, pp. 69–97.

44 B. Buckle, K. Kim and N. McLellan, 'The Impact of Monetary Policy on New Zealand Business Cycles and Inflation Variability', New Zealand Treasury Working Paper No. 03/09, 2003.

45 I. Claus, 'Changes in New Zealand's Production Structure: An Input Output Analysis', New Zealand Treasury Working Paper No. 03/01, 2003.

46 Brief information on this company's history is available at www.fisherpaykel.com.

47 D. Frame, 'Finland and New Zealand: A Cross-Country Comparison of Economic Performance', New Zealand Treasury Working Paper No. 00/1, 2000.

48 International Monetary Fund, *New Zealand: Selected Issues, op. cit.*; John Whitehead, 'New Zealand's Economic Growth: A Near and a Far View', paper presented to the New Zealand Association of Economists' Annual Conference, 30 June 2004.

49 Of course, that isolation also confers some benefits, as many New Zealanders realised after the recent terrorist attacks on the United States and Spain.

CHAPTER TWO MAORI ENTERPRISE: SHIPS AND FLOUR MILLS

1 Simon Ville, 'The Coastal Trade of New Zealand Prior to World War One', *New Zealand Journal of History*, 27(1), 1993, p. 85.

2 'History from below' is a form of historical narrative, developed following the Annales School, which was popularised in the 1960s. It focuses on the perspectives of ordinary individuals or aspects of history that were previously considered unimportant historically.

3 A New South Wales trading vessel purchased 7 to 8 tons of 'very fine' potatoes that year. R. P. Hargreaves, 'Changing Maori Agriculture in Pre-Waitangi New Zealand', *Journal of the Polynesian Society* (hereafter JPS), 72(2), June 1963, p. 103 and Rhys Richards and Jocelyn Chisholm, *Bay of Islands Shipping Arrivals and Departures 1803–1840*, The Paremata Press, Wellington, 1992.

4 William Dalton, *The Dalton Journal: Two Whaling Voyages to the South Seas 1823–1829*, Niel Gunson (ed.), National Library of Australia, Canberra, 1990, pp. 85–7.

5 King to Earl Camden, 30 April 1805, cited in R. McNab, *Historical Records of New Zealand*, vol. I, Government Printer, Wellington, pp. 254–5.

6 Log of Captain McKenzie of the *Samuel Robertson*, quoted in Richards and Chisholm, *op. cit.*, n.p.

7 Harry Morton found 'ample testimony' that Maori 'went whaling with delight' and that 'Captains liked to recruit Maoris': *The Whale's Wake*, McIndoe for The University of Otago Press, Dunedin, 1982, pp. 166–7. Moreover, concerning the Pacific more generally, Kerry Howe has suggested that there were probably more indigenous Pacific people than Europeans travelling during the early period of commercial interaction in the region: K. R. Howe, *Where the Waves Fall*, Allen and Unwin, Sydney, 1984, p. 108. David A. Chappell argued similarly in his book, *Double Ghosts: Oceanian Voyagers on Euroamerican Ships*, Armonk, New York, 1997.

8 By the end of 1836, Taiwhanga had twenty head of cattle and was regularly selling butter to a merchant at the Bay of Islands: Claudia Orange and Ormond Wilson, 'Taiwhanga Rawiri fl. 1818–1874', *Dictionary of New Zealand Biography*, vol. 1, Allen & Unwin/Dept. of Internal Affairs, Wellington, 1990, p. 418, updated 16 December 2003, http://www.dnzb.govt.nz/.

9 Angela Ballara, 'Tamati Waka Nene', *Dictionary of New Zealand Biography*, vol. 1, p. 306; and 'Eruera Maihi Patuone', *ibid.*, p. 338.

10 Andrew Sharp (ed.), *Duperrey's Visit to New Zealand in 1824*, Alexander Turnbull Library, Wellington, 1971, p. 27.

11 *Sydney Gazette*, 21 October 1826, cited in Richards and Chisholm, *Bay of Islands Shipping, op. cit.*, n.p.

12 Indeed, it appears that the figures recorded by the New South Wales Customs House differ quite significantly from the equivalent figures recorded at the Public Record Office in London: Peter Adams, *Fatal Necessity: British Intervention in New Zealand 1830–1847*, Auckland University Press, Auckland,

1977, p. 290. The importance of this trade to the New South Wales Governors and Council is likely to relate to that colony's shortage of suitable exports to offset their imports of tea and other foodstuffs, especially from China, and the barriers posed by the East India Company's monopoly over trade with the Chinese mainland and the islands of the East Indies: D. R. Hainsworth, *The Sydney Traders: Simeon Lord and his Contemporaries, 1788–1821*, Melbourne University Press, Melbourne, 1971, p. 157.

13   Montefiore, Haupokia and another Sydney merchant, Arthur Kemmis, departed on the brig *Argo* on 11 November 1830: John O. C. Ross, *William Stewart, Sealing Captain, Trader and Speculator*, Roebuck, Canberra, 1987, p. 154; and no author, 'The Early Traders on the West Coast', *Journal of the Auckland–Waikato Historical Societies*, 28, 1976, p. 19.

14   See, for example, William Endicott, *Wrecked Among Cannibals in the Fijis; A Narrative of Shipwreck and Adventure in the South Seas*, Marine Research Society, Salem (Mass.), 1923, pp. 17, 23.

15   Anne Salmond, *Between Worlds: Early Exchanges Between Maori and Europeans, 1773–1815*, Viking, Auckland, 1997, p. 441.

16   Patrick J. Grant, 'Late Holocene Histories of Climate, Geomorphology and Vegetation, and their Effects on the First New Zealanders', in Douglas G. Sutton (ed.), *The Origins of the First New Zealanders*, Auckland University Press, Auckland, 1994, p. 183; M. S. McGlone, A. J. Anderson and R. N. Holdaway, 'An Ecological Approach to the Polynesian Settlement of New Zealand', *ibid.*, pp.155–6.

17   Angela Ballara, 'Ruatara ? –1815', *Dictionary of New Zealand Biography*, *op. cit.*, p. 376, updated 16 Dec. 2003. Samuel Marsden eventually sent him a hand-operated flour mill from New South Wales.

18   A decline in Maori health and population due to dietary change, lack of immunity to new viruses, and the adoption of European clothing, gave credence to missionary assertions that theirs was a superior god. This, a desire for literacy, and the missionaries' role as peacemakers during a time of unprecedented violence increased rates of conversion and widened the acceptance of Christian tenets: Michael Jackson, 'Literacy, Communications and Social Change', in I. H. Kawharu (ed.), *Conflict and Compromise: Essays on the Maori since Colonisation*, A. H. and A. W. Reed, Wellington, 1975, pp. 30, 34; Judith Binney, 'Christianity and the Maoris to 1840: A Comment', *New Zealand Journal of History*, II, October 1969, p. 153.

19   J. W. Elder (ed.), *The Letters and Journals of Samuel Marsden, 1765–1838, Senior Chaplain in the Colony of New South Wales and Superintendent of the Mission of the Church Missionary Society in New Zealand*, Coulls, Somerville Wilkie and A. H. Reed for the Otago University Council, 1932, Dunedin, p. 189.

20   R. P. Wigglesworth, 'The New Zealand Timber and Flax Trade 1769–1840', Ph.D. thesis, Massey University, New Plymouth, 1981, pp. 129–30.

21   William Yate, *An Account of New Zealand*, Seeley and Burnside, London, 1835, p. 271.

22   Manuka Arnold Henare, 'The Changing Images of Nineteenth Century Maori Society – From Tribes to Nation', Ph.D. thesis, Victoria University of Wellington, Wellington, 2003, p. 160.

23   David McGill, *The Guardians at the Gate: The History of the New Zealand Customs Department*, Silver Owl Press for the New Zealand Customs Department, Wellington, 1991, p. 20; Binney, 'Christianity and the Maoris', *op. cit.*, p. 165. Jack Lee has noted the apparently anomalous situation whereby the shipping tonnage into the Bay of Islands was, at 22,206, the highest in New Zealand whereas the customs receipts of £3,728 15s 7d were below those of Auckland. His explanation for this is that shipping at the Bay consisted mostly of whalers which were very large vessels but handled little dutiable merchandise and generated little business: Jack Lee, *'I have named it the Bay of Islands . . .'*, Hodder and Stoughton, Auckland, 1983, p. 241.

24   Lee, *ibid.*, pp. 242–6. Mair was apparently in dire financial straits and Clendon was saved only by an injection of foreign capital.

25   J. L. Campbell to Dr Campbell, 24 October 1842, cited in R. C. J. Stone, *Young Logan Campbell*, Auckland University Press/Oxford University Press, Auckland, 1982, p. 108.

26   See, for example: the *New Zealander* (14 Mar. 1846, p. 3), concerning Maori seeking farm work in order to learn agricultural skills; the journal of missionary, John Morgan, concerning others being sent from the Waikato to earn money for the building of a chapel (John Morgan Journal, Dec. 1848, MS213, vol. 2, Auckland Museum); or Philip Andrews, *No Fear of Rusting*, (Rotorua and District Historical Society, Rotorua, 2001, p. 232), concerning a party from Maketu who went to Auckland to raise funds to pay off a ship and contribute towards another chapel.

27   'Te Rore School Anniversary [1880–1950]', p. 8, Waikato Museum, VG: Maori Collection: Archaeology/Plants/Religion etc., File 3B Flour Milling.

28   Dick Craig, *The King Country: New Zealand's Last Frontier (Rohe Potae)*, R. S. Craig, Te Awamutu, 1990, p. 35.

29   Nancy M. Taylor, *Early Travellers in New Zealand*, Clarendon Press, Oxford, 1959, p. 96.

30   W. Swainson, *Auckland, the Capital of New Zealand . . .*, Smith, Elder, London, 1853, reprinted Wilson & Horton, Auckland, 1971, pp. 33–4.

31   Muriel F. Lloyd Prichard, *An Economic History of New Zealand to 1939*, Collins, Auckland, 1970, pp. 34, 75; New Zealand Government, *New Zealand*

Statistics 1853–65, New Zealand Government, Auckland, 1858.

32   C. G. F. Simkin, *The Instability of a Dependent Economy: Economic Fluctuations in the Interwar Slump*, Oxford University Press, Oxford, 1951, p. 117; Lloyd Prichard, *op. cit.*, p. 73.

33   *New Zealander*, 11 Apr. 1855, p. 3.

34   For example, David Johnson, *New Zealand's Maritime Heritage*, Collins/Bateman, Auckland, 1987, p. 48.

35   A. D. Mead, *Richard Taylor: Missionary Tramper*, Reed, Wellington, 1966, pp. 206–7.

36   George Buttle to his sister, 23 Jun. 1855, 'Letters to and from members of the Newman Family, 1853–1868', MS 483, Auckland Museum.

37   Ville, 'The Coastal Trade in New Zealand', *op. cit.*, p. 75.

38   Johnson, *New Zealand's Maritime Heritage*, *op. cit.*, p. 50.

39   Edward Shortland, 'Evils', Shortland Papers, MS 20u, n.p., University of Auckland Library.

40   Chapman to Archdeacon Brown, 18 Aug. 1845, Thomas Chapman Letters and Journals, Folder 2, MS56, Auckland Institute and Museum.

41   *New Zealander*, 14 Mar. 1846, p. 3.

42   Morgan to Church Missionary Society (?), 11 Mar. 1846, Letters and Journals of John Morgan, vol. 1, MS 213, Auckland Institute and Museum.

43   Raymond Hargreaves calculated that at least thirty-seven mills were being or had been built for Maori owners in the Auckland Province between 1846 and 1860 (R. P. Hargreaves, 'Maori Flour Mills of the Auckland Province 1846–1860', JPS, 70(2), June 1961, p. 228), but at least six operated in Taranaki during the 1850s, as well as others in Wellington, Whanganui and elsewhere.

44   Grey to Earl Grey, 17 Mar. 1848, No. 37, *Great Britain Parliamentary Papers*, vol. 6, pp. 103–4.

45   *New Zealander*, 14 Mar. 1846, p. 3.

46   Most subsequent mills specified French burr stones.

47   Report for the Year 1851, Letters and Journals of John Morgan, MS213, vol. 2, Auckland Museum.

48   Morgan to Grey, 16 May 1853, GLNZ M44 (22), Auckland City Library.

49   Cited in W. H. Gifford and H. Bradney Williams, *A Centennial History of Tauranga*, Tauranga Centennial Committee and A. H. and A. W. Reed, Dunedin, 1940, p. 165. A mill was built at Maungatautari between 1847 and 1848. Costing £110, it was also equipped with scoria stones.

50   *New Zealander*, 13 Feb. 1847, p. 2. S. McD. Martin had earlier commented on the 'extravagance in living and drinking' of the Aucklanders, *New Zealand: in a Series of Letters*, Simmonds & Ward, London, 1845, p. 131.

51   *New Zealander*, 13 Feb. 1847, p. 3.

52   Young to the Colonial Secretary, 14 Nov. 1849, IA 1, 49/2307, ANZ, Wellington.

53   Grey to Earl Grey, No. 4 (No. 121), 30 Aug. 1851, *Great Britain Parliamentary Papers*, vol. 8, p. 23; *New Zealand Spectator and Cook's Strait Guardian*, 17 Nov. 1852.

54   Fenton to the Governor, 9 Jul. 1856, Report of a Board appointed by his Excellency the Governor to inquire into and report upon the state of Native Affairs, Paragraph 88, *Great Britain Parliamentary Papers*, vol. 10, p. 517.

55   Richard Taylor, *Te Ika a Maui; or, New Zealand and its Inhabitants …*, Wertheim and Macintosh, London, 1855, p. 214.

56   *Maori Messenger*, 24 Feb. 1853, p. 2.

57   Further purchases were made after 1860, but Maori were no longer predominant in the trade by then.

58   For further details concerning factors that obscured the extent of Maori ship ownership, see H. Petrie, ' "For a Season Quite the Rage"? Ships and Flourmills in the Maori Economy, 1840–1860s', Ph.D. thesis, University of Auckland, 2004, pp. 245, 270–4.

59   *Southern Cross*, 2 Jan 1852, p. 3; W. Dinwiddie, *Old Hawke's Bay*, Dinwiddie Walker, Napier, 1921, p. 13.

60   *Maori Messenger*, 15 Jan. 1852, pp. 2–4.

61   Pompallier to Moreau, 27 Feb. 1851, Letter 50, *The Pompallier Papers*, translated by E. R. Simmons, Auckland, 1978, vol. 5, p. 5. Thomas Chapman in the Bay of Plenty also resented his dependence on Maori shipping but other missionaries, such as Richard Taylor, appreciated their services: Richard Taylor Journal, 22 Feb. 1853, vol. 8, MS 302, Auckland Institute and Museum.

62   'Return of Vessels out of Auckland June 1852', *New Zealand Government Gazette, Province of New Ulster*, 12 Aug. 1852, p. 138; MA1 1860/221, Correspondence Register, Maori Affairs, ANZ, Wellington. Examples of licence seekers include Mr. Nicholas and his family who obtained permission to leave Thames in 1863 during the blockade with their cattle aboard the *George*, and trader, J. W. Harris, who appealed to Donald McLean, then Superintendent of Hawke's Bay, to allow the *Queen* to proceed to Gisborne with supplies for his station, *Southern Cross*, 6 Nov. 1863, p. 3; Harris to McLean, 22 Jan. 1866, HB 4/7 66/687, ANZ, Wellington.

63   J. L. Campbell to Dr J. Campbell, cited in Stone, *Young Logan Campbell*, *op. cit.*, p. 99.

64   *Ibid.*, p. 133.

65   David Rough, *Narrative of a Journey Through Parts of the North Island of New Zealand*, Home Friends, London, 1852, p. 30.

66   M. N. Pearson, 'Brown and Campbell in Early Auckland, 1840–56', M.A. thesis, University of Auckland, 1964, p. 21.

67   Auckland's population in 1856 was estimated at

15,335, *New Zealand Statistics 1853–56, op. cit.* With regard to the Maori contribution to the colonial economy, Richard Taylor commented concerning the Wanganui area: 'already is their trade of such value as to have chiefly contributed to the prosperity of the town': Taylor, *Te Ika a Maui, op. cit.*, p. 216. 'Wanganui Maori also sold big quantities of food and flax to Wellington' and William Pratt said of the 1840s that Wellington 'drew her chief supplies of produce, such as maize, pigs, potatoes, etc.' from Poverty Bay: James Watson, *Links: A History of Transport and New Zealand Society*, Ministry of Transport, Wellington, 1996, p. 66.

68   Simkin, *The Instability of a Dependent Economy, op. cit.*, p. 120.

69   R. P. Hargreaves, 'The Maori Agriculture of the Auckland Province in the Mid-nineteenth Century', *Journal of the Polynesian Society*, 68, Jun. 1959, p. 74.

70   Auckland's total revenues as well as the province's overseas imports and exports all declined in 1856: Lloyd Prichard, *An Economic History of New Zealand, op. cit.*, pp. 74, 82, 83.

71   See, for example, Petrie, 'For a Season Quite the Rage', *op. cit.*, pp. 305, 313.

72   *New Zealander*, 11 Apr. 1846, p. 2.

73   *Southern Cross*, 9 Mar. 1852, p. 3.

74   *Southern Cross*, 30 Nov. 1855, p. 3.

75   Memorandum, 2/2/5 (3?), 4 Sep. 1856, p. 24, Donald McLean Papers, Microfilm 0535, Reel 004, Alexander Turnbull Library. An intensification of bureaucratic regulation may be inferred from a notice published in the *Maori Messenger* in 1858 advising the owners of a number of Maori-owned vessels that they were required to produce the relevant Certificates of Registry so that an official number might be given to each. Owners were informed that, if they failed to do so, their vessels would 'be liable to seizure and confiscation': *Maori Messenger: Te Karere Maori*, 16 Aug. 1858, pp. 6–7.

76   C. W. Richmond, Memorandum by Responsible Advisers on Native Affairs, 29 Sep. 1858, *Great Britain Parliamentary Papers*, vol. 11, pp. 34–5.

77   Donald McLean, Memorandum of Assistant Native Secretary Relative to Native Territorial Rights Bill, 13 Oct. 1858, *Great Britain Parliamentary Papers*, vol. 11, p. 55.

78   11 Jul. 1856, *New Zealand Parliamentary Debates 1856–58*, p. 272. Until 1867, very few Maori were entitled to vote as the franchise was dependent on owning land under individual title.

79   *Maori Messenger*, 27 Jan. 1853, p. 1; Petrie, 'For a Season Quite the Rage', *op. cit.*, p. 207 fn.

80   BBAO 10526 1a: register of transactions subsequent to 1st reg, Archives New Zealand, Auckland.

81   *Maori Messenger: Te Karere Maori*, Mar. 1855, pp.

11–2. Te Hemera [*sic*] is reported as the master of the *Duke of Wellington* when it arrived at Auckland on 28 April 1857 with a cargo comprising 10,000 feet of sawn timber and twelve bags of wheat: *New Zealander*, 29 Apr. 1857, p. 2.

82   Rough, *Narrative of a Journey, op. cit.*, p. 35.

83   Arthur S. Thomson, *The Story of New Zealand: Past and Present, Savage and Civilized*, vol. II, Murray, London, 1859, p. 224.

84   M. P. K. Sorrenson, 'Maori and Pakeha', in W. H. Oliver and B. R. Williams (eds), *The Oxford History of New Zealand*, Clarendon Press, Oxford and Wellington, 1981, p. 186.

CHAPTER THREE HOBSON TO HUBBING: CHANGE AND CONTINUITY IN AUCKLAND'S MARITIME HISTORY

1   R. C. J. Stone, *From Tamaki-Makau-Rau to Auckland*, Auckland University Press, Auckland, 2001, pp. 242–6.

2   David Johnson, *New Zealand's Maritime Heritage*, Collins/Bateman, Auckland, 1987, p. 52.

3   S. Musgrove (ed.), *The Hundred of Devonport: A Centennial History*, Devonport Borough Council, Auckland, 1986, p. 15.

4   R. C. J. Stone, *Young Logan Campbell*, Auckland University Press/Oxford University Press, Auckland, 1982, p. 134.

5   Johnson, *Maritime Heritage, op. cit.*, p. 48.

6   *Ibid.*, p. 47.

7   Elsie Locke and Janet Paul, *Mrs Hobson's Album*, Auckland University Press in association with the Alexander Turnbull Library, Auckland, 1990, p. 14.

8   For a pictorial survey of recreational use of the harbour, see: Robin Elliott and Harold Kidd, *The Logans: New Zealand's Greatest Boatbuilding Family*, David Ling, Auckland, 2001; Robin Elliott, Harold Kidd and T. L. Rodney Wilson, *Winkelmann's Waitemata: Classic Auckland Yachting*, David Ling in association with the Auckland War Memorial Museum, Auckland, 1998; and Di Miller and William Owen, *Images of the Hauraki Gulf*, Hodder & Stoughton, Auckland, 1990.

9   *New Zealand Official Year-Book 1893*, Government Printer, Wellington, 1893, p. 97.

10   M. N. Watt, *Index to the New Zealand Section of the Register of All-British Ships 1840–1950*, New Zealand Ship & Marine Society, Wellington, 1961, Section 2, p. 15.

11   Duncan Mackay, *Frontier New Zealand: The Search for Eldorado 1800–1920*, HarperCollins, Auckland, 1992, p. 105.

12   See Anthony G. Flude, 'Henderson and Macfarlane's Circular Saw Line: The Fleet That Helped to Build a City', http://homepages.ihug.co.nz/~tonyf/CSL/index.html.

13   Jack Churchouse, *Sailing Ships of the Tasman Sea*, Millwood Press, Wellington, 1984, pp. 1–4.

14   Johnson, *op. cit.*, p. 57.

15   Malcolm McKinnon (ed.), *New Zealand Historical Atlas*, David Bateman in association with the Department of Internal Affairs, Auckland, 1997, Plate 52b.

16   Two former scow men have written about the scow: P. A. Eaddy, *'Neath Swaying Spars*, Whitcombe & Tombs, Christchurch, 1939, and Ted Ashby, *Phantom Fleet: The Scows and Scowmen of Auckland*, A. H. and A. W. Reed, 1975. Cliff Hawkins has written about their construction in *A Maritime Heritage, the Lore of Sail in New Zealand*, Collins, Auckland, 1978.

17   *Southern Cross*, 26 Jun. 1873.

18   Eaddy, *'Neath Swaying Spars*, *op. cit.*, p. 40.

19   Johnston, *New Zealand's Maritime Heritage*, *op. cit.*, p. 115.

20   See Cliff Furniss, *Servants of the North: Adventures on the Coastal Trade With the Northern Steam Ship Company*, A. H. and A. W. Reed, Wellington, 1977.

21   R. C. J. Stone, *Makers of Fortune: A Colonial Business Community and its Fall*, Auckland University Press/Oxford University Press, Auckland, 1973, p. 79.

22   Johnston, *Maritime Heritage*, *op. cit.*, p. 76.

23   *New Zealand Official Year-Book*, Government Printer, Wellington, 1915.

24   See Robin Elliott and Harold Kidd, *The Logans: New Zealand's Greatest Boatbuilding Family*, David Ling in association with the Auckland War Memorial Museum, Auckland, 2001 and Elliott, Kidd and Rodney Wilson, *Winkelmann's Waitemata*, *op. cit.*

25   Neill Atkinson, *Crew Culture: New Zealand Seafarers Under Sail and Steam*, Te Papa Press, Wellington, 2001, p. 124.

26   Atkinson, *Crew Culture*, *op. cit.*, p. 128.

27   Quoted in Neill Atkinson, 'Against the Tide: The Auckland Seamen's Union 1880–1914', in Pat Walsh (ed.), *Trade Unions, Work and Society: The Centenary of the Arbitration System*, Dunmore Press, Palmerston North, 1994, p. 90.

28   *New Zealand Official Year-Book, 1915*, Government Printer, Wellington, 1915, p. 118.

29   *New Zealand Official Yearbook, 1971*, Government Printer, Wellington, 1971, p. 66.

30   *Cyclopedia of New Zealand, vol. 2: Auckland Provincial District*, The Cyclopedia Company, Christchurch, 1902, p. 135.

31   G. W. A. Bush, *Decently and in Order: The Government of the City of Auckland 1840–1971, the centennial history of the Auckland City Council*, published for the Auckland City Council by Collins, Auckland, 1971, p. 109.

32   A. H. McLintock, *The Port of Otago*, Otago Harbour Board, Dunedin, 1951, p. 251.

33   Anna Green, *British Capital, Antipodean Labour: Working the New Zealand Waterfront, 1915–1951*, University of Otago Press, Dunedin, 2001, p. 33.

34   W. A. Laxon, *Steamers Down the Firth*, self-published, Auckland, 1966, p. 37.

35   Harry Julian, *Sea in My Blood*, H. L. Julian, Auckland, 1999, p. 102.

36   John Rose, *Akarana: The Ports of Auckland*, Auckland Harbour Board, Auckland, 1971, p. 196.

37   'New Zealand Ports and Shipping Developments', p. 1068, supplemented by data from the 1982 *Yearbook*.

38   In 1972, ACT and ANL (Australian National Line) introduced a limited four-ship container service (five from 1974) from Wellington and Lyttelton.

39   Freight forwarders contracted with Railways to hire wagons and sold space in them to customers, offering them door-to-door service.

40   'For the Record', *New Zealand Marine News*, New Zealand Ship & Marine Society, 52/3, 2004, p. 143.

41   Johnson, *New Zealand's Maritime Heritage*, *op. cit.*, p. 133. Nancy M. Taylor, *The New Zealand People at War: The Home Front*, vol. II, Historical Publications Branch, Department of Internal Affairs, Wellington, 1986, p. 741, gives slightly different figures: fifty small wooden tugs, twenty-two steel sea-going tugs, and fifteen powered lighters; later wooden barges, oil barges, five small general-purpose vessels for servicing Pacific Islands and more wooden tugs for the British.

42   http://www.alloyyachts.co.nz/news.html

43   Don Brash, 'New Zealand's Remarkable Reforms', address to the Institute of Economic Affairs, London, 1996, http://www.rbnz.govt.nz/speeches/0031201.html

44   *Report of the Waterfront Industry Restructuring Authority*, 1991, F.10, *AJHR* 1991–3, p. 5.

45   Tasman Express Line minutes, 15/16 Feb. 1990, McKay Shipping Ltd.

46   Geoff Vazey, 'New Zealand Ports – We Can Do Better Yet', speech to Shipping Conference, 29 May 1998.

47   http://www.poal.co.nz/about/about.htm

48   *Dominion Post*, 5 Feb. 2005.

49   Stone, *From Tamaki-Makau-Rau to Auckland*, *op. cit.*, p. 246.

50   http://www.poal.co.nz/community/community.htm

CHAPTER FOUR FINANCIAL MANAGEMENT STRATEGIES IN THE AUCKLAND GAS COMPANY, 1862–1915

1   G. W. A. Bush, *Decently and in Order: The Government of the City of Auckland 1840–1971, the centennial history of the Auckland City Council*, published for the Auckland City Council by Collins, Auckland, 1971, p. 76.

2   C. W. Firth, *Water Supply of Auckland, New Zealand*, Auckland Regional Authority, Auckland, 1967, pp. 11–12

3   *The New Zealand Herald*, 17 Apr. 1865, p. 4.

4   J. Barr, *The City of Auckland, New Zealand, 1840–1947*, Whitcombe and Tombs, Auckland, 1922, p. 197.

5   Bush, *Decently and in Order*, *op. cit.*, pp. 161–5.

6   Statistical and financial data on the Auckland Gas Company are sourced from the company's annual reports and the minutes of its directors' meetings. Share price data from those sources have been augmented with data from weekly reports in *The New Zealand Herald*.

7   General biographical data on Whitaker in these paragraphs are drawn from R. C. J. Stone, 'Whitaker, Frederick 1812–1891', *Dictionary of New Zealand Biography*, vol. 1 (1769–1869), Allen and Unwin and the Department of Internal Affairs, Wellington, 1990, pp. 586–7. More specific data on Whitaker's careers in banking and the law are drawn from, respectively, B. A. Moore and J. S. Barton, *Banking in New Zealand*, New Zealand Bank Officers' Guild, Wellington, 1935, and R. Cooke (ed.), *Portrait of a Profession: The Centennial Book of the New Zealand Law Society*, A. H. and A. W. Reed, Wellington, 1969.

8   W. P. Reeves, *The Long White Cloud: Ao Tea Roa*, Tiger Books International, Twickenham, 1998, p. 195.

9   *The Daily Southern Cross*, 9 Jul. 1862, p. 4.

10   *Ibid.*

11   *Ibid.*

12   Auckland Gas Company Ltd., Directors' Meetings Minute Book, p. 13.

13   *Ibid.*, p. 5.

14   William Smellie Grahame had emigrated from Scotland in 1840 and made his fortune in Auckland as a merchant, farmer and land speculator before leaving in 1857 to live in London: D. A. Rae, 'William Smellie Grahame: an almost unknown founder of Auckland', *Journal of the Auckland–Waikato Historical Societies*, 28, 1976, pp. 27–30.

15   Auckland Gas Company Ltd., Annual Report 1864. (The company's annual reports are not paginated.)

16   *Ibid.*

17   Auckland Gas Company Ltd., Directors' Meetings Minute Book, p. 13.

18   The material for this paragraph and the previous paragraph has been sourced from the minutes of the directors' meetings of the period.

19   Auckland Gas Company Ltd., Directors' Meetings Minute Book, p. 43.

20   *Ibid.*

21   *Ibid.*, p. 50.

22   *Ibid.*, p. 62.

23   *New Zealand Herald*, 17 Apr. 1865, p. 4.

24   *Ibid.*, p. 3.

25   Auckland Gas Company Ltd., Annual Report 1865.

26   Auckland Gas Company Ltd., Annual Report 1885.

27   Auckland Gas Company Ltd., Annual Report 1913.

28   Auckland Gas Company Ltd., Annual Report 1907.

29   Auckland Gas Company Ltd., Directors' Meetings Minute Book, p. 104.

30   Anonymous, *Auckland Savings Bank Centenary, 1847–1947*, Whitcombe and Tombs, Auckland, 1947, p. 37.

31   *New Zealand Herald*, 5 May 1866, p. 4.

32   Auckland Gas Company Ltd., Annual Report 1866.

33   Auckland Gas Company Ltd., Annual Report 1875.

34   After the share-split (of each £5 share into five shares of £1) 'shareholders quickly increased in number from 694 to 1,055': Auckland Gas Company Ltd, Annual Report 1913.

35   Auckland Gas Company Ltd, Annual Report 1914.

CHAPTER FIVE GUILT BY ASSOCIATION: ATTEMPTS AT DOMINATION OF THE LATE-NINETEENTH- AND EARLY-TWENTIETH-CENTURY AUCKLAND TIMBER TRADE

1   Kenneth E. Jackson, 'Forest Policy and Trade: The New Zealand Experience', in John Dargavel and Richard Tucker (eds), *Changing Pacific Forests: Historical Perspectives on the Forest Economy of the Pacific Basin*, Forest History Society, Durham (N.C.), 1992, p. 126.

2   G. T. Bloomfield, *New Zealand: A Handbook of Historical Statistics*, G. K. Hall, Boston (Mass.), 1984, p. 280.

3   E. P. Neale, 'Economics Notes', *The Accountants Journal*, 20 Apr. 1925, p. 322.

4   J. B. Condliffe, *New Zealand in the Making*, 2nd edn, Unwin Brothers, London, 1959, p. 912.

5   Bloomfield, *New Zealand: A Handbook*, *op. cit.*, pp. 280–1.

6   M. M. Roche, 'The New Zealand Timber Economy. 1840–1935', *Journal of Historical Geography*, vol. 16, 1990, p. 302.

7   Acland, Final Report of the Reconstruction Committee of the Forestry Sub-Committee Cd [8881] *British Parliamentary Papers*, XVII, 1917–18, p. 423.

8   T. J. Stobart, *Timber Trade of the United Kingdom*, vol 1, London, 1937, p. 31.

9   Neale, 'Economics Notes', *op. cit.*, p. 322.

10   Kenneth E. Jackson, 'The Economics of Forestry Policy in New Zealand to the 1920s', in Jan Whitwell, & Mary Anne Thompson (eds), *Society and Culture: Economic Perspectives*, vol. 1, NZAE, Wellington, 1991, pp. 238–9.

11   Jackson, 'Forest Policy and Trade', *op. cit.*, pp. 132–3.

12   This finding comes from the work of Matt McGlone, David Whitehead, Richard Duncan and Rob

Allen. 'Why the leaves don't fall in Autumn',
Marsden Fund Newsletter, 28, Jul. 2004, p. 2. http:
//www.rsnz.org/funding/marsden_fund/news28/
index.php#leaves, accessed 21 Aug. 2004.

13   L. Macintosh Ellis, *Forest Conditions in New Zealand*,
Government Printer, Wellington., 1920, p. 8;
Condliffe, *New Zealand in the Making*, *op. cit.*, p. 135
has a longer quotation.

14   Stephanie McWhinnie, *Economic Extinction Theory:
Three Alternatives and New Zealand Kauri*, B.A.
(Hons) dissertation, University of Otago, 1996.

15   E. M. Bilek and G. P. Horgan, 'Organisational and
Administrative Challenges Involving Large Scale
Transfer of Public Assets to the Private Sector: New
Zealand's Experience', paper presented to the *XIXth
World Congress, International Union of Forest Research
Organisations, Montreal, 1990*, p. 2.

16   Roche, 'The New Zealand Timber Economy', *op.
cit.*, p. 295.

17   K. H. Fleet, *New Zealand's Forests*, Heinemann,
Auckland, 1984, pp. 48–50, 80–1.

18   G. W. A. Bush, *Decently and In Order: The
Government of the City of Auckland 1840–1971:
The centennial history of the Auckland City Council*,
published for the Auckland City Council by Collins,
Auckland, 1971, pp. 154–8.

19   J. O. Shearer, 'The Control of Monopoly in New
Zealand', M.A. thesis, University of New Zealand,
1929, p. 89.

20   J. E. Le Rossignol, and W. D. Stewart, *State Socialism
in New Zealand*, Harrap, London, 1910, p. 298.

21   Shearer, 'The Control of Monopoly in New Zealand',
op. cit., pp. 332–5.

22   R. C. J. Stone, *Makers of Fortune: A Colonial Business
Community and its Fall*, Auckland University Press/
Oxford University Press, Auckland, 1973, p. 93.

23   *Bretts Auckland Almanac*, Auckland, 1886, p. 160.

24   Stone, *Makers of Fortune*, *op. cit.*, pp. 95–6.

25   Statistics in the respective Official Year Books tell
us that by 1880 the 123 mills in the South Island
employed some 1920 people, compared to the 2278
employed in the North Island's 100 mills. Forty-three
of these mills were to be found in Auckland. By 1890
there were forty-nine mills in Auckland; over half of
them involved with the kauri timber combine.

26   M. M. Roche, *Forest Policy in New Zealand: An
Historical Geography 1840–1919*, Dunmore Press,
Palmerston North, 1987, p. 27.

27   Kenneth E. Jackson, 'Of Trees Trade and Clearance:
When Kauri was King', Working Papers in Economics, No. 69, University of Auckland, 1990, p. 24.

28   Shearer, 'The Control of Monopoly in New Zealand',
op. cit., p. 29.

29   *Ibid.*, p. 172.

30   Benita Carter, 'The Kauri Timber Company 1888–
1914', M.A. thesis, University of Melbourne, 1972.

31   *Ibid.*, p. 19.

32   Suzanne Loughlin (compiler), University of
Auckland Archives Manuscript and Archives
Collection 90/4 Inventory of the Records of Kauri
Timber Company, Auckland, 1991.

33   *Ibid.*

34   Carter, 'The Kauri Timber Company 1888–1914', *op.
cit.*, p. 135.

35   *Ibid.*, p. 139.

36   *Ibid.*, p. 140.

37   *Ibid.*, pp. 146–7.

38   *Ibid.*, pp. 176–9.

39   *Ibid.*, p. 187.

40   University of Auckland MSS & Archives, 90/4 Box
18.

41   Shearer, *The Control of Monopoly in New Zealand*, *op.
cit.*, p. 29.

CHAPTER SIX MAKING SPACE: CLUSTERS AND DISTRICTS IN AUCKLAND MANUFACTURING 1889–1908

1   G. T. Bloomfield, 'The Growth of Auckland 1840–
1966', in J. S. Whitelaw (ed.), *Auckland in Ferment*,
New Zealand Geographical Society, Miscellaneous
Series No. 6, New Zealand Geographical Society,
Auckland, 1967.

2   Carville Earle observes that first centrifugal
then centripetal forces dominated American city
growth in alternating periods of expansion in an
'extend-and-fill' process. Spatial consolidation
and involution ensued when centripetal forces
took charge as attention switched to policies to
stimulate aggregate demand through improved
housing and transport developments. New radial
routes and 'peninsular urban corridors' connected
'insular industrial suburbs' to the 'urban mainland'.
Thus, US cities experienced 'fairly sustained if
multi-staged suburban expansion', with periods
of expansion (1790–1830, 1880–1930, 1980–2000)
punctuated by periods of consolidation: C. Earle, *The
American Way: A Geographical History of Crisis and
Recovery*, Rowman and Littlefield, Lanham, 2003,
pp. 370–1.

3   Bush gives the City a population of 30,847 in 1882: G.
W. A. Bush, *Decently and in Order: The Government
of the City of Auckland 1840–1971, the centennial
history of the Auckland City Council*, published for the
Auckland City Council by Collins, Auckland, 1971.

4   Bush, *Decently and In Order*, *op. cit.*; Bloomfield, 'The
Growth of Auckland', *op. cit.*

5   This is much the same process as that identified in
Canada and the United States by Richard Harris and
Robert Lewis, who argue that suburbs were diverse
and that, for the period 1900–50, distinctions between
city and suburbs have been overstated. Industry 'has
been decentralizing for decades before Burgess made
the assumption that it was concentrated around

the CBD': R. Harris and R. Lewis, 'Constructing a Fault(y) Zone: Misrepresentations of American Cities and Suburbs, 1900–1950', *Annals of the Association of American Geographers*, 88(4), 1998, pp. 622–39. See, also, R. Harris, 'Self-Building in the Urban Housing Market', *Economic Geography*, 67, 1991 pp. 1–21; R. Harris, *Unplanned Suburbs: Toronto's American Tragedy, 1901–1951*, John's Hopkins University Press, Baltimore, 1996.

6   Earle, *The American Way*, *op. cit.*, pp. 370–1.

7   G. J. R. Linge, 'The Diffusion of Manufacturing in Auckland, New Zealand', *Economic Geography*, 39(1), 1963, pp. 23–39. See, also, G. J. R. Linge, 'The Geography of Manufacturing in New Zealand 1840–1936', in New Zealand Geographical Society (Inc.), Canterbury Branch, *Proceedings of the Second New Zealand Geography Conference, Christchurch, August 1958*, New Zealand Geographical Society Conference Series No. 2, Simpson and Williams, Christchurch, pp. 40–8; and G. J. R. Linge, 'Manufacturing in Auckland: Its Origins and Growth 1840–1936', *New Zealand Geographer*, 14, 1958, pp. 47–64.

8   Linge, 'The Diffusion of Manufacturing', *op. cit.*, p. 25.

9   *Ibid.*, p. 25. Auckland grew rapidly after 1930, adding 130 square kilometres to the existing 100 square kilometres of built-up area, and 165,000 people. Manufacturing suburbanised in this expansion phase. Where the 13,000 workers employed in inner-zone factories in 1931 accounted for 85 per cent of urban area manufacturing employment, by 1956 the zone's 19,000 workers comprised only 43 per cent of factory employment. This suburbanisation of manufacturing involved completely new factories and enterprises.

10   R. Lewis, 'Restructuring and the Formation of an Industrial District in Montreal's East End, 1850–1914', *Journal of Historical Geography*, 20, 1994, pp. 143–57.

11   *Statistics of the Dominion of New Zealand*. David R. Meyer, 'The National Integration of Regional Economies, 1860–1920', in Robert D. Mitchell and Paul A. Groves (eds), *North America: The Historical Geography of a Changing Continent*, Rowman and Littlefield, Totowa (N.J.), 1987, pp. 321–46.

12   G. J. R. Linge, 'Manufacturing in New Zealand: Four Years in a Century of Growth', in R. F. Watters (ed.), *Land and Society in New Zealand: Essays in Historical Geography*, A. H. and A. W. Reed, Wellington, 1965, pp. 139–59.

13   Robert A. J. McDonald, *Making Vancouver: Class, Status and Social Boundaries, 1863–1913*, University of British Columbia Press, Vancouver, 1996, p. 122.

14   G. J. R. Linge, 'The Forging of an Industrial Nation: Manufacturing in Australia 1788–1913', in *Australian Space, Australian Time: Geographical Perspectives*, Oxford University Press, Melbourne, 1975, pp. 163–65.

15   Linge, 'Manufacturing in New Zealand', *op. cit.*

16   Paul A. Groves, 'The Northeast and Regional Integration, 1800–1860', in *North America: the Historical Geography of a Changing Continent*, *op. cit.*, pp. 207–14. See, also, R. W. Armstrong, 'Auckland By Gaslight: An Urban Geography of 1896', *New Zealand Geographer*, 15, 1959, pp. 173–89.

17   E. Muller and P. Groves, 'The Emergence of Industrial Districts in Mid-Nineteenth Century Baltimore', *Geographical Review*, 54, 1979, pp. 159–78.

18   R. Lewis, 'Restructuring and the Formation of an Industrial District in Montreal's East End, 1850–1914', *Journal of Historical Geography*, 20, 1994, pp. 143–57.

19   G. Gad, 'Location Patterns of Manufacturing: Toronto in the Early 1880s', *Urban History Review*, XXII(2), 1994, pp. 113–38.

20   R. Lewis, 'The Development of an Early Suburban Industrial District: The Montreal Ward of Saint-Ann, 1851–71', *Urban History Revue*, XIX(3), 1991, pp. 166–80. A. E. Mosher, ' "Something Better Than the Best": Industrial Restructuring, George McMurtry and the Creation of the Model Industrial Town of Vandergrift, Pennsylvania, 1883–1901', *Annals of the Association of American Geographers*, 85(1), 1995, pp. 84–107. G. M. Winder, 'The North American Manufacturing Belt in 1880: A Cluster of Regional Industrial Systems or One Large Industrial District?', *Economic Geography*, 75(1), 1999, pp. 71–92. R. Walker and R. Lewis, 'Beyond the Crabgrass Frontier: Industry and the Spread of the City, 1850–1950', *Journal of Historical Geography*, 27(1), 2001, pp. 3–19.

21   A. Grey, *Aotearoa and New Zealand: A Historical Geography*, Canterbury University Press, Christchurch, 1994, pp. 212–17. B. Stott, *Prices of Thames*, Allied Press, Dunedin, 1983.

22   R. Arnold, *New Zealand's Burning: The Settlers' World in the Mid 1880s*, Victoria University Press, Wellington, 1994.

CHAPTER SEVEN STOCK AND STATION AGENTS AND WOOL BROKERS

1   See G. R. Hawke, *The Making of New Zealand: An Economic History*. Cambridge University Press, Cambridge, 1985, pp. 31–5; W. J. Gardner, 'A Colonial Economy', in W. H. Oliver and B. R. Williams (eds), *Oxford History of New Zealand*, Oxford University Press, Auckland, 1988 reprint, pp. 70, 74, 78; W. Vamplew (ed.), *Australians. Historical Statistics*. Fairfax, Syme & Weldon Associates, Broadway (N.S.W.), 1987, pp. 82, 188. The author would like to acknowledge the helpful comments of the editors, referee and conference

participants in the preparation of this chapter.

2 For a history of the industry in Australia and New Zealand, see S. Ville, *The Rural Entrepreneurs: A History of the Stock and Station Agent Industry in Australasia*, Cambridge University Press, Melbourne, 2000. There are a number of individual studies of New Zealand firms: L. Anderson, *Throughout the East Coast: The Story of Williams and Kettle Ltd.*, New Zealand Pictorial Publications, Hastings, 1974; J. H. Angus, *Donald Reid Otago Farmers Ltd: A History of Service to the Farming Community of Otago*, Donald Reid Otago Farmers, Dunedin, 1978; J. C. Irving, *A Century's Challenge. Wright Stephenson and Co. Ltd., 1861–1961*, Wright Stephenson, Wellington, 1961; G. Parry, *NMA. The Story of the First Hundred Years of the National Mortgage and Agency Company of New Zealand Ltd., 1864–1964*, National Mortgage and Agency, Dunedin, 1964; P. G. Stevens, *Pyne, Gould, Guinness Ltd.*, Pyne, Gould Guinness, Christchurch, 1970; W. Vaughan-Thomas, *Dalgety. The Romance of a Business*, H. Melland, London, 1984; Falconer Larkworthy, *Ninety-one Years: Being the Reminiscences of Falconer Larkworthy* (Harold Begbie, ed.), Mills and Boon, London, 1924; R. Gore, *Levins, 1841–1941*, Levins, Wellington, 1956.

3 Wrightson Archives, Wright Stephenson (hereafter WS) 0001, Annual Report.

4 In its simplest form, the costs of specifying, negotiating and monitoring a business contract or agreement are its transaction costs.

5 Positive externalities are unanticipated beneficial outcomes of a transaction.

6 A. Barnard, *The Australian Wool Market, 1840–1900*, Melbourne University Press, Melbourne, 1958, pp. 7–8.

7 See S. Ville 'The Relocation of the International Market for Australian Wool', *Australian Economic History Review*, 45(1), 2005, for an account of a similar trend in Australia.

8 Known as skirting and rolling.

9 J. Stacpoole, 'Buckland, Alfred 1825–1903', *Dictionary of New Zealand Biography*, updated 16 December 2003 http://www.dnzb.govt.nz/. NMA began weekly auctions at Dunedin in 1864 and Wright Stephenson there the following year. Several Wellington agents, including Levins and Bethune & Hunter, conducted regular auctions from 1871. Parry, *NZMA, op. cit.*, pp. 24, 218; Irving, *A Century's Challenge, op. cit.*, p. 24; Gore, *Levins, op. cit.*, pp. 26–7.

10 Barnard, *The Australian Wool Market, op. cit.*, pp. 110, 154–5; University of Melbourne Archives (UMA) Dennys Lascelles collection 62, 12, Conran, out-letters, 1892; Angus, *Donald Reid, op. cit.*, pp. 27–8. Sydney had periodically had central wool sales from the 1860s.

11 *Dalgety Annual Wool Review*.

12 Auckland Public Library, NZ MSS 270.

13 Wellington Woolbrokers Association minutes, MSY 4136, National Library of New Zealand.

14 Mean, median and mode are all six, providing a normal bell-curve distribution.

15 The two-firm share is a coefficient of concentration to describe the share held by the largest two firms. 1.0 constitutes the entire market.

16 Wool Research Organisation of New Zealand, 'Wools of New Zealand. Buying New Zealand Wool' (www.woolsnz.com), pp. 1–6.

17 G. R. Hawke, 'The Growth of the Economy', in W. H. Oliver and B. R. Williams (eds), *Oxford History of New Zealand*, Oxford University Press, Auckland, 1988 reprint, p. 382.

18 Hocken Archives, University of Otago, NMA collection, UN 28 General Manager's letters to Auckland 23.9.1919; 23.4.1924; 11.10.1926.

19 Irving, *A Century's Challenge, op. cit.*, pp. 113, 121–3; WS 0001, Annual Reports.

20 Stacpoole, 'Buckland', *op. cit.*; Parry, *NZMA, op. cit.*, p. 217.

21 New Zealand Livestock Auctioneers Association minutes, MSY 4142, National Library of New Zealand.

22 NZLMA collection 76-291, 1892 Annual General Meeting, National Library of New Zealand.

23 WS minute book 2, 1917 30.

24 R. C. J. Stone, *Makers of Fortune. A Colonial Business Community and its Fall*, Auckland University Press/ Oxford University Press, Auckland, 1973, p. 25.

25 Stone, *ibid.*, pp. 20, 23.

26 NZLMA, minutes February 1879. The minute books contain detail of loans made by the firm.

27 Stone, *Makers of Fortune, op. cit.*, p. 52; N. M. Chappell, *New Zealand Banker's Hundred. A History of the Bank of New Zealand, 1861–1961*, Bank of New Zealand, Wellington, 1961, p. 117.

28 See Larkworthy, *Ninety-one Years, op. cit.*; Stone, *Makers of Fortune, op. cit.*, p. 23.

29 See S. Ville, 'Social Capital Formation in Australian Rural Communities: the Enhancing Role of the Stock and Station Agent', *Journal of Interdisciplinary History*, 36(2), 2005, for a discussion of the nature and magnitude of these investments.

30 S. Ville and G. Fleming, 'The Nature and Structure of Trade-Financial Networks: Evidence from the New Zealand Pastoral Sector, 1860–1939', *Business History*, 42(1), 2000, pp. 41–58; S. Ville and G. Fleming, 'Financial Intermediaries and the Design of Optimal Loan Contracts in the Australasian Pastoral Sector', *Financial History Review*, 7(2), 2000, pp. 201–18.

31 Stone, *Makers of Fortune, op. cit.*, pp. 121–2. Highwic was purchased by the Auckland City Council and the New Zealand Historic Places Trust in 1978 and opened to the public in 1981.

32   R. C. J. Stone, *The Father and his Gift*, Auckland University Press, Auckland, 1987, pp. 123–4, cites the main advantages of being part of the limited circle, notably prestige, inside commercial information, generous overdrafts, directors' fees and share bonuses.

33   R. C. J. Stone, 'The New Zealand Frozen Meat and Storage Company', *New Zealand Journal of History*, 5, 1971, p. 182. NZLMA had a sizeable ownership stake in the company and a director on the board.

34   Auckland had joined the NZWBA by 1911.

35   MSY 4137, NZWBA minutes.

36   MSY 4133, NZWBA minutes, 1911.

37   MSY 4127, Wellington Woolbrokers Association minutes.

38   M. Kay, *Inside Story of Farmers*, The Farmers Trading Company, Auckland, 1953.

39   See Ville, *Rural Entrepreneurs, op. cit.*, ch. 2, for a more detailed analysis.

40   Irving, *A Century's Challenge, op. cit.*, pp. 161–5.

41   L. V. Castle, *A Study of New Zealand Manufacturing*, Victoria University of Wellington, Wellington, 1966.

42   WS 001 annual reports, 31.3.1924. The company was also in the process of 'erecting extensive premises' at Auckland in 1919, although it is unclear whether this refers to the fertiliser works or additional expansion: WS 0595.

43   UN 28, General Manager letterbooks.

44   For example, in 1916: 'The majority of our directors, as you know, belong to Invercargill, Dunedin, and Gore, and their interests are not so much concerned about the North Island as Mr Hunt [Chairman] and myself.': WS 0022 J. T. Martin to A. M. Howden.

45   A company enquiry undertaken after the Second World War looked at the possibility of transferring control to New Zealand, largely as a tax avoidance strategy, but the proposal was rejected: UN 133 Lord Glenconner's Memorandum – Transfer of Control to New Zealand.

46   Ville, *Rural Entrepreneurs, op. cit.*, Table 2.3 pp. 32–3.

47   See G. Fleming, D. Merrett and S. Ville, *Big Business and Corporate Leadership in Twentieth-Century Australia*, Cambridge University Press, Melbourne, 2004, ch. 5.

48   WS 0022.

49   Abraham & Williams had in turn acquired G. W. Binney.

50   Irving, *A Century's Challenge, op. cit.*, pp. 121–3.

CHAPTER EIGHT A 'BUSINESS TO BUSINESS RELATIONSHIP': THE ORIGIN AND DEVELOPMENT OF AUCKLAND NEWSPAPERS, 1841–2004

1   *Cyclopedia of New Zealand*, 1902, cited in R. C. J. Stone, *Makers of Fortune: A Colonial Business Community and its Fall*, Auckland University Press/ Oxford University Press, Auckland, 1973, p. 47.

2   Two valuable sources on the history of the New Zealand press are Guy Scholefield, *Newspapers in New Zealand*, A. H. and A. W. Reed, Wellington, 1958, and Patrick Day, *The Making of the New Zealand Press, A Study of the Organisational and Political Concerns of New Zealand Newspaper Controllers 1840–1880*, Victoria University Press, Wellington, 1990. A useful source on more recent developments and issues relating to the New Zealand press is Paul Norris's 'News Media Ownership in New Zealand', in Judy McGregor and Margie Comrie (eds), *What's News: Reclaiming Journalism in New Zealand*, Dunmore Press, Palmerston North, 2002, ch. 2, pp. 33–56. Jenifer Curnow, Jane McRae and Ngapare Hope (eds), *Rere Atu, Taku Manu! Discovering History, Language and Politics in the Maori Language Newspapers*, Auckland University Press, Auckland, 2002, is an important source on Maori language newspapers.

3   This phrase is used by Shirley Leith in 'Business and the Media', in John Deeks and Peter Enderwick (eds), *Business and New Zealand Society*, Longman Paul, Auckland, 1994, ch. 6, pp. 280–92, at p. 285.

4   The paper was suppressed under a series of New South Wales anti-press laws, instituted by Governor Darling in the 1827–30 period. See Patrick Day, 'The Political Role of the Early New Zealand Press', Working Paper No. 14, *Conference of the Social Association of Australia and New Zealand, University of Waikato, Hamilton, November 1981*, p. 2.

5   Scholefield, *Newspapers in New Zealand, op. cit.*, pp. 69–72.

6   One official, George Graham, estimated that by the end of 1841 the European population of Auckland exceeded 3000. However, R. C. J. Stone describes this figure as 'somewhat exaggerated': *Young Logan Campbell*, Auckland University Press/Oxford University Press, Auckland, 1982, p. 99.

7   A balance sheet published on 27 November 1871 indicated there was £1,398 in unpaid debts owing to the company. See Day, *Making of New Zealand Press, op. cit.*, p. 70.

8   Scholefield, *Newspapers in New Zealand, op. cit.*, pp. 72–3.

9   Graeme Hunt, *Hustlers, Rogues and Bubble Boys: White Collar Mischief in New Zealand*, Reed, Auckland, 2001, p. 114.

10   Scholefield, *Newspapers in New Zealand, op. cit.*, p. 73.

11   Patrick Day, 'Political Role of the Early New Zealand Press', *op. cit.*, pp. 10–2; Scholefield, *op. cit.*, pp. 74–5.

12   Stone, *Young Logan Campbell, op. cit.*, p. 100.

13   Scholefield, *Newspapers in New Zealand, op. cit.*, pp. 74–5.

14   *Ibid.*, p. 75.

15 *Ibid.*, p. 77. In Day's *Making of New Zealand Press* (p. 36), this motto is translated more elaborately as 'If I have been extinguished, yet there rise/A thousand beacons from the spark I bore.'

16 *Southern Cross, New Zealand Gazette and Auckland, Thames and Bay of Islands Advertiser*, Saturday, 22 Apr. 1843, vol. 1, p. 1.

17 See R. C. J. Stone's *Young Logan Campbell, op. cit.*, and *The Father and His Gift*, Auckland University Press, Auckland, 1987, for detailed accounts of this successful Auckland business and the men who owned it.

18 *Southern Cross*, 22 Apr. 1843, vol. 1, p.1.

19 *Ibid.*

20 John Horsman, *The Coming of the Pakeha to Auckland Province*, Hicks Smith, Wellington, 1971, p. 65.

21 Although the desired gold boom did not occur at this point in time, largely due to problems of access, the discovery was an important one: gold from the Coromandel would later play an important part in invigorating the faltering Auckland economy.

22 Reprinted in *Nelson Examiner and New Zealand Chronicle*, 8 Jun. 1844, cited in Day, *Making of New Zealand Press, op. cit.*, p. 36.

23 Scholefield, *Newspapers in New Zealand, op. cit.*, p. 77. The most notable of these appointments was Robert Creighton, who was hired by Brown in Britain and sent to act as editor and manager of the *Southern Cross* from 1861 until 1865. The *Southern Cross* was acquired by Julius Vogel in 1869. See Day, *Making of New Zealand Press, op. cit.*, pp. 131, 142.

24 Scholefield, *ibid.*, pp. 79–80.

25 Day, *Making of New Zealand Press, op. cit.*, pp. 92–5.

26 *Ibid.*, pp. 93–5.

27 *Ibid.*, pp. 70–1. Wilson became practical manager of the *New Zealander* in 1848.

28 *Ibid.*, p. 71.

29 *Ibid.*

30 Stone, *Makers of Fortune, op. cit.*, p. 8.

31 *Ibid.*, p. 14.

32 Day, *Making of New Zealand Press, op. cit.*, p. 175.

33 *Ibid.*

34 *New Zealand Herald*, 13 Nov. 1863, p. 4.

35 Day, *Making of New Zealand Press, op. cit.*, p. 132.

36 'Herald as Shop Window for Advertisers', 14 Nov. 1863, *New Zealand Herald* Clippings Files 1959–1966.

37 *New Zealand Herald*, 13 Nov. 1863, p. 4.

38 Stone, *Makers of Fortune, op. cit.*, p. 9.

39 *Ibid.*

40 *Ibid.*, p. 36.

41 *New Zealand Herald*, 13 Nov. 1863, p. 1.

42 *Ibid.*, 18 Nov. 1863, p. 2.

43 *Ibid.*, 20 Nov. 1863, p. 3.

44 *Ibid.*

45 The *Weekly News*, a pictorial weekly which commenced in 1863, was originally owned and published by Robert Creighton and Alfred Scales. At the time of the amalgamation, it was owned by the Daily Southern Cross and Weekly News Company Limited. From 1877 to 1934, the paper was known as the *Auckland Weekly News*. From 1934 until its demise in 1971, it was called the *Weekly News*. See Scholefield, *Newspapers in New Zealand, op. cit.*, p. 86.

46 See Day, *Making of New Zealand Press, op. cit.*, p. 142, for a summary of the paper's proprietors between Vogel's acquisition in 1869 and Horton's purchase in 1876.

47 *Ibid.*, p. 136.

48 Michael Horton, 'Alfred George Horton', in *Dictionary of New Zealand Biography*, vol. 2, Allen and Unwin/Department of Internal Affairs, Wellington, p. 229.

49 See Day, *Making of New Zealand Press, op. cit.*, p. 230.

50 From 15 papers in 1859, the country's total number of newspapers had reached 109 in 1879: *ibid.*, p. 137.

51 *Ibid.*, pp. 138–42.

52 *Ibid.*, p. 137.

53 Scholefield, *Newspapers in New Zealand, op. cit.*, p. 88.

54 *Ibid.* The motto is a light adaptation of the verse from G. Linnaeus Banks.

55 *Auckland Star Diamond Jubilee Edition*, 7 May 1930, p. 2.

56 Michael Brett, 'Henry Brett', *Dictionary of New Zealand Biography*, vol. 2, *op. cit.*, p. 56.

57 *Ibid.*

58 Day, *Making of New Zealand Press, op. cit.*, pp. 206–7. For a colourful account of the antics employed to deny rivals access to the telegraph, see A. R. Brett's *The Race for the Wires; Old Time Journalism: Some Reminiscences of the later Sir Henry Brett*, Auckland Star, Auckland, 1927.

59 Scholefield, *Newspapers in New Zealand, op. cit.*, p. 89.

60 Leith, 'Business and the Media', *op. cit.*, p. 285.

61 Day, *Making of New Zealand Press, op. cit.*, p. 235.

62 Terence Hodgson, *The Heart of Colonial Auckland, 1865–1910*, Random Century, Auckland, 1992, p. 38.

63 Horton, 'Alfred George Horton', *op. cit.*, p. 229.

64 'William Scott Wilson', in Guy Scholefield (ed.), *A Dictionary of New Zealand Biography*, vol. 2, Department of Internal Affairs, Wellington, 1940, p. 525.

65 'Henry Brett', *ibid.*, vol. 1, p. 93.

66 Janice C. Mogford, 'Thomson Wilson Leys', in *Dictionary of New Zealand Biography*, vol. 2, *op. cit.*, p. 271.

67 *Ibid.*

68 Obituary of J. L. Wilson, 18 Aug. 1902, *New Zealand Herald* Clipping Files 1896–1934.

69 Scholefield, *Newspapers in New Zealand, op. cit.*,

pp. 89–90.

70   *Ibid.*, p. 90.

71   9 Aug. 1961, *New Zealand Herald* Clipping Files 1959–1966.

72   Day, *Making of New Zealand Press*, *op. cit.*, p. 243.

73   *New Zealand Herald – Special Commemorative Issue*, 13 Nov. 1923, p. 1.

74   *Auckland Star Jubilee Edition*, 7 May 1930, p. 5.

75   *Ibid.*, p. 19.

76   'Farmer's Largest Advertisement', 29 Nov. 1958, *New Zealand Herald* Clipping Files 1896–1958.

77   'Record Classified Ads', 18 Aug. 1960, *New Zealand Herald* Clippings Files 1959–1966.

78   E. J. Keating, MP for Hastings, during a Budget debate in the House, *New Zealand Herald* Clipping Files 1959–1966, 17 July 1959.

79   Prime Minister Walter Nash, 23 Jan. 1959, *New Zealand Herald* Clipping Files 1959–1966.

80   *New Zealand Herald Centennial Record*, 13 Nov. 1963, p. 7.

81   'Herald as Shop-Window for Advertisers', 14 Nov. 1963, *New Zealand Herald* Clipping Files 1959–1966.

82   'Many Old Firms Represented at Gathering', 15 Nov. 1963, *New Zealand Herald* Clipping Files 1959–1966.

83   See Michael Bassett's pamphlet 'Our Newspapers', Auckland University Labour Club, Auckland, 1970, and Gordon Parry's book *Behind the Headlines*, McIndoe, Dunedin, 1969.

84   S. W. Bradley, *Newspapers: An Analysis of the Press in New Zealand*, Heinemann Educational, Auckland, 1973, p. 6.

85   Norris, 'News Media Ownership', *op. cit.*, pp. 36–7.

86   N. A. Griffiths, *Reading New Zealand Newspapers*, Reed Educational, Auckland, 1973, p. 8.

87   Norris, 'News Media Ownership', *op. cit.*, pp. 33–53.

88   The reasons for this trend were complex and varied, although the competing attractions of other media such as television doubtless played a significant part.

89   Julienne Molineux, 'Concentration of Ownership in the New Zealand Daily Newspaper Industry', *New Zealand Journal of Media Studies*, 2, 1995, p. 9.

90   The front page of the final edition of the *Auckland Star* contains an account of the financial failure that necessitated the paper's closure, under the simple headline 'Goodbye'.

91   Robson proclaimed that after each successive restructuring, 'we have been defeated by the general state of the New Zealand economy': *Auckland Star*, Friday, 16 Aug. 1991, p. 1.

92   Warwick Roger, 'Can Gavin Ellis and Granny Herald do Show Business?', *North and South*, Oct. 1996, p. 55, cited in Brian Gordon Stanney, 'Reforming the *Herald*: A Comparative Analysis of Front Section News Content in the *New Zealand Herald*, 1995 and 2001', M.A. thesis, University of Auckland, 2001, p. 7.

93   Norris, 'News Media Ownership', *op. cit.*, p. 38. The publishers of the *Herald* are APN New Zealand Ltd.

94   For a detailed account of the changes to 2001, see Stanney 'Reforming the *Herald*', *op. cit.*

95   In a response to competition for the weekend market from Fairfax Sunday Newspapers' popular *Sunday Star-Times*, however, *Herald* publishers APN New Zealand launched a new Sunday newspaper, the *Herald on Sunday*, in October 2004. Wilson and Horton had established a separate Sunday paper entitled the *Sunday Herald* in 1971, but this only lasted until 1975. Again, the depressed national economy was cited as the reason for that paper's demise: 27 Apr. 1975, *New Zealand Herald* Clipping Files.

96   See Joe Atkinson, 'Tabloid Democracy', in Raymond Miller (ed.), *New Zealand Government and Politics*, 3rd ed., Oxford University Press, Auckland, 2003, pp. 305–19, and Margie Comrie, 'Spin in the News', in McGregor and Comrie(eds), *op. cit.*, ch. 10, pp. 158–72.

CHAPTER NINE RETAIL INNOVATION AND THE FARMERS TRADING COMPANY: AUCKLAND'S BIG STORE

1   See A. B. Stephenson and N. G. Stephenson, *Samuel Stephenson: Pioneer Merchant of Russell, 1804–1885*, N. G. and A. B. Stephenson, Auckland, 1984.

2   Edward Markham, *New Zealand or Recollections of It*, R. E. Owen, Government Printer, Wellington, 1963, p. 63.

3   Robert Graham, Journal of a Passage from Greenock to Auckland, New Zealand on board the *Jane Gifford*, 18 June–16 November 1842, Auckland Institute and Museum Library, MS 121, p. 27.

4   As it did in 1862, following the discovery of gold the previous year at Gabriel's Gully, Otago.

5   'Imports and Exports', *Statistics of the Dominion of New Zealand for the Year 1910*, John Mackay, Government Printer, Wellington, 1911.

6   See, for example, D. A. Hamer, 'Towns in Nineteenth-Century New Zealand', *New Zealand Journal of History*, 13(1), 1979, pp. 15–8.

7   Briscoe and Co. was established in Wolverhampton in 1768. By 1881, the firm had branches in London, Melbourne (1852), Dunedin (1862), Sydney (1878) and Invercargill (1881).

8   See *Cyclopedia of New Zealand, vol. 4: Otago and Southland*, The Cyclopedia Company, Christchurch, 1905.

9   Kim Humphery, *Shelf Life: Supermarkets and the Changing Cultures of Consumption*, Cambridge University Press, Cambridge, 1998, pp. 30–1.

10   *Cyclopedia of New Zealand, vol. 4: Otago and Southland*, *ibid.*, pp. 306–7.

11   Issuing £30,000 of debentures at 5.5 per cent to do

so. Prospectus, 13 Jul. 1916, Whitcombe and Tombs Ltd., Papers, Misc-MS-1743, Hocken Library.

12   *Cyclopedia of New Zealand, vol. 4: Otago and Southland*, *ibid.*, p. 846.

13   *Cyclopedia of New Zealand, vol. 3: Canterbury*, The Cyclopedia Company, Christchurch, 1903, pp. 314–5.

14   Helen Laurenson in her thesis on Auckland department stores notes: 'Department store shopping in the 1920s, with its service, comfort and overwhelming goods, its freshly reconstructed buildings with their facades of colour, glass, and light, was an exciting experience. It drew men, women, and children into the heart of the city of Auckland to enter these imposing structures, and to savour what was new and modern in the twentieth century.': Helen Laurenson, 'Going up? – going down! The Rise and Fall of Auckland Department Stores, 1920–1960', M.A. thesis, University of Auckland, Auckland, 2003, p. 18.

15   K. A. Tucker, *Milne and Choyce: A One Hundred Year Business History, 1867–1967*, Milne and Choyce, Auckland, 1968, p. 41.

16   Humphery, *Shelf Life*, *op. cit.*, p. 36.

17   Joseph A. Schumpeter, *Capitalism, Socialism and Democracy*, George Allen Unwin, London, 1976, p. 132.

18   See Ian Hunter, *Robert Laidlaw: Man for our Time*, Castle, Auckland, 1999, pp. 30–51.

19   The capital he had saved at this point to start his concern amounted to £280.

20   Laidlaw Papers, Private Collection, Laidlaw Leeds Catalogue No. 1, 1910.

21   *Ibid.*, p. 1.

22   Laidlaw Papers, Private Collection, Laidlaw Leeds Cash Analysis Book, 1910.

23   See, for example, David Yerex, *Empire of the Dairy Farmers*, NZ Dairy Exporter Books in association with Ampersand Publishing Associates, Petone, 1989. Also, G. R. Hawke, *The Making of New Zealand: An Economic History*, Cambridge University Press, Cambridge, 1985.

24   See D. A. Hamer, 'Towns in Nineteenth-Century New Zealand', *op. cit.*, pp. 5–24.

25   See for example, S. R. H. Jones and D. R. Paul, 'Concentration and Regulation in the New Zealand Brewing Industry, 1850–1970', *Australian Economic History Review*, 31(2), 1991, pp. 66–93.

26   See Simon Ville, 'The Coastal Trade of New Zealand Prior to World War One', *New Zealand Journal of History*, 27(1), 1993, pp. 75–89.

27   See Dorothy Davis, *A History of Shopping*, Routledge & Kegan Paul, London, 1966, pp. 289–91.

28   On at least one occasion visiting evangelists addressed the staff, and Laidlaw himself wrote a gospel tract, 'The Reason Why', which he distributed among the staff.

29   Laidlaw Papers, Private Collection, *The Optimist*, 1(4), 1910, p. 11.

30   Early adopters of scientific management principles in the American retail environment included Ernest Katz at R. H. Macy's, where systematically recorded operating facts were gathered to help manage the day-to-day operations of the business, and, in particular, stock inventory, which was later improved by Filen's in the 1930s in the form of the model stock plan: Ronald Savitt, 'Innovation in American Retailing, 1919–39: Improving Inventory Management', *International Review of Retail, Distribution and Consumer Research*, 9(3), July 1999, pp. 307–20.

31   The payment was 2s 6d for each staff suggestion put into action.

32   The Quality of Working Life (QWL) movement is concerned with the interaction between the workplace and an individual's level of job satisfaction. It is argued that if the workplace environment is improved, including such aspects as work systems, tools, job design, physical layout and employee benefits, then employee satisfaction levels will increase with attendant benefits, including lower stress, less fatigue, lower absenteeism, lower rates of labour turnover and enhanced productivity.

33   Laidlaw also kept a personal management book library which he made available to staff.

34   Tucker, *Milne and Choyce*, *op. cit.*, app. B.

35   The merged cooperative was called the Farmers Co-operative Wholesale Federation. Other department stores by this time were also offering mail-order sales, although not on the scale of Laidlaw.

36   Gordon Ogilvie, *Ballantynes, The Story of Dunstable House 1854–2004*, J. Ballantyne & Co., Christchurch, 2004, p. 190.

CHAPTER TEN ROSS & GLENDINING AND THE CLOTHING, FOOTWEAR, AND TEXTILE INDUSTRIES IN NEW ZEALAND, 1938–1966: A CASE OF STRATEGIC AND MANAGEMENT FAILURE

1   W. B. Sutch, *The Quest for Security in New Zealand*, Oxford University Press, Wellington, 1966, pp. 223–5.

2   Annual Report, 1 Sep. 1939, AG 512 8/8. These archives are held in Hocken Library and Archives, University of Otago.

3   Unpublished paper on industrial location, AG 512 8/8.

4   Half Yearly Analysis, 1928–53, AG 515 15/13; Factory Returns, 1922–1946, AG 512 19/9.

5   J. V. T. Baker, *War Economy*, Department of Internal Affairs, Wellington, 1965, p. 314.

6   Annual Report, 9 Sep. 1941, AG 512 8/8; Factory Returns, 1922–1946, AG 512 19/9.

7   Annual Report, 9 Sep. 1941, *ibid.*; Operational

Survey, May 1963, app. E, AG 512 19/1.

8   Unpublished MS, Box 10, AG 512.

9   Baker, *op. cit.*, pp. 160–6; 600-02, Tables 36–39.

10   Factory Returns, 1922–46, AG 512 19/9; Annual General Meeting 14 Sep. 1944, AG 512 8/8.

11   *Ibid.*, p. 467; *New Zealand Draper and Allied Retailer*, 7 Mar. 1943, p. 3.

12   *New Zealand Draper*, *ibid.*, p. 5; 7 Apr. 1944, p. 6.

13   Head office to London office, 18 Feb. 1941, 28 Mar. 1942, AG 512 6/6.

14   Head office to London office, 25 Feb. 1943, AG 512 6/6.

15   *New Zealand Draper*, 7 May 1943, p. 3.

16   *Ibid.*, 7 Apr. 1944, p. 7.

17   *Ibid.*, 7 Nov. 1944.

18   Factory Returns, 1922–46, AG 512 19/9.

19   *New Zealand Official Year Book*, Government Printer, Wellington, 1956, pp. 297, 319.

20   Annual Reports, 12 Sep. 1946, 19 Sep. 1947, AG 512 8/8.

21   Ross & Glendining employment figures, 12 July 1937, AG 513 Box 8.

22   Annual Reports, 9 Sep. 1941 and 15 Sep. 1949, AG 512 8/8; National Archives, IC1 9/13 pt. 1.

23   Archives New Zealand, IC1 9/13 pt. 1.

24   Unpublished MS, Box 10, AG 512.

25   Annual Report, 1946–1951, AG 512 8/8; J. W. Wrightson to D. I. Ross, 28 Mar. 1952, AG 512 Box 8.

26   Half Yearly Analysis, 1928–53, AG 512 15/13; Annual General Meeting, 10 Sep. 1948, AG 512 8/8.

27   Annual Report, 15 Sep. 1949, AG 512 8/8.

28   Annual Reports, 15 Sep. 1949 and 14 Sep. 1950, AG 512 8/8.

29   *New Zealand Official Year Book*, Government Printer, Wellington, 1963, p. 731.

30   Annual Report, 14 Sep. 1951, AG 512 8/8.

31   Annual Report, 18 Sep. 1952, AG 512 8/8.

32   Annual Report, 8 Oct. 1956, AG 512 8/8.

33   Operational Survey, May 1963, pp. 1, 11. AG 512 19/1.

34   *Ibid.*, pp. 2–3.

35   Wise's *Auckland Provincial Directory*, 1949, p. 1158a, 1953/4, p. 1095.

36   Operational Survey, May 1963, pp. 2–3, 5, AG 512 19/1.

37   Annual Report, 15 Sep. 1949, AG 512 8/8.

38   Annual Report, 18 Sep. 1952, AG 512 8/8.

39   Annual Reports, 17 Sep. 1953 and 3 Sep. 1954, AG 512 8/8.

40   Operational Survey, May 1963, pp. 9, 11, AG 512 19/1.

41   Annual Report, 5 Oct. 1955, AG 512 8/8.

42   Annual Reports, 5 Oct. 1955, 8 Oct. 1956, AG 512 8/8.

43   *Ibid.*

44   Operational Survey, May 1963, pp. 16–8, AG 512 19/1.

45   *Ibid.*, p. 16.

46   Annual Report, 14 Oct. 1958, AG 52 8/8.

47   Annual Reports, 2 Oct. 1959, 18 Oct. 1960, AG 512 8/8.

48   Operational Survey, May 1963, p. 17, AG 512 19/1.

49   *Ibid.*

50   Report from Underwear Factory, 9 July 1963; Report of Footwear Meeting, 14 Aug. 1963, AG 512 19/1.

51   Operational Survey, May 1963, p. 12, AG 512 19/1.

52   *Ibid.*

53   *Ibid.*, p. 10.

54   *Ibid.*, p. 10.

55   Annual Report, 18 Oct. 1960, AG 512 8/8.

56   Annual Report, 31 Oct. 1962, AG 512 8/8.

57   Operational Survey, May 1963, pp. 17–8, AG 512 19/1.

58   Annual Report, 18 Oct. 1960, AG 512 8/8.

59   Operational Survey, May 1963, pp. 17–8, AG 512 19/1.

60   *R & G Reporter*, 2(1), 1965, p. 4, AG 512 Box 10.

61   *Ibid.*, pp. 3, 6–7, 11.

62   *Ibid.*, Chart 1.

63   *Ibid.*, pp. 22–4.

64   *R & G Reporter*, 1(1), 1964, pp. 1–8, AG 512 Box 10.

65   *Ibid.*, pp. 5–6.

66   *Ibid.*, p. 4.

67   *Ibid.*, p. 3.

68   Annual Report, 29 Oct. 1964, p. 12, AG 512 8/8.

69   *R & G Reporter*, 2(6), 1965, p. 3, AG 512 Box 10.

70   *Ibid.*, 1(2), 1964, p. 3.

71   Annual Report, 4 Nov. 1965, AG 512 8/8.

72   *Ibid.*

73   *R & G Reporter*, 1(2), 1964, pp. 1, 3; *R & G Reporter*, 2(1), 1965, p. 7, AG 512, Box 19; Annual Report, 20 Oct. 1964, AG 512 8/8.

74   *R & G Reporter*, 2(6), 1965, p. 1, AG 512 Box 10.

75   *R & G Reporter*, 3(1), 1966, p. 1; *R & G Reporter*, 3(2), 1966, p. 3, AG 512 Box 10.

76   Statement by Ross & Glendining to the New Zealand Stock Exchange, 21 Apr. 1966, AG 512 19/2.

77   Directors' meeting, 4 Apr. 1966, minutes, AG 512 19/2.

78   Letter to all shareholders of Ross & Glendining, 21 Apr. 1966, AG 512 19/2.

79   Calculation of Asset Backing of Shares as at 19th January, 1966, AG 512 19/2.

80   C. R. Grey to D. I. Ross, 5 Apr. 1966, AG 512 19/2.

81   D. I. Ross to C. R. Grey, 15 Apr. 1966, AG 512 19/2.

82   Directors' meeting, 4 Apr. 1966; Statement by Ross & Glendining to the New Zealand Stock Exchange, 21 Apr. 1966, AG 512 19/2.

83   Memorandum to Customers, 30 Sep. 1966, AG 512 19/2; *Unibox* (U.E.B. Group Magazine), 1966, AG 512 Box 10.

84   Peter J. Stewart, *Patterns on the Plain: A Centennial History of Mosgiel Woollens Limited*, Mosgiel Woollens, Dunedin 1975, pp. 97–8.

85   S. R. H. Jones, 'The Establishment and operation of European Business', in P. Enderwick and J. Deeks (eds), *Business and New Zealand Enterprise*, Longman Paul, Auckland, 1994, pp. 43–67.

CHAPTER ELEVEN FROM LOCAL TO GLOBAL: AUCKLAND ACCOUNTING PARTNERSHIPS

1   Brown *et al.* suggested the growth of PMBs (professional managed bureaucracies), in J. L. Brown, D. J. Cooper, R. Greenwood and C. R. Hinings, 'Strategic Alliances Within a Big-six Accounting Firm: A Case Study', *International Studies of Management & Organization*, 26(2), 1996, pp. 59–80. Other organisational studies use synonymous acronyms such as GBAFs (Global Business Firms) in T. Rose and C. R. Hinings, 'Global Client Demands Driving Change in Global Business Advisory Firms', in D. M. Brock, M. J. Powell and C. R. Hinings (eds), *Restructuring the Professional Organization: Accounting, Health Care and Law*, Routledge, London, 1999, pp. 41–67.

2   D. M. Brock, M. J. Powell and C. R. Hinings, 'The Changing Professional Service Firm: Towards New Archetypes and Typology', unpublished working paper, University of Auckland, 2002.

3   This study uses multiple sources, including professional notices in practitioner literature, newspapers and trade directories, a survey of 488 partners in the Big 8 firms in New Zealand, and interviews with forty partners from all firms.

4   Formed in 1898.

5   Eighteen accountants in Auckland were in the list of accountants in Wise's 1904 *Trade Directory*.

6   They were later better known as Watkins Hull Wheeler and Johnston.

7   Clark Menzies was always spoken of with the Scottish pronunciation: Clark 'Mingies'.

8   J. O. McKinsey, 'Modern Tendencies in Accounting Practice', *The Accountants Journal*, Dec. 1925, pp. 171–4.

9   R. C. J. Stone, *Makers of Fortune: A Colonial Business Community and its Fall*, Auckland University Press/ Oxford University Press, Auckland, 1973, pp. 82–3.

10   With the acronym GGPP, this was unceremoniously referred to as 'Horse's Piss'.

11   *The Accountants Journal*, 41, 1963, p. 343.

12   Announced in the February 1972 issue of *The Accountants Journal*.

13   A newspaper article stated that Deloitte Haskins & Sells goes back to 1872 when the first of the firms were established: A. Henry, 'Major Firms to Join Forces', *Auckland Star*, 11 Dec. 1989, p. A11. This is probably a reference to W. C. Reid, as the other firms were later than 1872.

14   This is fully documented in Rachel Morley and John Beechey, 'An application of Adams' Theory of (In)equity to Partnership Income Allocation', paper presented at the 2004 AFAANZ conference, Alice Springs, Australia.

15   Doug Watson, Touche Ross partner.

16   Ernst & Young, KPMG, Deloitte Touche Tohmatsu and PricewaterhouseCoopers.

17   They were W. C. Crump, B. H. Eliott, C. C. Holloway, R. C. Wheatcroft and J. M. Wiseman.

18   *New Zealand Herald*, 15 Sep. 1987, Section 4, p. 6.

19   T. Rose and C. R. Hinings, 'Global Client Demands', *op. cit.*

20   The mergers did not occur in the United Kingdom and Australia; in the United Kingdom, the Deloitte partners went to Coopers, and in Australia they joined KPMG.

21   There is no connection to the firm of McCulloch and Partners in Invercargill. This was a spin-off from Ernst & Young. The firm McCullochs, in Gisborne, was formed from disaffected partners from KPMG in 1992.

22   Deloitte Touche Tohmatsu partner.

23   T. Morris and L. Empson, 'Organisation and Expertise: An Exploration of Knowledge Bases and the Management of Accounting and Consulting Firms', *Accounting Organisations and Society*, 23(5/6), 1998, pp. 609–24.

24   www.greenink.co.nz

25   The effect of the Registered Securities Limited settlement on Arthur Young is documented in *The Dominion*, 17 Sep. 1993, p. 1. Arthur Young paid $37.5 million to investors, after being sued for $140 million following the 1988 collapse of RSL.

26   The 'Non-Big 8' share has been fluctuating between 13 per cent and 17 per cent of the listed company audit market in the period 1987–2001, with 17.2 per cent in 2001.

AFTERWORD

1   See, for example, Todd S. Purdum, 'Electoral Affirmation of Shared Values Provides Bush a Majority', *New York Times*, 4 Nov. 2004.

2   Gary Hawke, evidence presented to Waitangi Tribunal, re Wai–686, Sep. 2000, p. 5.

3   *Southern Cross*, Auckland, 15 Jun. 1844. (Report of Legislative Council debate.)

4   William Fox, *The Six Colonies of New Zealand*, Parker, London, 1851, p. 40.

5   See G. T. Bloomfield, *NZ: A Handbook of Historical Statistics*, G. K. Hall, Boston, 1984, p. 181.

6   The role of merchants in Auckland in the 1860s is best covered in G. C. Dunstall, 'Colonial Merchant: J. T. Mackelvie and Brown Campbell and Company, and the Business Community, 1865–71', M.A. thesis, University of Auckland, 1971. This thesis has stood the test of time extraordinarily well.

7   This refers to the Piako swamp, the clandestine

purchase of which from the Vogel Government by a syndicate led by Whitaker and Russell was a continuing political scandal in the 1870s.

8   Lawyers representing Thomas Russell, Thomas Morrin, Robert Graham and others in a Native Land Court hearing at Cambridge presided over by Judge Rogan during 1874–5 ferociously competed for the Hungahunga block near Waharoa in the Upper Thames Valley.

9   For more on this company, see Co A-34. Dead companies file at Archives New Zealand, Mt Wellington, Auckland.

10   Thomas Buddle to Thomas Russell, 4 Aug. 1875, Thomas Buddle Letterbook, 1867–75, Special Collections, Auckland City Libraries.

11   Information provided by John O. Lusk, of the law firm of Harmos, Horton and Lusk. I acknowledge my indebtedness to John Lusk, Tony Frankham and Murray Weatherston whom I interviewed on modern Auckland business. But I alone must bear responsibility for conclusions drawn from their information.

12   Audrey Young, 'Labour's Mr Fixit Makes His Mark', *New Zealand Herald*, 13 Nov. 2004, B4. (The words cited are Young's.)

13   *Bold Century: The New Zealand Insurance Company Limited, 1859–1869*, NZI Co. Ltd, Auckland, 1959, pp. 7–11.

14   C. W. Vennell, *Risks and Rewards*, Wilson & Horton, Auckland, 1972, pp. 3–14.

15   N. M. Chappell, *New Zealand Banker's Hundred: A History of the Bank of New Zealand, 1861–1961*, Bank of New Zealand, Wellington, 1971, pp. 19–29.

16   It is ironic that the main trading banks in New Zealand have once again in the twenty-first century fallen under the control of Australian and other overseas owners.

17   Information provided by Anthony N. Frankham,

18   Bloomfield, *NZ: A Handbook of Historical Statistics*, *op. cit.*, Table 11.10, p. 57. Much of the suburban increase came from the conversion in the statistical records of outer districts, which had previously been regarded as rural, into 'suburbs'.

19   *Ibid.*, ch. 10; Chappell, *New Zealand Banker's Hundred*, *op. cit.*, ch. 13; *Appendices to the Journal of the House of Representatives*, 1896, 1-6.

20   *New Zealand Official Yearbook 2002*, Wellington, 2002, p. 99.

21   John Waugh to Editor, *New Zealand Herald*, 2 Mar. 2002.

22   Graeme Hunt, 'The $200 Million Men', *Metro*, Issue 281, Nov. 2004, p. 28. This article is most illuminating.

23   *New Zealand Official Yearbook 2002*, p. 95.

24   *Ibid.*

25   *Ibid.*, p. 99.

26   The Port of Tauranga is becoming, however, a formidable rival and is threatening the previous monopoly position of the Ports of Auckland. The Port of Tauranga is promoting diversification, helped by the ripening of its friendly relations with Toll NZ Railways. It has offset against a drop in log exports, an increase in export of dairy and horticultural products, it is planning to be a main point of entry for the new Huntly thermal power complex, and is using its container facility to rail imports from foreign suppliers directly to the Auckland market. See, for example, *New Zealand Herald*, 7 Oct. 2004, C1.

27   *Weekend Herald*, 25–26 Sept. 2004, C5.

28   Matt Philp, 'Hard Times on Mahogany Row', *Metro*, 4 Jul. 2004, pp. 42–50; a perceptive article.

29   See, for example, 'Is the Queen City too big for its boots?', *Sunday Star-Times*, 20 Jun. 2004, C2, p. 3.

Auckland accountant and company director.

SELECT BIBLIOGRAPHY

Adams, Peter, *Fatal Necessity: British Intervention in New Zealand 1830–1847*, Auckland University Press/ Oxford University Press, Auckland, 1977.

Anderson, L., *Throughout the East Coast: The Story of Williams and Kettle Ltd.*, New Zealand Pictorial Publications, Hastings, 1974.

Andrews, Philip, *No Fear of Rusting*, Rotorua and District Historical Society, Rotorua, 2001.

Angus, John H., *Donald Reid Otago Farmers Ltd: A History of Service to the Farming Community of Otago,* Donald Reid Otago Farmers, Dunedin, 1978.

—— *The Ironmasters: The First One Hundred Years of H.E. Shacklock Limited*, H. E. Shacklock, Dunedin, 1973.

Angus, John H., *Papermaking Pioneers: A History of New Zealand Paper Mills Limited and Its Predecessors*, New Zealand Paper Mills, Mataura, 1976.

Armstrong, R. W., 'Auckland By Gaslight: An Urban Geography of 1896', *New Zealand Geographer*, 15, 1959, pp. 173–89.

Arnold, R., *New Zealand's Burning: The Settlers' World in the Mid 1880s*, Victoria University Press, Wellington, 1994.

Arnold, R. D., *The Farthest Promised Land*, Victoria University Press, Wellington, 1981.

Ashby, Ted, *Phantom Fleet: The Scows and Scowmen of Auckland*, A. H. and A. W. Reed, Auckland, 1975.

Atkinson, Neill, *Crew Culture: New Zealand Seafarers Under Sail and Steam*, Te Papa Press, Wellington, 2001.

Baker, B. V. T., *The New Zealand People at War: War Economy,* Department of Internal Affairs, Wellington, 1973.

Barnard, A., *The Australian Wool Market, 1840–1900,* Melbourne University Press, Melbourne, 1958.

Bassett, Michael, *Our Newspapers*, Auckland University Labour Club, Auckland, 1970.

—— *The State in New Zealand 1840–1984*, Auckland University Press, Auckland, 1998.

Bedford, R. D., Bedford, C. E., Ho, E. S., and Lidgard, J. M., 'The Globalization of Migration in New Zealand', *New Zealand Population Review*, 28(1), 2002, pp. 69–97.

Belich, James, *Paradise Reforged: A History of the New Zealanders from the 1880s to the Year 2000*, Penguin, Auckland, 2001.

Binney, Judith, 'Christianity and the Maoris to 1840: A Comment', *New Zealand Journal of History*, II, October, 1969, pp. 143–65.

Bloomfield, G. T., 'The Growth of Auckland 1840–1966', in J. S. Whitelaw (ed.), *Auckland in Ferment*, New Zealand Geographical Society Miscellaneous Series, No. 6, New Zealand Geographical Society, Auckland, 1967.

Bradley, S. W., *Newspapers: An Analysis of the Press in New Zealand*, Heinemann Educational, Auckland, 1973.

Brett, A. R., *The Race for the Wires: Old Time Journalism: Some Reminiscences of the Late Sir Henry Brett*, Auckland Star, Auckland, 1927.

Brown, J. L., Cooper, D. J., Greenwood, R., and Hinings, C. R., 'Strategic Alliances Within a Big-Six Accounting Firm: A Case Study', *International Studies of Management & Organization*, 26 (2), 1996, pp. 59–80.

Brownie, S., and Dalziel, P., 'Shift-Share Analyses of New Zealand Exports, 1970–1984', *New Zealand Economic Papers*, 27(2), 1993, pp. 233–49.

Buckle, B., Kim, K., and McLellan, N., 'The Impact of Monetary Policy on New Zealand Business Cycles and Inflation Variability', New Zealand Treasury Working Paper No. 03/09, 2003.

Bush, G. W. A., *Decently and in Order: The Government of the City of Auckland 1840–1971, the centennial history of the Auckland City Council*, published for the Auckland City Council by Collins, Auckland, 1971.

Cain, P. J. and Hopkins, A. G., *British Imperialism: Crisis and Deconstruction, 1914–1990*, Longman, London, 2003.

—— *British Imperialism: Innovation and Expansion, 1688–1914*, Longman, London, 2003.

Capie, F., 'Australian and New Zealand Competition in the British Market 1920–39', *Australian Economic History Review*, 18(1), 1978, pp. 46–63.

Cashin, P. A., 'Real GDP in the Seven Colonies of Australasia: 1861–1991', *Review of Income and Wealth*, 41(1), 1995, pp. 19–39.

Chandler, Alfred D., *Strategy and Structure*, MIT Press, Cambridge (Mass.), 1962.

Chappell, David A., *Double Ghosts: Oceanian Voyagers on Euroamerican Ships*, Armonk, New York, 1997.

Chappell, Norman, *New Zealand Banker's Hundred: A History of the Bank of New Zealand, 1861–1961*, Bank of New Zealand, Wellington, 1961.

Churchouse, Jack, *Sailing Ships of the Tasman Sea*, Millwood Press, Wellington, 1984.

Cleveland, Les, 'Structure and Functions of the New Zealand Press', Ph.D. thesis, Victoria University of Wellington, Wellington, 1970.

Condliffe, J. B., *New Zealand in the Making*, George Allen & Unwin, London, 1930.

Craig, Dick, *The King Country (Rohe Potae)*, R. S. Craig, Te Awamutu, 1990.

Curnow, Jenifer, McCrae, Jane, and Hopa, Margaret (eds), *Rere Atu, Taku Manu! Discovering History, Language and Politics in the Maori Language Newspapers*, Auckland University Press, Auckland, 2002.

Dalton, William, *The Dalton Journal: Two Whaling Voyages to the South Seas 1823–1829*, (Niel Gunson, ed.), National Library of Australia, Canberrra, 1990.

Dalziel, P., 'New Zealand's Economic Reforms: An Assessment', *Review of Political Economy*, 14(2), 2002, pp. 31–46.

Dalziel, P., and Lattimore, R., *The New Zealand Macroeconomy: A Briefing on the Reforms and their Legacy*, 4th edn, Oxford University Press, South Melbourne, 2001.

Davis, Dorothy, *A History of Shopping*, Routledge & Kegan Paul, London, 1966.

Day, Patrick, *The Making of the New Zealand Press: A Study of the Occupational and Political Concerns of the New Zealand Newspaper Controllers, 1840–1880*, Victoria University Press, Wellington, 1990.

Deane, R. S., *Foreign Investment in New Zealand Manufacturing*, Sweet & Maxwell, Wellington, 1970.

Deeks, John, and Enderwick, Peter (eds), *Business and New Zealand Society*, Longman Paul, Auckland, 1994.

Dinwiddie, W., *Old Hawke's Bay*, Dinwiddie Walker, Napier, 1921.

Drummond, I. M., *Imperial Economic Policy 1917–1939*, George Allen & Unwin, London, 1974.

Earle, C., *The American Way: A Geographical History of Crisis and Recovery*, Rowman and Littlefield, Lanham, 2003.

Easton, B., *The Nationbuilders*, Auckland University Press, Auckland, 2001.

—— *In Stormy Seas: The Post-War New Zealand Economy*, University of Otago Press, Dunedin, 1997.

Elder, J. W. (ed.), *The Letters and Journals of Samuel Marsden, 1765–1838, Senior Chaplain in the Colony of New South Wales and Superintendent of the Mission of the Church Missionary Society in New Zealand*, Coulls, Somerville Wilkie, Ltd, and A. H. Reed for the Otago University Council, Dunedin, 1932.

Elliott, Robin, and Harold Kidd, *The Logans: New Zealand's Greatest Boatbuilding Family*, David Ling, Auckland, 2001.

Endicott, William, *Wrecked Among Cannibals in the Fijis; A Narrative of Shipwreck and Adventure in the South Seas*, Marine Research Society, Salem (Mass.), 1923.

Endres, T., 'The Development of Economists' Policy Advice in New Zealand, 1930–4: With Particular Reference to Belshaw's Contribution', *Australian Economic History Review*, 30(1), 1990, pp. 64–78.

—— 'The Economics of Wages and Wage Policy in the Depression and Recovery Period: Distinctive Elements in the New Zealand Debate', *New Zealand Journal of Industrial Relations*, 15, 1990, pp. 1–18.

Endres, T., and Jackson, K., 'Policy Responses to the Crisis: Australasia in the 1930s', in W. R. Garside (ed.), *Capitalism in Crisis: International Responses to the Great Depression*, Pinter, London, 1993, pp. 148–65.

Evans, L., Grimes, A., and Wilkinson, B., with Teece, D., 'Economic Reform in New Zealand 1984–95: The Pursuit of Efficiency', *Journal of Economic Literature*, 34(4), 1996, pp. 1856–902.

Fleming, G., 'Agricultural Support Policies in a Small Open Economy: New Zealand in the 1920s', *Economic History Review*, 52(2), 1999, pp. 334–54.

—— 'Economists and Mortgage Relief in New Zealand in the 1930s', *Australian Economic History Review*, 37(1), 1997), pp. 54–68.

—— 'Keynes, Purchasing Power Parity and Exchange Rate Policy in New Zealand during the 1930s Depression', *New Zealand Economic Papers*, 31, 1997, pp. 1–14.

Fleming, G., Merrett, D., and Ville, S., *Big Business and Corporate Leadership in Twentieth-Century Australia*, Cambridge University Press, Melbourne, 2004.

Flude, Anthony G., *Henderson and Macfarlane's Circular Saw Line*, Henderson Borough Council, Auckland, 1993.

Furniss, Cliff, *Servants of the North: Adventures on the Coastal Trade With the Northern Steam Ship Company*, A. H. and A. W. Reed, Wellington, 1977.

Gad, G., 'Location Patterns of Manufacturing: Toronto in the Early 1880s', *Urban History Review*, XXII (2), 1994, pp. 113–38.

Gardner, W. J., 'A Colonial Economy', in W. H. Oliver and B. R. Williams (eds), *Oxford History of New Zealand*, Oxford University Press, Auckland, 1988 reprint.

Gifford, W. H., and Bradney Williams, H., *A Centennial History of Tauranga*, published for Tauranga Centennial Committee by A. H. and A. W. Reed, Dunedin, 1940.

Gore, R., *Levin, 1841–1941*, Levin, Wellington, 1956.

Gould, J. D., *The Rake's Progress: The New Zealand Economy Since 1945*, Hodder & Stoughton, Auckland, 1982.

Grant, Patrick J., 'Late Holocene Histories of Climate, Geomorphology and Vegetation, and their Effects on the First New Zealanders', in Douglas G. Sutton (ed.), *The Origins of the First New Zealanders*, Auckland University Press, Auckland, 1994.

Greasley, D., and Oxley, L., 'Globalization and Real Wages in New Zealand 1873–1913', *Explorations in Economic History*, 41(1), 2004, pp. 26–47.

—— 'Growing Apart? Australia and New Zealand Growth Experiences, 1870–1993', *New Zealand Economic Papers*, 33(2), 1999, pp. 1–14.

—— 'Outside the Club: New Zealand's Economic Growth, 1870–1993', *International Review of Applied Economics*, 14(2), 1999, pp. 173–92.

—— 'Regime Shift and Fast Recovery on the Periphery: New Zealand in the 1930s', *Economic History Review*, 55(4), 2002, pp. 697–720.

—— 'A Tale of Two Dominions: Comparing the Macroeconomic Records of Australia and Canada Since 1870', *Economic History Review*, 51(2), 1998, pp. 294–318.

Green, Anna, *British Capital, Antipodean Labour: Working the New Zealand Waterfront, 1915–1951*, University of Otago Press, Dunedin, 2001.

Grey, A., *Aotearoa and New Zealand: A Historical Geography*, Canterbury University Press, Christchurch, 1994.

Griffith, N. A., *Reading New Zealand Newspapers*, Reed, Auckland, 1973.

Guest, M. W., and Singleton, J., 'The Murupara Project and Industrial Development in New Zealand 1945–65', *Australian Economic History Review*, 39(1), 1999, pp. 52–71.

Gustafson, B., *His Way: A Biography of Robert Muldoon*, Auckland University Press, Auckland, 2000.

Hainsworth, D. R., *The Sydney Traders: Simeon Lord and his Contemporaries, 1788–1821*, Cassell, Sydney, 1971.

Hall, Noeline V., *I Have Planted … A Biography of Alfred Nesbit Brown*, Dunmore Press, Palmerston North, 1981.

Hamer, D., 'Towns in Nineteenth-Century New Zealand', *New Zealand Journal of History*, 13(1), 1979, pp. 5–24.

Hargreaves, R. P., 'Changing Maori Agriculture in Pre-Waitangi New Zealand', *Journal of the Polynesian Society*, 72(2), June 1963, pp. 101–17.

—— 'Maori Flour Mills of the Auckland Province 1846–1860', *Journal of the Polynesian Society*, 70(2), June 1961, pp. 227–32.

—— 'The Maori Agriculture of the Auckland Province in the mid-nineteenth century', *Journal of the Polynesian Society*, 68(2), June 1959, pp. 61–79.

Harris, R., 'Self-Building in the Urban Housing Market', *Economic Geography*, 67, 1991, pp. 1–21.

Hawke, G. R., 'Depression and Recovery in New Zealand', in R. G. Gregory and N. G. Butlin (eds.), *Recovery from the Depression: Australia and the World Economy in the 1930s*, Cambridge University Press, Cambridge, 1988, pp. 113–34.

——'The Growth of the Economy' in W. H. Oliver and B. R. Williams (eds), *Oxford History of New Zealand*, Auckland, Oxford University Press, 1988 reprint.

—— *The Making of New Zealand. An Economic History*, Cambridge University Press, Cambridge, 1985.

—— *The Thoroughbred Among Banks in New Zealand: 1872–1947, the early years*, vol. 1, National Bank of New Zealand, Wellington, 1997.

Henare, Manuka Arnold, 'The Changing Images of Nineteenth Century Maori Society — From Tribes to Nation', Ph.D. thesis, Victoria University of Wellington, Wellington, 2003.

Hodgson, Terence, *The Heart of Colonial Auckland,* Random Century, Auckland, 1992.

Holmes, Sir Frank, *The Thoroughbred Among Banks in New Zealand*, vol. 3, National Bank of New Zealand, Wellington, 2003.

Hopkins, A. G., 'Gentlemanly Capitalism in New Zealand,' *Australian Economic History Review*, 43(3), 2003, pp. 287–97.

Horsman, John, *The Coming of the Pakeha to Auckland Province*, Hicks Smith, Wellington, 1971.

Howe, K. R., *Where the Waves Fall*, Allen and Unwin, Sydney, 1984.

Humphery, Kim, *Shelf Life: Supermarkets and the Changing Cultures of Consumption*, Cambridge University Press, Cambridge, 1998.

Hunt, Graeme, *Hustlers, Rogues and Bubble Boys: White Collar Mischief in New Zealand*, Reed, Auckland, 2001.

Hunter, Ian, *Robert Laidlaw: Man for Our Time*, Castle, Auckland, 1999.

Irving, J. C., *A Century's Challenge. Wright Stephenson and Co. Ltd., 1861–1961*, Wright Stephenson and Co., Wellington, 1961.

Jackson, Michael, 'Literacy, Communications and Social Change', in I. H. Kawharu (ed.), *Conflict and Compromise: Essays on the Maori since Colonisation*, A. H. and A. W. Reed, Wellington, 1975.

Johnson, David, *New Zealand's Maritime Heritage*, Collins/Bateman, Auckland, 1987.

Jones, S. R. H., 'The Establishment and operation of European Business', in P. Enderwick and J. Deeks, *Business and New Zealand Enterprise*, Longman Paul, Auckland, 1994, pp. 43–67.

—— 'Government Policy and Industry Structure in New Zealand, 1900–1970', *Australian Economic History Review*, 39(3), 1999, pp. 191–212.

Jones S. R. H. and Paul, D. R., 'Concentration and Regulation in the New Zealand Brewing Industry, 1850–1970', *Australian Economic History Review*, 31(2), 1991, pp. 66–93.

Julian, Harry, *Sea in My Blood*, H. L. Julian, Auckland, 1999.

Kay, M., *Inside Story of Farmers*, Farmers Trading Company, Auckland, 1953.

Kindleberger, C. P., 'Competitive Currency Depreciation Between Denmark and New Zealand', *Harvard Business Review*, 12, 1934, pp. 416–26.

Larkworthy, F., *Ninety-one Years: Being the Reminiscences of Falconer Larkworthy*, (Harold Begbie, ed.), Mills and Boon, London, 1924.

Laurenson, Helen, 'Going up?—going down! The Rise and Fall of Auckland Department Stores, 1920–1960', M.A. thesis, University of Auckland, Auckland, 2003.

Lee, Jack, *I Have Named It the Bay of Islands*, Hodder and Stoughton, Auckland, 1983.

Lewis, R., 'The Development of an Early Suburban Industrial District: The Montreal Ward of Saint-Ann, 1851–71', *Urban History Revue*, XIX(3), 1991, pp. 166–80.

——'Restructuring and the Formation of an Industrial District in Montreal's East End, 1850–1914', *Journal of Historical Geography*, 20, 1994, pp. 143–57.

Linge, G. J. R., 'The Diffusion of Manufacturing in Auckland, New Zealand', *Economic Geography*, pp. 23–39.

——'Manufacturing in Auckland: Its Origins and Growth 1840–1936', *New Zealand Geographer*, 14, 1958, pp. 47–64.

Lloyd Prichard, Muriel F., *An Economic History of New Zealand to 1939*, Collins, Auckland, 1970.

Mabbett, D., *Trade, Employment and Welfare: A Comparative Study of Trade and Labour Market Policies in Sweden and New Zealand, 1880–1980*, Clarendon Press, Oxford, 1995.

McAloon, J., 'Gentlemanly Capitalism and Settler Capitalists: Imperialism, Dependent Development and Colonial Wealth in the South Island of New Zealand', *Australian Economic History Review*, 42(2), 2002, pp. 204–23.

McGill, David, *The Guardians at the Gate: The History of the New Zealand Customs Department*, Silver Owl

Press for the New Zealand Customs Department, Wellington, 1991.

McGlone, M. S., Anderson, A. J., and Holdaway, R. N., 'An Ecological Approach to the Polynesian Settlement of New Zealand', in Douglas G. Sutton (ed.), *The Origins of the First New Zealanders*, Auckland University Press, Auckland, 1994.

McGregor, Judy (ed.), *Dangerous Democracy: News Media Politics in New Zealand*, Dunmore Press, Palmerston North, 1996.

McGregor, Judy and Comrie, Margie (eds), *What's News: Reclaiming Journalism in New Zealand*, Dunmore Press, Palmerston North, 2002.

McKinnon, M., *Treasury: 160 Years of the New Zealand Treasury*, Auckland University Press in association with the Ministry for Culture and Heritage, Auckland, 2003.

McKinsey, J. O., 'Modern Tendencies in Accounting Practice', *The Accountants Journal*, Dec., 1925, pp. 171–4.

McLean, Gavin, *Captain's Log: New Zealand's Maritime History*, Hodder Moa Beckett, Auckland, 2001.

—— *The Southern Octopus: The Rise of a Shipping Empire*, New Zealand Ship and Marine Society/ Wellington Harbour Board Maritime Museum, Wellington, 1990.

—— *We Were Different: The Tasman Express Line Story*, Ventures Two, Auckland, 2004.

Macmillan, H., *At the End of the Day, 1961–1963*, Macmillan, London, 1973.

McNab, R., *Historical Records of New Zealand*, vol. I, Government Printer, Wellington, 1908–14.

Maddison, A., *Dynamic Forces in Capitalist Development*, Oxford University Press, Oxford, 1991.

Markham, Edward, *New Zealand or Recollections of It*, Government Printer, Wellington, 1963.

Martin, S. McD., *New Zealand: In a Series of Letters*, Simmonds & Ward, London, 1845.

Mead, A. D., *Richard Taylor: Missionary Tramper*, Reed, Wellington, 1966.

Meiklejohn, G. M., *Early Conflict of Press and Government: The Story of the First New Zealand Herald and the Founding of Auckland*, Wilson and Horton, Auckland, 1953.

Miller, Raymond (ed.), *New Zealand Government and Politics*, 3rd edn, Oxford University Press, Auckland, 2003.

Molineux, Julienne, 'Concentration of Ownership in the New Zealand Daily Newspaper Industry', *New Zealand Journal of Media Studies*, 2(2), 1995, pp. 3–11.

Morris, T., and Empson, L., 'Organisation and Expertise: An Exploration of Knowledge Bases and the Management of Accounting and Consulting Firms', *Accounting Organisations and Society*, 23(5/6), 1998, pp. 609–24.

Morton, Harry, *The Whale's Wake*, McIndoe for the University of Otago Press, Dunedin, 1982.

Muller, E., and Groves, P., 'The Emergence of Industrial Districts in Mid-Nineteenth Century Baltimore', *Geographical Review*, 54, 1979, pp. 159–78.

Olgivie, Gordon, *Ballantynes, The Story of Dunstable House 1854–2004*, J. Ballantyne & Co., Christchurch, 2004.

Oliver, W. H., and Orange, Claudia (gen. eds), *The Dictionary of New Zealand Biography*, vol. 1–4, Allen and Unwin/ Department of Internal Affairs, Wellington, 1990–98. (Now also available online at: http://www.dnzb.govt.nz/.)

Parry, G., *NMA: The Story of the First Hundred Years of the National Mortgage and Agency Company of New Zealand Ltd., 1864–1964*, National Mortgage and Agency Company, Dunedin, 1964.

Parry, Gordon, *Behind the Headlines*, McIndoe, Dunedin, 1969.

Pearson, M. N., 'Brown and Campbell in Early Auckland, 1840–56', M.A. thesis, University of Auckland, 1964.

Petrie, Hazel, ' "For a Season Quite the Rage"? Ships and flourmills in the Maori Economy, 1840–1860s', Ph.D. thesis, University of Auckland, 2004.

Richards, Rhys, and Chisholm, Jocelyn, *Bay of Islands Shipping Arrivals and Departures 1803–1840*, Paremata Press, Wellington, 1992.

Rose, John, *Akarana: The Ports of Auckland*, Auckland Harbour Board, Auckland, 1971.

Rose, T., and Hinings, C. R., 'Global Client Demands Driving Change in Global Business Advisory Firms', in D. M. Brock, M. J. Powell and C. R. Hinings (eds), *Restructuring the Professional Organization: Accounting, Health Care & Law*, Routledge, London, 1999, pp. 41–67.

Rosenberg, Bill, 'News Media Ownership: How New Zealand is Foreign Dominated', *Pacific Journalism Review*, 8, Jun. 2002.

Ross, John O. C., *William Stewart, Sealing Captain, Trader and Speculator*, Roebuck, Canberra, 1987.

Rough, David, *Narrative of a Journey Through Parts of the North Island of New Zealand*, Home Friends, London, 1852.

Salmond, Anne, *Between Worlds: early exchanges between Maori and Europeans, 1773–1815*, Viking, Auckland, 1997.

Savitt, Ronald, 'Innovation in American Retailing, 1919–39: Improving Inventory Management', *International Review of Retail, Distribution and Consumer Research*, 9(3), July 1999, pp. 307–20.

Scholefield, G. (ed.), *A Dictionary of New Zealand Biography*, Department of Internal Affairs, Wellington, 1940.

Scholefield, Guy, *Newspapers in New Zealand*, A. H. and A. W. Reed, Wellington, 1958.

Schumpeter, Joseph A., *Capitalism, Socialism and Democracy*, George Allen Unwin, London, 1976.

Sharp, Andrew (ed.), *Duperrey's Visit to New Zealand in 1824*, Alexander Turnbull Library, Wellington, 1971.

Silverstone, B., Bollard, A., and Lattimore, R. (eds), *A Study of Economic Reform: The Case of New Zealand*, Elsevier, Amsterdam, 1996.

Simkin, C. G. F., *The Instability of a Dependent Economy: Economic Fluctuations in New Zealand 1840–1914*, Oxford University Press, Oxford, 1951.

Singleton, J., 'New Zealand: Devaluation without a Balance of Payments Crisis', in T. Balderston (ed.), *The World Economy and National Economies in the Interwar Slump*, Palgrave, Basingstoke, 2003, pp. 172–90.

Singleton, J., and Robertson, P. L., *Economic Relations between Britain and Australasia 1945–1970*, Palgrave, Basingstoke, 2002.

Stanney, Brian Gordon, 'Reforming the *Herald*: A Comparative Analysis of Front Section News Content in the *New Zealand Herald*, 1995 and 2001', M.A. thesis, University of Auckland, 2001.

Stephenson, A. B., and Stephenson, N. G., *Samuel Stephenson: Pioneer Merchant of Russell, 1804–1885*, N. G. and A. B. Stephenson, Auckland, 1984.

Stewart, Peter, *Patterns on the Plain: A Centennial History of Mosgiel Woollens Limited*, Mosgiel Woollens, Dunedin, 1975, pp. 97–8.

Stone, R. C. J., *The Father and His Gift*, Auckland University Press, Auckland, 1987.

——*Makers of Fortune. A Colonial Business Community and Its Fall*, Auckland University Press/Oxford University Press, Auckland, 1973.

——'The New Zealand Frozen Meat and Storage Company', *New Zealand Journal of History*, 5(2), 1971, pp. 171–84.

——*Young Logan Campbell*, Auckland University Press/Oxford University Press, Auckland, 1982.

Swainson, W., *Auckland, the Capital of New Zealand …* , Smith, Elder, London, 1853, reprinted by Wilson and Horton, Auckland, 1971.

Taylor, Nancy M., *Early Travellers in New Zealand*, Clarendon Press, Oxford, 1959.

Tucker, K. A., *Milne and Choyce: A One Hundred Year Business History, 1867–1967*, Milne and Choyce, Auckland, 1968.

Ville, S., *The Rural Entrepreneurs: A History of the Stock and Station Agent Industry in Australia and New Zealand*, Cambridge University Press, Melbourne, 2000.

Ville, Simon, 'Business Development in Colonial Australia', *Australian Economic History Review*, 38(1), 1998, pp. 16–41.

—— 'The Coastal Trade of New Zealand Prior to World War One', *New Zealand Journal of History*, 27(1), 1993, pp. 75–89.

—— 'The Growth of Specialization in English Shipowning, 1750–1850', *Economic History Review*, 46(4), 1993, pp. 702–22.

Ville, Simon, and Fleming, Grant, 'The Nature and Structure of Trade-Financial Networks: Evidence from the New Zealand Pastoral Sector', *Business History*, 42(1), 2000, pp. 41–58.

Walker, R., and Lewis, R., 'Beyond the Crabgrass Frontier: Industry and the Spread of the City, 1850–1950', *Journal of Historical Geography*, 27(1), 2001, pp. 3–19.

Watson, James, *Links: A History of Transport and New Zealand Society*, Ministry of Transport/Te Manatu Waka, Wellington, 1996.

Wigglesworth, R. P., 'The New Zealand Timber and Flax Trade 1769–1840', Ph.D. thesis, Massey University, New Plymouth, 1981.

Winder, G. M., 'The North American Manufacturing Belt in 1880: A Cluster of Regional Industrial Systems or One Large Industrial District?' *Economic Geography*, 75(1), 1999, pp. 71–92.

Yate, William, *An Account of New Zealand: and of the formation and progress of the Church Missionary Society's Mission in the Northern Island*, Seeley and Burnside, London, 1835.

Yerex, David, *Empire of the Dairy Farmers*, NZ Dairy Exporter Books in association with Ampersand Publishing Associates, Petone, 1989.